Service, Society and Social Change

Post-War Clubs from the *Valley Times* Newspaper

Edited by Christine Adolph

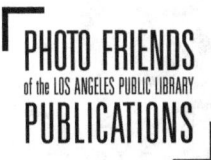

PHOTO FRIENDS
of the LOS ANGELES PUBLIC LIBRARY
PUBLICATIONS

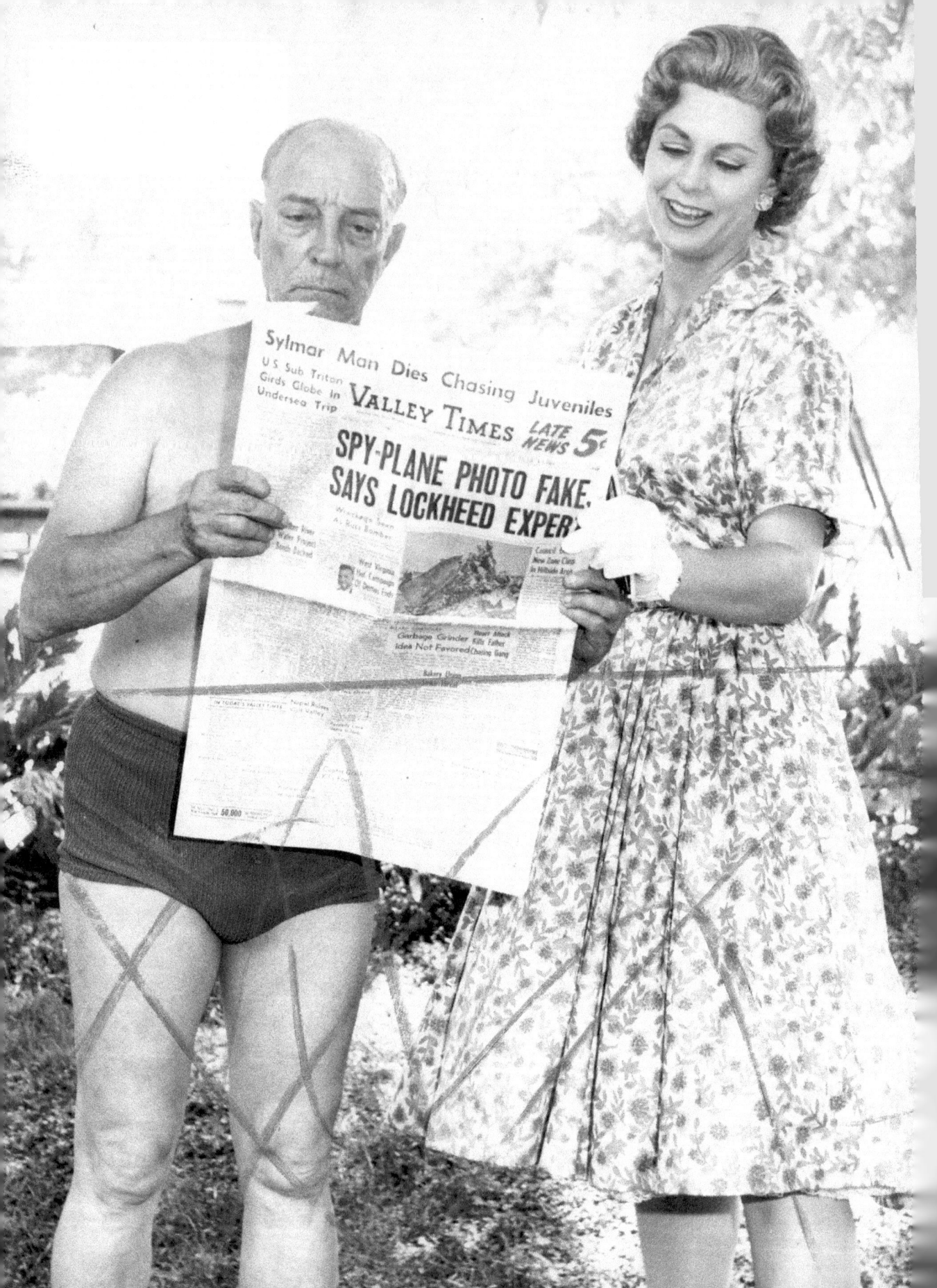

Contents

"Actor Buster Keaton, honorary mayor of Woodland Hills, looks over copy of the *Valley Times* in new large Imperial type. Model Maggie Heisick explains to veteran comedian that type face makes Valley's daily newspaper easy reading for its customers." May 18, 1960.

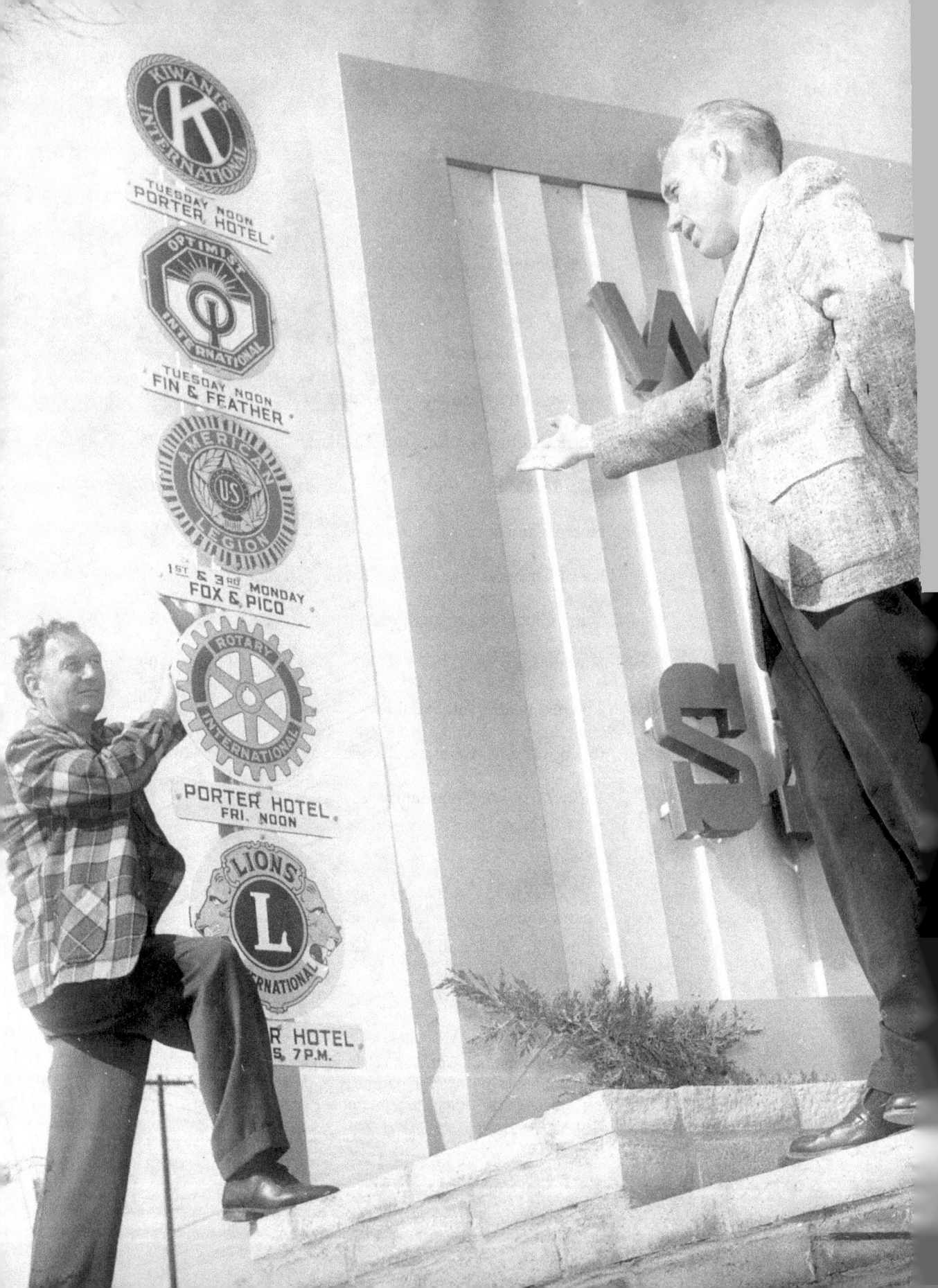

Introduction

In the post-war era the San Fernando Valley rapidly transformed into the quintessential American suburb. Tract homes, swimming pools and shopping centers replaced dairy and fruit farms and vast ranches. With the availability of affordable housing and jobs from the thriving aerospace, aircraft, and manufacturing industries, the Valley's population boomed. The promise of prosperity inspired new opportunities for leisure time, family life and civic engagement. Membership in social and service clubs soared. Whether people united through shared identities or shared interests in hobbies, civics or philanthropy, the prevalence of club life defined the Valley's growing community.

The *Valley Times* newspaper, published from 1946 to 1970, documented the changes to the Valley's physical landscape through suburban development, but also revealed how social networks impacted society. Throughout the country, attendance in established national and international service organizations rose to new heights after a decline during the Depression and World War II. It was not uncommon to see club logos tacked on the welcome signs of most American towns, and the Valley was no exception. Chapters of Rotary, Optimists, Kiwanis

Opposite: "San Fernando officials Marshall W. Julian, right, city's administrative officer, and Ray E. Walker, superintendent of public works, check uniform signs of community service clubs that greet motorists on Truman street approach to San Fernando from Los Angeles. New plaques replace odd shapes and sizes that officials terms 'unsightly'." March 23, 1961.

and Lions clubs, as well as fraternal orders like the Elks were chartered in almost all the Valley's distinct neighborhoods. Men often joined clubs for camaraderie and professional networking, but they also donated time, money and services to the community, especially to children in need, the visually impaired and veterans. Since many service clubs at the time were divided by gender, women were excluded from membership. However, women found ample opportunities to engage in civic life through federated clubs that promoted their interests. The League of Women Voters, the American Association of University Women (AAUW), Soroptimist International, the Zontas and the Business and Professional Women (BPW) clubs provided community service and advocated for education and career development. Through local chapters the California Federation of Women's Clubs, the Assistance League, and auxiliary clubs, women became a vital force in volunteerism and philanthropy.

The majority of formal service clubs reflected the Valley's homogenous white demographic. Mexican Americans and the Japanese Nisei community, who had strong roots in the area but were underrepresented, engaged in civic culture through community centers and church organizations. The post-war jobs brought many African Americans to the Valley, but racial discrimination in the newly built suburban home developments kept neighborhoods segregated. A large and active African American community formed in Pacoima. During the civil rights movement of the 1960s, involvement in churches and the local chapters of the National Association for the Advancement of Colored People (NAACP) and the Congress of Racial Equality (CORE) forged opportunities for integration through the fight for fair housing and employment practices.

The activities of organizations representing all aspects of the community dominated the pages of the *Valley Times*. The variety of clubs from the American Legion to the PTAs, all participated in fundraising drives to support schools, hospitals, churches, synagogues, community centers and local charities that were necessary to accommodate the increasing population. Staff photographers documented the numerous benefits—bake sales and bazaars, fashion shows and festivals, luncheons and luaus, poolside barbecues and theme parties. The photographers approached their jobs with creativity and enthusiasm, promoting these events with imagery that was unlike anything seen in any other Los Angeles area

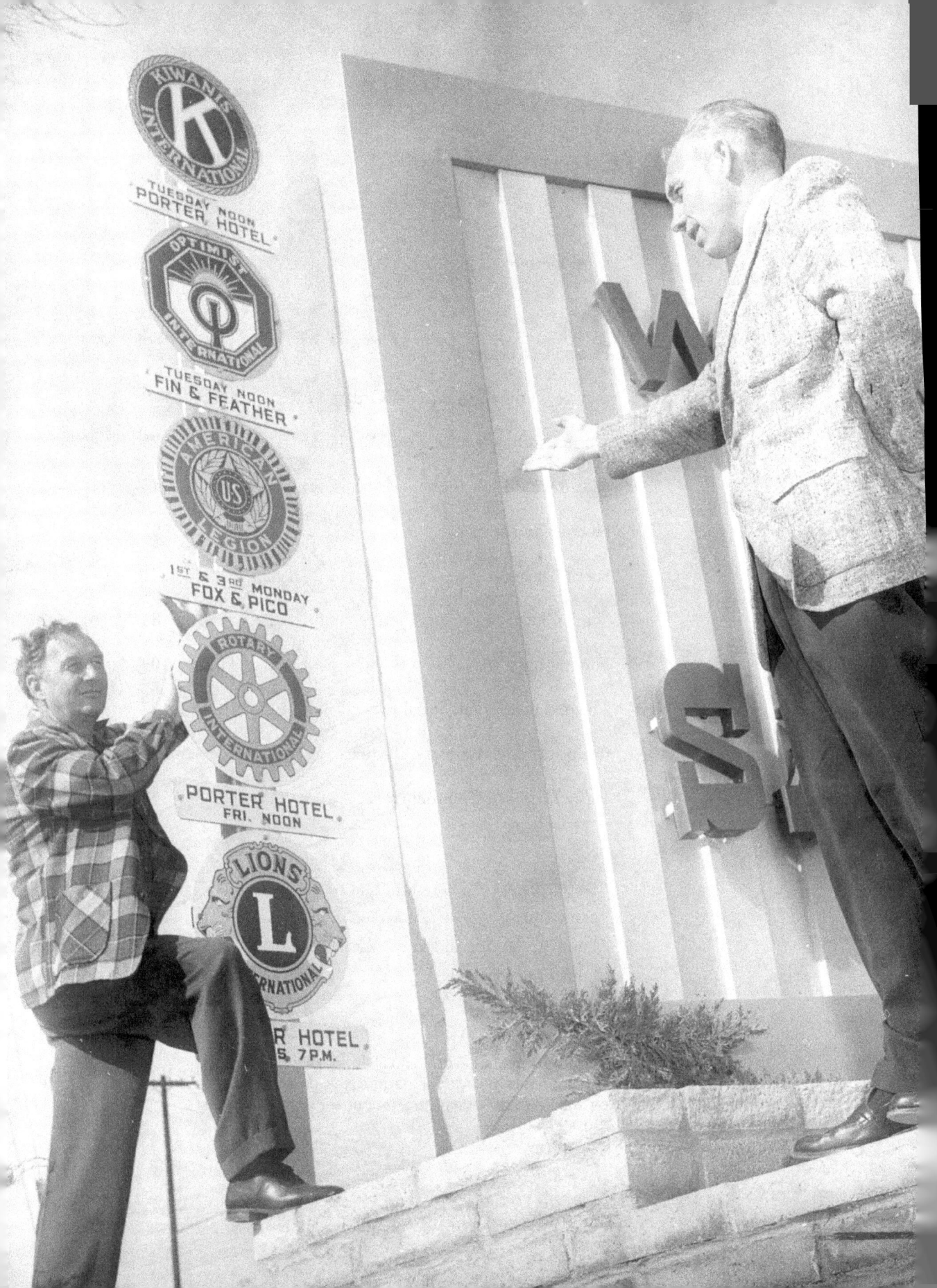

Contents

"Actor Buster Keaton, honorary mayor of Woodland Hills, looks over copy of the *Valley Times* in new large Imperial type. Model Maggie Heisick explains to veteran comedian that type face makes Valley's daily newspaper easy reading for its customers." May 18, 1960.

publications. They captured the pioneer picnics and square dancing that recalled the Valley's rural past, and the cars, music, theater and youth that contributed to a new cultural environment. The proximity to the entertainment industry meant that many celebrities made their home in the Valley. The regional Chambers of Commerce designated famous actors and musicians as honorary mayors who passed gavels at club installations and took pride in community service with earnestness and accessibility. At its core, the *Valley Times* had the sensibility of a small town newspaper that was ingrained in neighborhood life. Readers were invited to see the interworking of its North Hollywood offices, and many staff members, some who were actual members of Valley clubs, were often photographed as active participants in local affairs.

While social and service clubs are by no means extinct, they were an integral part of the social fabric of the post-war era that differs from the way we construct our social lives today. The *Valley Times* collection provides a unique visual history of the ways people connect to build a community.

—Christine Adolph
Los Angeles Public Library - *Valley Times* Archivist
June 2016

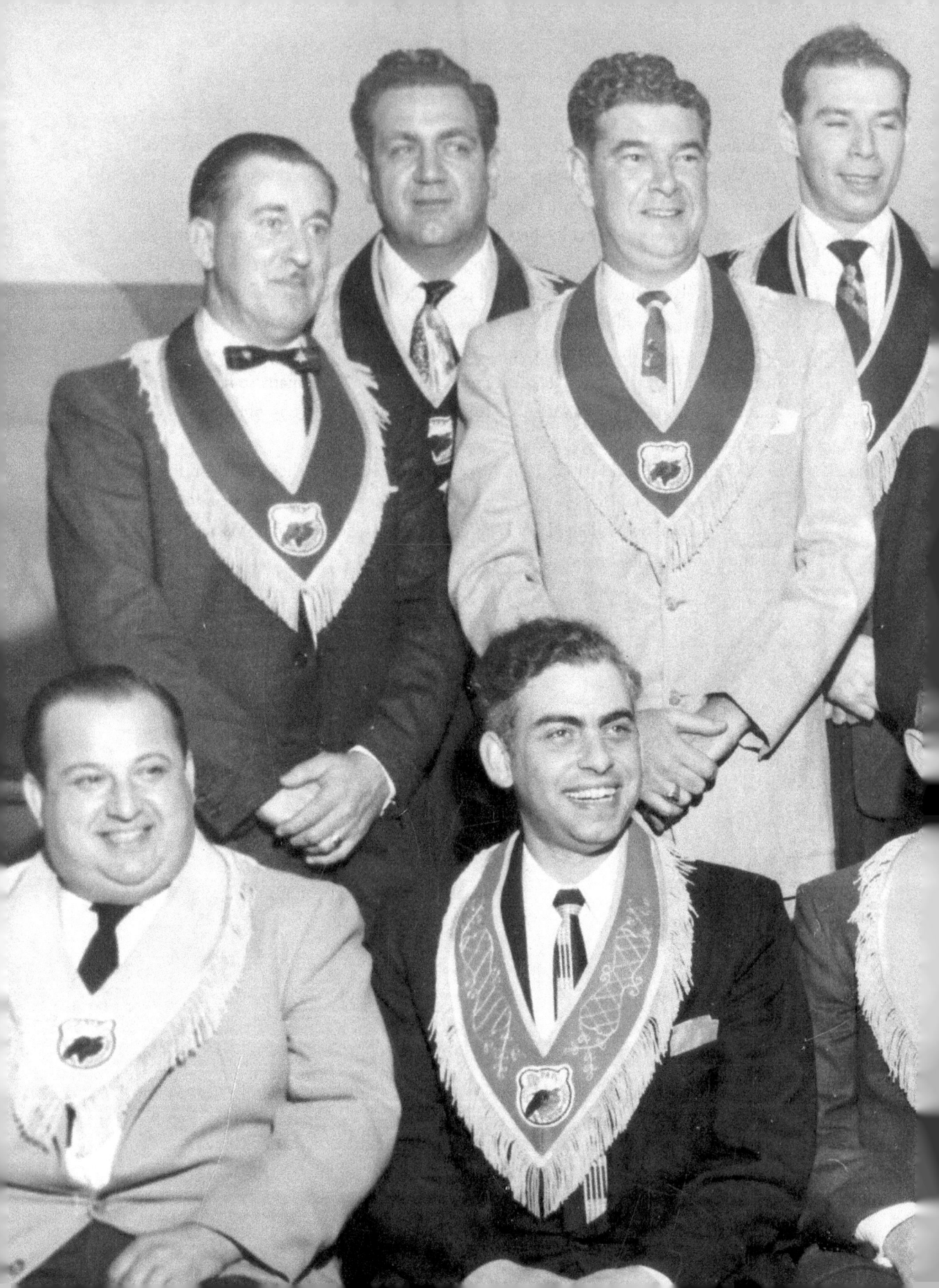

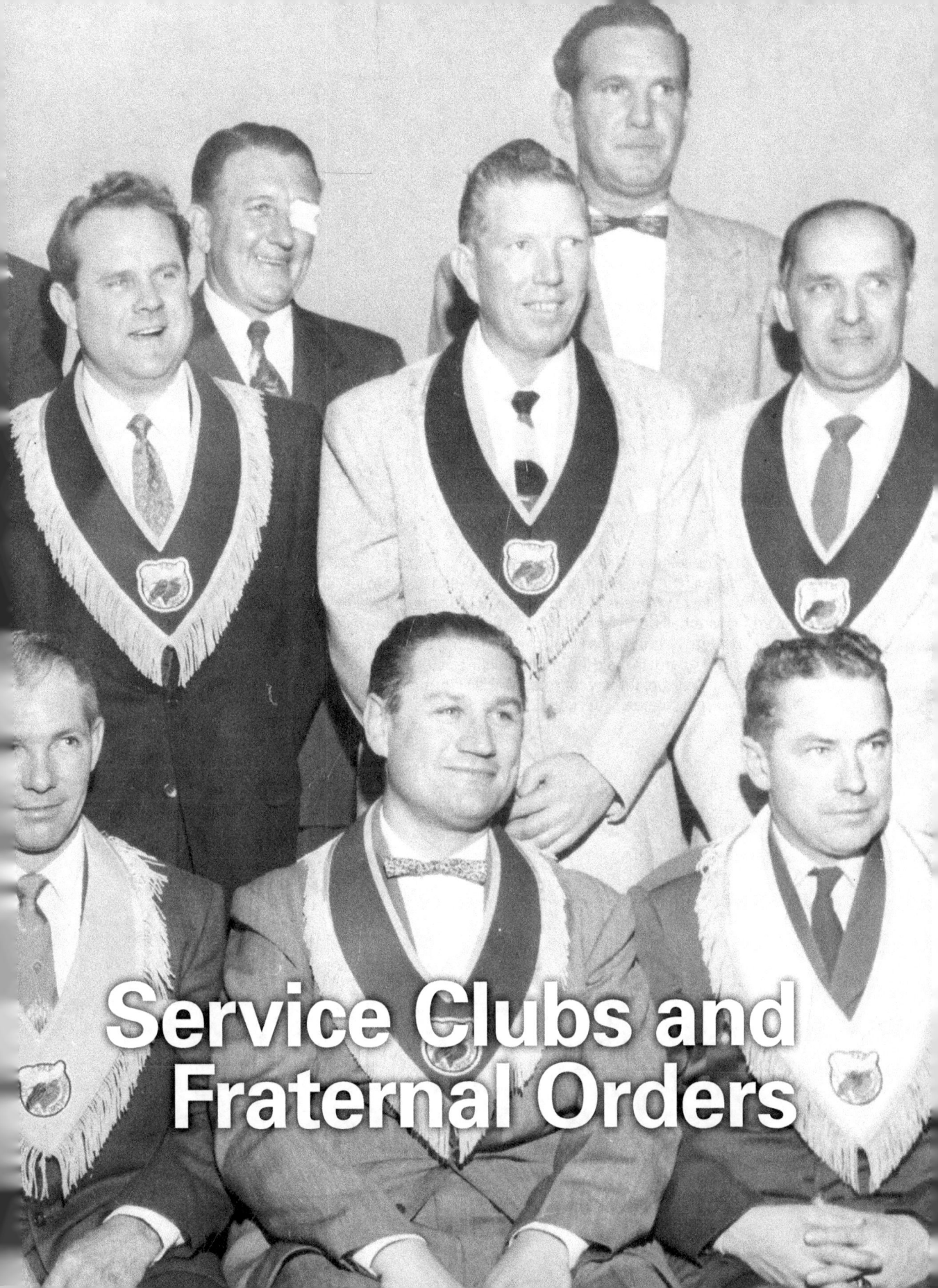

Service Clubs and Fraternal Orders

Overleaf: "These new officers of North Hollywood Lodge 1789, Loyal Order of the Moose, will preside at first meeting Wednesday. From left are (seated) Harry Liebman, assistant sergeant at arms; David L. Tratner, governor; Max Slusher, junior governor; Mitchell Kuhn, secretary, and John E. D. Moore, prelate; (standing) Robert Kruger, past governor; Louis Letizia, inner guard; Louis E. Berroyer, treasurer; Mark Brown, outer guard; Donald Ames, one-year trustee; George Blake, membership director; Guy Wilson, three-year trustee; Bill Hammon, sergeant at arms, and Lloyd E. Wood, two-year trustee." February 20, 1956.

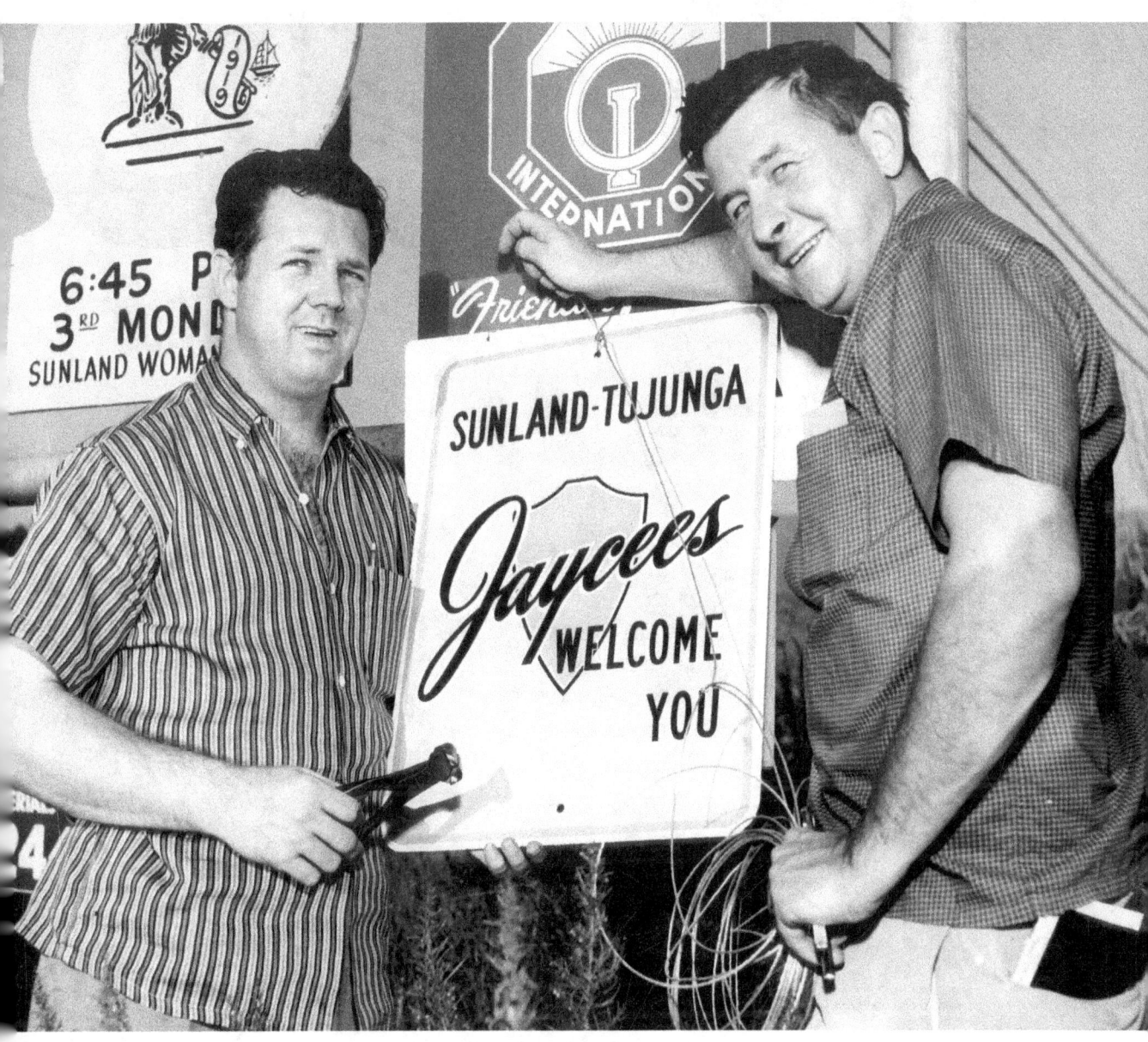

"George Beckley (left), immediate past president of Sunland-Tujunga Junior Chamber of Commerce, helps Robert Christopher, president, hang signs welcoming visitors to twin communities. Signs are posted at all entrances to city." October 27, 1959.

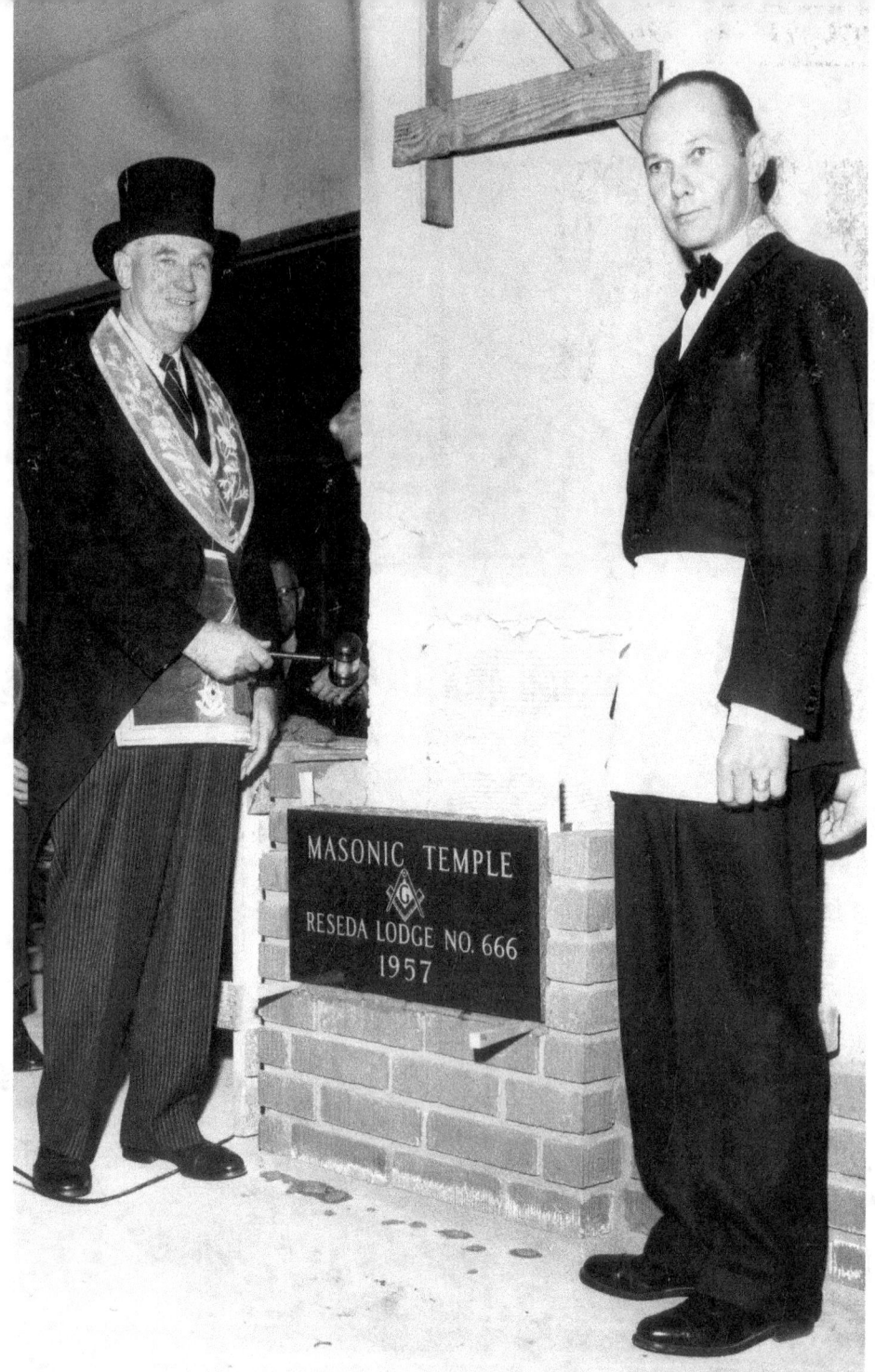

"Members of Reseda Masonic Lodge 666 take part in dedication ceremonies of their $250,000 temple at 6701 Darby Ave., Reseda. Leo Anderson (left), of Arcadia, Grand Master of California Jurisdiction, tests cornerstone with gavel. Karl Wood is Grand Master of Reseda lodge, which was founded in 1929. October 14, 1957.

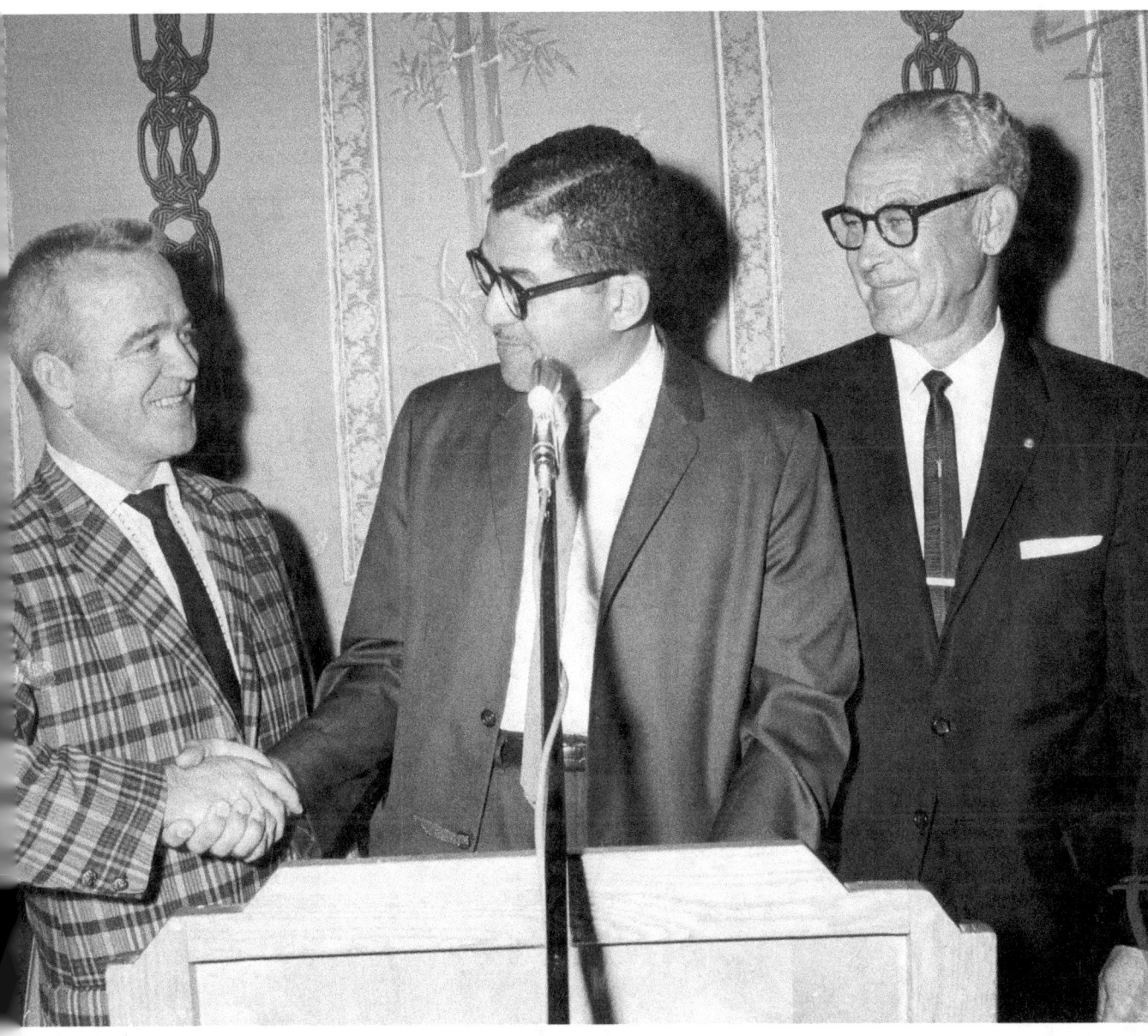

"The Rev. James Edward Jones, a candidate for Los Angeles City Board of Education Office No. 2 in next Tuesday's election, is flanked by Jack Forsythe (left), North Hollywood Rotary club, and club president Joe Oswald. Mr. Jones addressed the group yesterday at Arthur Wong's New Far East Terrace." May 18, 1965. (George Brich)

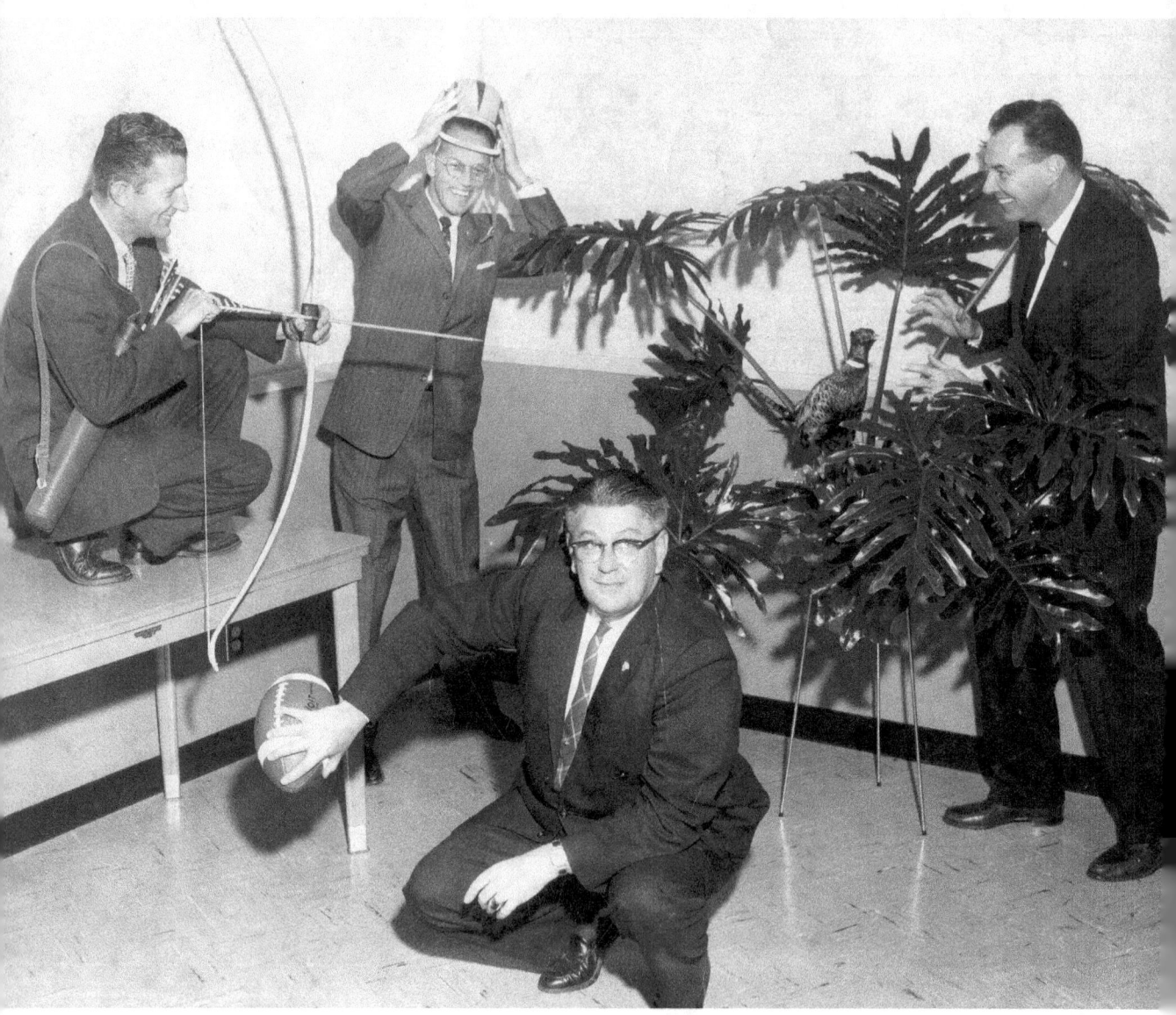

"North Hollywood service club presidents display athletic equipment to be purchased for local YMCA with proceeds of benefit dinner party on Nov. 26 at the Colonial House in North Hollywood. Left to right are Charles Jones, Lions; Frank Baudino, Kiwanis; Carl Lange, Opti-mist, and Peter Fritz, Rotary." November 20, 1958.

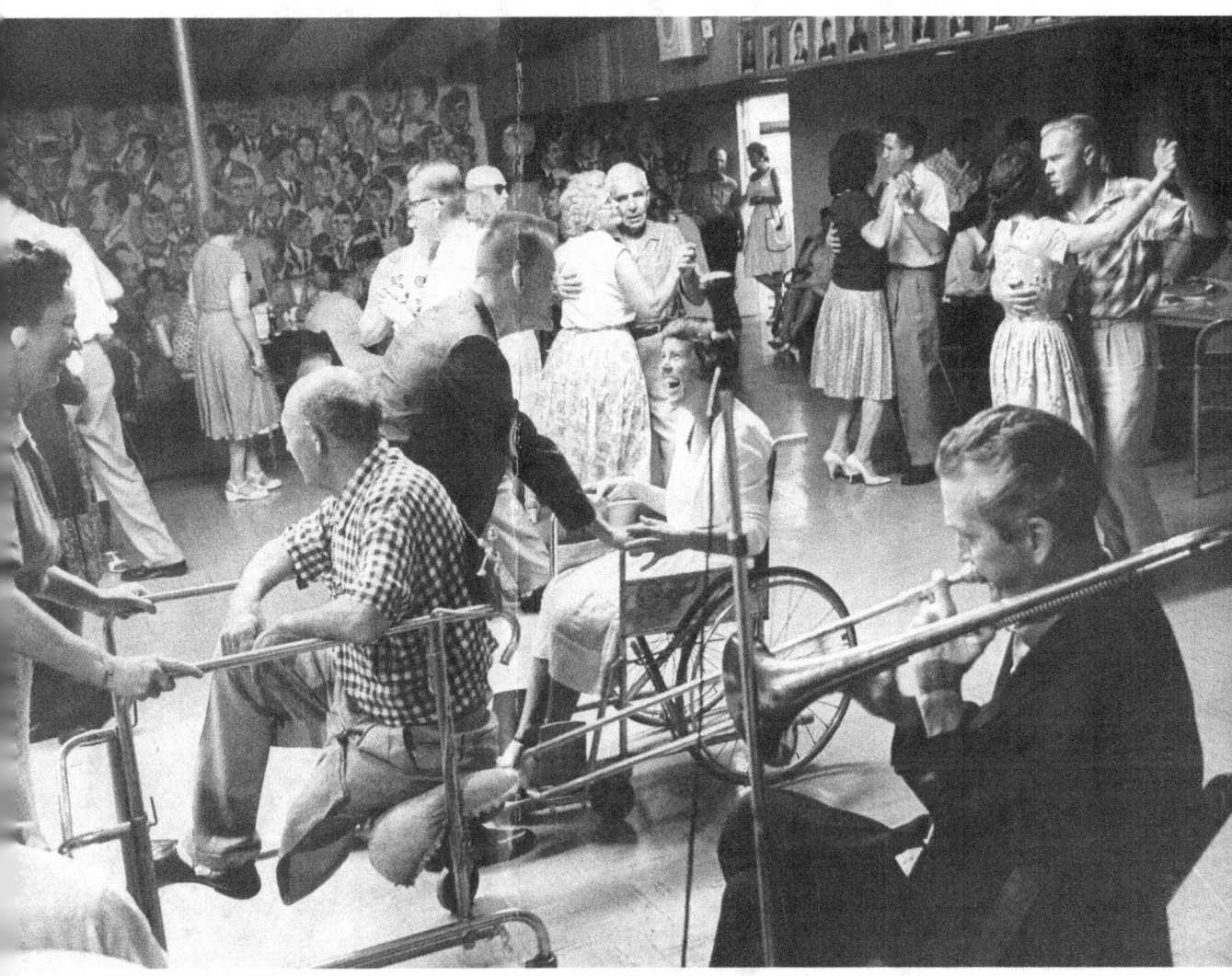

"Dancing partners Kenneth Buth and Ruth Meyers (center), Burbank, join in fun at monthly party sponsored by Exchange Club of Burbank and auxiliary, the Exchangettes. The club has held monthly parties for the handicapped since 1956 at the Burbank American Legion Post No. 150, 940 W. Olive Ave." August 3, 1962. (George Brich)

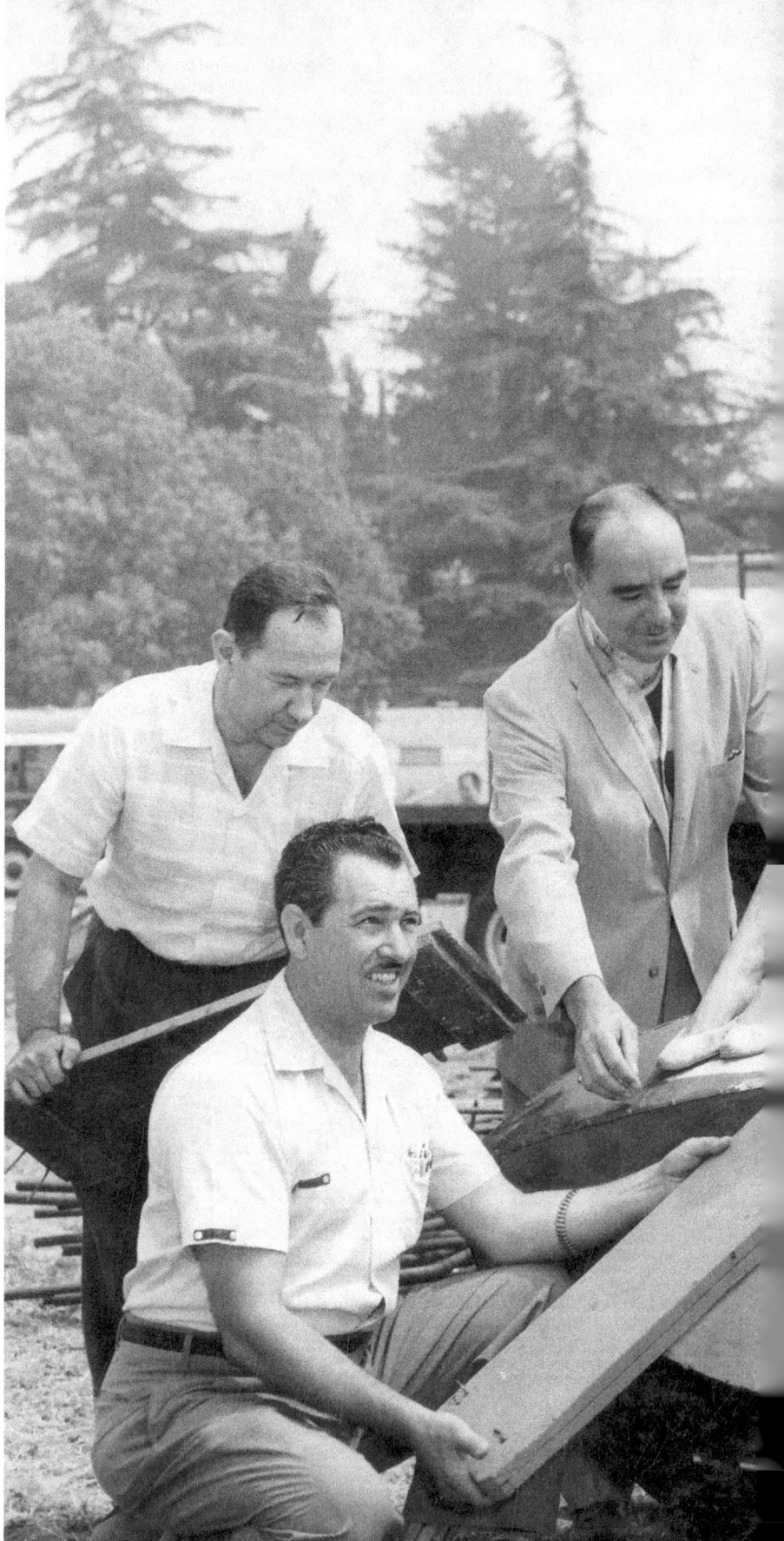

"Members of Van Nuys Elks Lodge 2028 get some decorative assistance from two Elks queen candidates as they put up final booth for four-day carnival which opens tonight in Van Nuys. From left are Rudy Jackson, Joe Kohler, Roy Nunnally, Phyllis Hechter, 15; Ced Downs and Gayle Morce, 16." September 4, 1958.

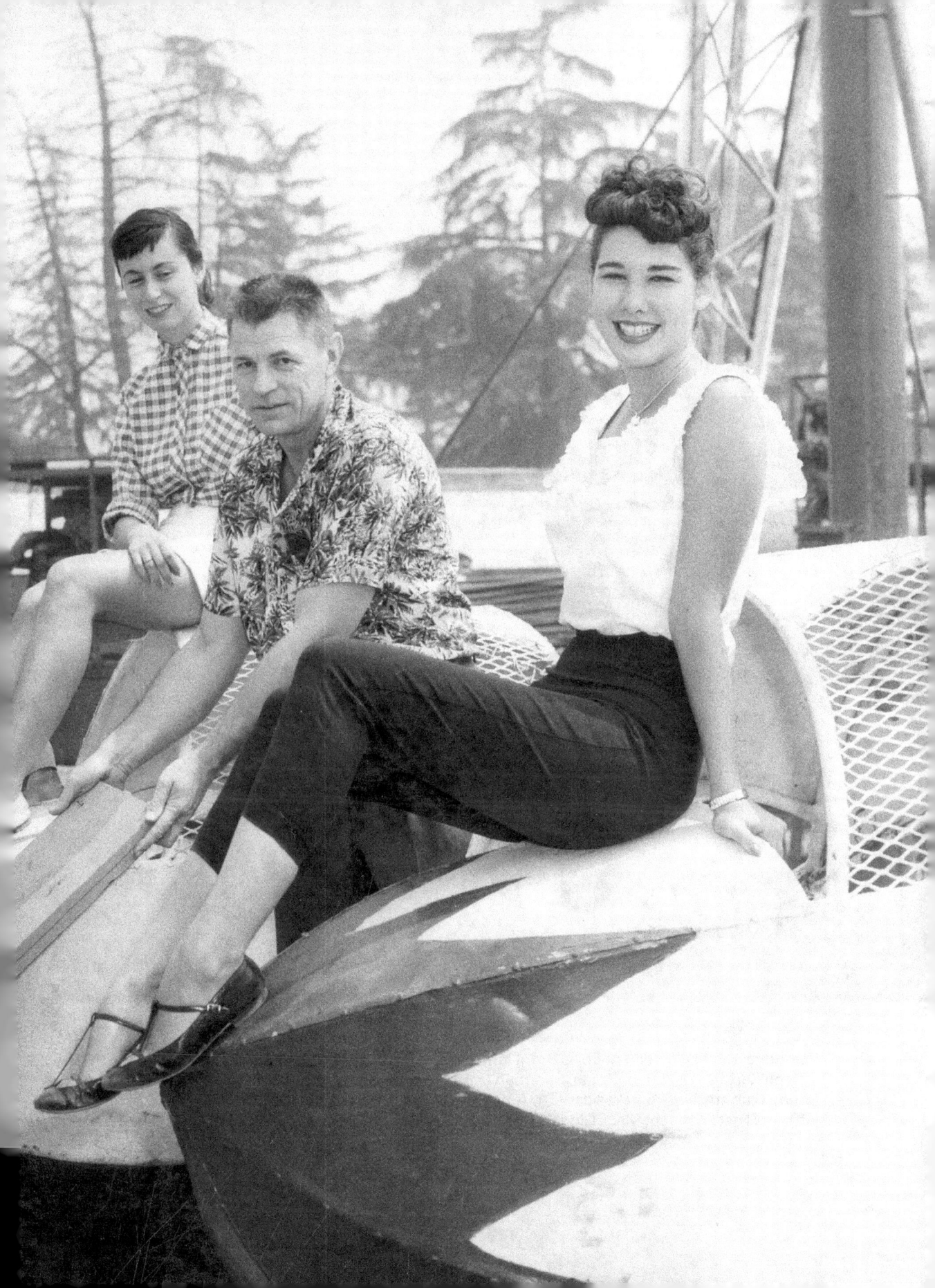

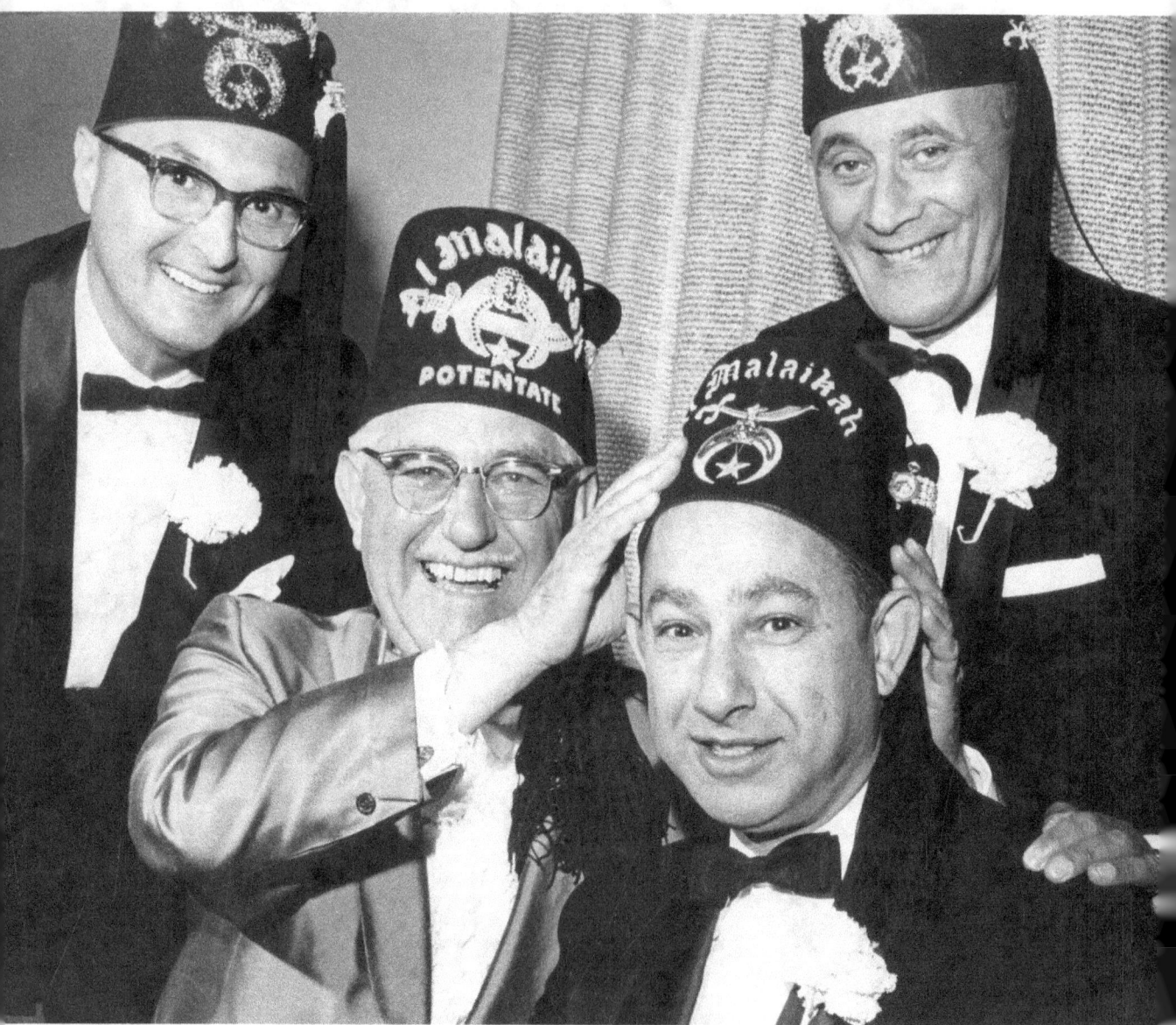

"Potentate J. B. Finney, Los Angeles (front left), confers the emblem of the presidency on Dr. Joseph Kaplan, 3701 Regal Vista, Sherman Oaks (front right). Other officers of the West Valley Shrine Club are First Vice President Dr. Arnold E. Weyman, 19143 Marilla St., Northridge (rear left), and Past President Mack Glorit, 6467 Petit Ave., Encino." March 21, 1961. (George Brich)

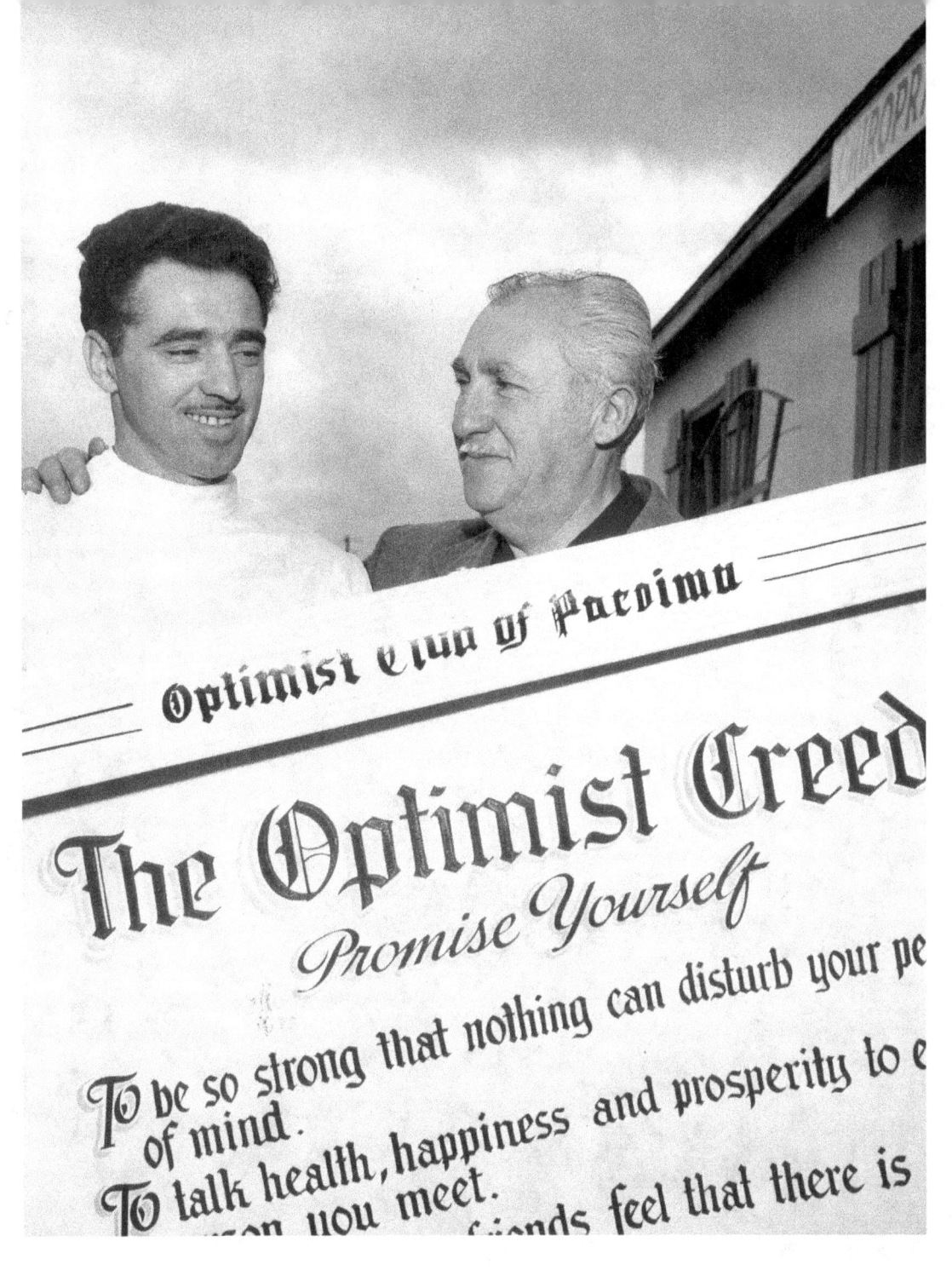

"H. Jay Ulis (right) of sponsoring Sepulveda Club, and Dr. Angelo Macchiarella, charter president of new Pacoima Optimist Club, pose with sign bearing creed of organization." February 1, 1955.

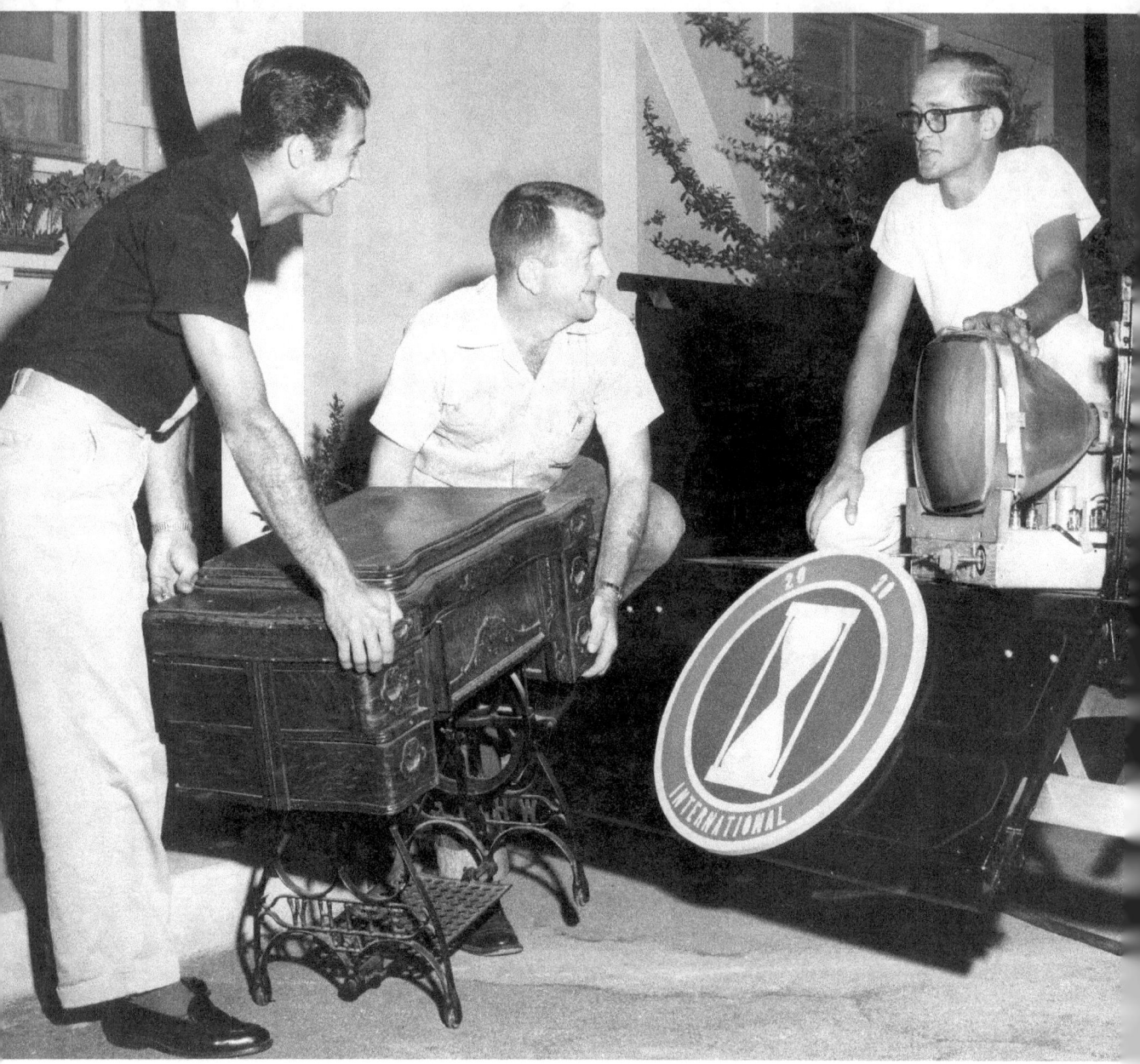

"Canoga Park 20-30ians collecting items for benefit auction at 6578 Winnetka Ave., Canoga Park. Stock piling goods for event are (from left) Bill Miklos, Neil Pefley and Bob Copeland. Proceeds will be used to purchase therapy equipment for handicapped children." July 26, 1958.

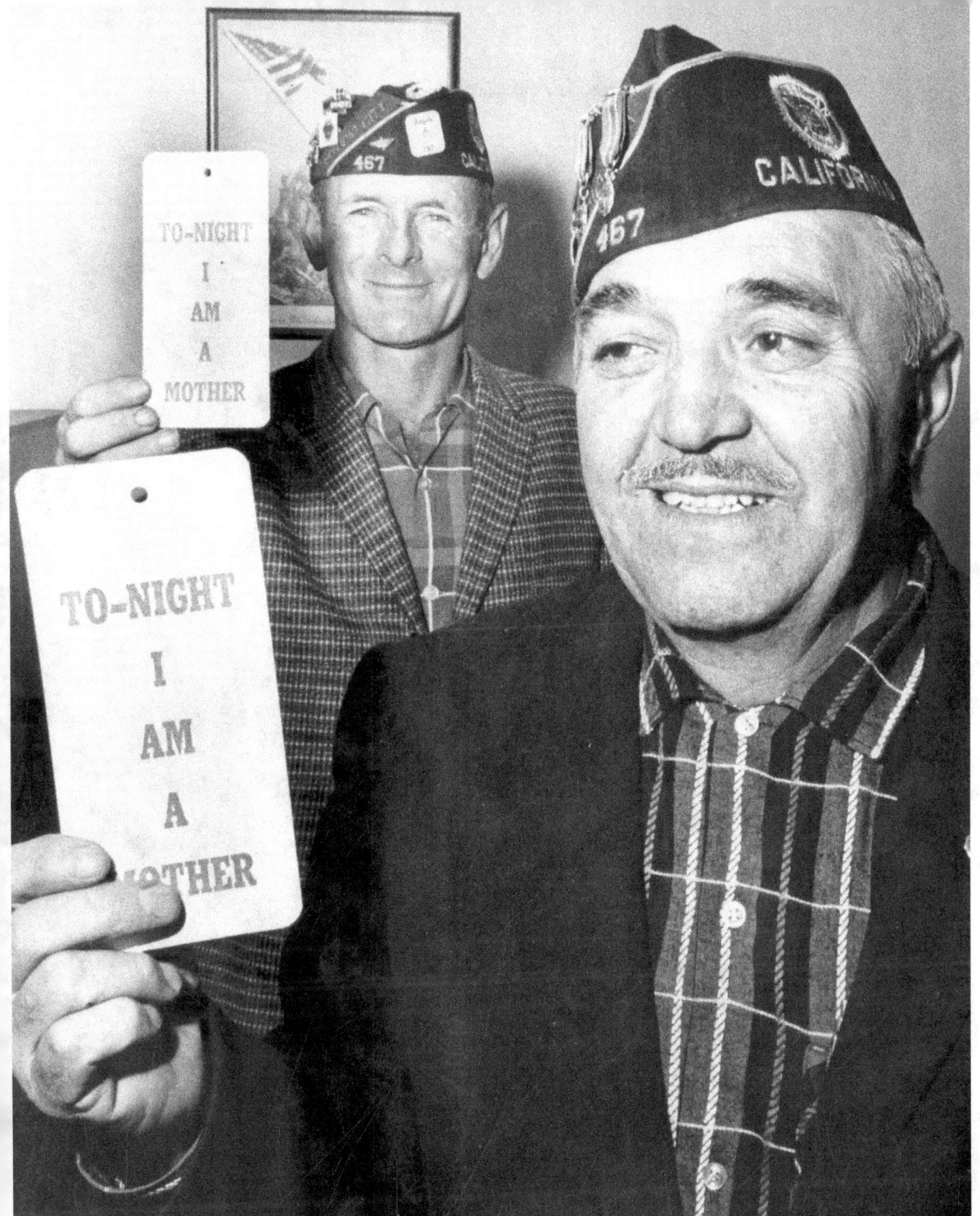

"Members of American Legion Post 467 will lend a helping hand in the Mothers March for the 1962 March of Dimes by calling at homes in the hilly areas of Studio City. Bill Sanford, commander of the post (back), and Bernard Pellegrini display placards they will carry." January 23, 1962. (Jeff Goldwater)

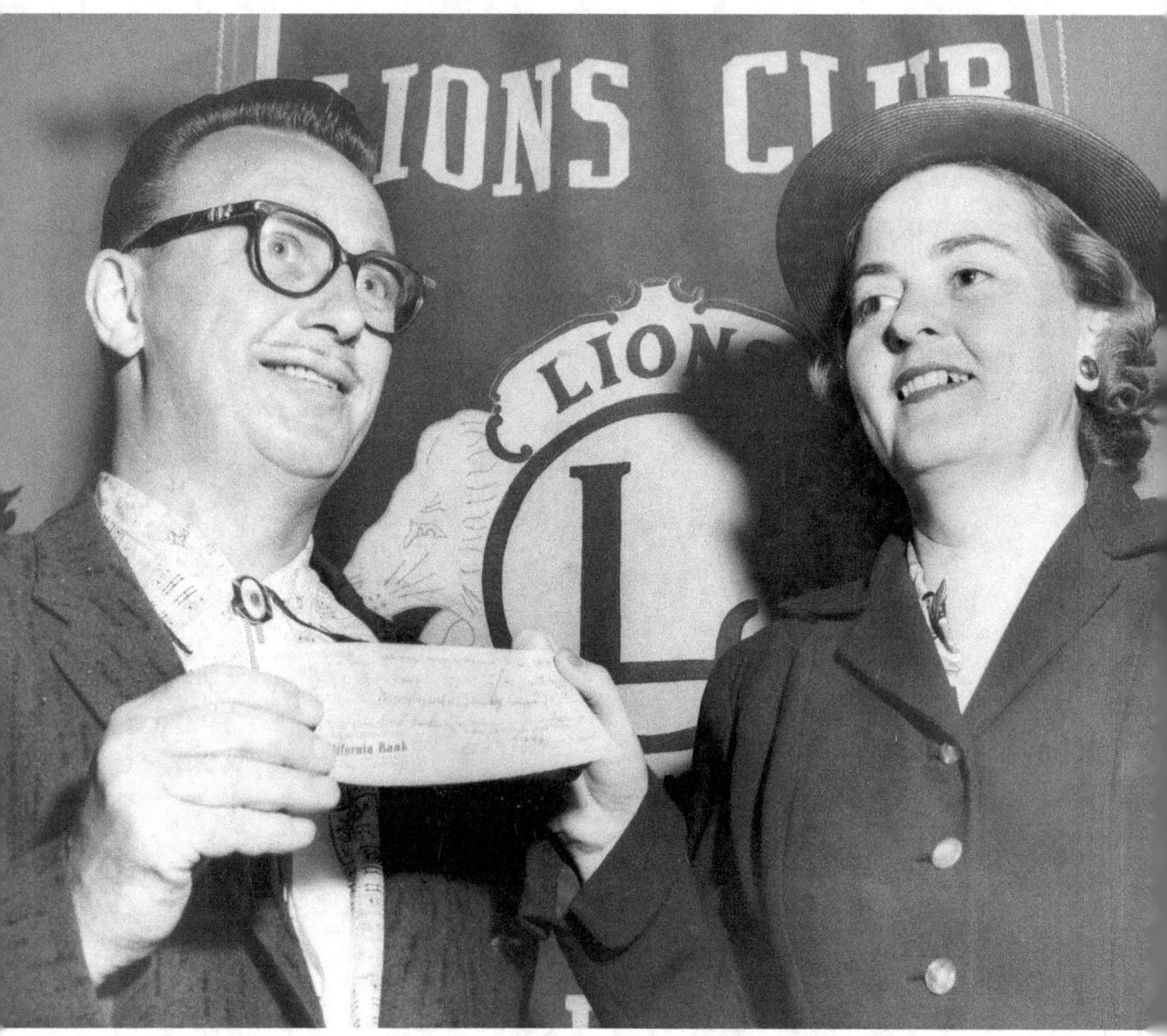

"E. Jay Page, president of North Hollywood Lions Club, gives Mrs. W. D. Lowry, secretary of a Los Angeles nursery school for visually handicapped children, a check for $700." Lions have donated from proceeds of club's salvage store. May 22, 1956.

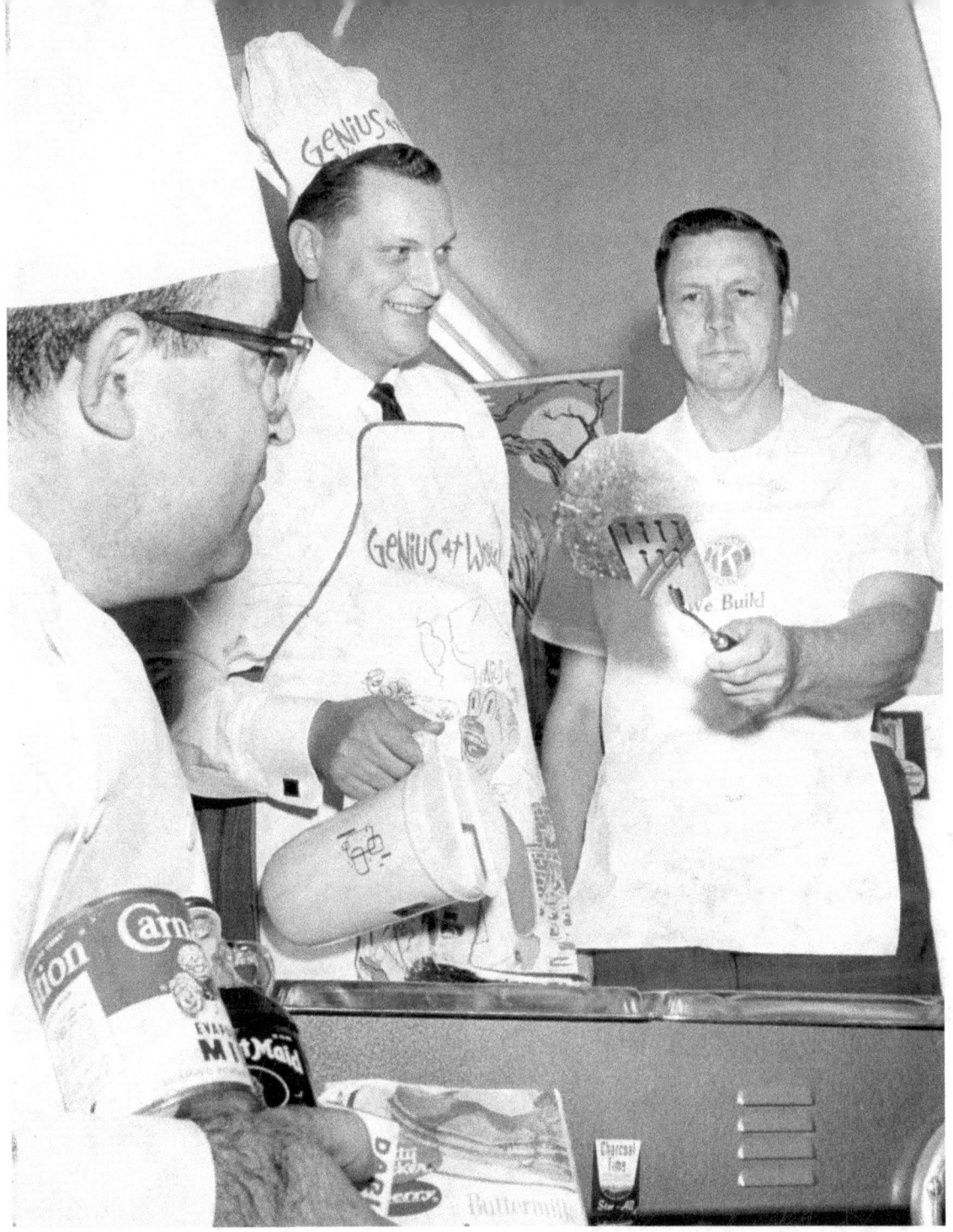

"Dr. Fred Bowers, president of Sepulveda-Mission Hills Kiwanis, right, demonstrates technique on griddle to Bob Hattem (left), while Jim Marcus pours batter." Trio is preparing for Kiwanis Pancake Breakfast at McDaniels Food Market, 10400 Sepulveda Blvd., Mission Hills. October 6, 1960. (George Brich)

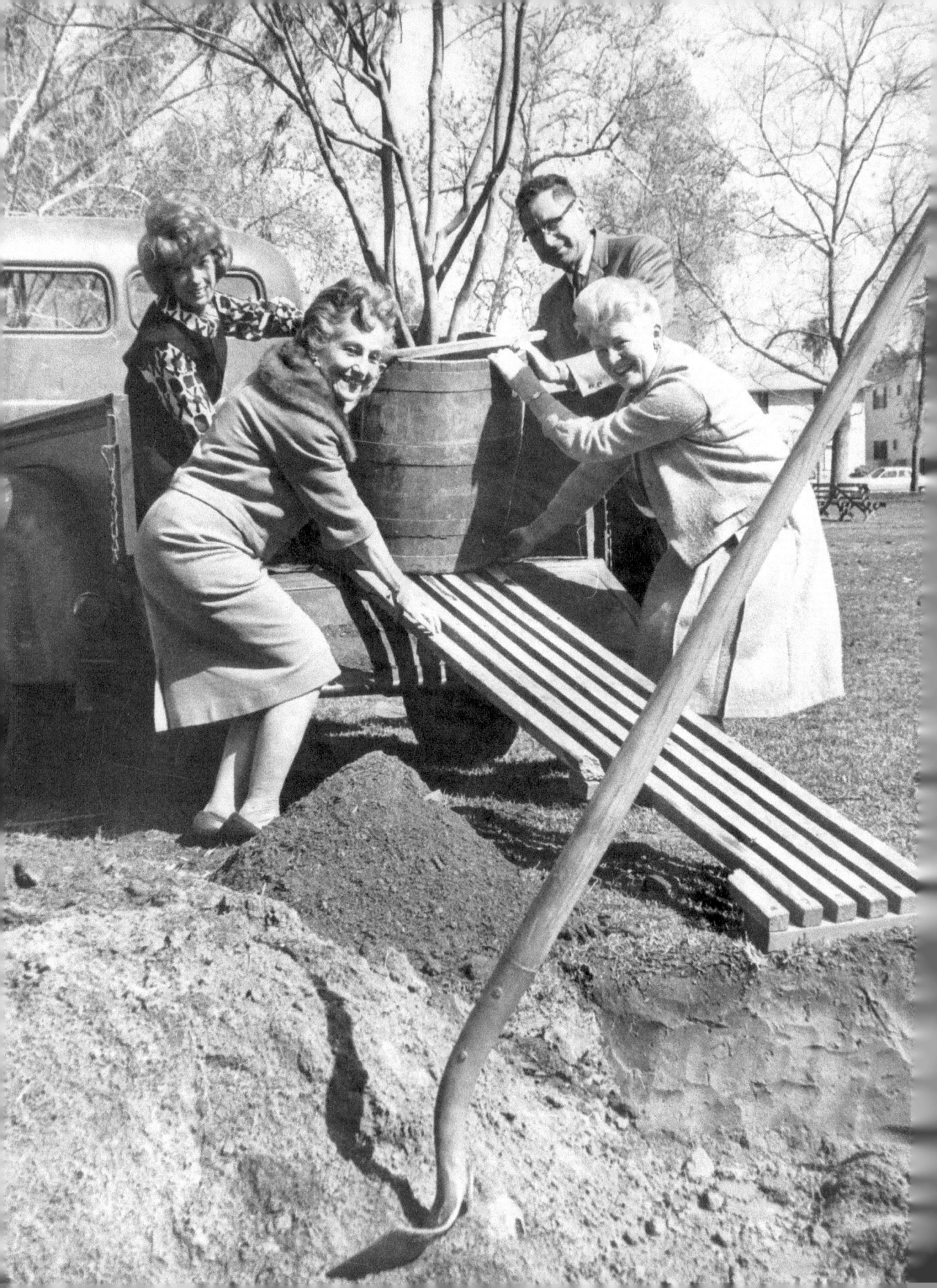

Women's Organizations and Auxiliaries

Page 24: "Unloading a double pink crepe myrtle tree in North Hollywood Park are Erwin Williams of the Los Angeles Recreation and Parks Dept. and members of the Laurel Garden Club who donated the tree for planting. From left are Mrs. Harold Hood, who sponsored the tree planting; Mrs. Fred Lanko, club president, and Mrs. R. B. Spensley, the club's conservation chairman." March 13, 1964. (Jeff Robbins)

Page 25: "Valley area members of the League of Women Voters demonstrate on the scale what they believe to be unnecessary detail in the State Constitution. At right is their conception of a trimmed-down version. Members shown (from left) are Mrs. Donald Weber, 8515 Delco Ave., Canoga Park; Mrs. Norbert Grengs, 5630 Le Sage Ave., Woodland Hills, and Mrs. Jack Hoffenberg, 13511 Rand Ave., Sherman Oaks." Interviews of Valley legislators will be reported at the League's meeting at Glen Air Country Club, 3910 Stansbury Dr., Sherman Oaks. January 16, 1961. (George Brich)

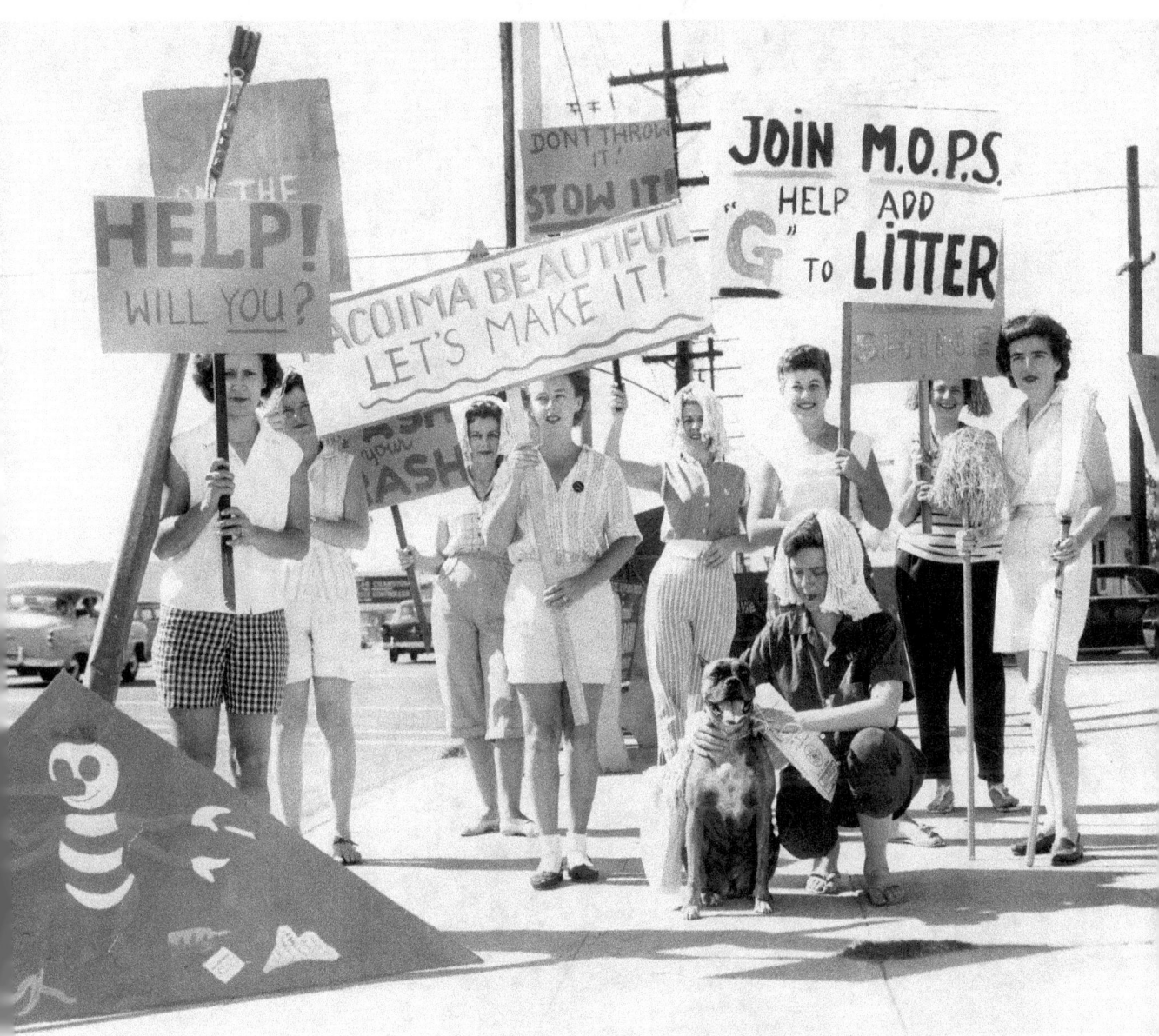

"Members of Pacoima Woman's Club began picketing on community streets today to point up campaign for Pacoima Beautiful. All participants in strike dolled themselves up in mop-hats and raggedy clothes. They intend to promote interest among citizens in cleaning up and enhancing appearance of neglected areas of community." October 20, 1958.

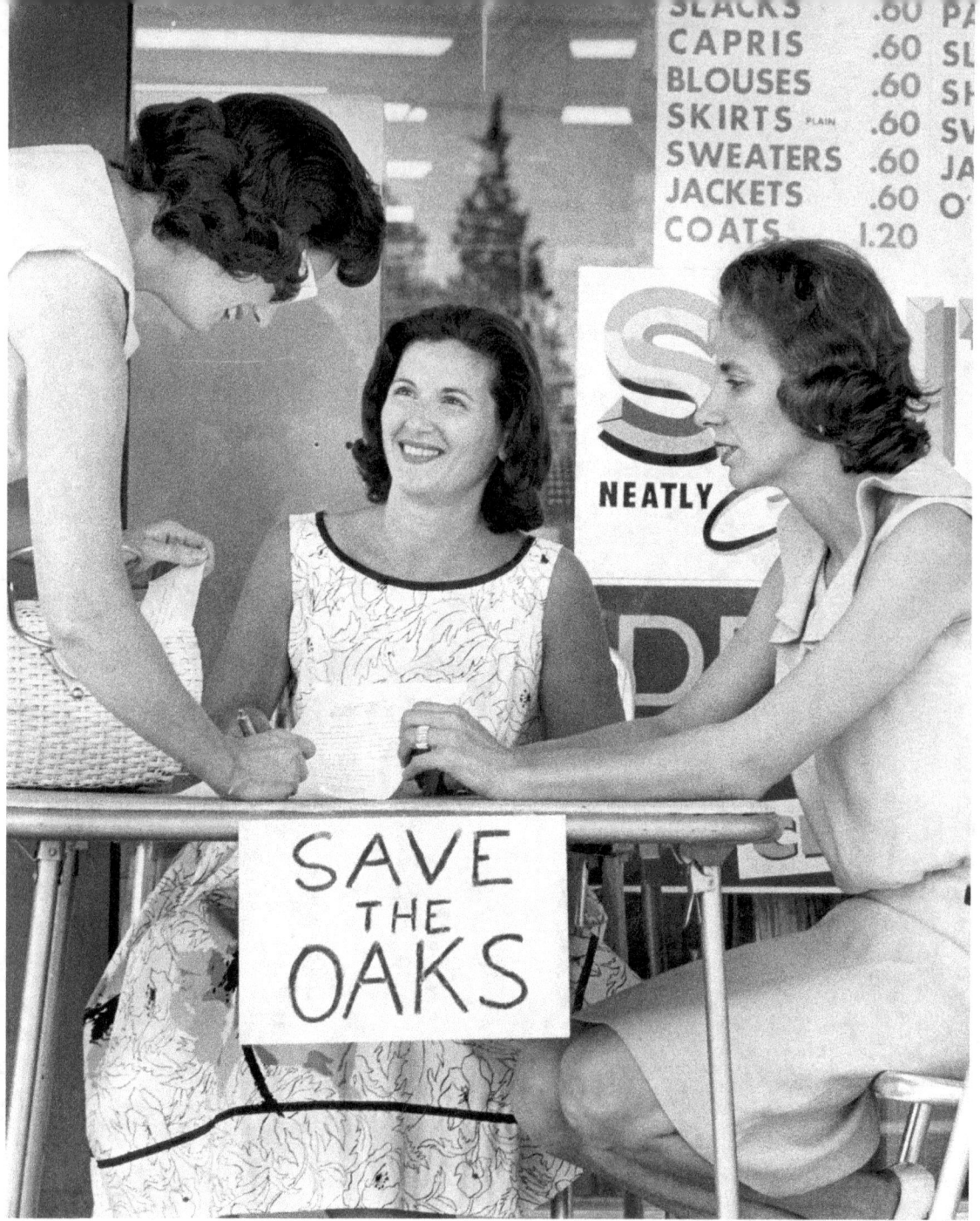

"The Chatsworth Junior Women's Club is obtaining signatures on petitions to save oak trees of great age and beauty, which will be destroyed unless the present plan for rerouting Santa Susana Ave. in Chatsworth is changed. The oak trees are located at 10870 Santa Susana Ave. and adjacent thereto. Hard at work on the project are (from left) Mmes. Bruce Magill, James Cicchi, and Garvin Aulepp." The drive was held outside Hughes Market in Chatsworth. July 11, 1964. (George Brich)

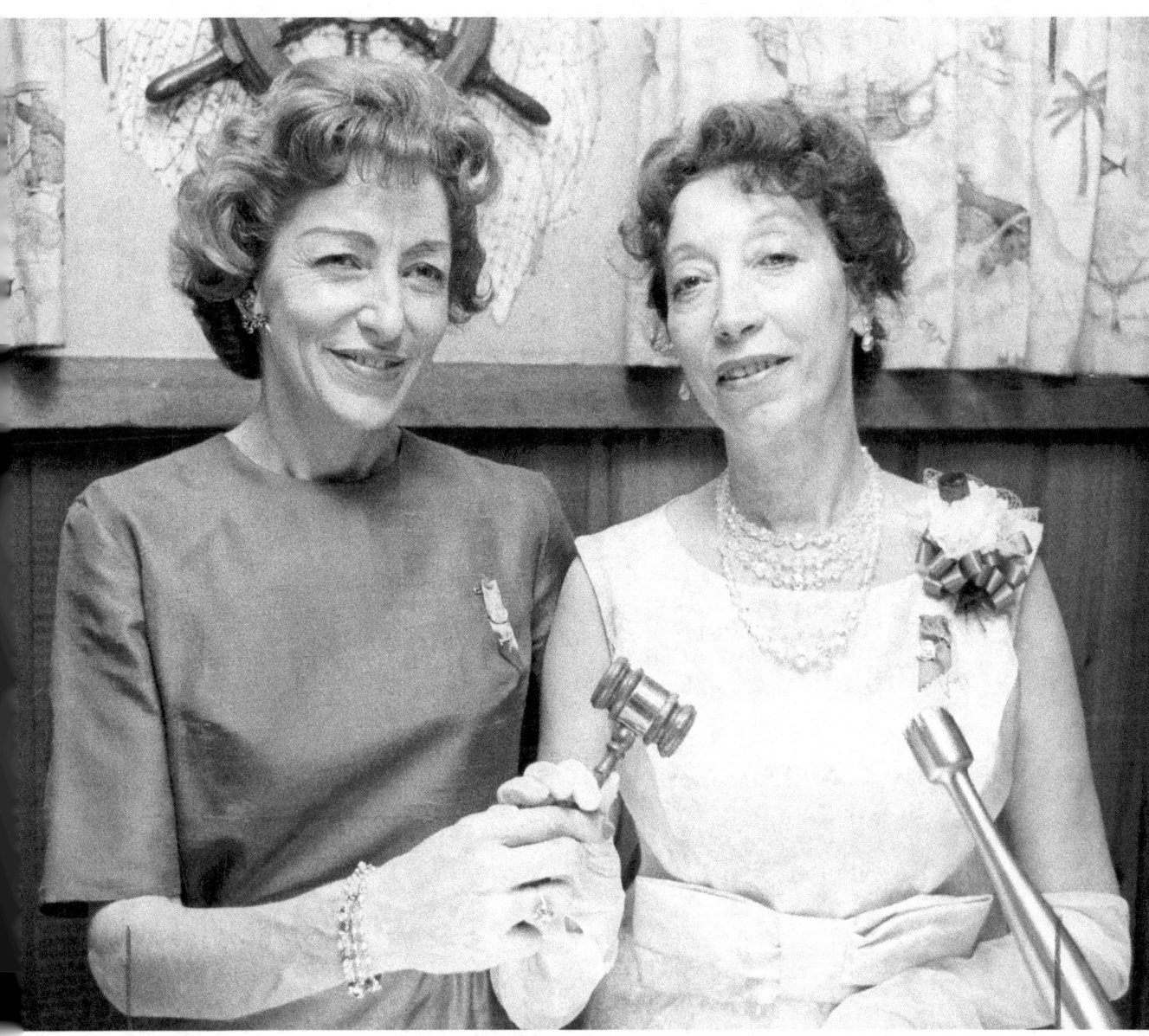

"Mrs. Leona Paine (left), retiring president of the San Fernando Business and Professional Women's Club, turns gavel over to new president, Mrs. Jeanne Anderson, at recent installation dinner at the Fin and Feather Restaurant, San Fernando." Mrs. Paine is the San Fernando city deputy treasurer. May 26, 1964. (Steve Young)

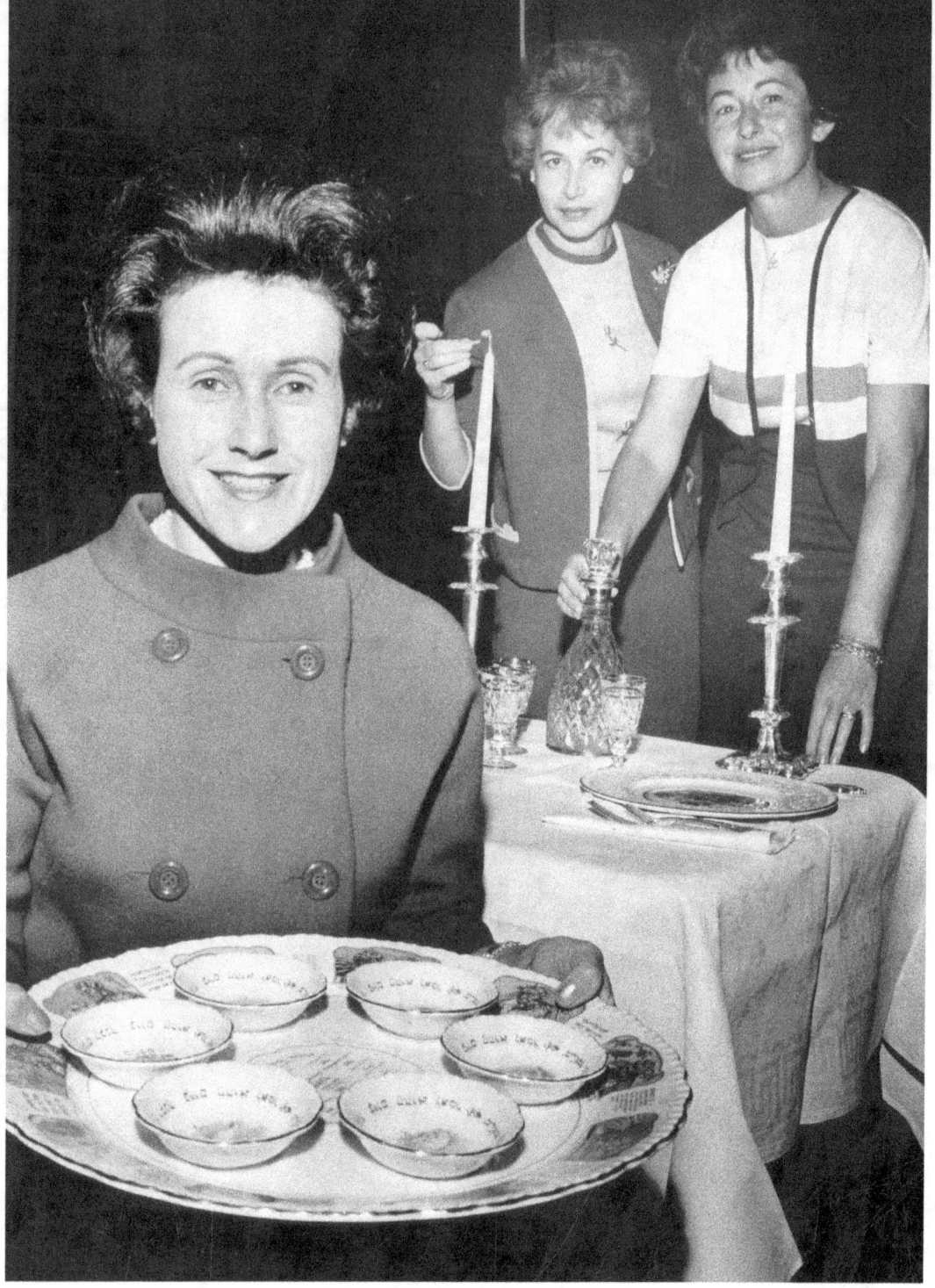

"The Temple Beth Hillel Sisterhood members welcome women of all religious denominations at their Inter-faith Dessert Tea in the temple social hall, 12326 Riverside Dr., North Hollywood. From left to right, Mmes. Saltsman, Dinkin, and Laundres." February 5, 1963. (George Brich)

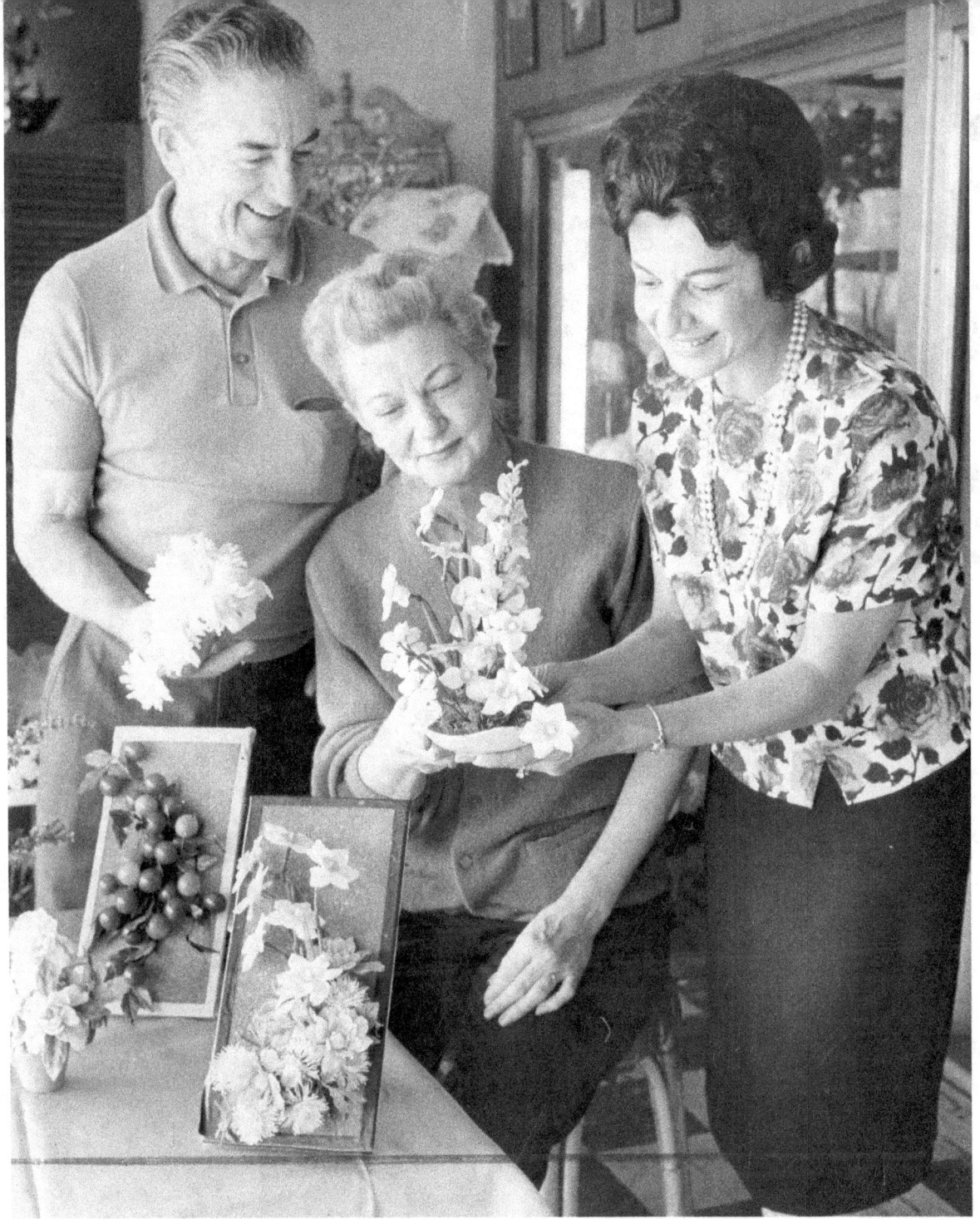

"Mr. and Mrs. Ted McMichael, owners of the Merry Macs Flower Pot, North Hollywood, show arrangements created by children of Lowman School for the Handicapped to Mrs. James Sullivan, corresponding secretary for North Hollywood, Toluca Lake, Studio City Soroptimist Club, sponsoring organization for the project." November 12, 1963. (Larry Leach)

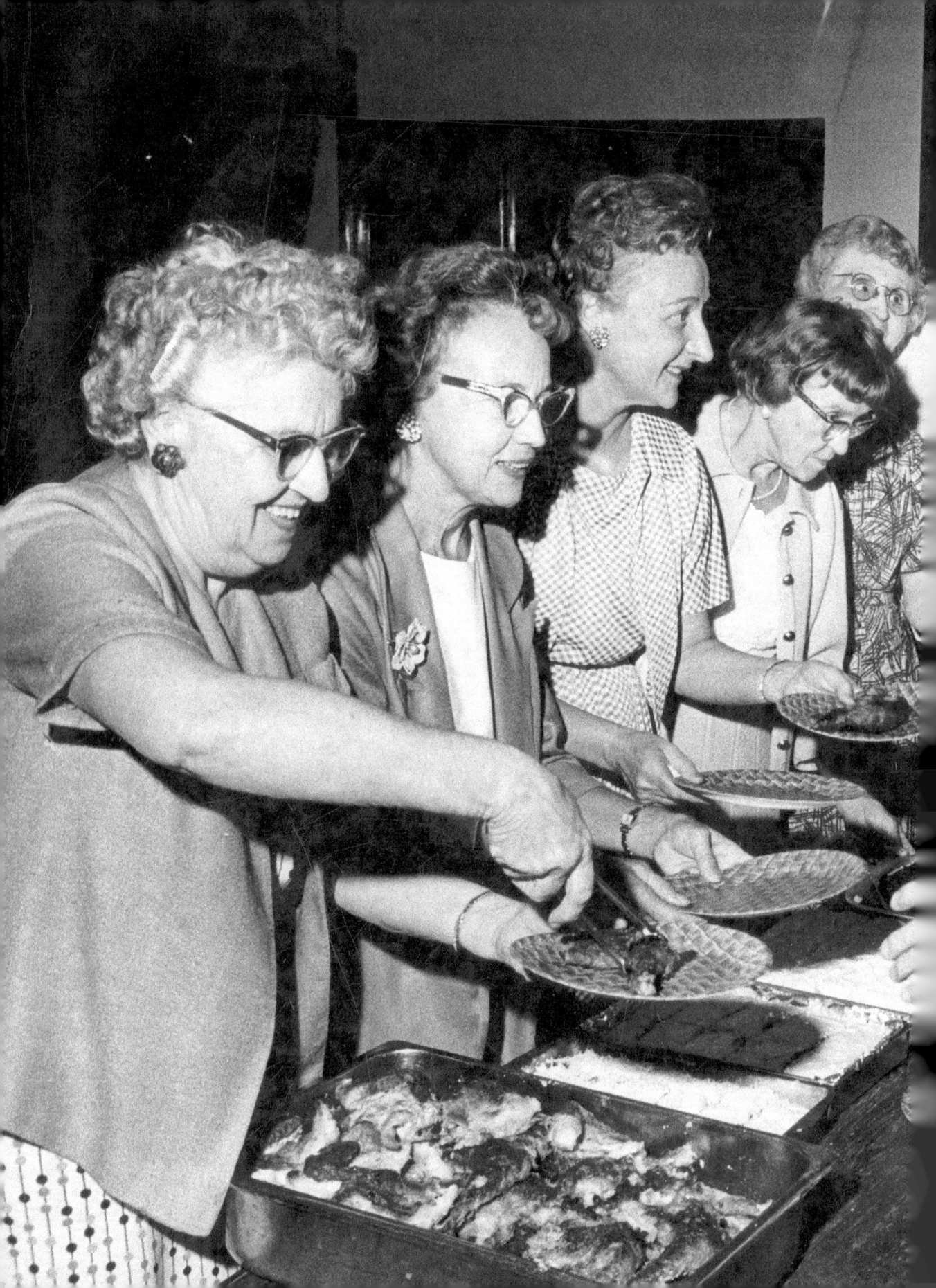

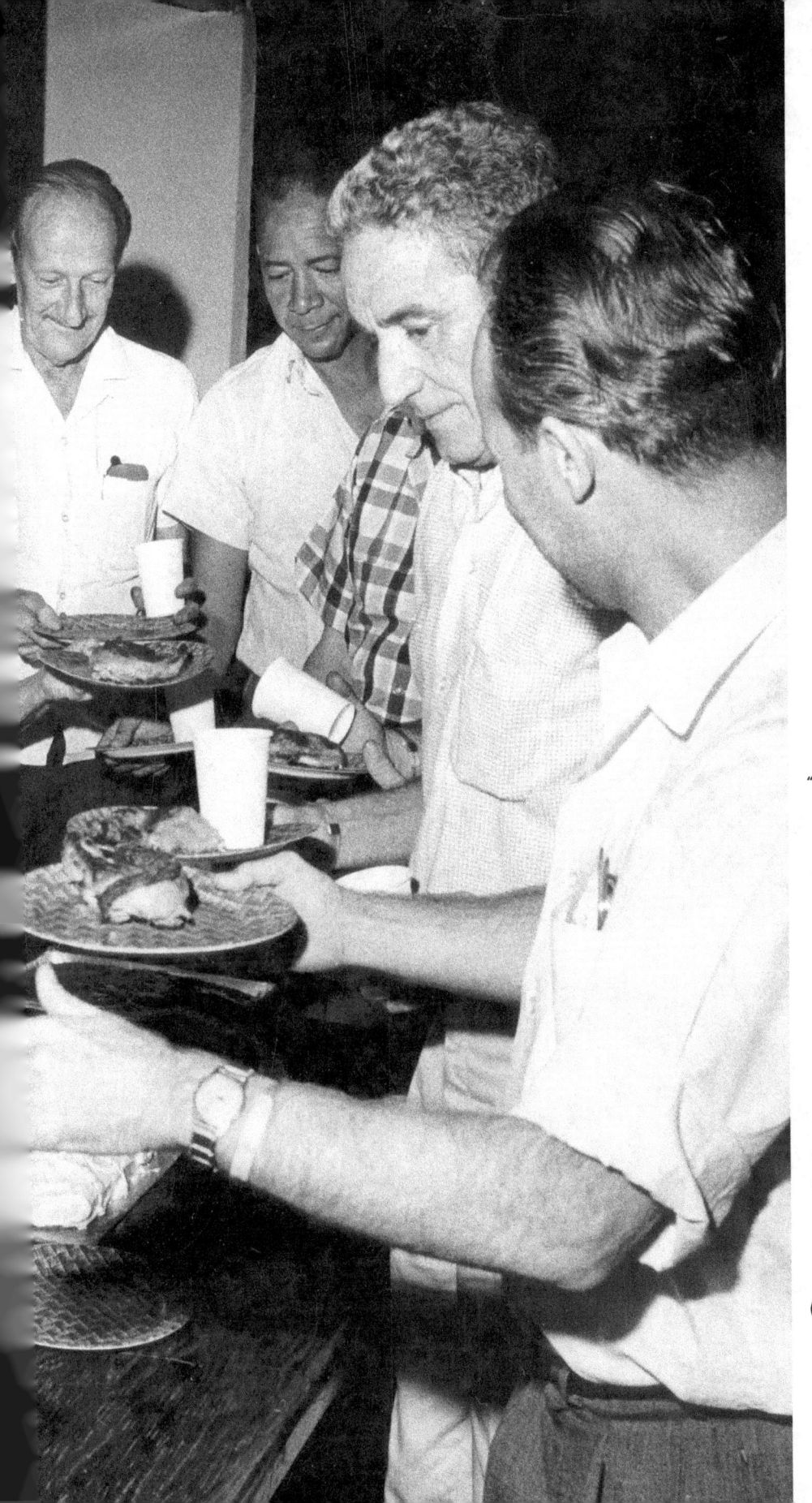

"Serving veterans at annual cookout sponsored by the North Hollywood Woman's Club at the San Fernando Valley Veterans Hospital are (from left) Mmes. H. C. Millerberg, William S. Morrow, Broox Davis, club president; George Worsham and Harriet Ponder, veterans' affairs chairman. Also assisting was Mrs. B. W. Kemper." September 14, 1964.
(George Brich)

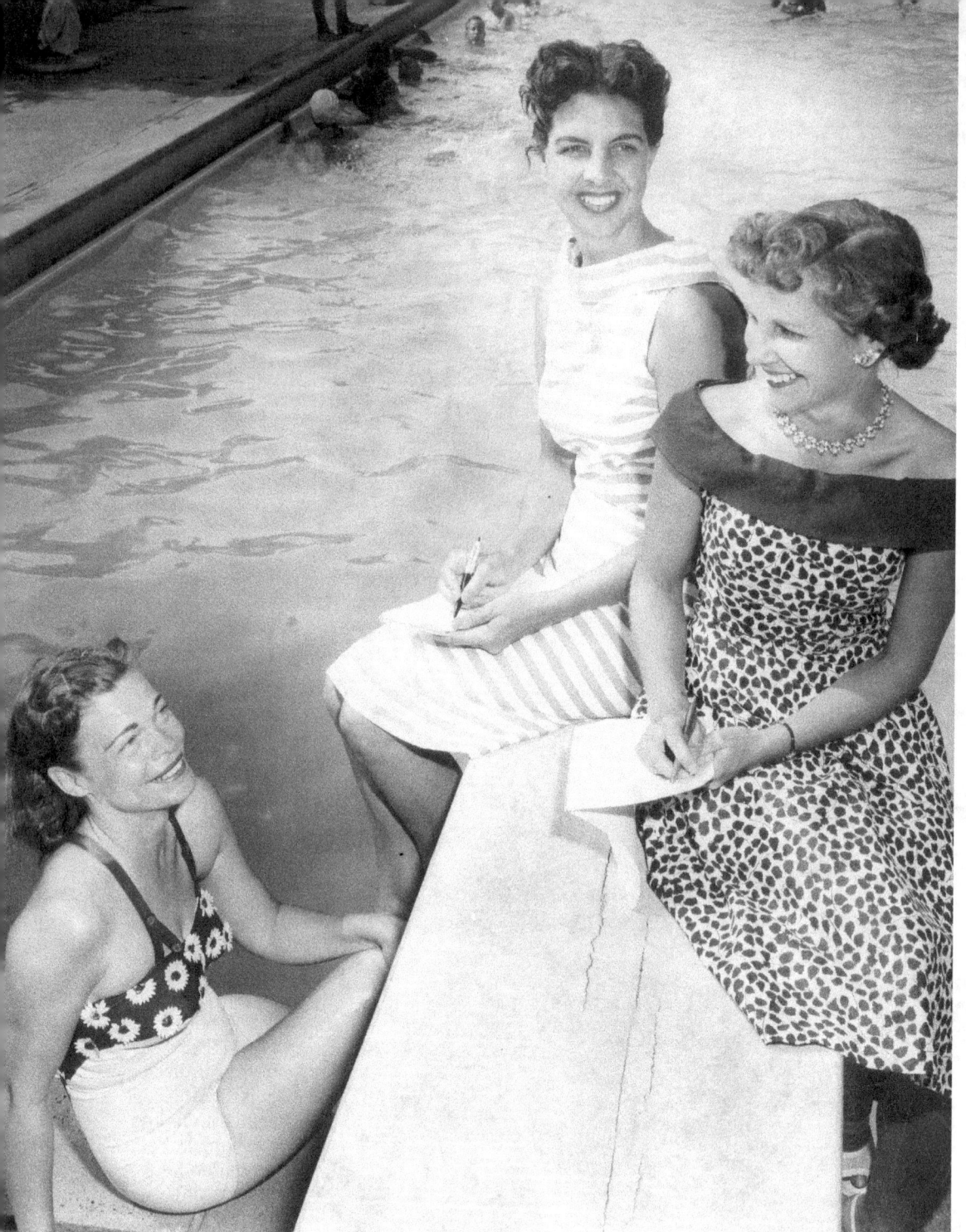

"Poolside inspirations of Mrs. Richard Turner (at left) are recorded by Mrs. Calvin Scroggins and Mrs. A. B. Clarke, members, for potluck dinner and swim party being planned by West Valley Y W Wives Club." July 23, 1958.

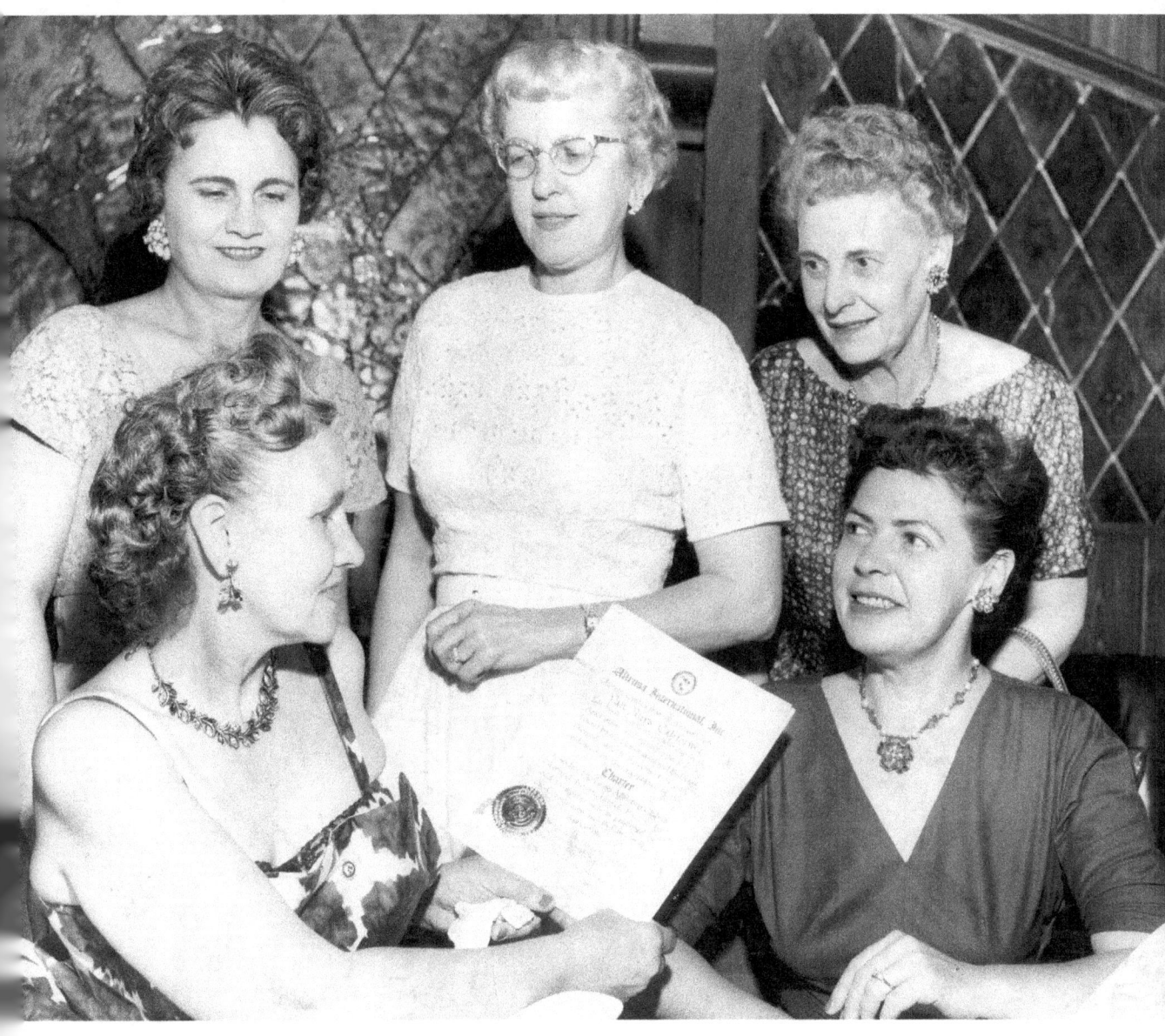

"Newly installed leaders of Altrusa Club of Van Nuys admire charter from Altrusa International after induction at charter dinner. Seated (from left), is Mary Farmer, charter president, with Laura Larson, treasurer. Standing are Mildred Patterson, vice president; Hazel Reeves and Mary O'Neill secretaries (from left)." June 29, 1959.

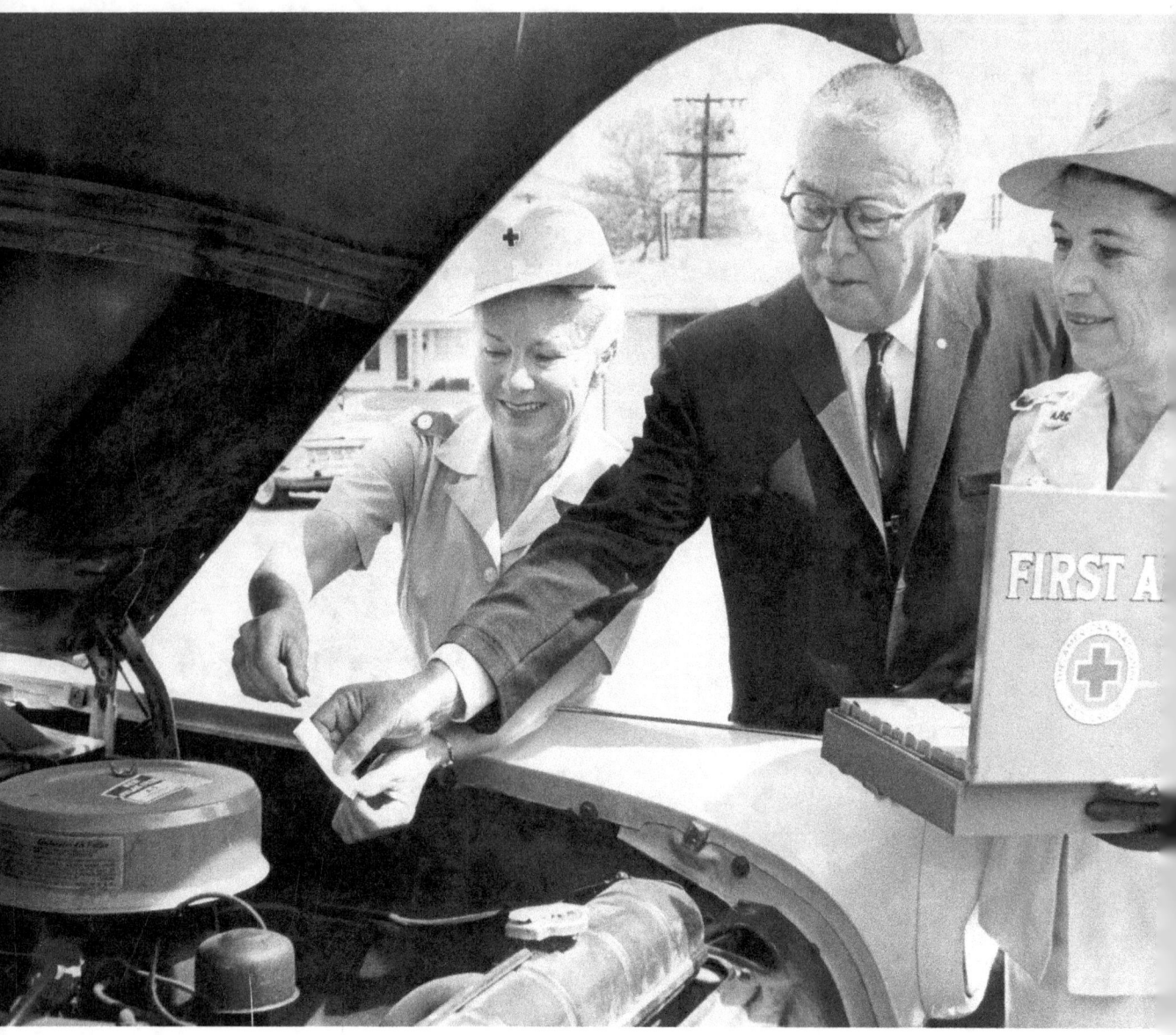

"Burbank Red Cross workers give 'first aid' to the engine of their used station wagon. From left are Mrs. Jack Leaverton, member, Woman's Club of Burbank, and chairman of the Burbank Red Cross volunteer Motor Corps, Benjamin Watson, chapter chairman, and Mrs. G. Ray Sherwood, past club president and a Red Cross driver for 20 years. The station wagon is the only car available to transport local Red Cross workers to the scene of a disaster." April 6, 1963. (Jeff Goldwater)

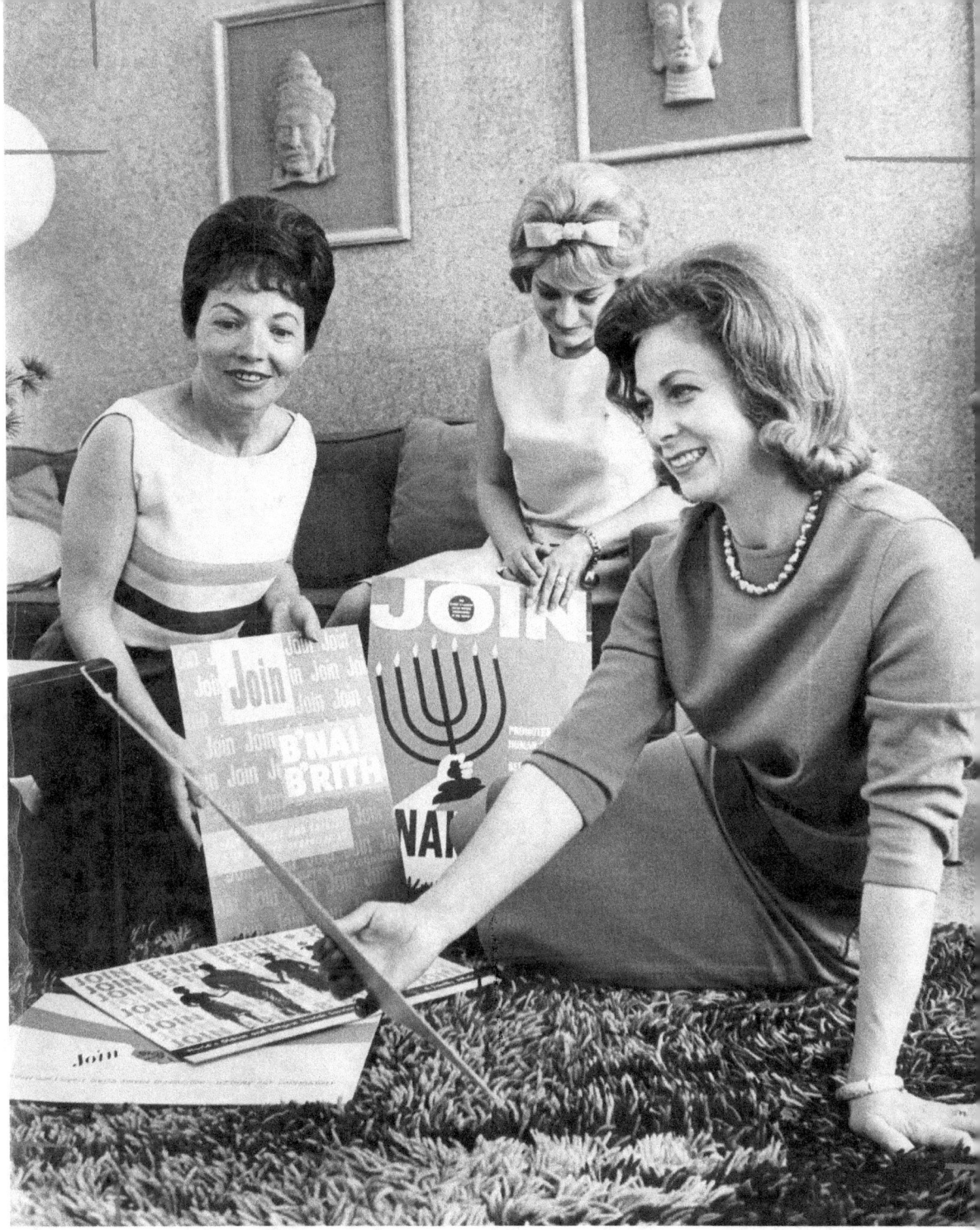

"Davida Chapter of B'nai B'rith Women will sponsor a membership evening in the Encino home of Mrs. Arthur Provisor. Discussing plans for the event with the hostess (left) are Mrs. Maurice Bachelis, Granada Hills, and Seymour Lehrer, Studio City." June 9, 1964. (Gordon Dean)

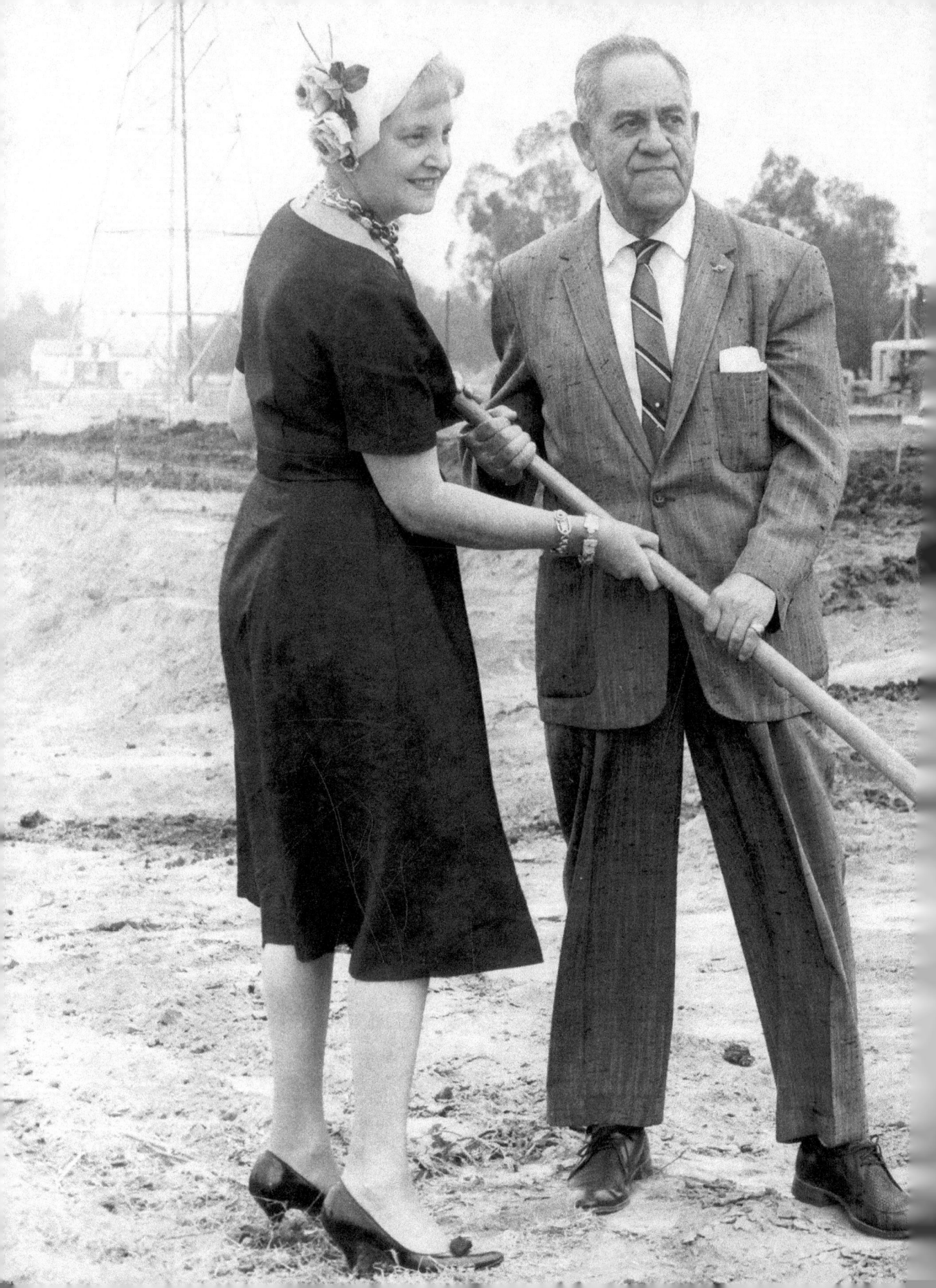

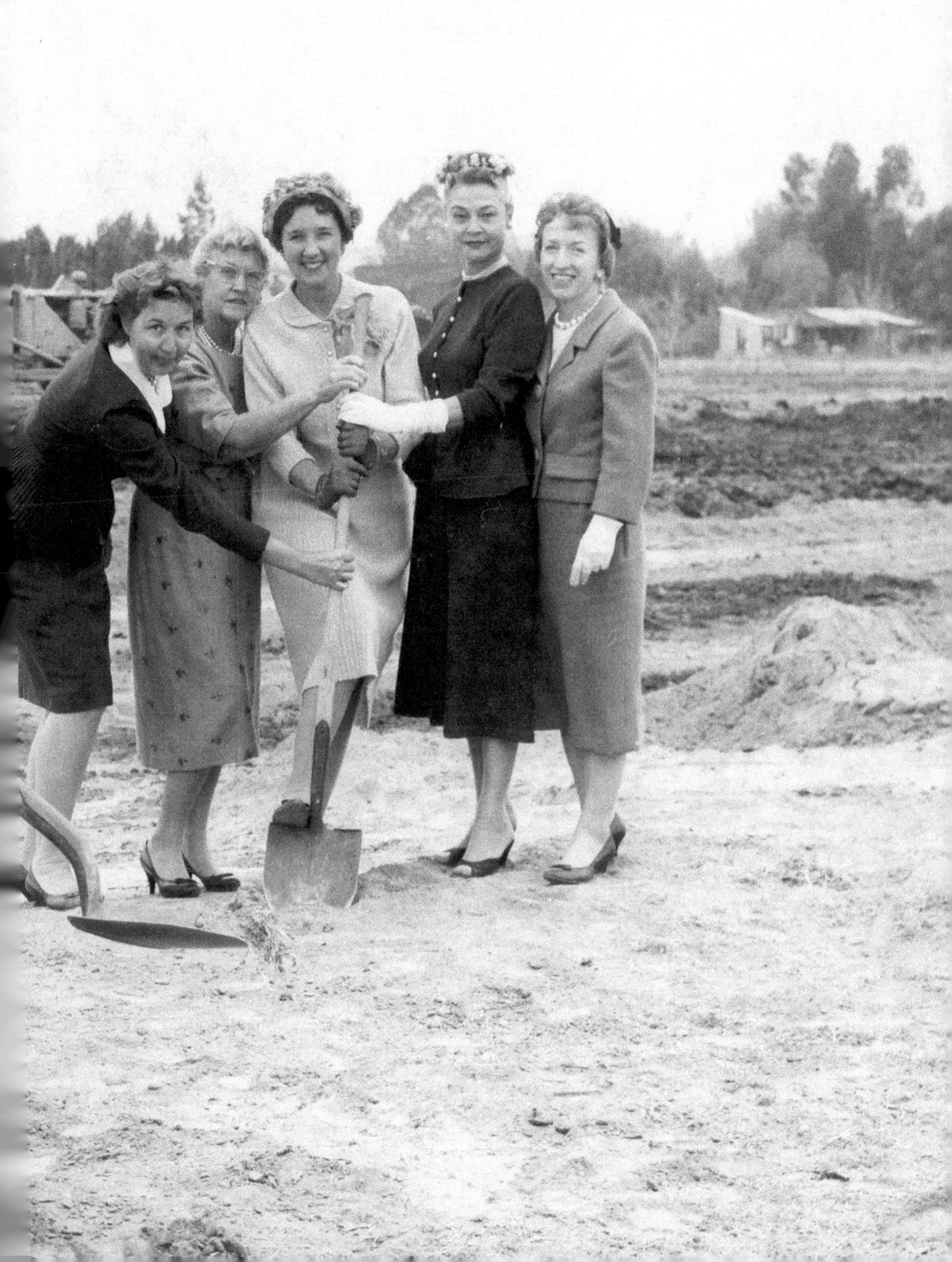

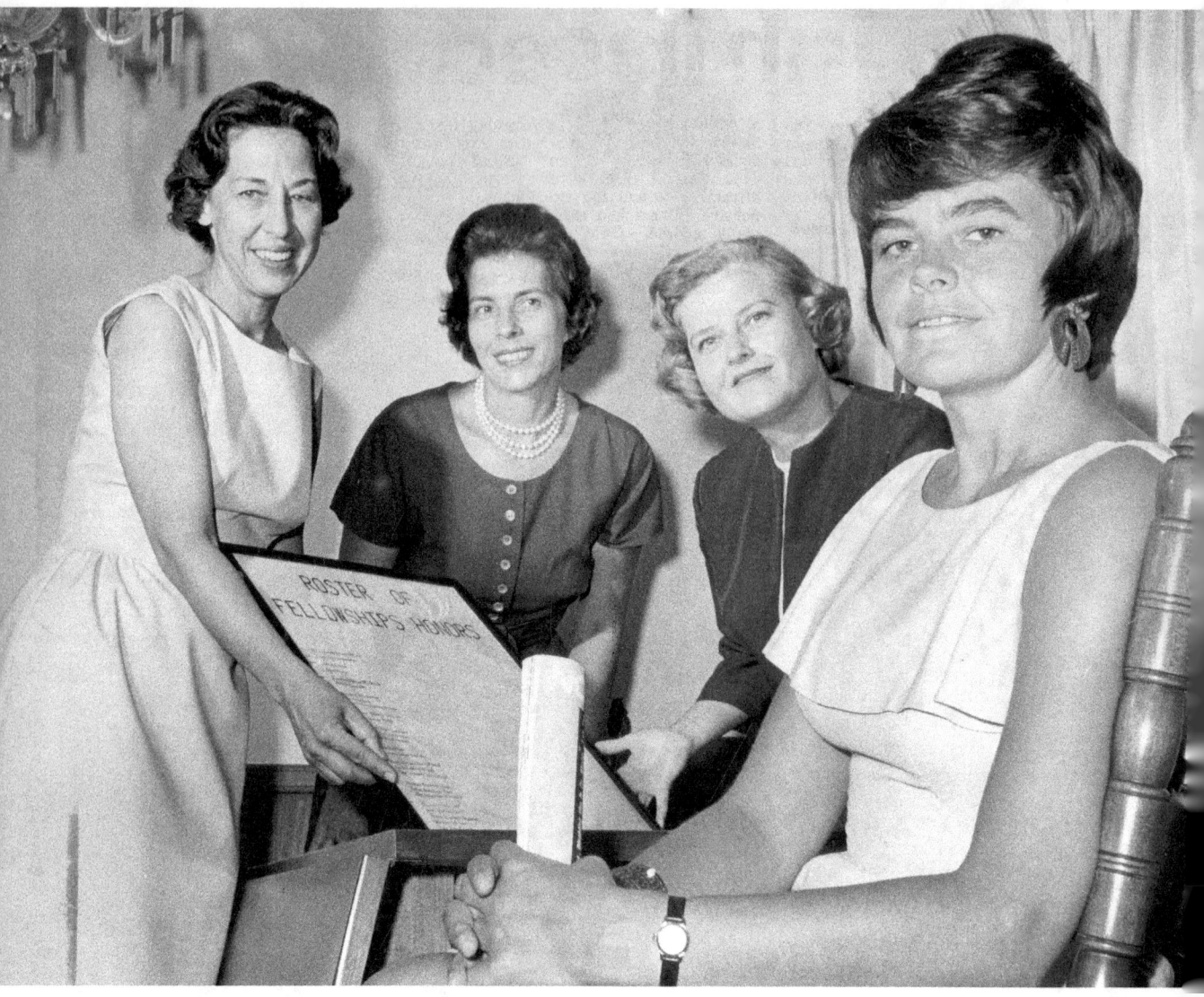

"Three Valley members of the American Association of University Women, Mmes. John Skjelstad (left) of San Fernando; Henry R. Senf of Encino and Wilfred Bryant of Van Nuys, admire the $2,500 fellowship on which their names have been placed as they meet the recipient of the fellowship, Ildri Bie, right, of Norway." October 2, 1962. (George Brich)

Overleaf: "Participating in groundbreaking ceremonies for the new $106,000 Northridge Woman's Club building are club president Mrs. William Hunter (foreground), with Northridge Chamber of Commerce president Nathan Freedman and Mmes. William Bennett (left rear); Frank Park, Ben F. Wetzel, Raymond Saltonstall and George Drake, members of the club building committee. The clubhouse will be located at 18401 Lassen St. in Northridge." April 17, 1961.

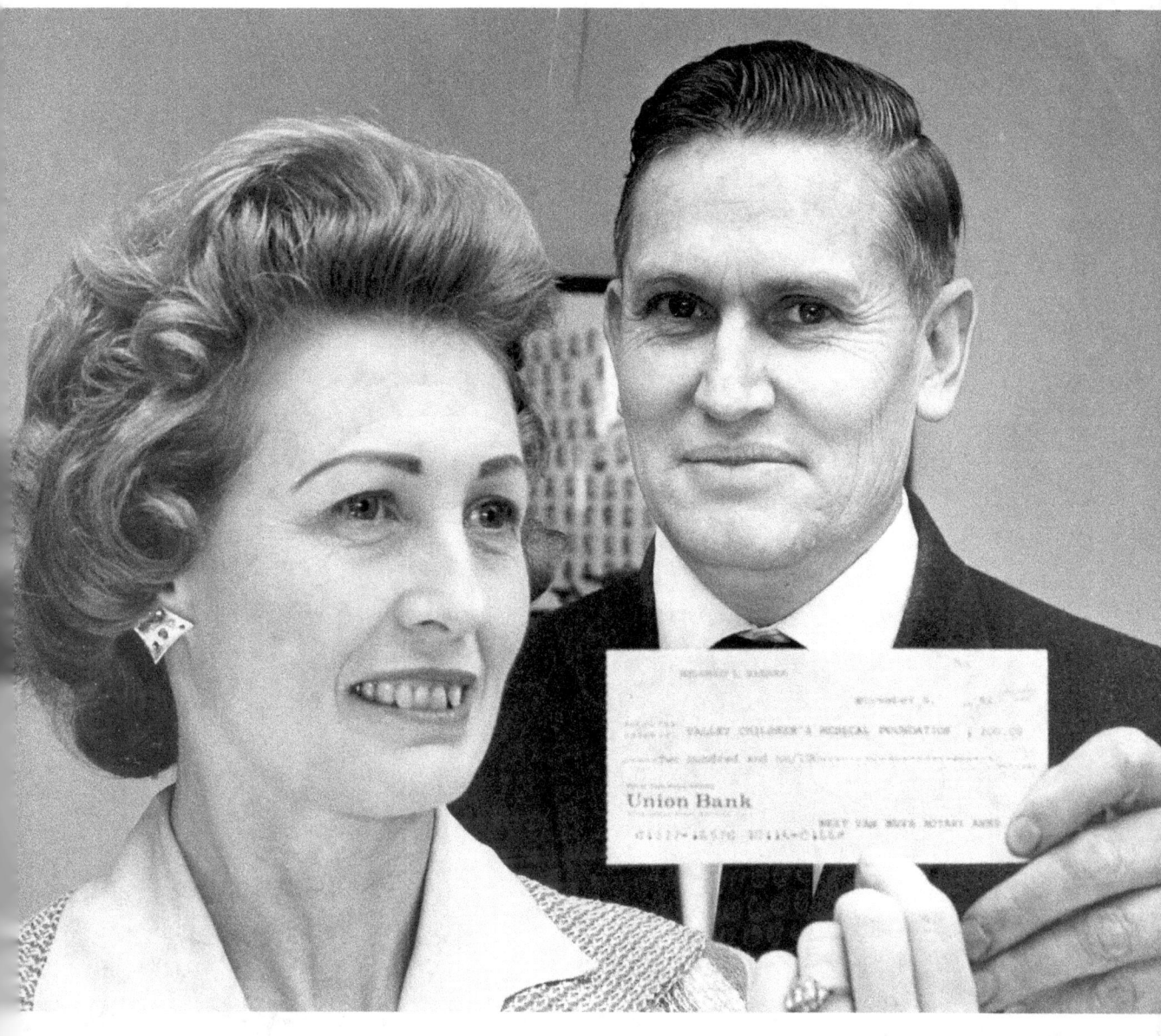

"Mrs. Joseph Barnes, president of the West Van Nuys Rotary Anns, presents a $200 check to Clayton J. Burrell, president of the board of directors of the newly-formed Valley Children's Medical Foundation. The women's club hopes to raise interest in establishing a children's medical facility in the Valley." November 13, 1961. (Jon Woods)

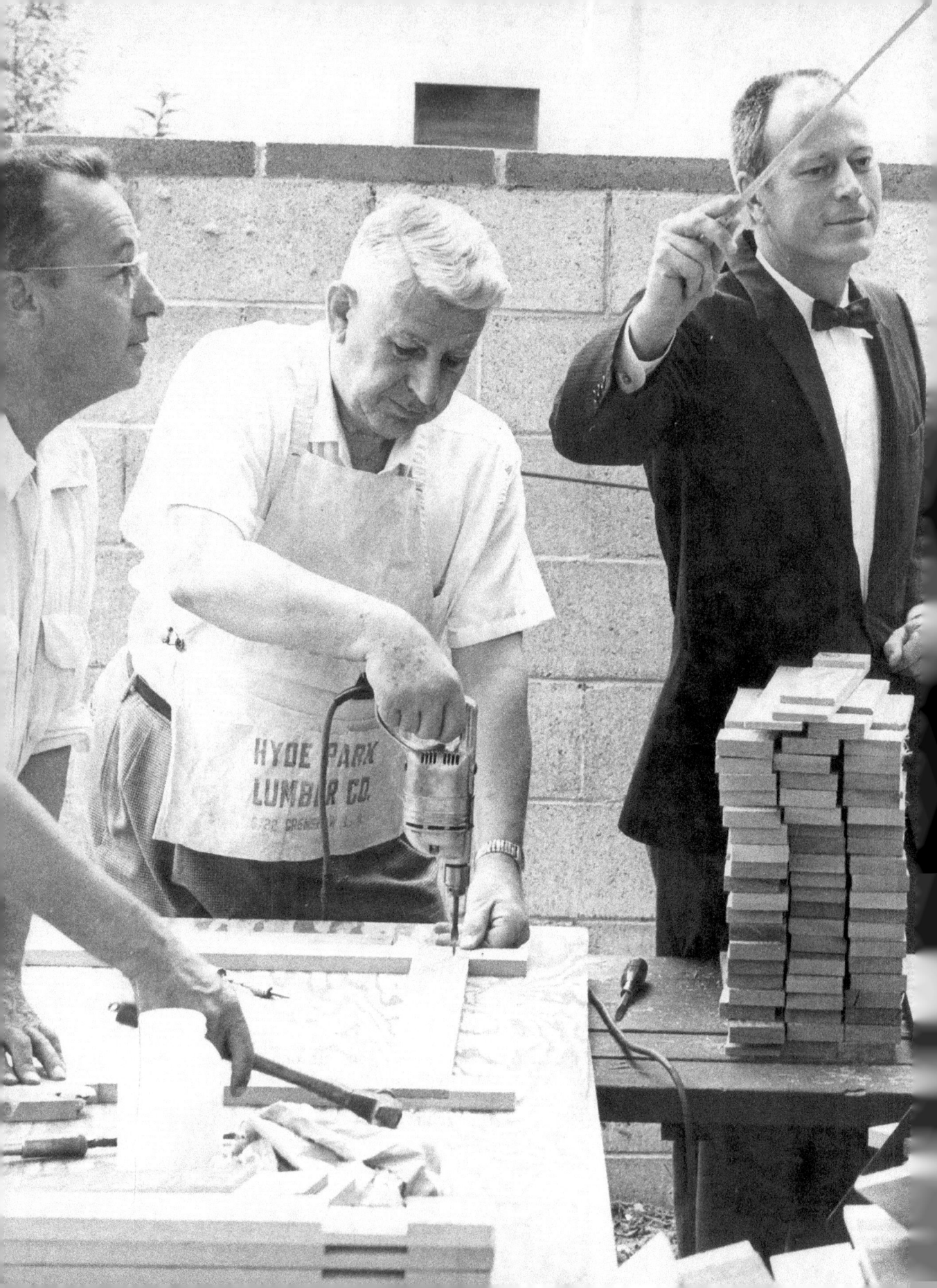

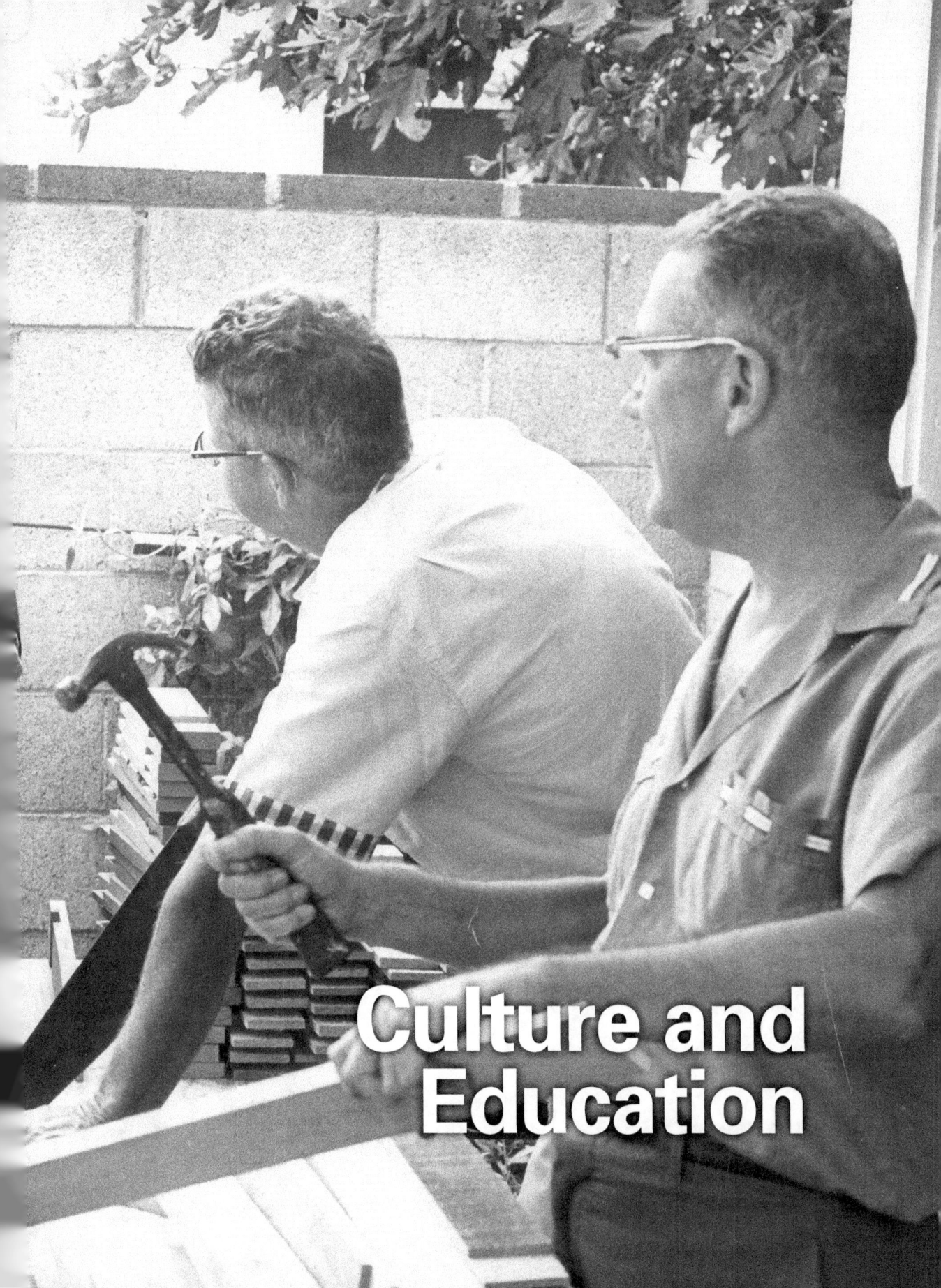

Culture and Education

Overleaf: 'Members of the San Fernando Valley Symphony Association lend their talents to constructing wooden risers for their concert season. Leading the group (baton in hand) is Musical Director James A. Swift. Aiding in the project are (from left) Winton Greening, association member; Paul Garver, vice president of the association; Ralph Warner, association member and teacher at Grant High School, and Karl Kunze, president of the association. Members build the wooden platforms at the home of association president Karl R. Kunze, 5629 Bellingham Ave., North Hollywood." September 20, 1961.

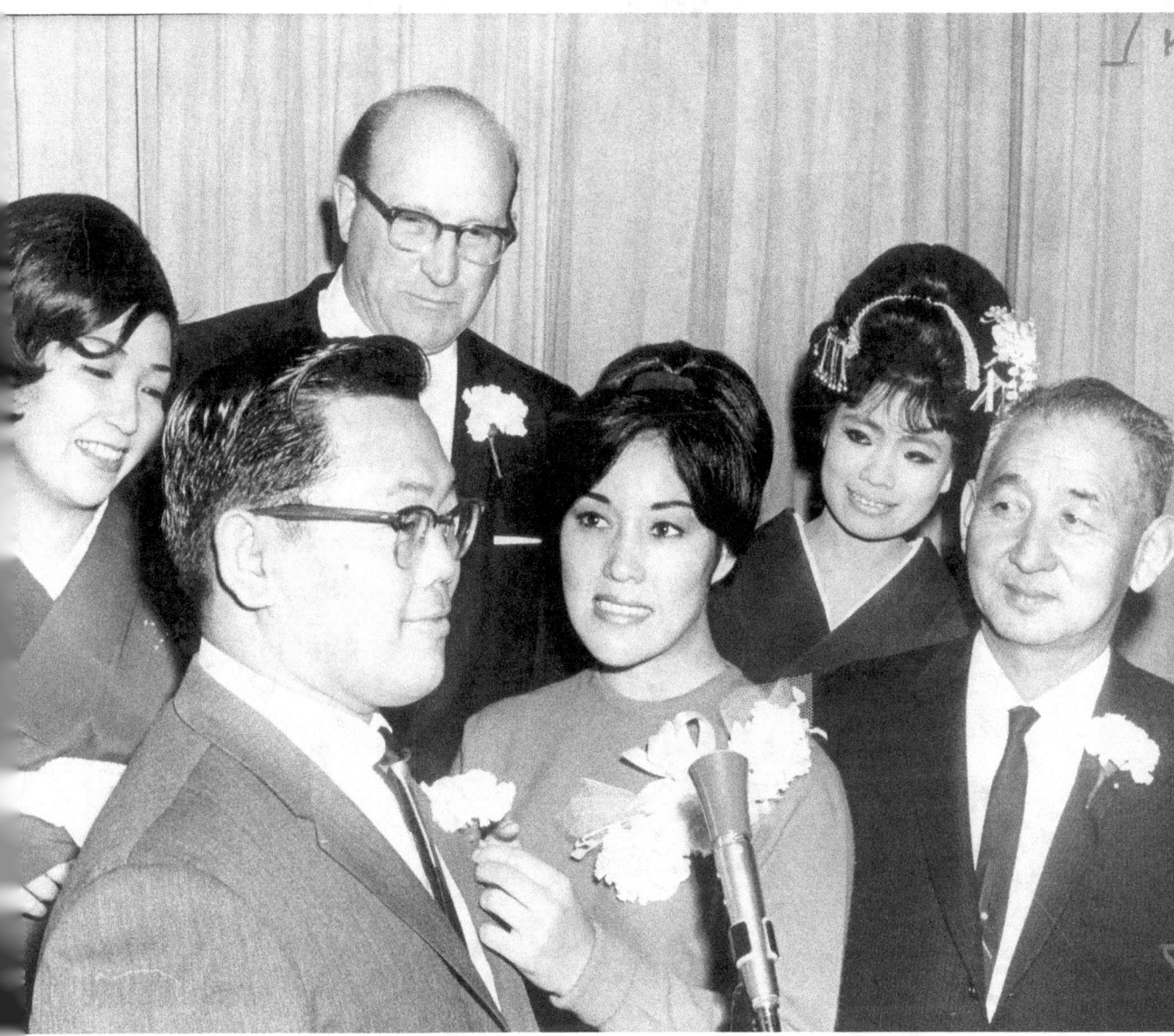

"Roy Murakami, new president of the San Fernando Valley Japanese-American Center in Pacoima, gets a flower pinned on his lapel by pretty Shigemi Matsumoto, Valley Nisei Week Queen, while ex-Center prexy Fumio Muto (right) looks on. Also at the ceremony last night were (rear row, from left) Mimiko Kumata, San Francisco; Councilman Louis R. Nowell and Hozuhiro Hanayagi, North Hollywood." January 23, 1965. (Bob Martin)

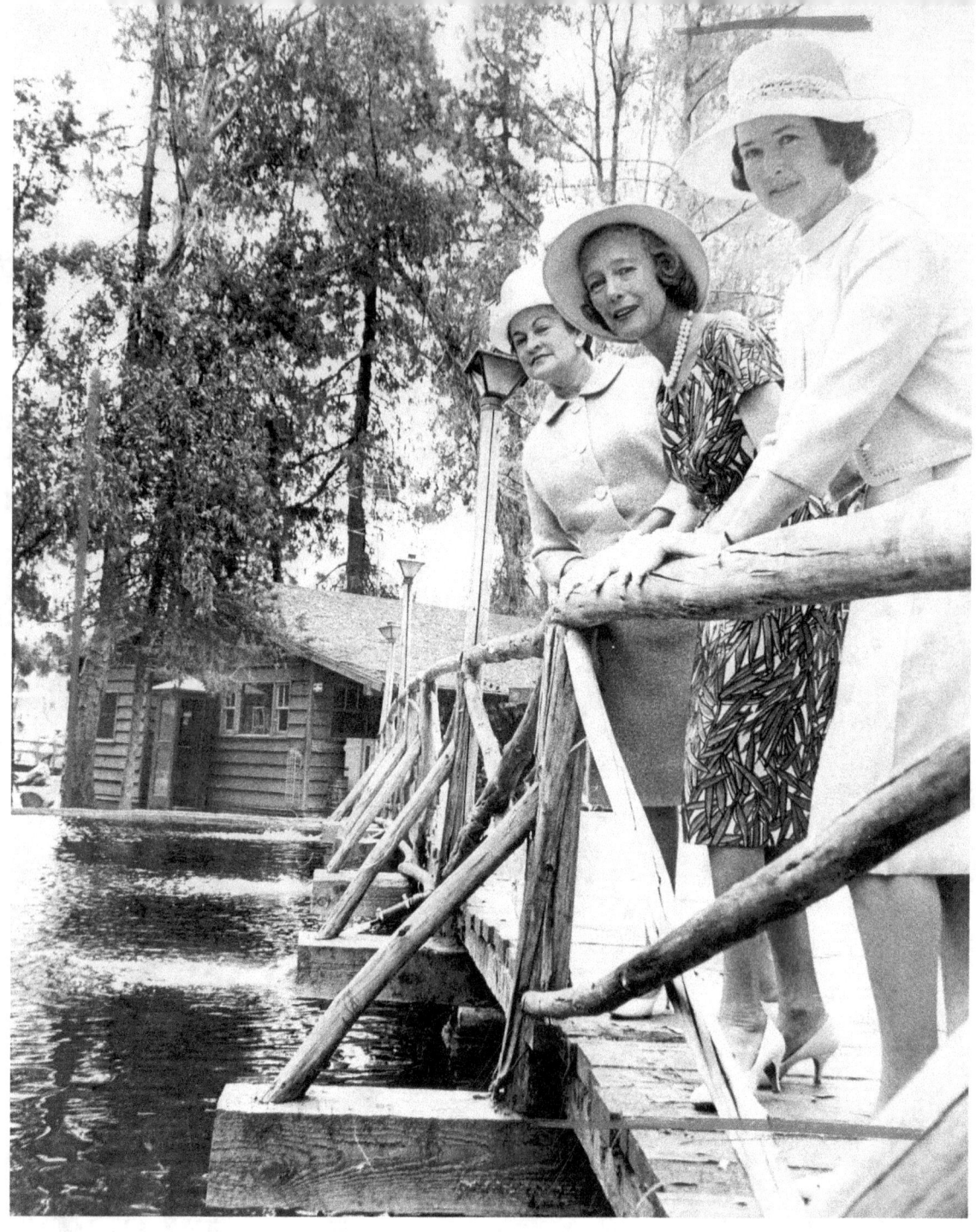

"Los Angeles Philharmonic committee hostesses of a morning musicale at the Sportmen's Lodge—Mmes. Harry Levey, Clement Atwater, George Fouche." May 15, 1963. (Jeff Goldwater)

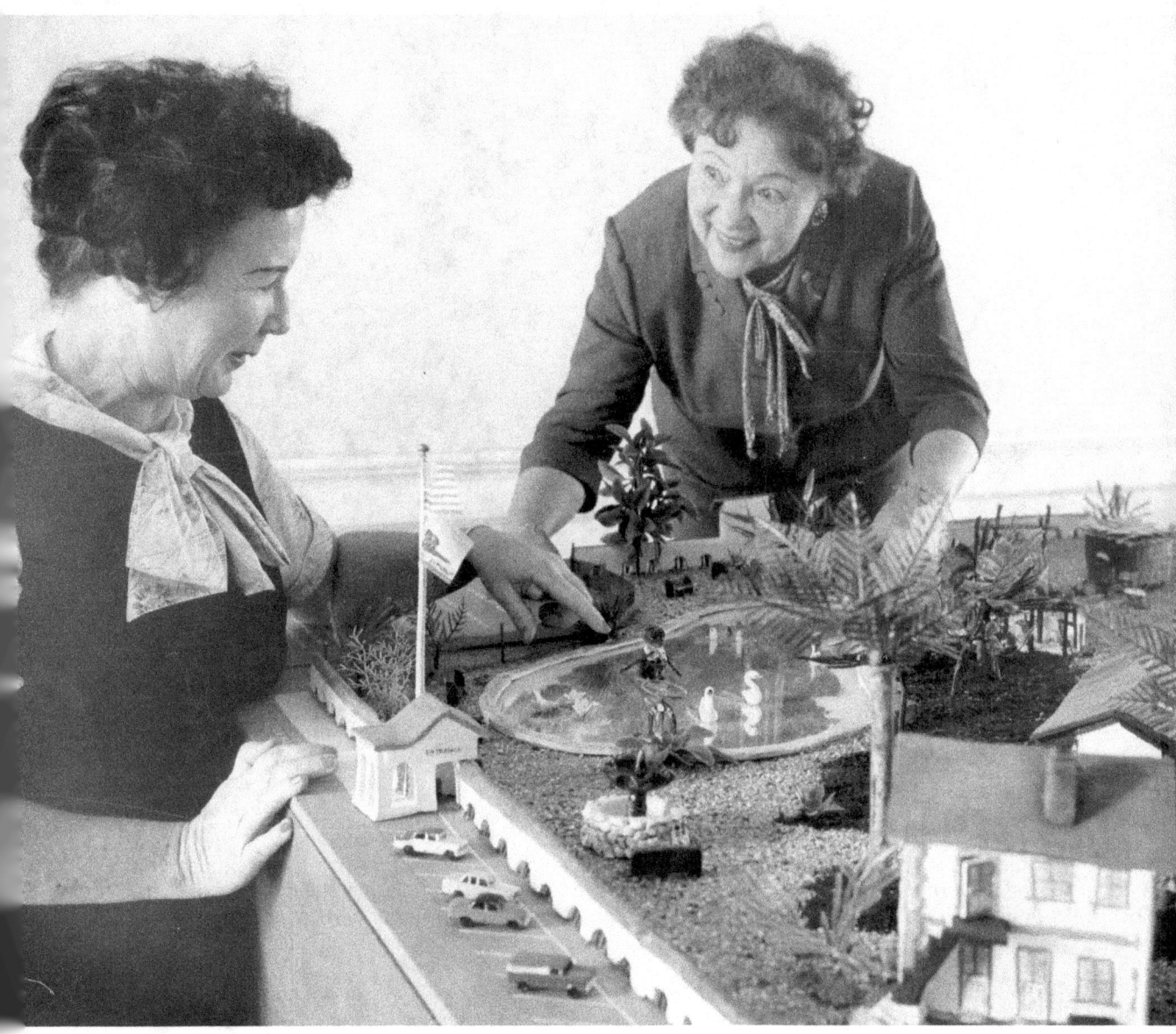

"Mrs. J. Earl Stewart, president of the Encino Historical Society, shows model of Los Encinos State Historical Monument renovation project to Mrs. Carolyn Boniface." October 23, 1961.

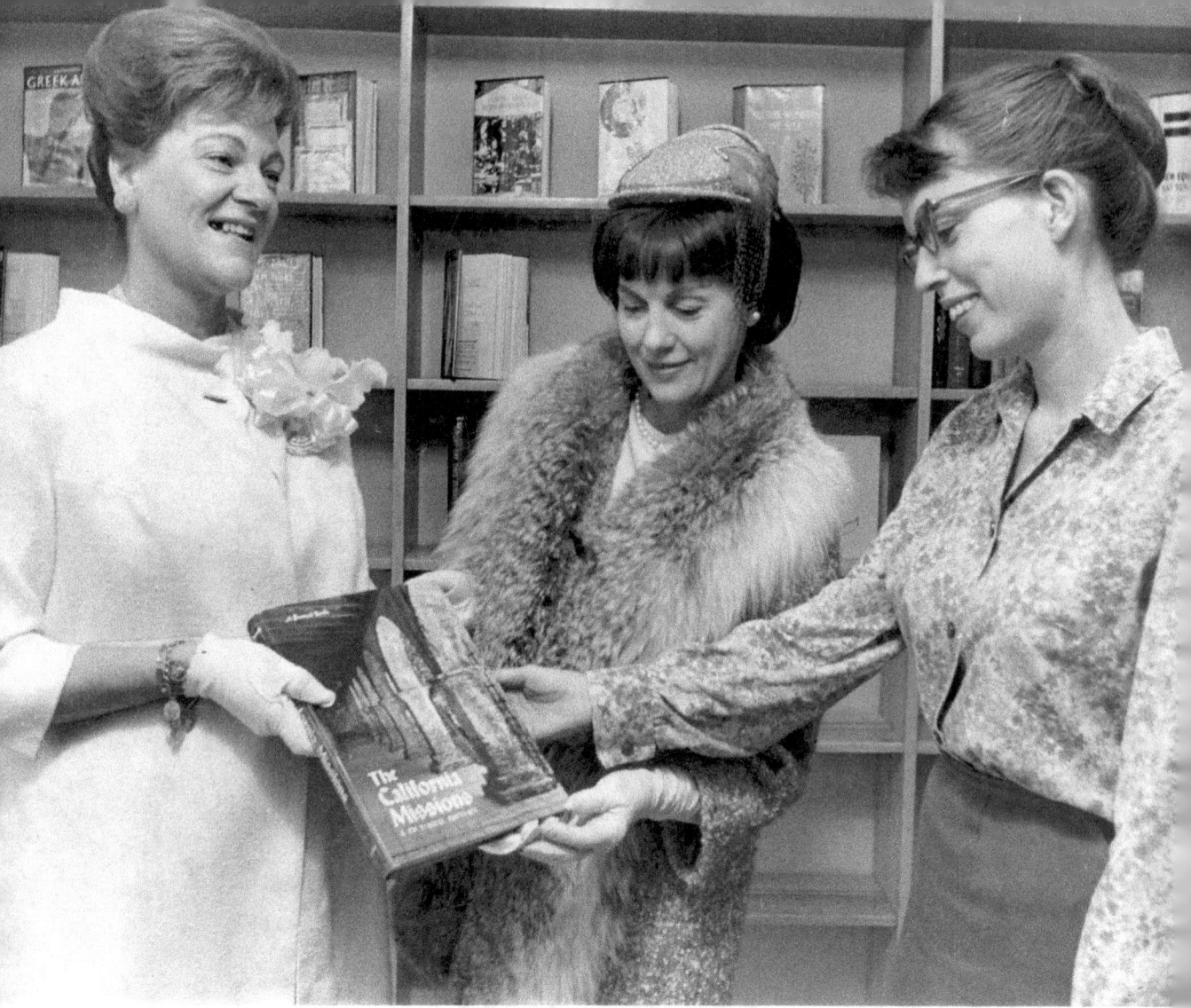

"Grand president of the Native Daughters of the Golden West, Mrs. Fern Adams, presents book, *The California Missions,* to Mrs. Lois Brown, head librarian at Granada Hills Library, as part of her official visit to El Camino Real Parlor. Looking on is Mrs. Charles Huenergardt, parlor president." April 9, 1965. (Tom Kravitz)

Opposite: "All-night parties for graduating high school seniors have been arranged with the Valley PTAs acting as sponsors and chaperones. Pickwick Recreation Center, 1001 Riverside Dr., Burbank, will be open to seniors of Birmingham and Grant High Schools, Thursday, and Polytechnic, Van Nuys, Taft, Sylmar, Canoga Park and Reseda High Schools, Friday. Dancing, bowling and skating have been arranged by (front) Mrs. Gene Bryan, senior activities chairman, Polytechnic; (back) Mrs. Eugene Bedal, activities chairman, Taft, and Mrs. Royal S. Crane, senior activities chairman, Del North Council PTA, for the entertainment of the seniors." January 28, 1963. (Jeff Goldwater)

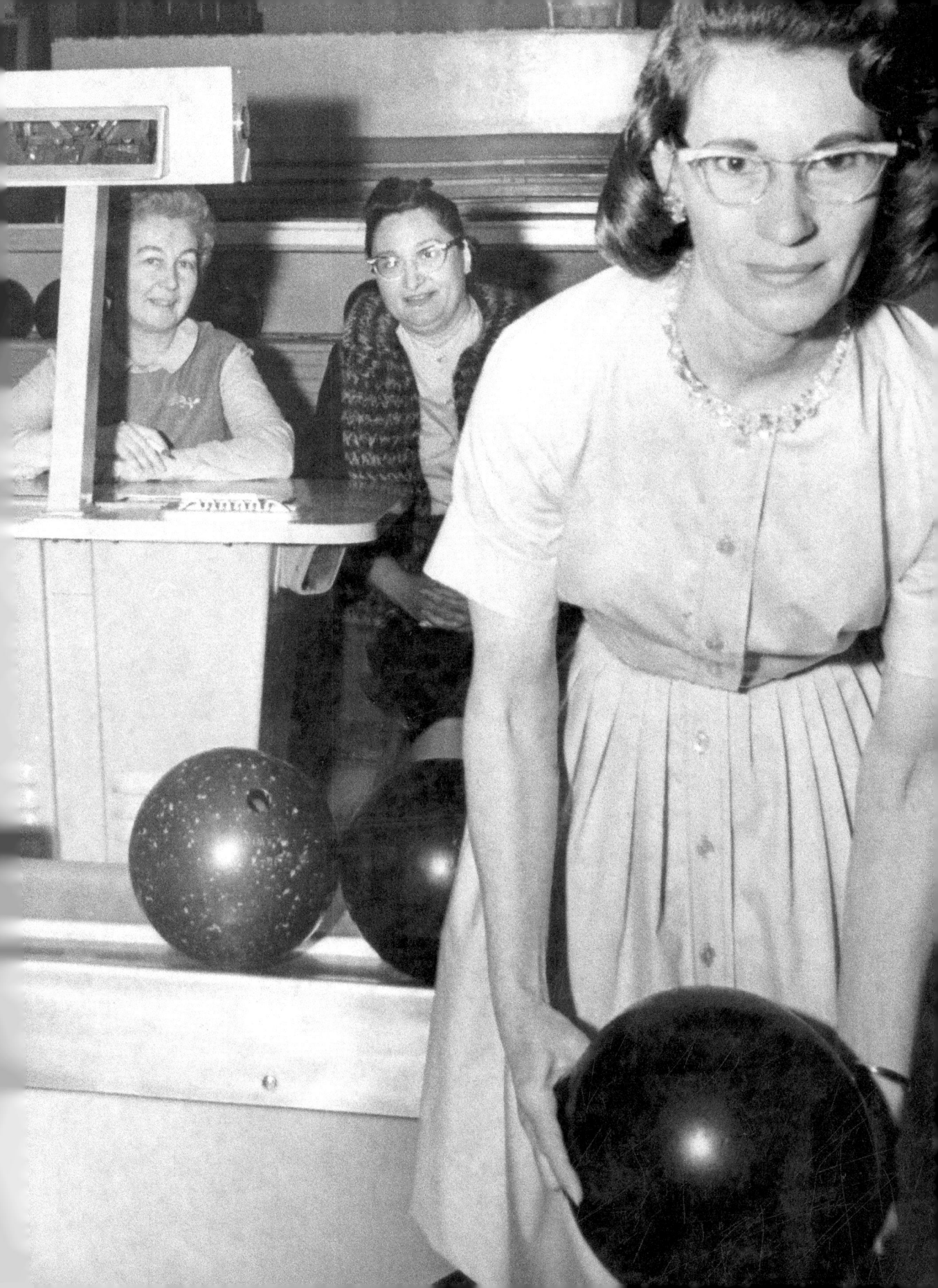

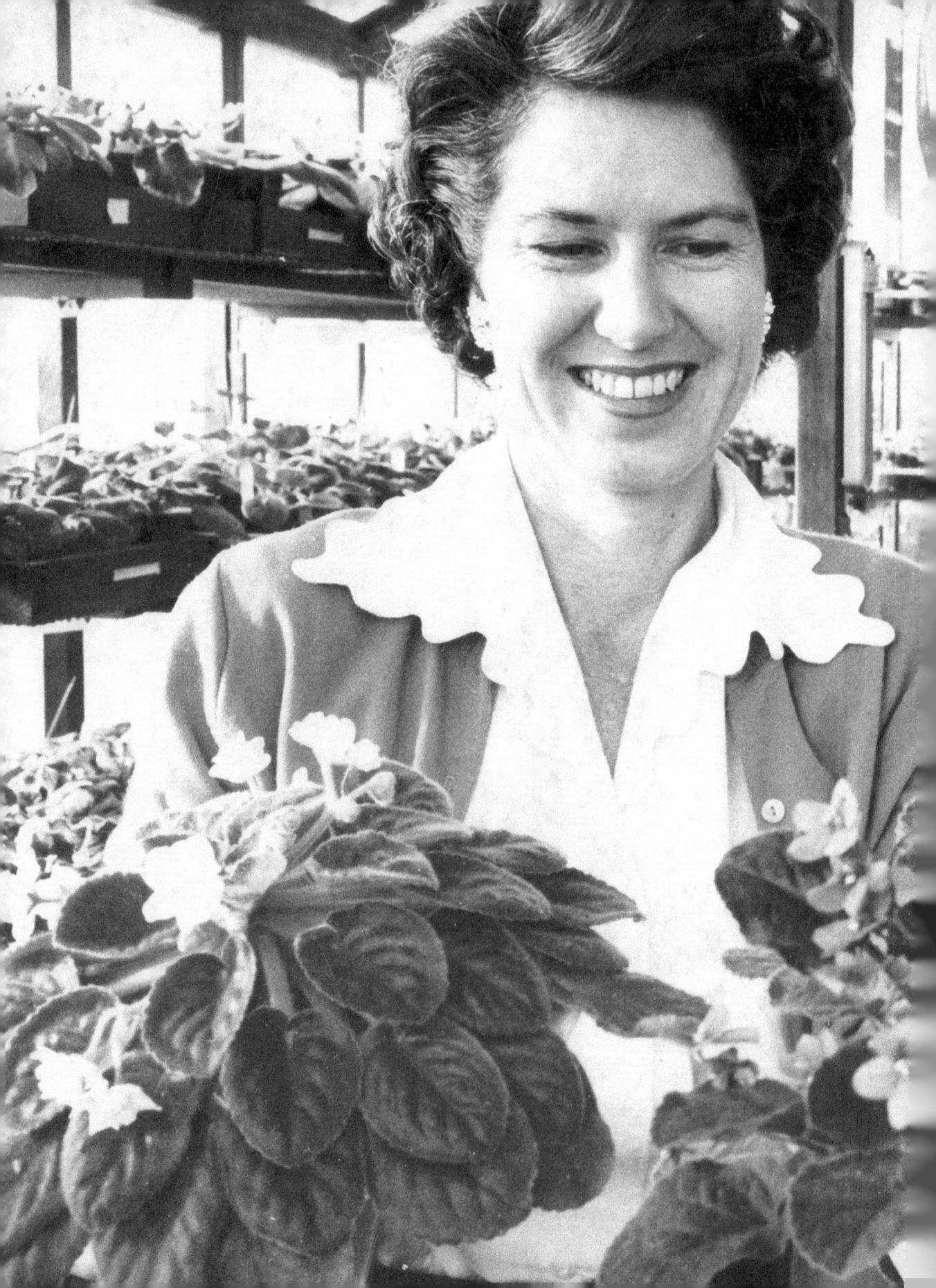

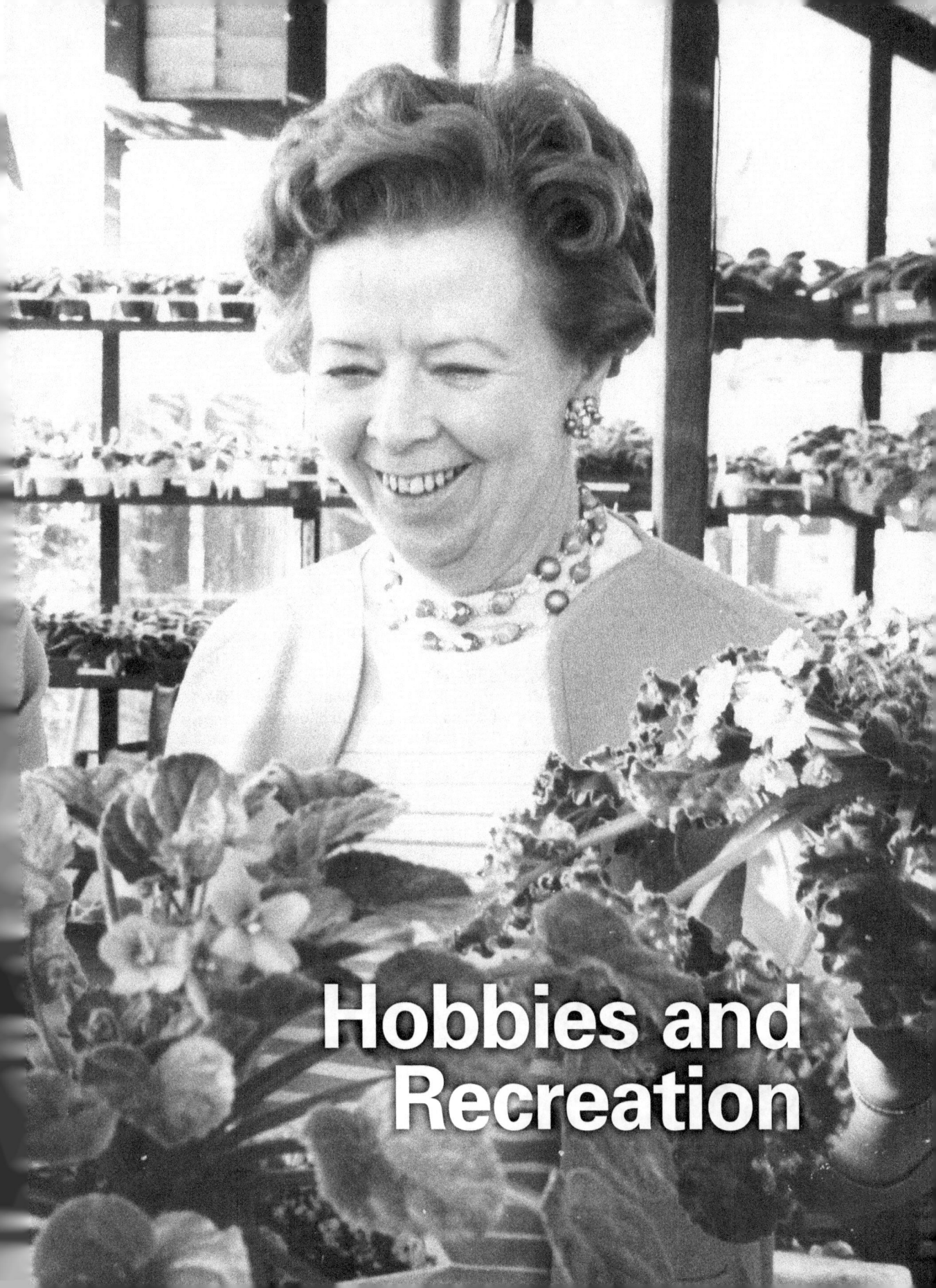

Hobbies and Recreation

Opposite: "The North Hollywood Figure Skating Club has been accepted as a member club by the United States Figure Skating Association, the North Hollywood club's president said today. Mrs. H. A. Schultz, Burbank, leader of the group, noted that her skaters use USFSA figures—basic skating turns, edges and changes—when they meet each Tuesday evening at 5:30 at the Schramm Ice Skating Rink, 7111 Vineland Ave., North Hollywood." Pictured are (from back to front), Mmes. Gardner, Megowan, Dr. Ervin, and Mrs. Schultz." July 20, 1961. (George Brich)

Overleaf: "Second annual African Violet Show of San Fernando Valley African Violet Society to be held at the Van Nuys Woman's Club, 14836 Sylvan St. Show chairman Mrs. R.L. Hutchens (left), of Sepulveda, who also serves as club president, shares preview of coming attractions with Mrs. Clarence E. Wescott, Van Nuys." March 27, 1963. (George Brich)

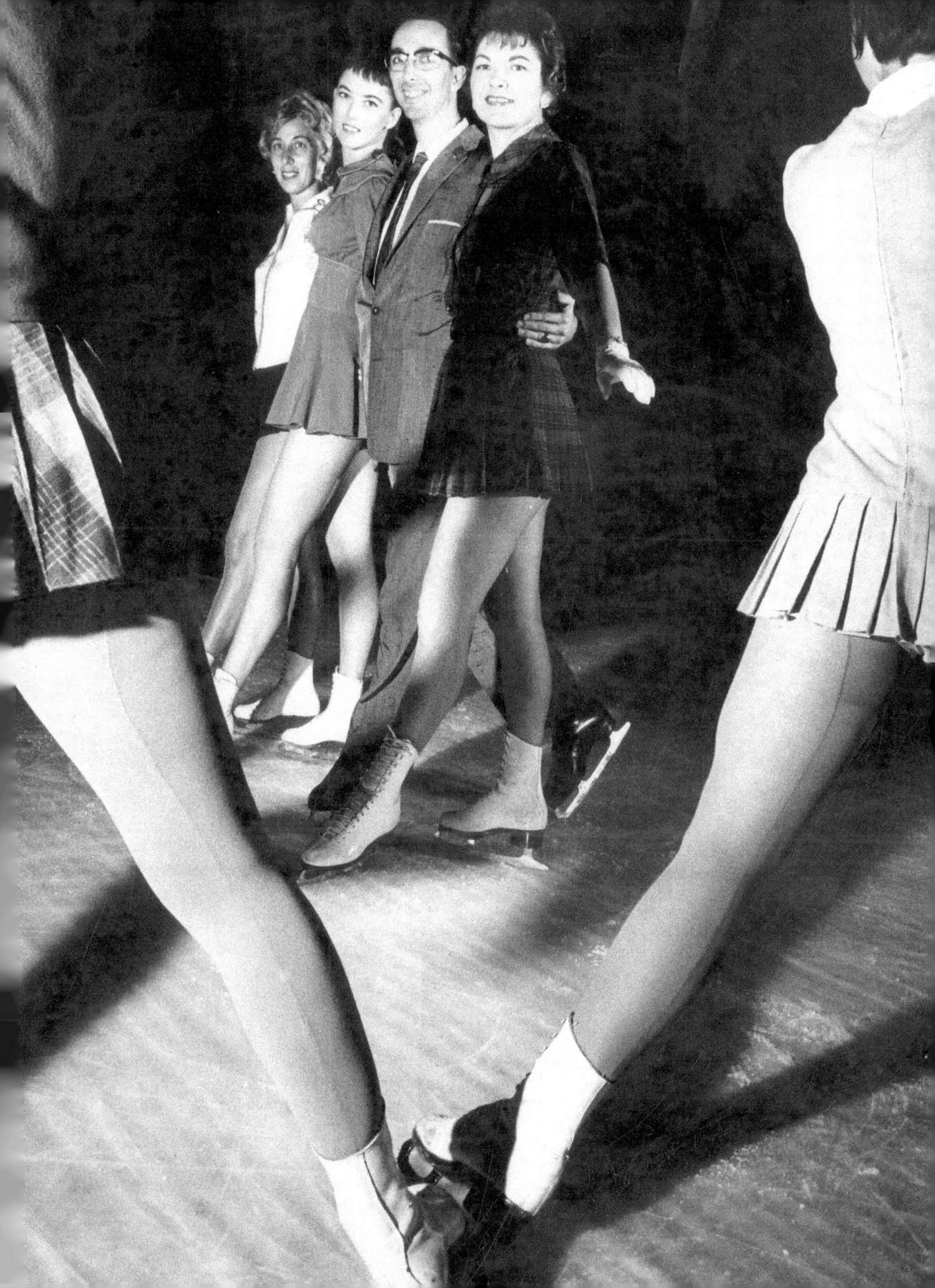

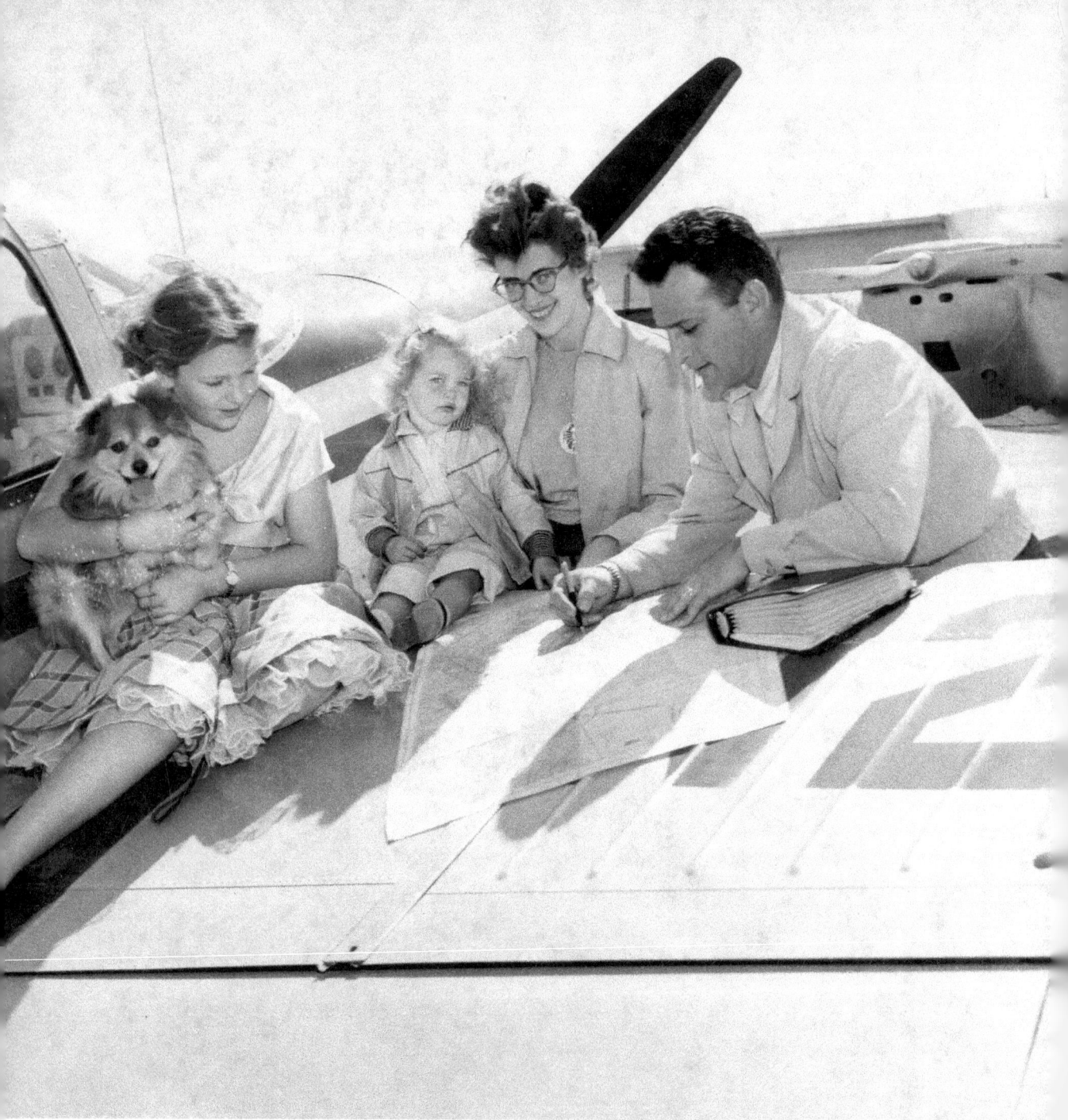

"Icarians plan flight—Matt Jacobson of Burbank, charter member and president of Icarian Flying Club, maps out flight plan for group's Las Vegas trip. Linda Deltour, 11, of Northridge and 'Zipper' watch with Mrs. Charles Sword and two-year-old daughter Bonnie." March 15, 1956. (Jess Westerfield)

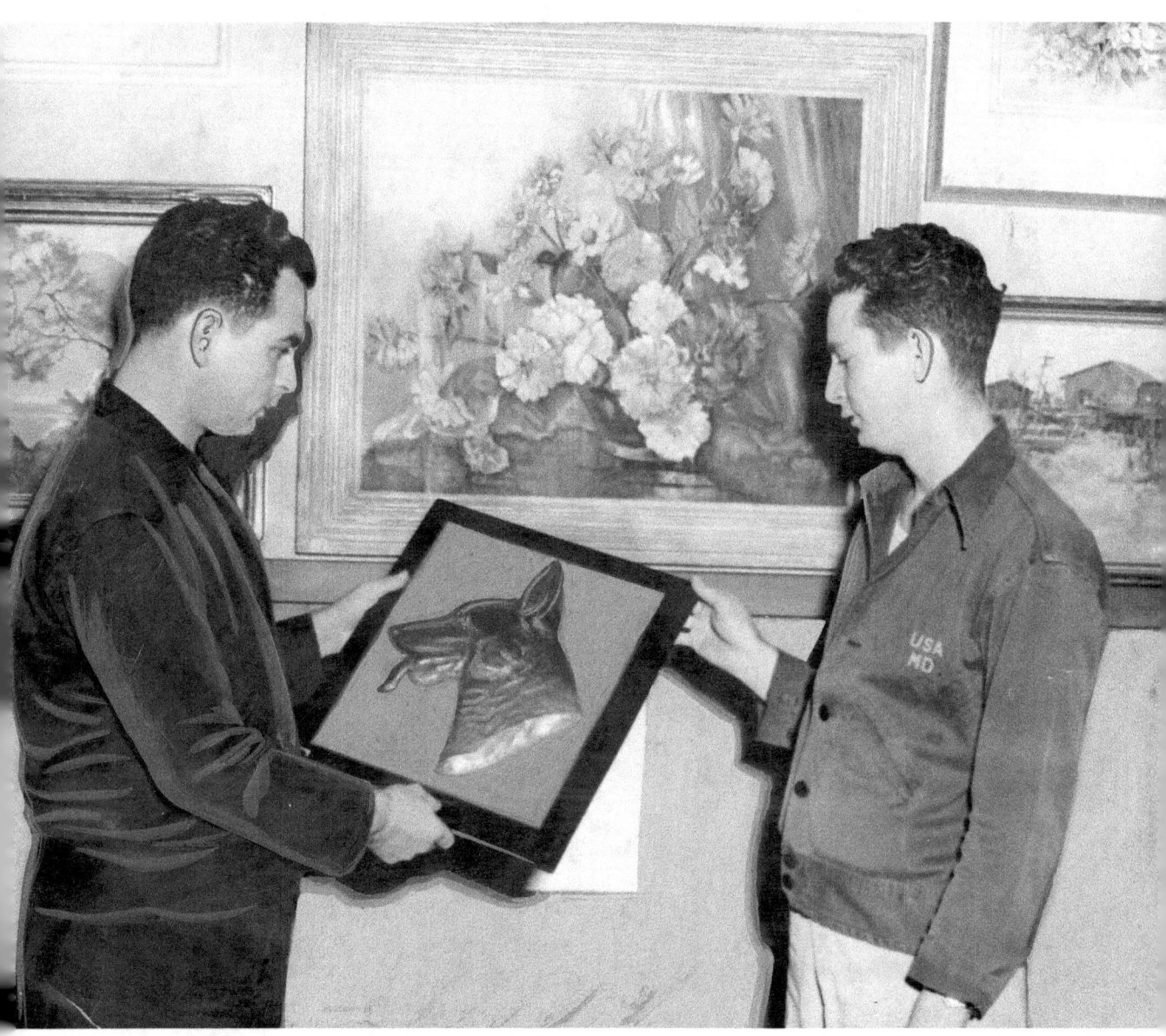

"San Fernando Valley Art Club at the Birmingham Hospital. Eugene Philpott of Glendale (left) and Grady Cleveland of North Hollywood (right), look over art for the upcoming Veteran's sale." January 23, 1947.

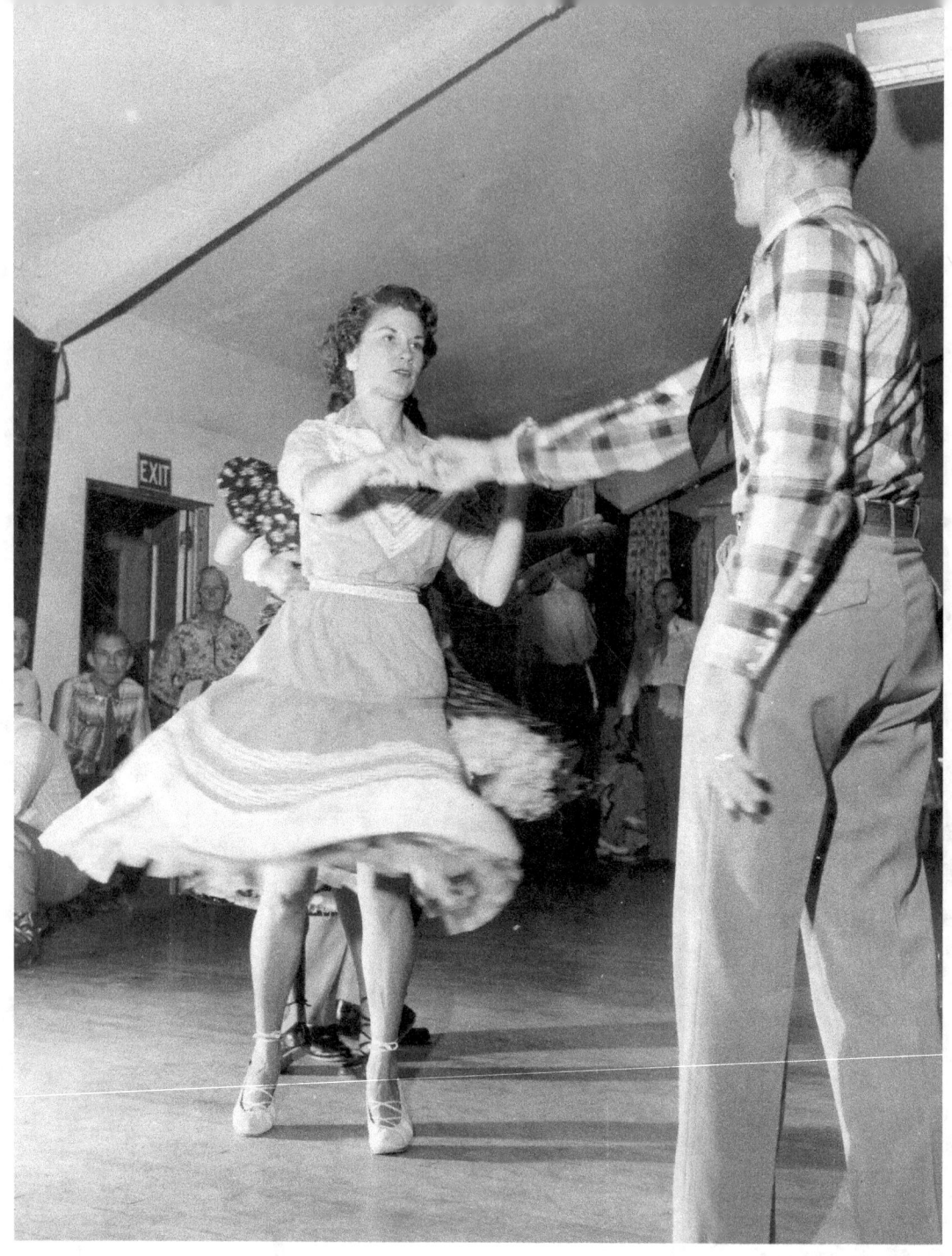

"Twirling skirts and stomping boots symbolize square dance garb is Gerald Shephard swings Mrs. Bill Howell of Las Caudrillas Club around square in left allemande step. Dance clubs and classes meet almost every night of week in Valley playgrounds and private halls." December 14, 1957.

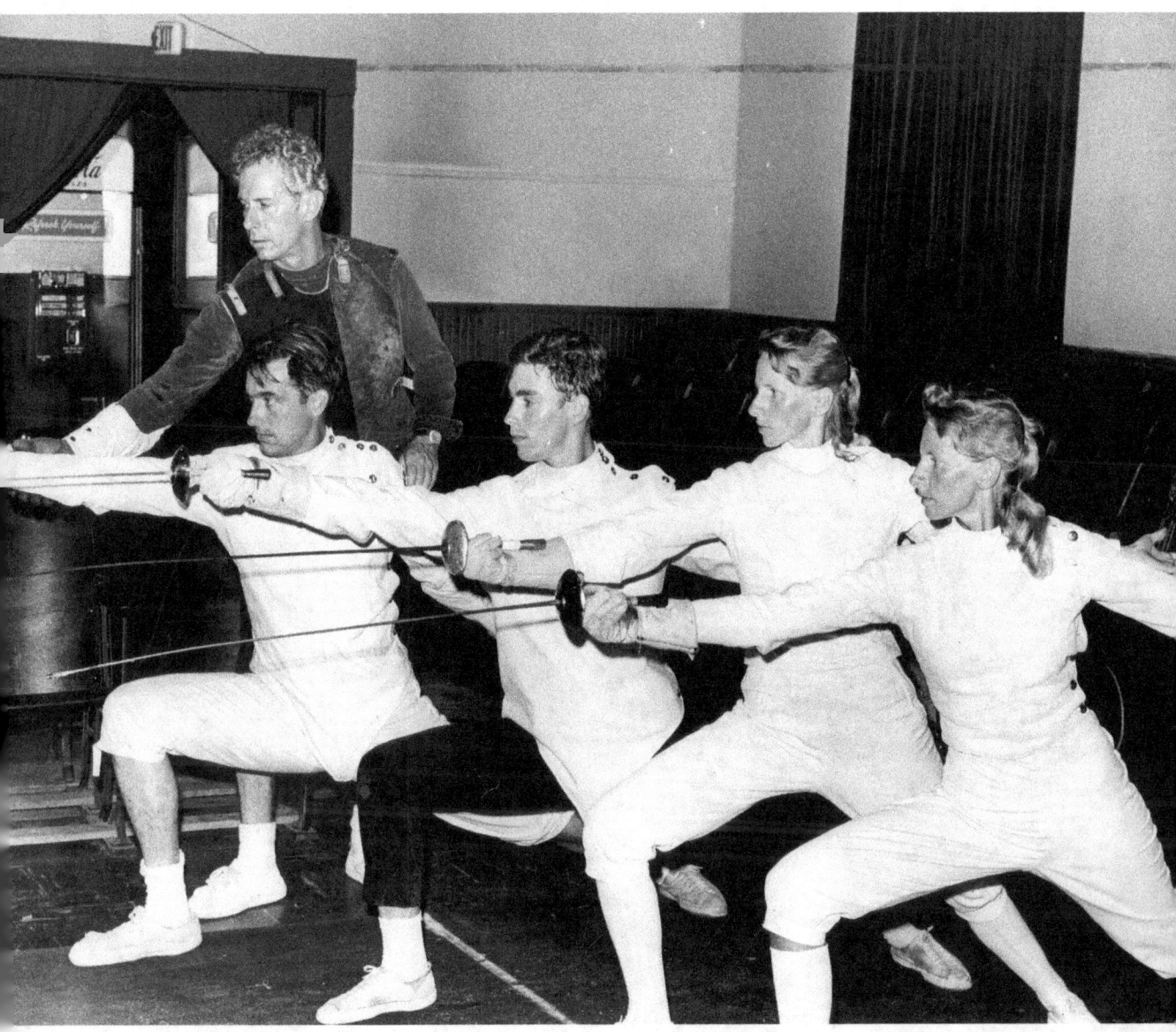

"Lunging with foils are (from left) Delmar Calvert, fencing master and coach, and students Halton Arp, Paul DeWolf, Betty Drago and Bonnie Linkmeyer, of the newly formed North Hollywood Fencing Club. The club meets at the North Hollywood Playhouse, 11043 Magnolia Blvd." August 22, 1963. (Jeff Robbins)

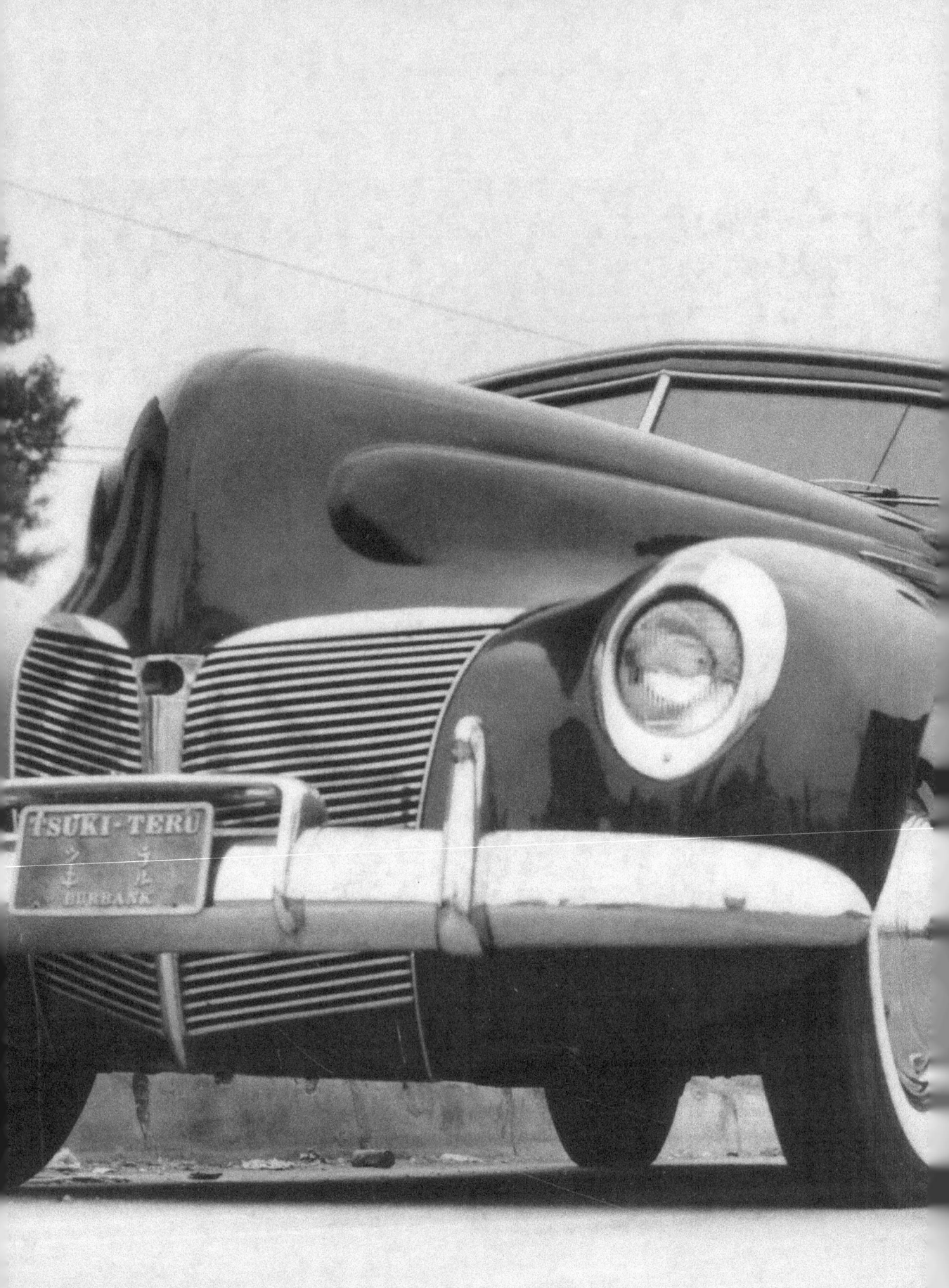

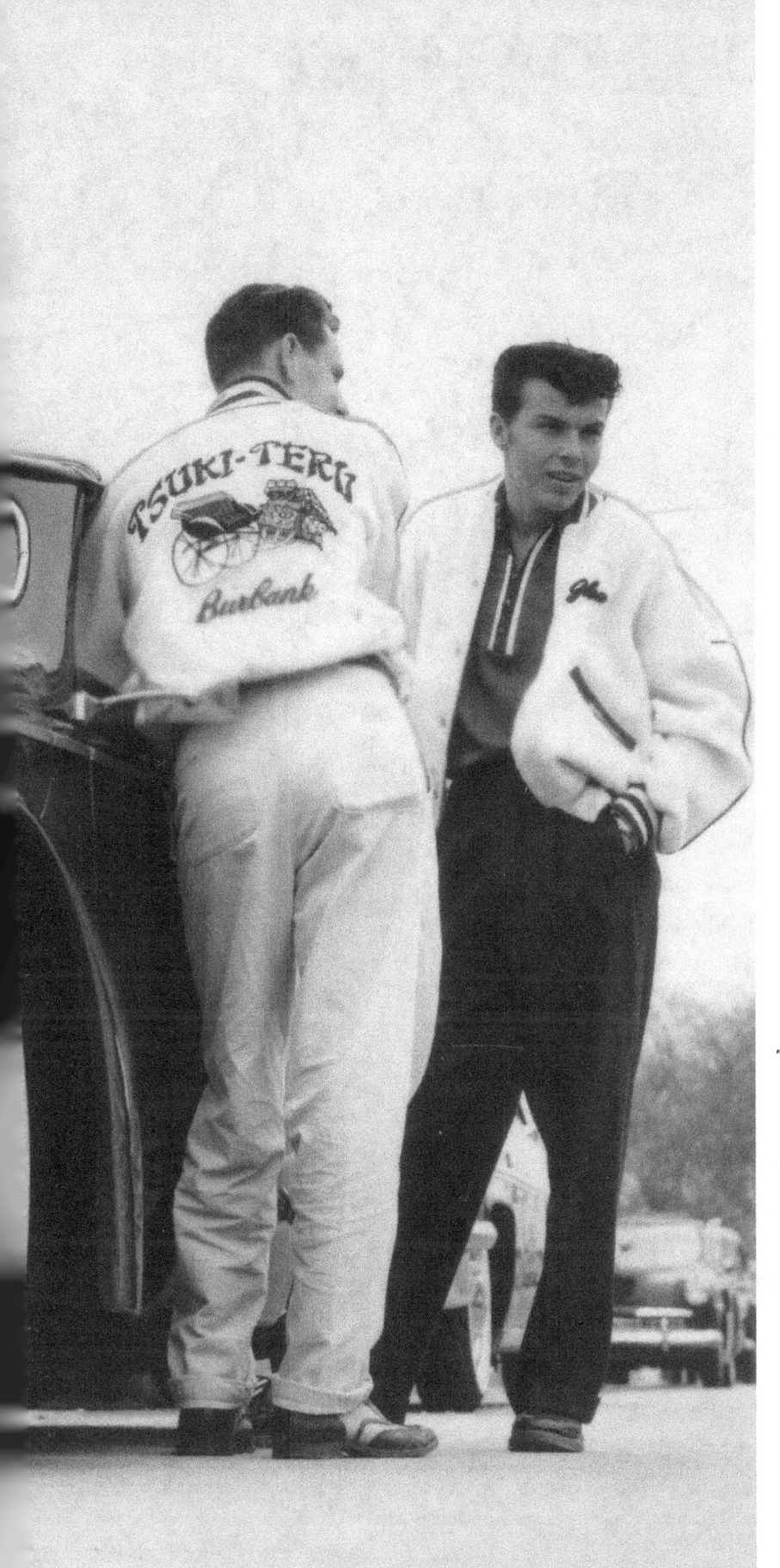

"Burbank's Tsuki-Teru Car Club includes among top club secrets meaning of name, whose Far Eastern characters are inscribed on club plaque. Beautiful jackets are made of 100 per cent Orlon, softest and lightest in weight of synthetic fabrics. Left to right are President Dick Lewis and Glen Hooker, vice president." August 24, 1954. (Larry Paulson)

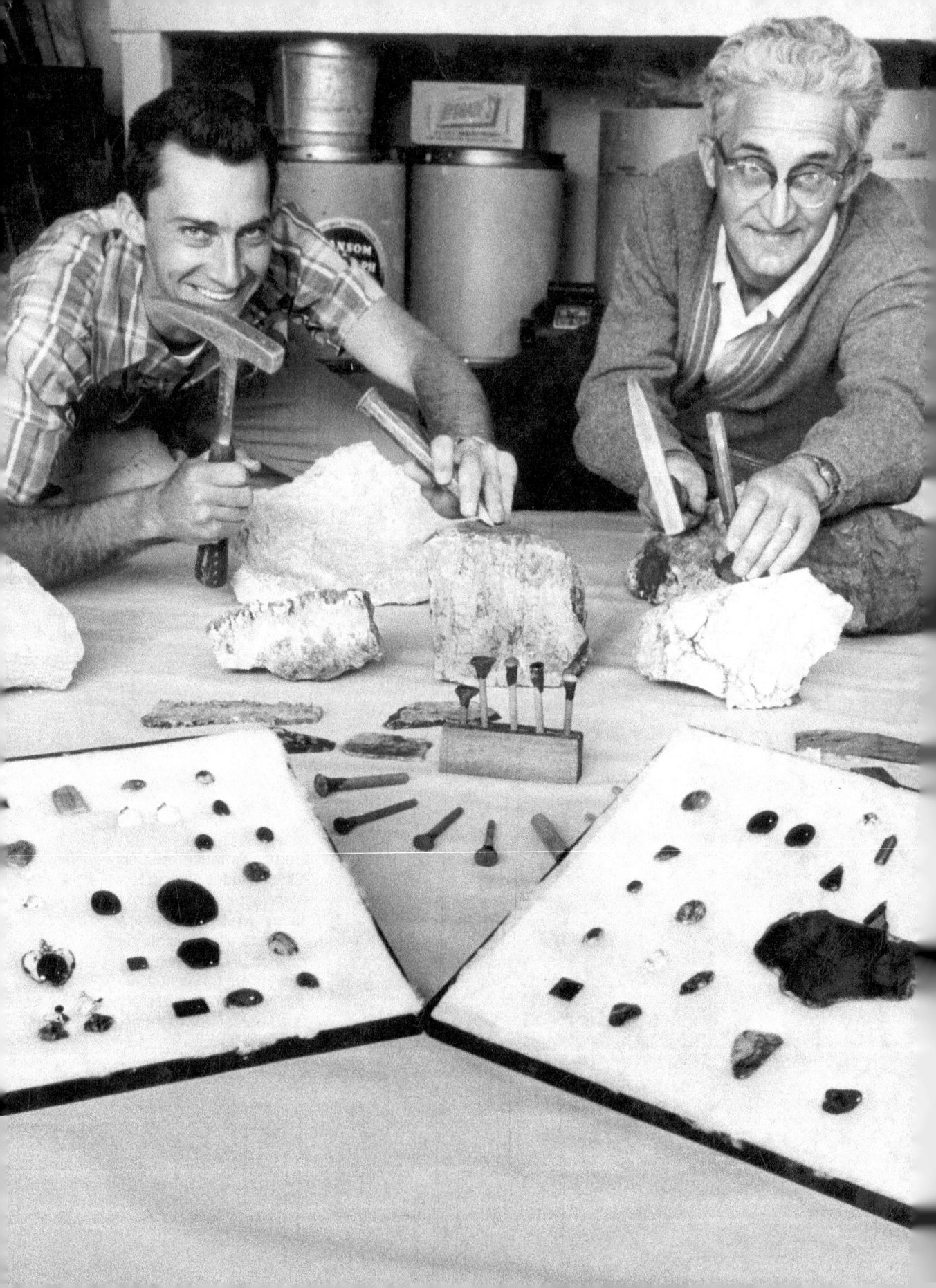

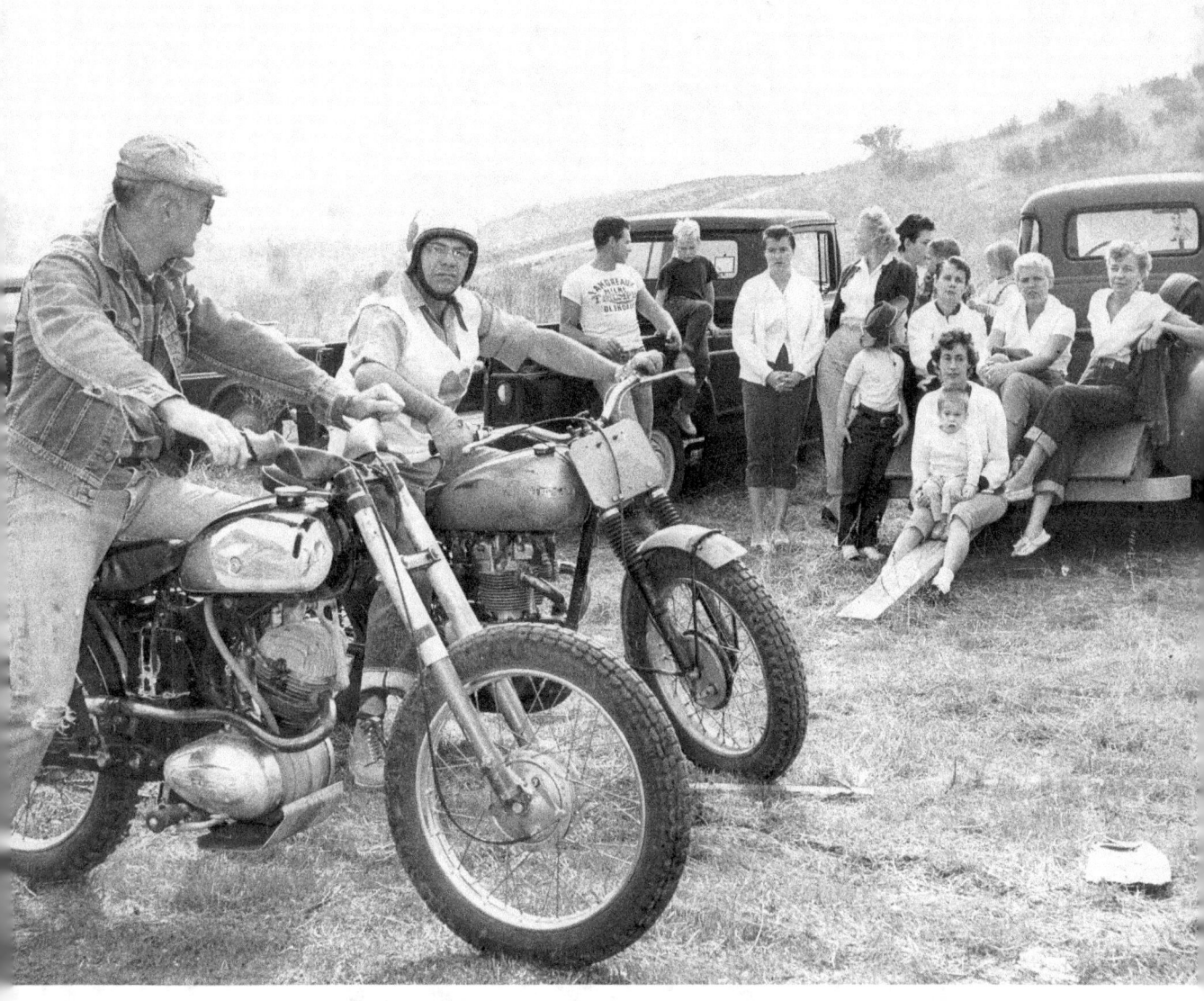

"Wives and children of Shamrock Motorcycle Club members relax in background between competition events...Talking over day's activities are Bob James (left) and Johnny Simpson of Tujunga. Women do not ride but belong to club auxiliary and serve refreshments during outings." December 6, 1957.

Opposite: "Members of Rock Hound Societies of San Fernando Valley, who'll be hosts at the Golden Bear Gem Fair, Pomona, prepare their displays: Melvin Ward, left, 3107 Wyoming Ave., and Lloyd Ward, 1910 N. Ontario St., both Burbank, attack small rocks with big tools as lapidary instruments rest in middle ground and finished products shine in foreground." June 8, 1961. (George Brich)

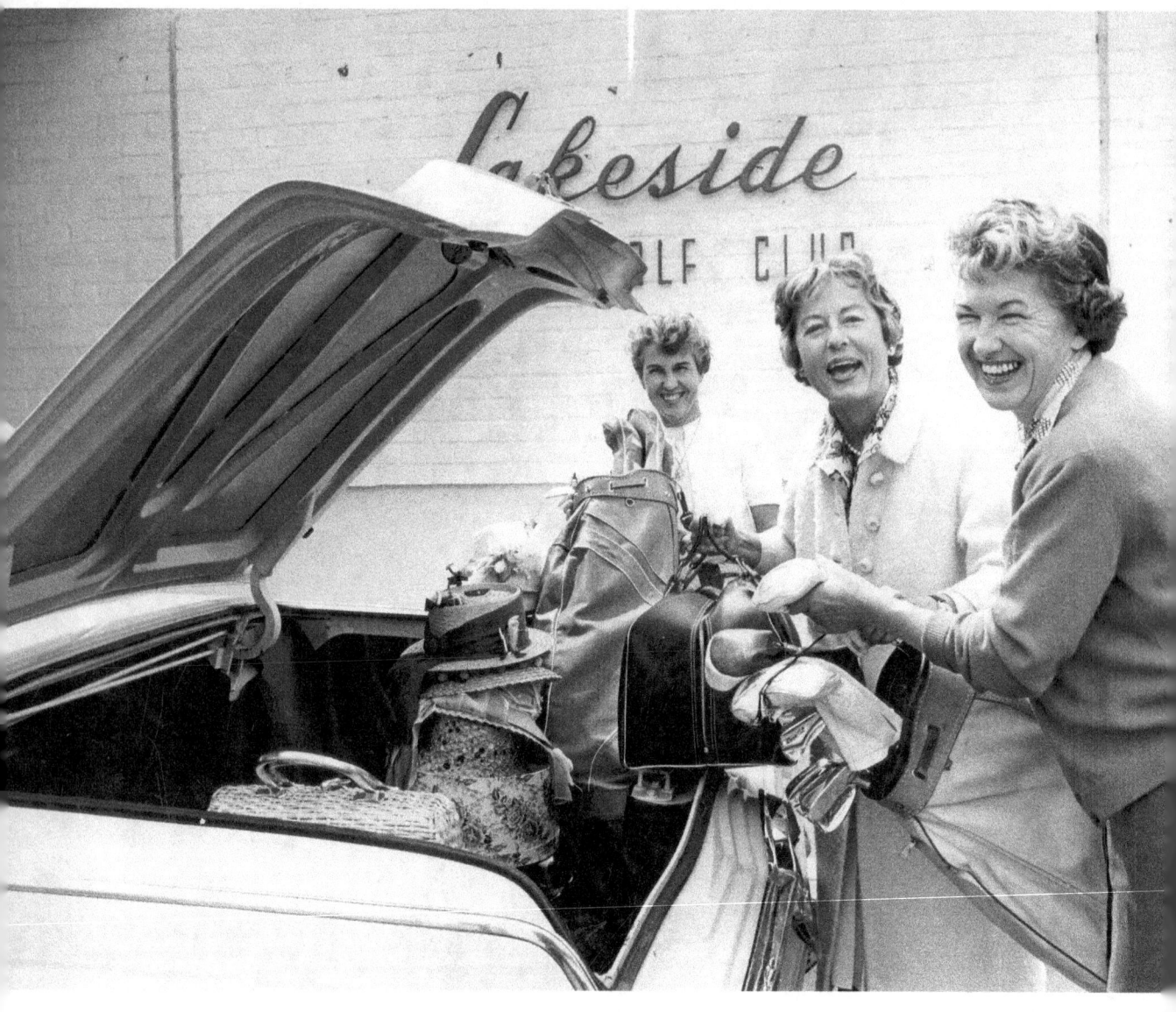

"Packing their equipment for Women's Southern California Golf Association annual Desert Event are (from left) Mmes. James A. McCoy, Woodland Hills Country Club; Sherry Shrouds, Thunderbird Country Club, and George Dutton, Lakeside Country Club." The women are in front of the Lakeside Golf Club located in Burbank, California. May 7, 1964. (George Brich)

Opposite: "Dick Nelson, Mrs. Jim Firth, and Ray Coutchie, rear, prepare a display for the Polaris Astronomical Society open house to be held in the Reseda Park recreational building at 18411 Victory Blvd. Exhibits of telescopes, mirror-making equipment, celestial photographs, books, charts and unusual instruments will be on display." May 10, 1962. (George Brich)

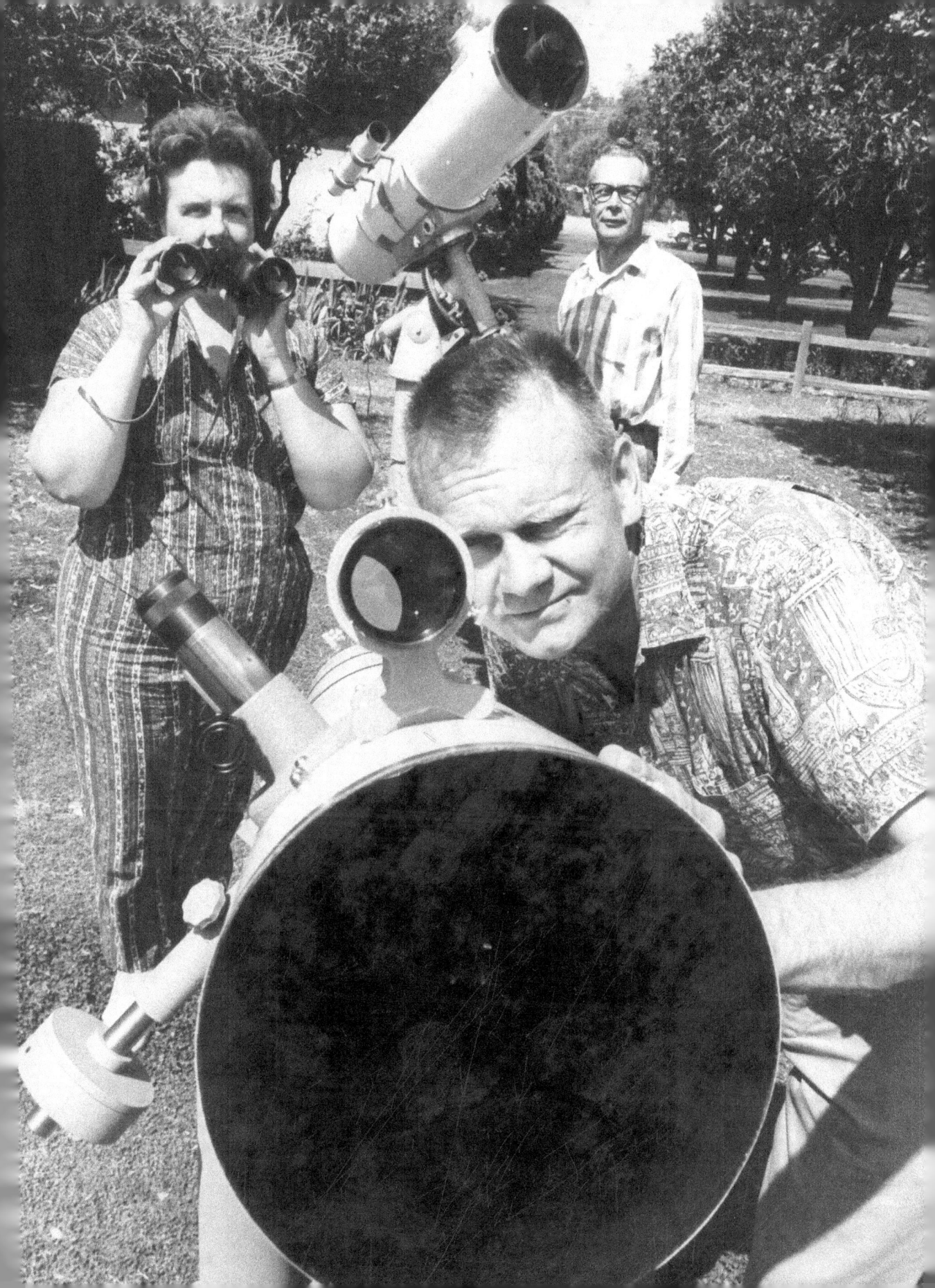

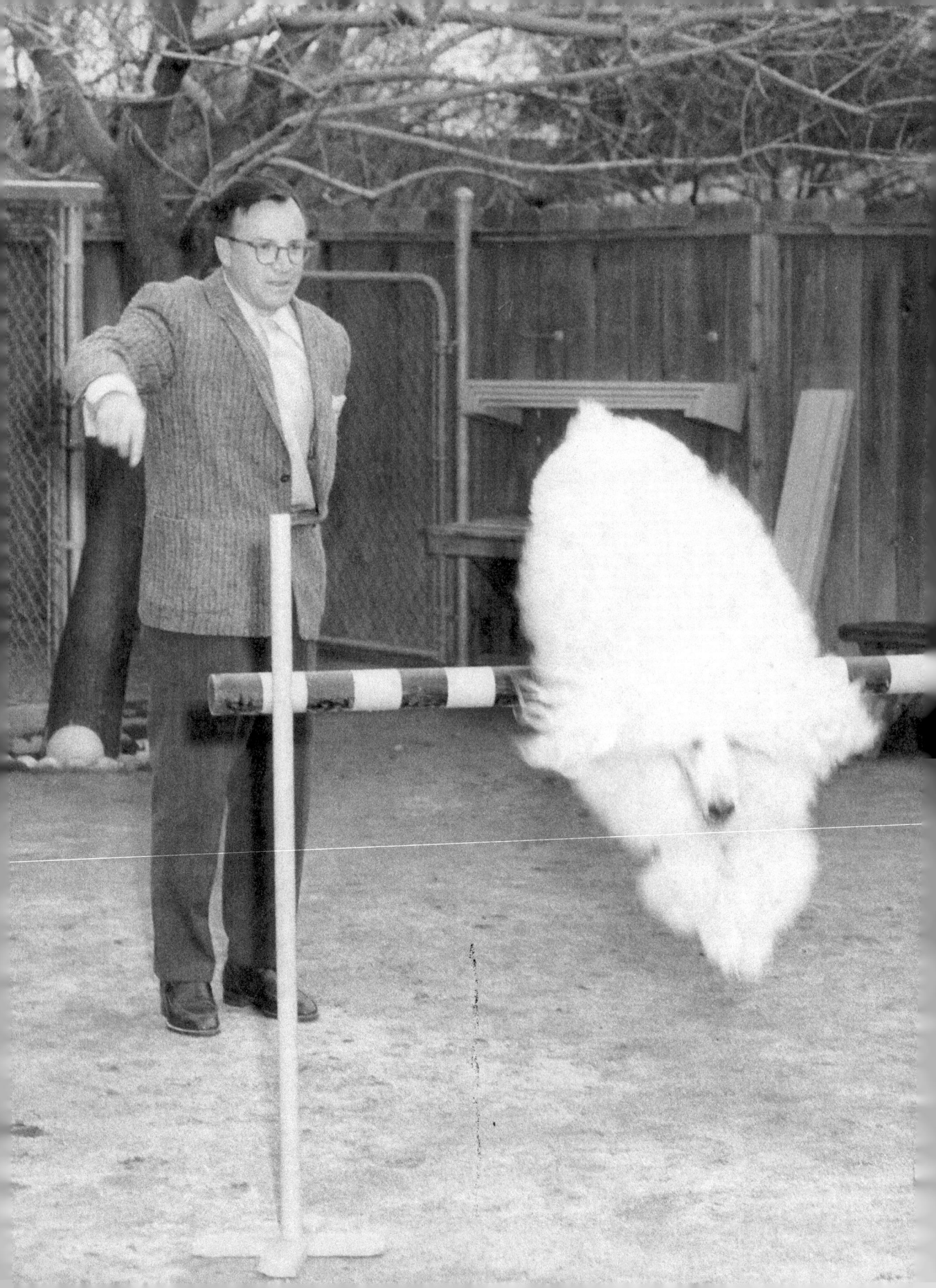

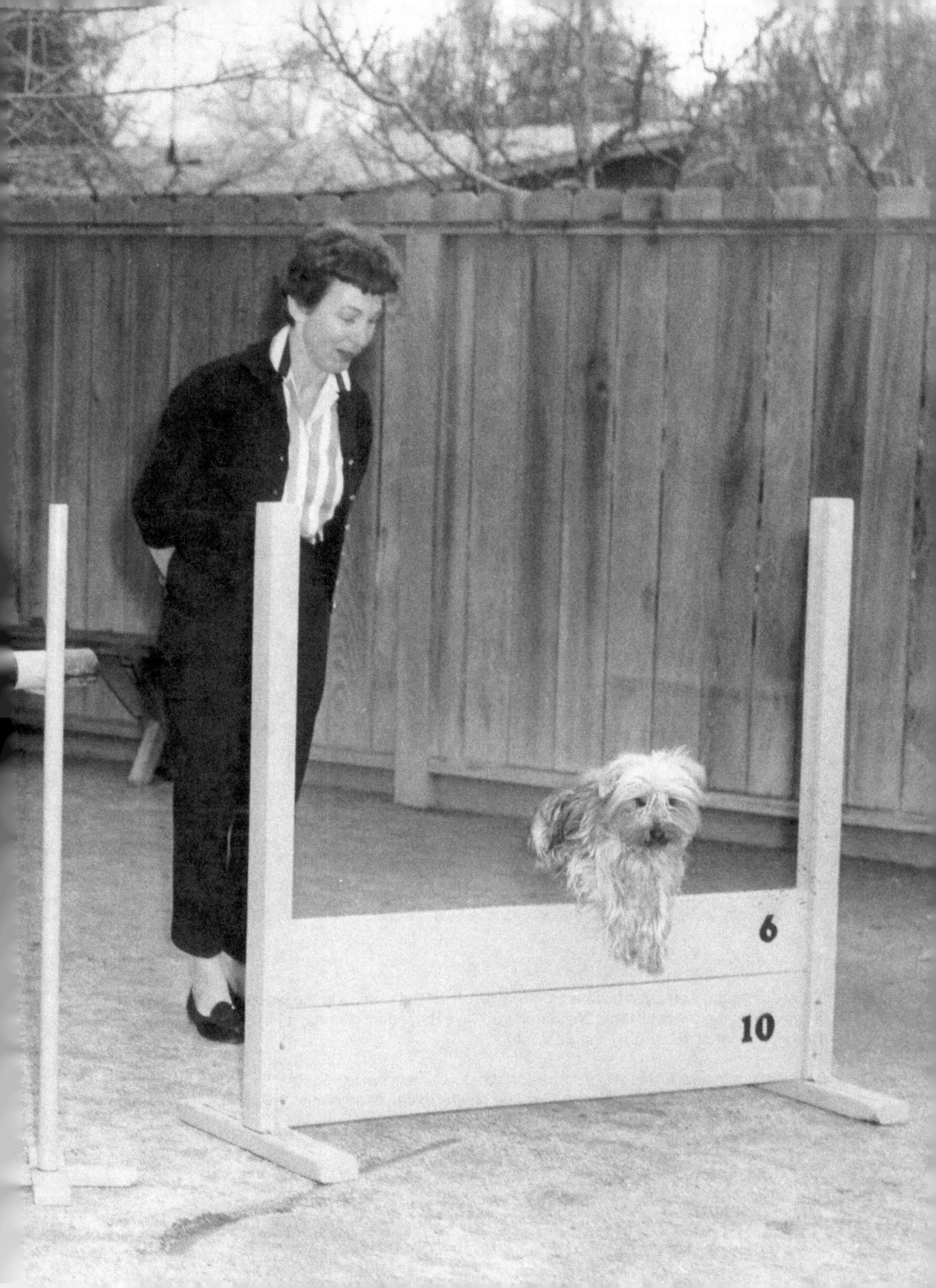

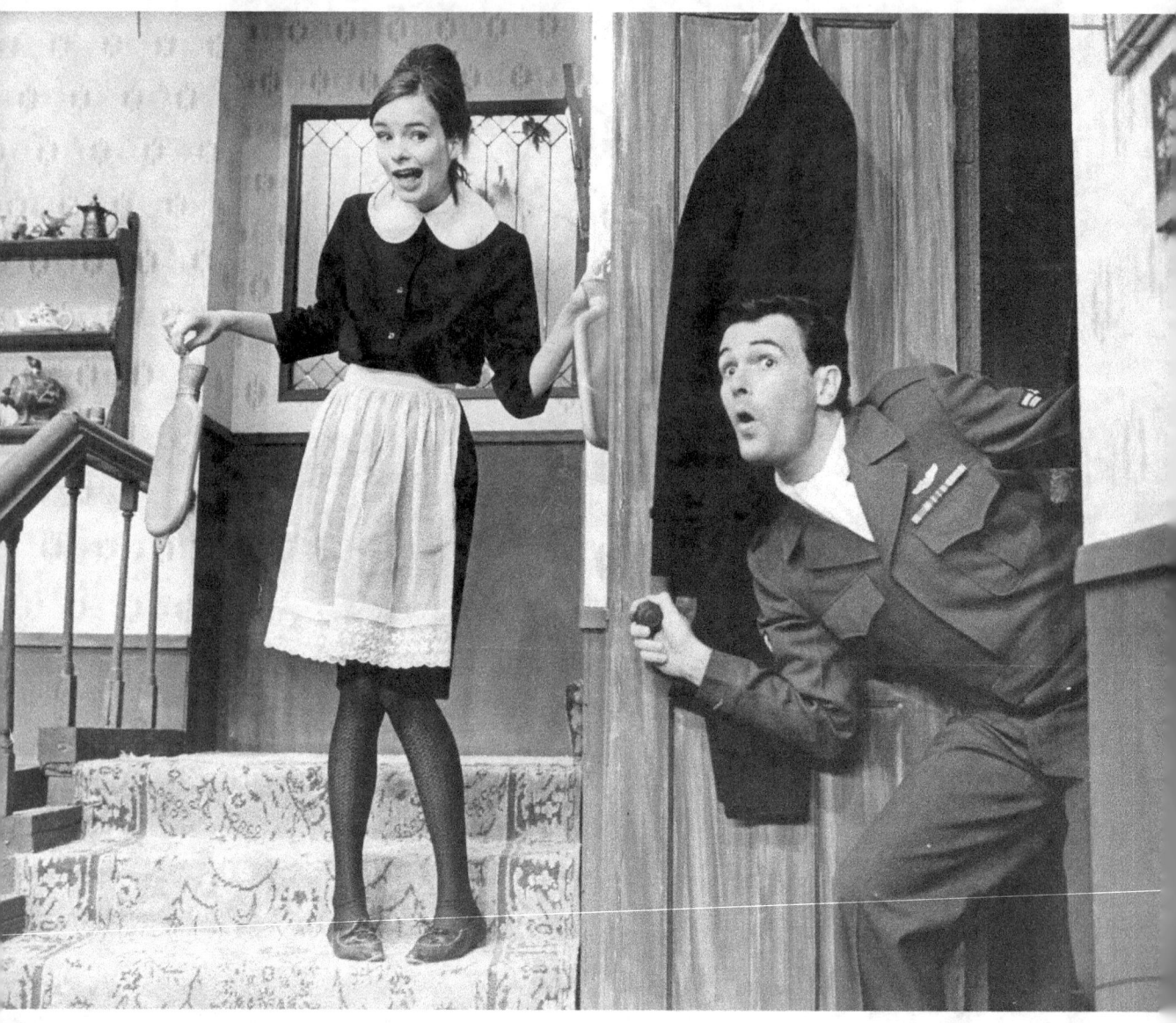

"Zany doings are portrayed by Shannon Stewart and Paul Corfino in the production of *See How They Run* at the Burbank Little Theater at the Olive Recreation Center, 1111 West Olive Ave., Burbank." March 18, 1965. (George Brich)

Overleaf: "Yorkshire Terrier, Mr. Boo, jumps over low fence, while poodle Beau takes the high hurdles with owners Harry Lieb and Mrs. Lois Noyes of Van Nuys during Valley Obedience Club class in Reseda." April 9, 1959.

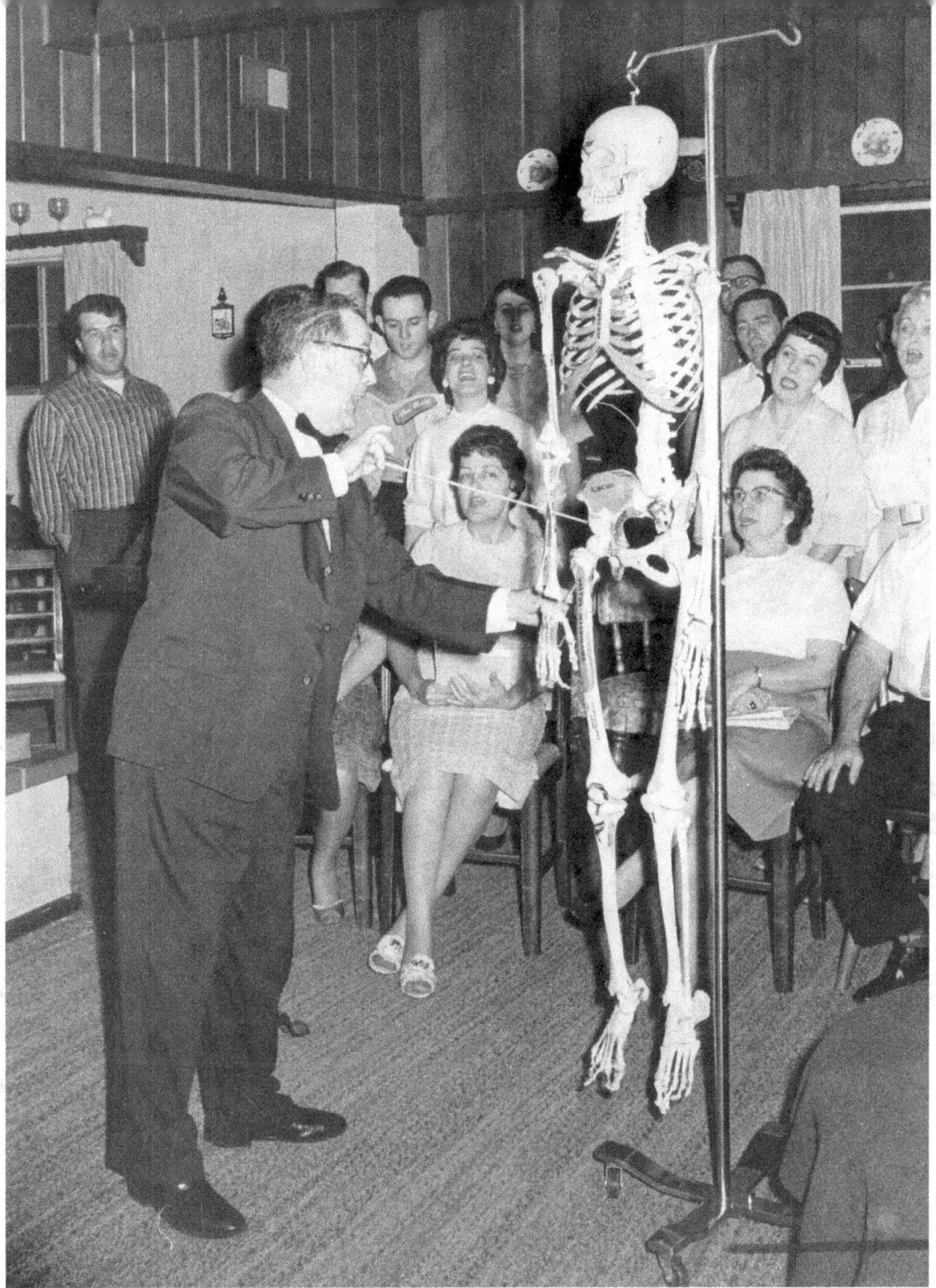

"Will Blailock Chorale in a practice session in a Van Nuys home, as director Blailock leads. The 30-voice chorus of housewives and working men borrowed this skeleton from a hospital for realism in the song, 'Dry Bones.' The group practices every Monday night at 6923 Tyrone Ave., Van Nuys, and plans a concert April 10 at Sherman Oaks Woman's Club. The singers range in age from 20 to 50." March 30, 1961. (Alan Hyde)

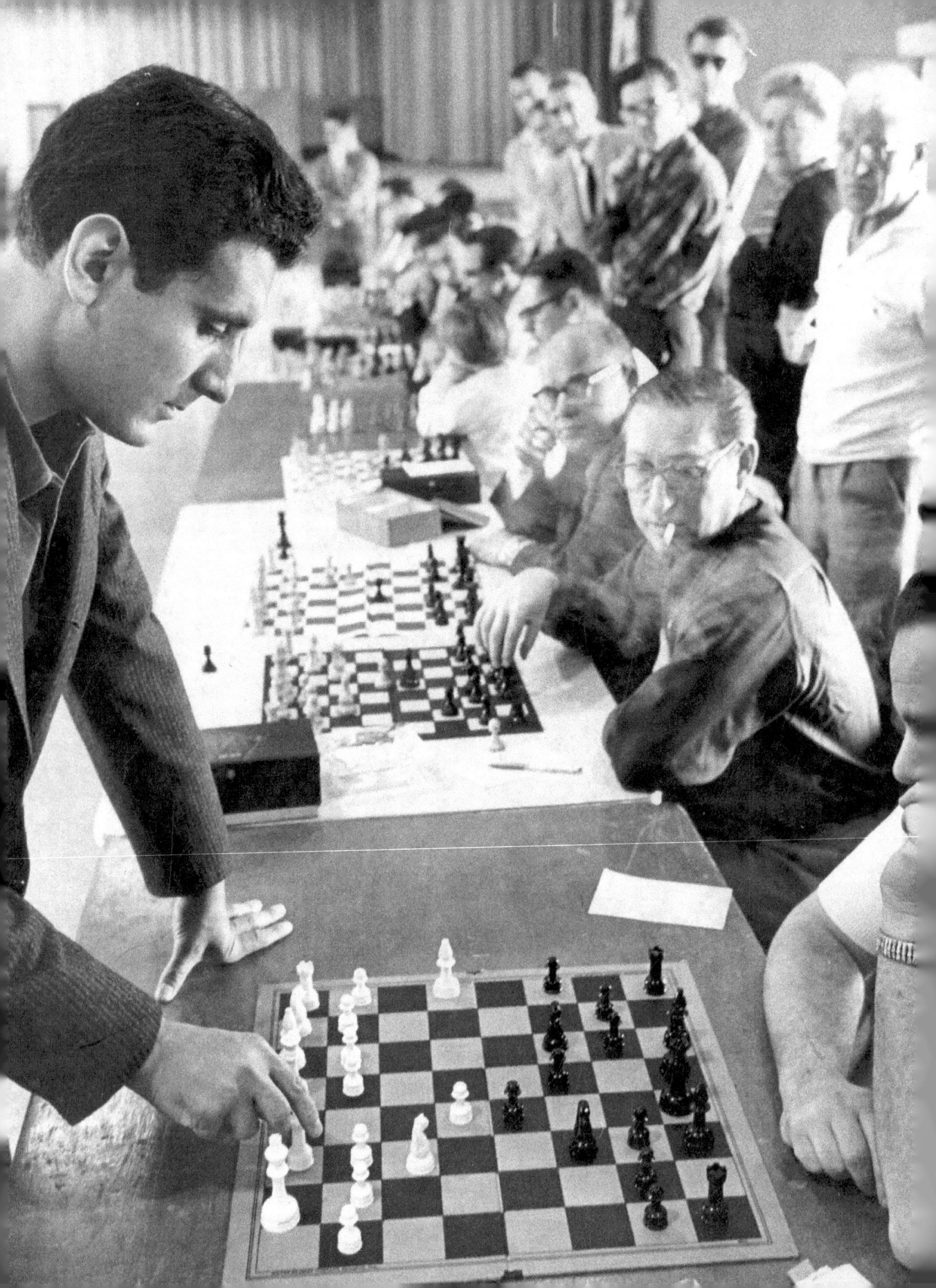

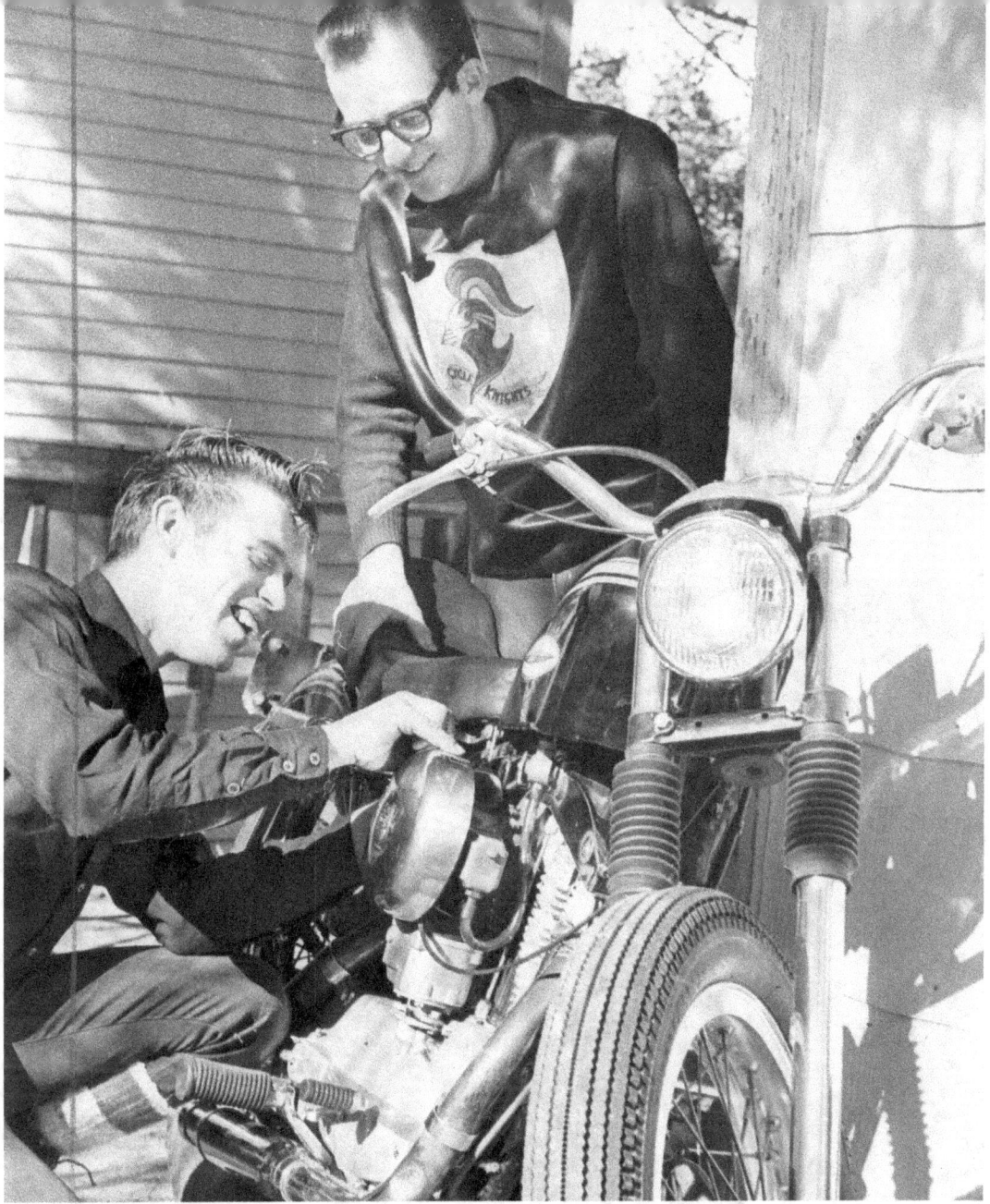

"Pictured doing maintenance work on motorcycle are Bob Waltrip (left) and Mike Radner, members of the Cycle Knights motorcycle club. In addition to being a pleasure club, the group has worked to improve the public image of motorcyclists by giving aid to motorists in trouble, keeping up a blood bank and participating in charity projects. January 24, 1963. (Jeff Goldwater).

Opposite: "Members of the Van Nuys Chess Club today were recovering from the beating they took Sunday from former U. S. Chess Champion Larry Evans. Evans played 50 simultaneous games—and won 48, drew 2, and lost none. Evans (left) makes move on the board of Lee Baumstein, 6611 Lindley Ave., Reseda." February 7, 1961. (Jon Woods)

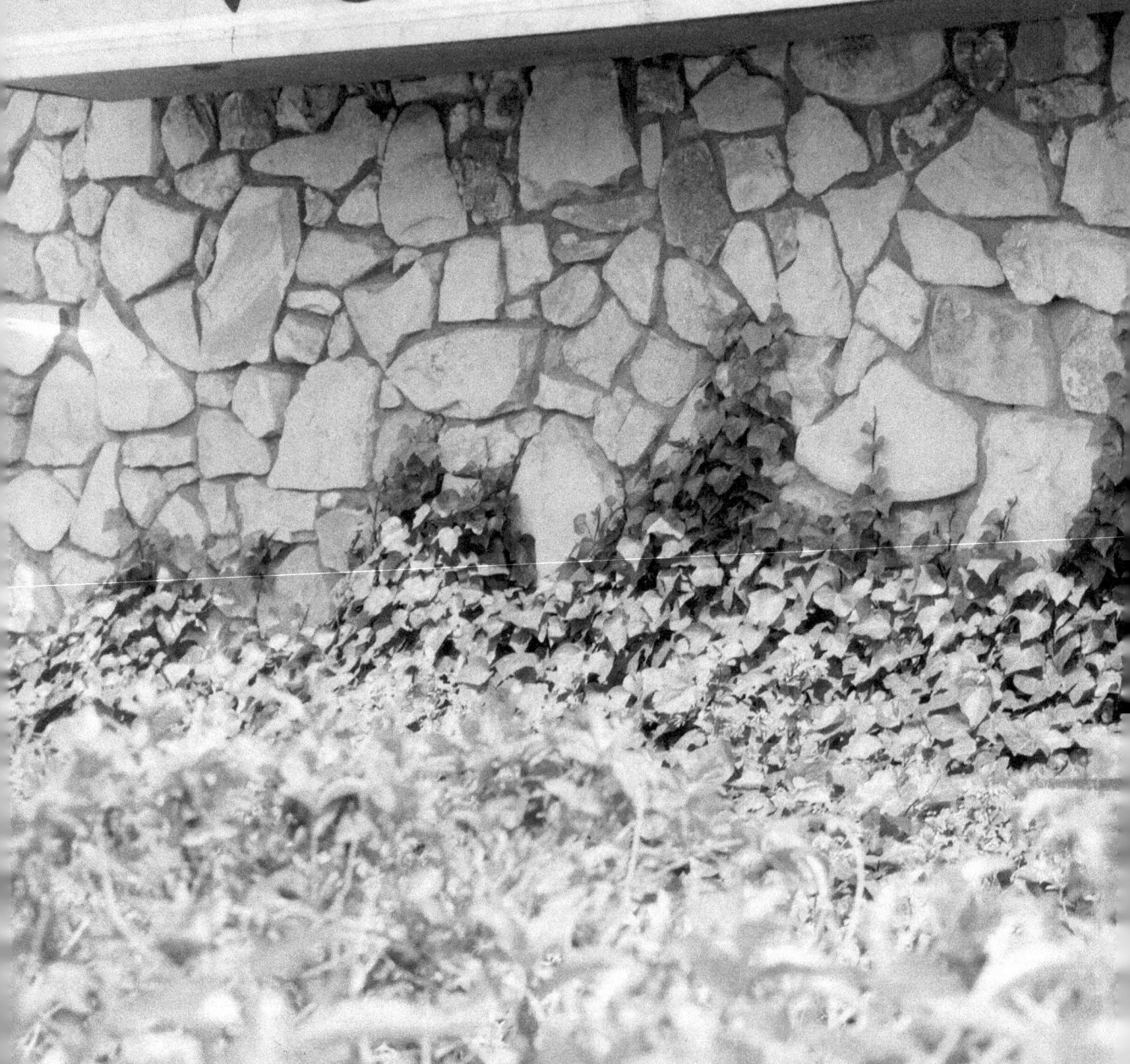

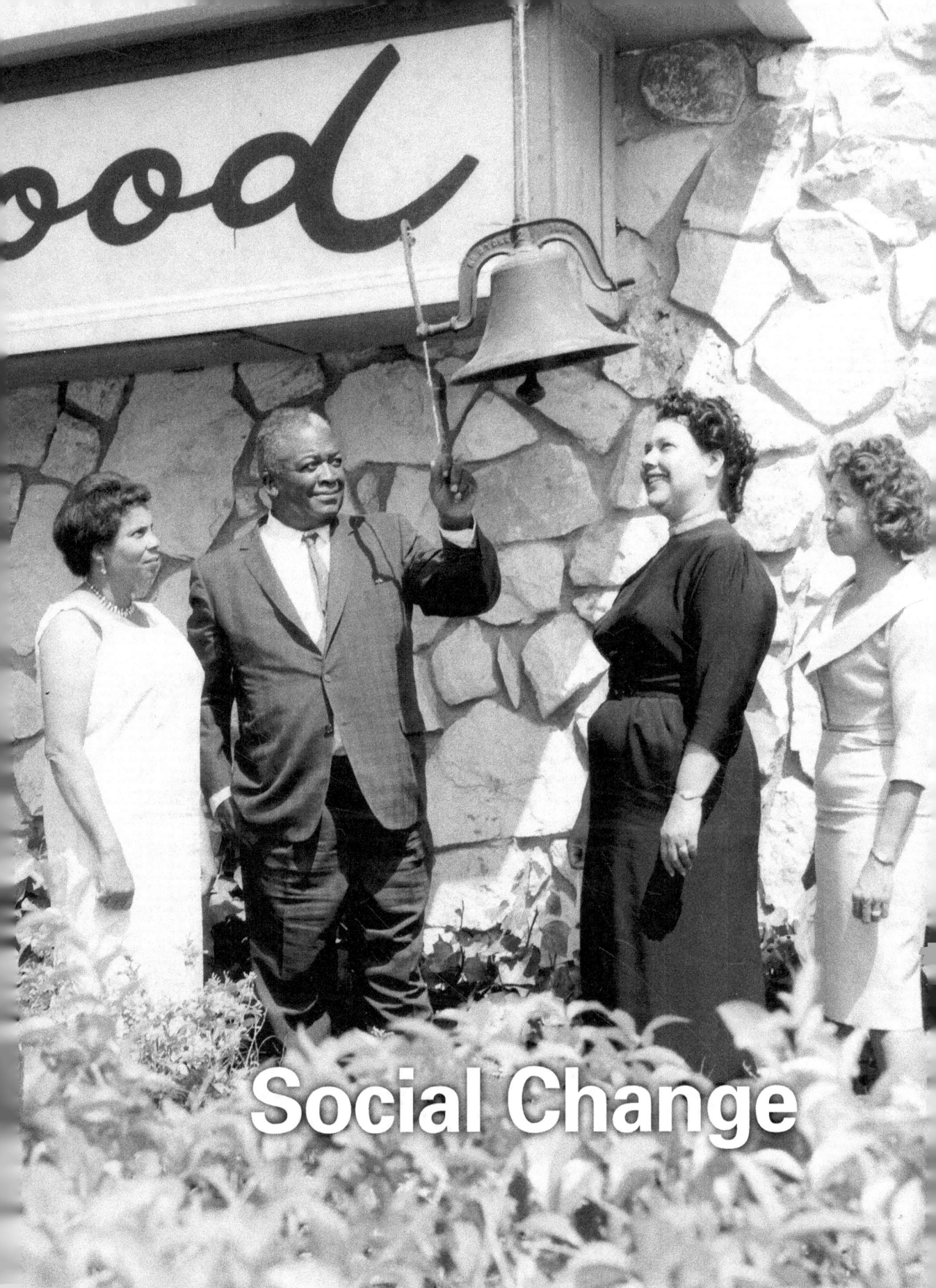

Social Change

Overleaf: "A ball celebrating the traditional Freedom Day for Texas and Oklahoma Negros will be held by the NAACP Valley Branch at Knollwood Country Club, Granada Hills. Inspecting the bell that will dominate the decorations are (from left) Mrs. Edward Melfort, co-chairman of the affair; Dr. Vernon Collins, M.D., toastmaster; Mrs. Theodore Larkin of the Valley Fair Housing Council, and Mrs. A. L. Calvin of the NAACP Women's Auxiliary. The bell was cast at Fulton, Kentucky, in a formerly slave-operated foundry." June 18, 1964.

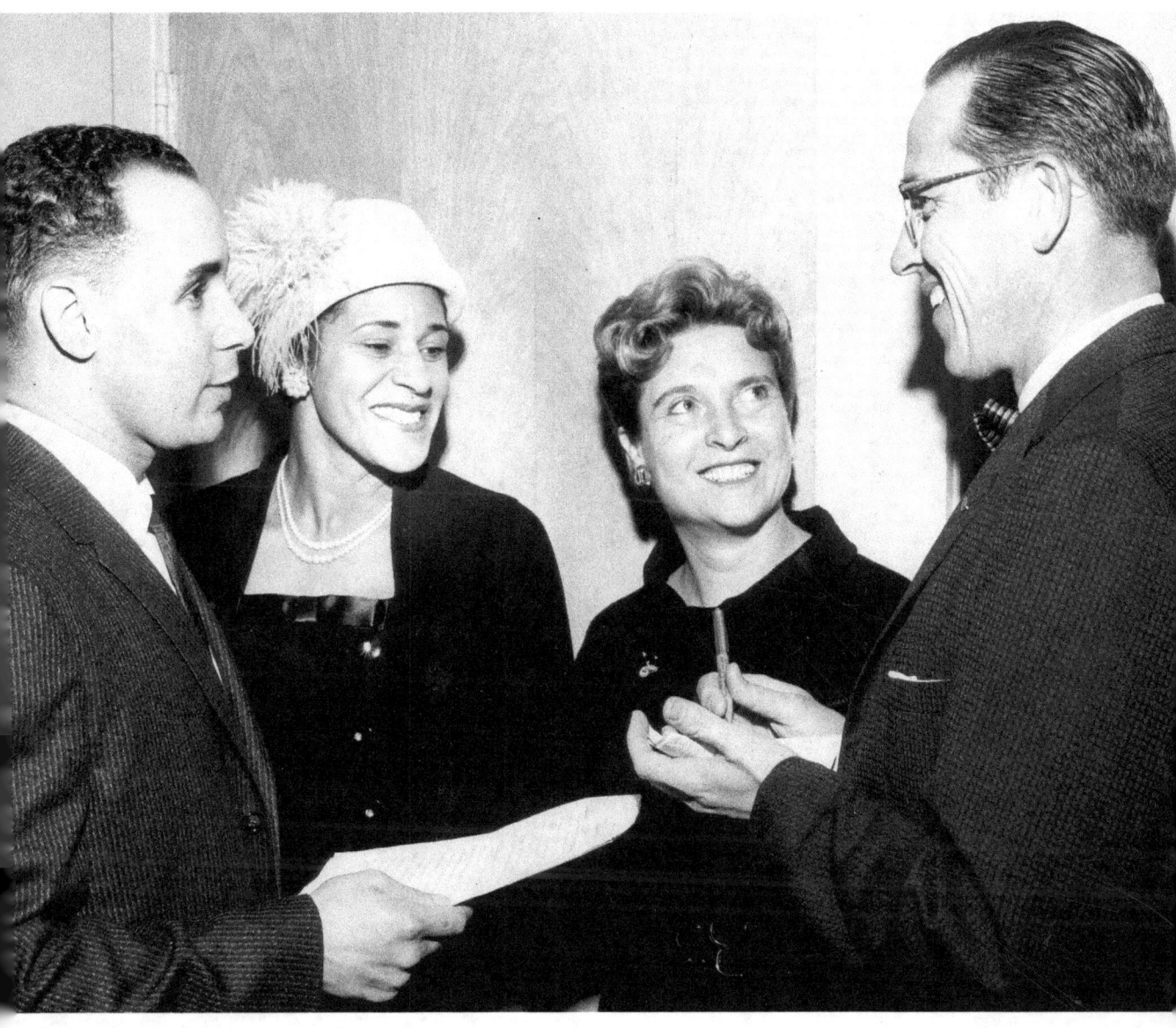

"Panelists for North Valley Human Relations Council meeting compare notes on questions raised during session at Panorama City Presbyterian Church on 'Roots of Prejudice.' From left are William T. White, County Commission on Human Relations consultant; Mrs. James Avery, past president of Valley Branch, NAACP and member of North Valley Human Relations Committee; Mrs. Al Newman, past president of San Fernando Coordinating Council, and John Buchanan, college teacher and committee member." November 5, 1959.

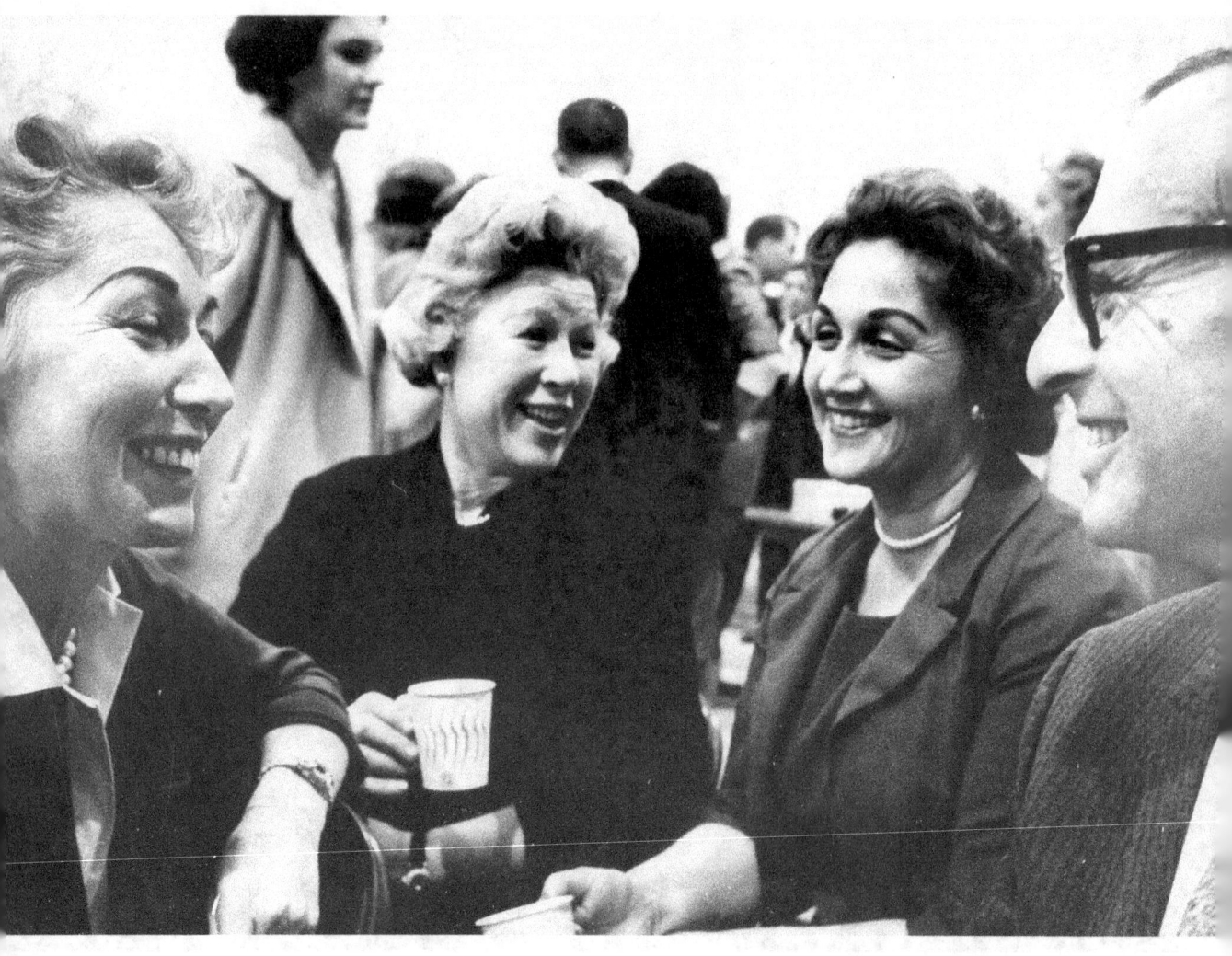

"Valley Parents Without Partners members, Mildred Saxs of Encino (from left), Helen Gardner and Bea Schwartz of Sherman Oaks, and Sam Friedland of North Hollywood, relax after the club's monthly business meeting to share ideas, new plans and progress concerning their mutual problem of raising children alone. Social activities are planned for children of the members, including parties, field trips, athletic events and trips to places of amusement." Meetings are held in the Victory-Vanowen Playground Auditorium, North Hollywood. January 18, 1961.

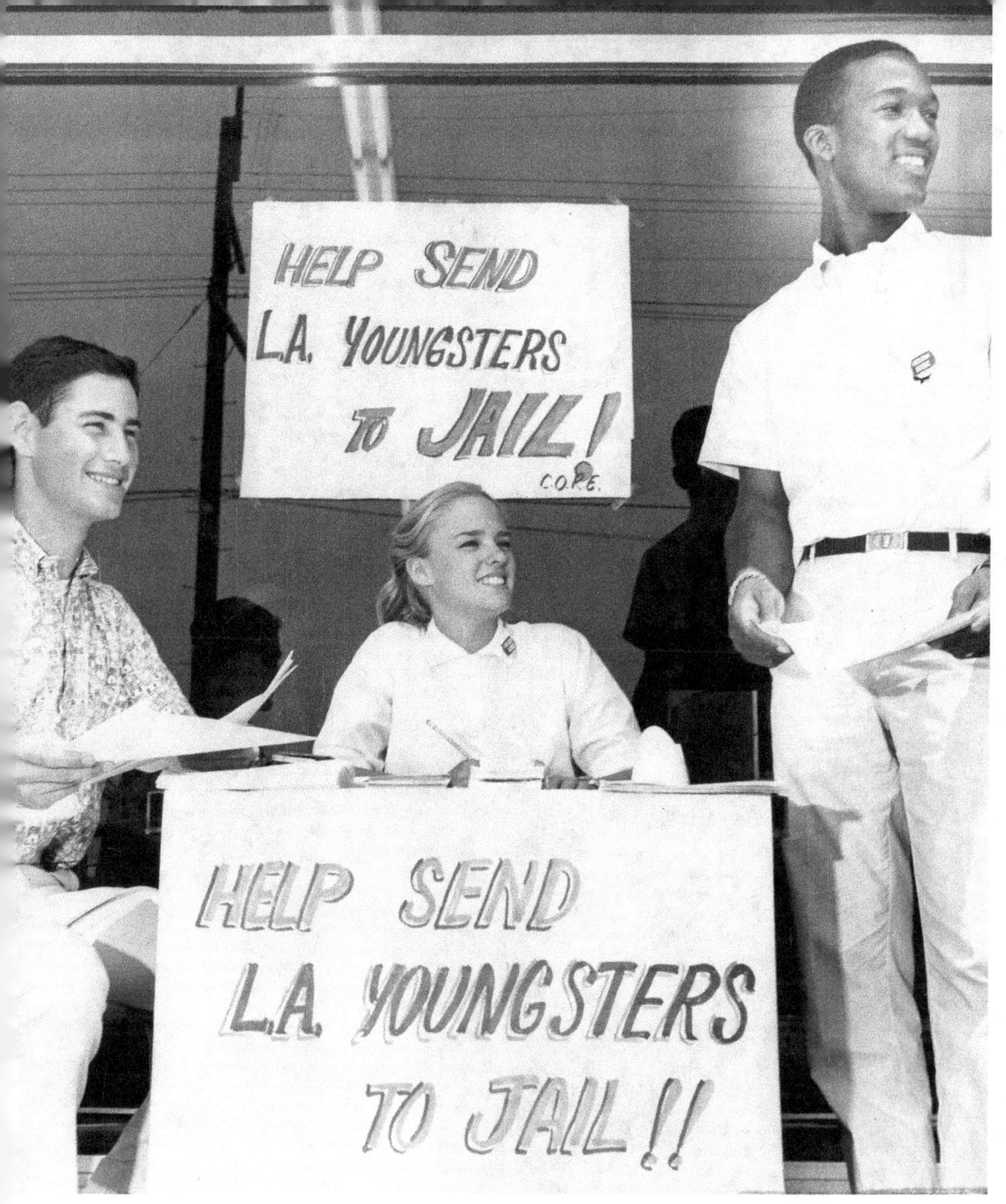

"Members of CORE (Congress of Racial Equality) pass out pamphlets protesting the jailing of Freedom Riders. Shown distributing the sheets in Pacoima are (from left) Michael Haimovitz, 19, 5529 Lemona Ave., Van Nuys, a student at the University of California; Stevie Lipney, 17, 3921 Woodcliff Rd., Sherman Oaks, a student at Van Nuys High School, and Ernie Dillard, 23, 8109 Genesta St., Van Nuys, an electronics salesman." July 24, 1961.

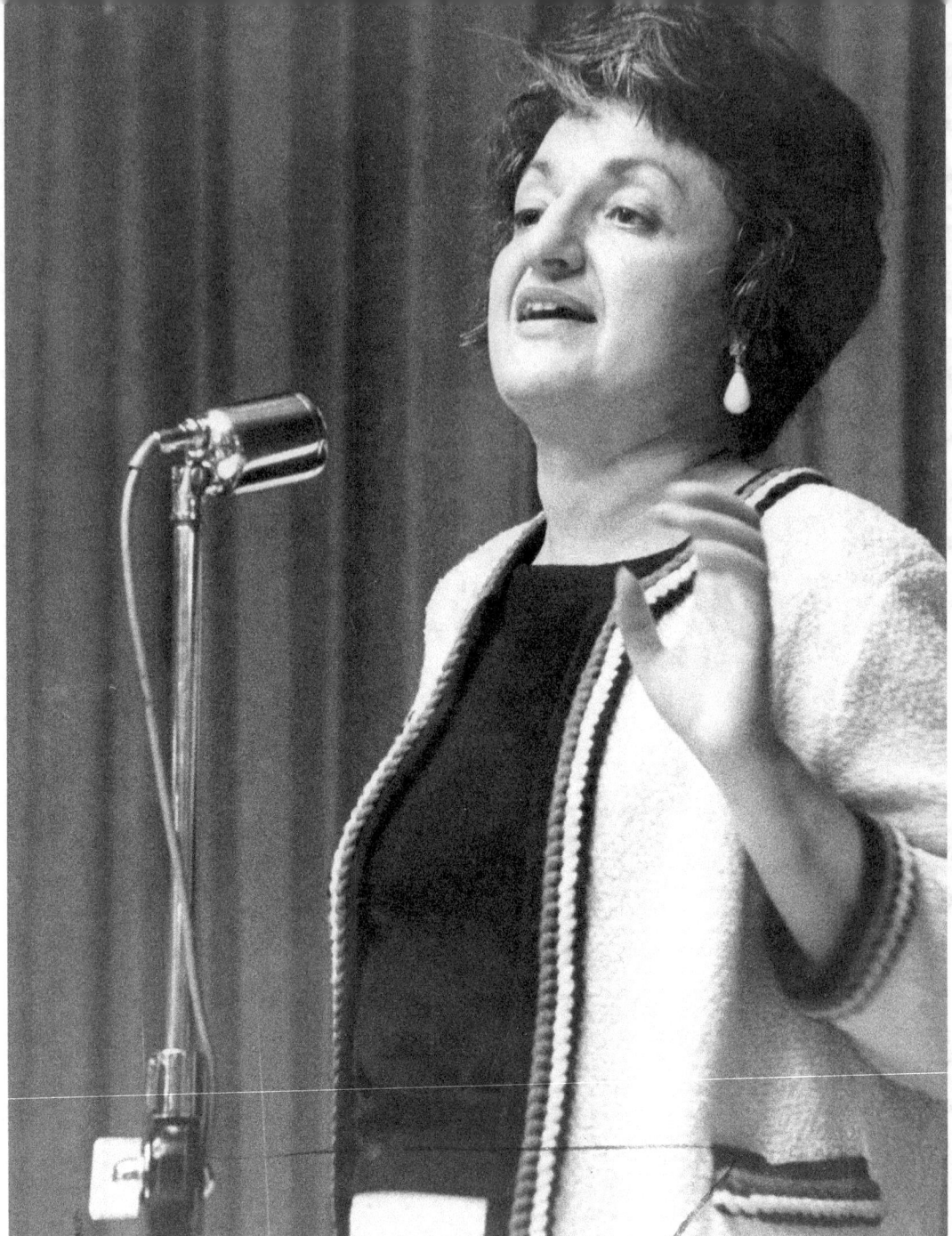

"Betty Friedan, who spoke recently to the Valley branch of the American Association of University Women, claims the American woman, 'buried in her dishpans,' has been brainwashed into believing that the only commitment for women is the 'fulfillment of their own femininity...' The first step in finding oneself, Mrs. Friedan said, is to 'recognize that housework is not a career, but something that must be done as quickly and efficiently as possible. The second step is to see marriage as it really is—not necessarily as the final fulfillment of life...Men are not holding women back in America,' she said. 'It's our own self-degradation.'" April 13, 1964. (Bob Martin)

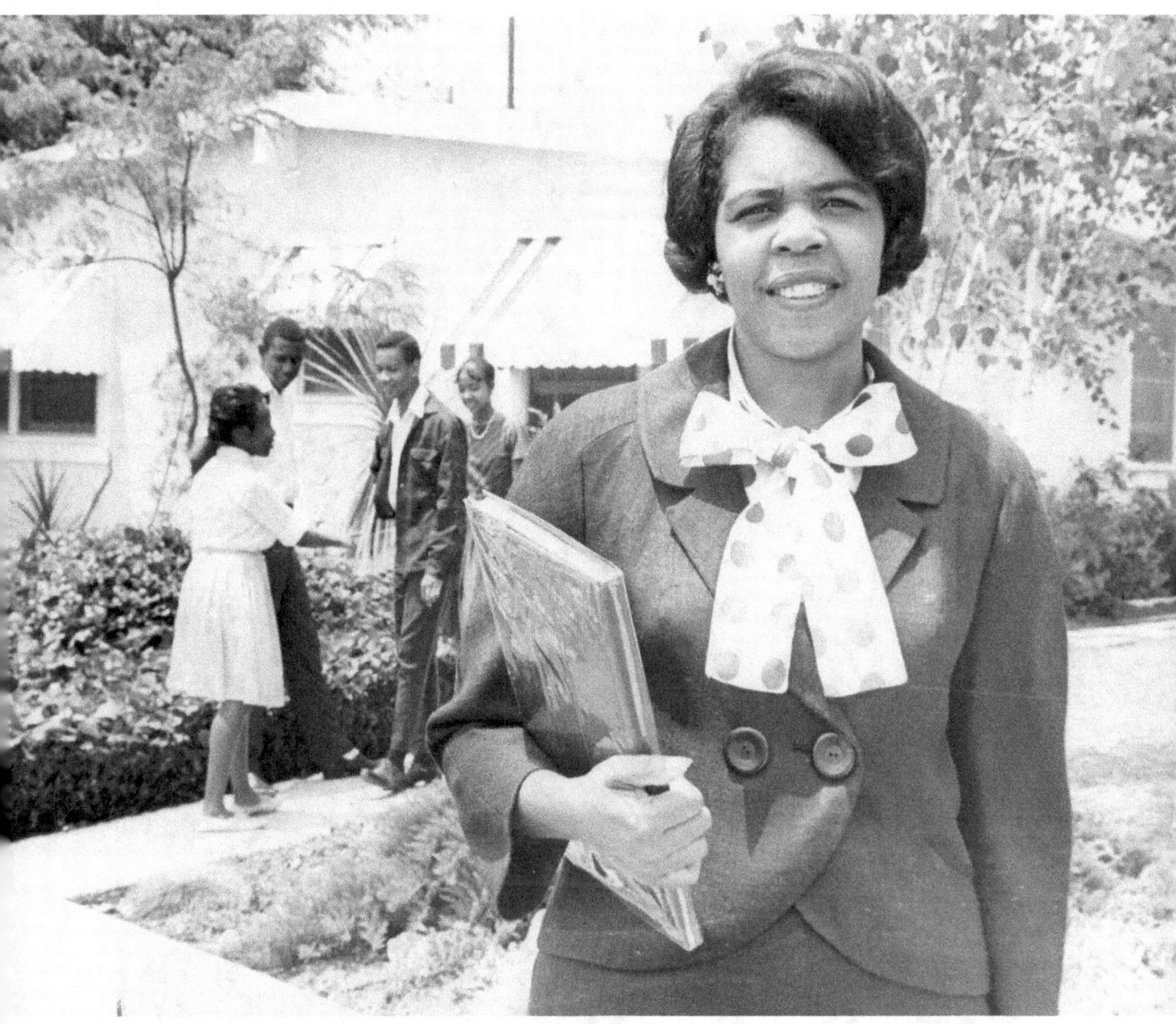

"A Valley integration leader says there is much that local chambers of commerce and service clubs could do if they seriously wanted to aid desegregation in the Valley...'But no one has offered any help to us. There is a lot they could do, but they haven't made the effort,' says Georgia Taylor, president of the Valley chapter of the National Association for the Advancement of Colored People (NAACP). Mrs. Taylor, a 38-year-old Negro who lives with her husband and five children in an almost completely Negro neighborhood in Pacoima, has a project that she says chambers of commerce and service clubs could handle. A major problem in the Valley, she holds, is the fact that many Southern Negros and whites have come to California bringing their segregation practices with them." August 3, 1963. (Gordon Dean)

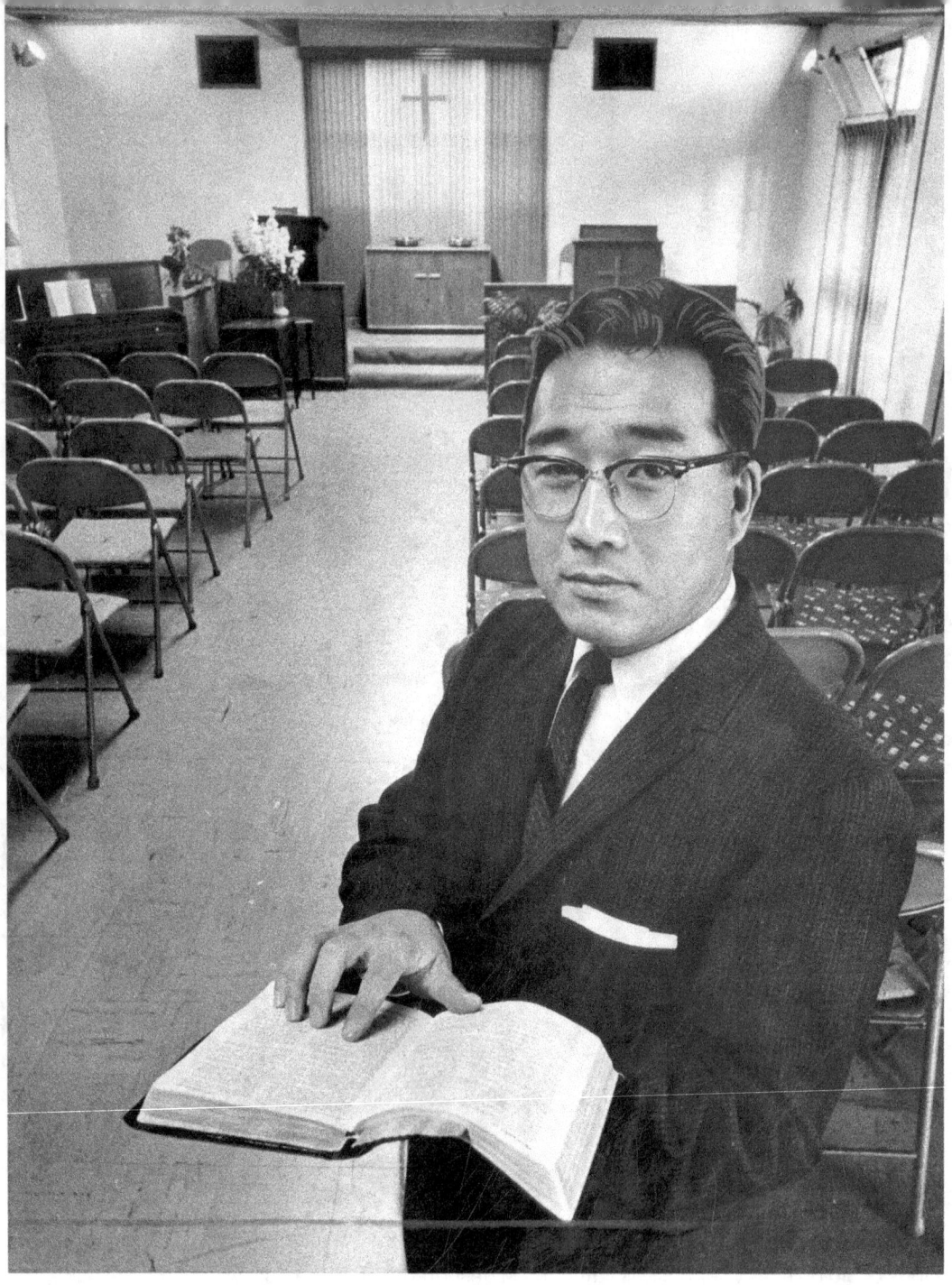

"We want to get ahead and be like everyone else," said the Rev. George Toda, "but because we are a minority group we have found it isn't always easy." Mr. Toda, Japanese-American-born pastor of the San Fernando Holiness Church, which serves the Nisei population in the Valley, expressed the feelings of his small Pacoima congregation. January 26, 1963. (George Brich)

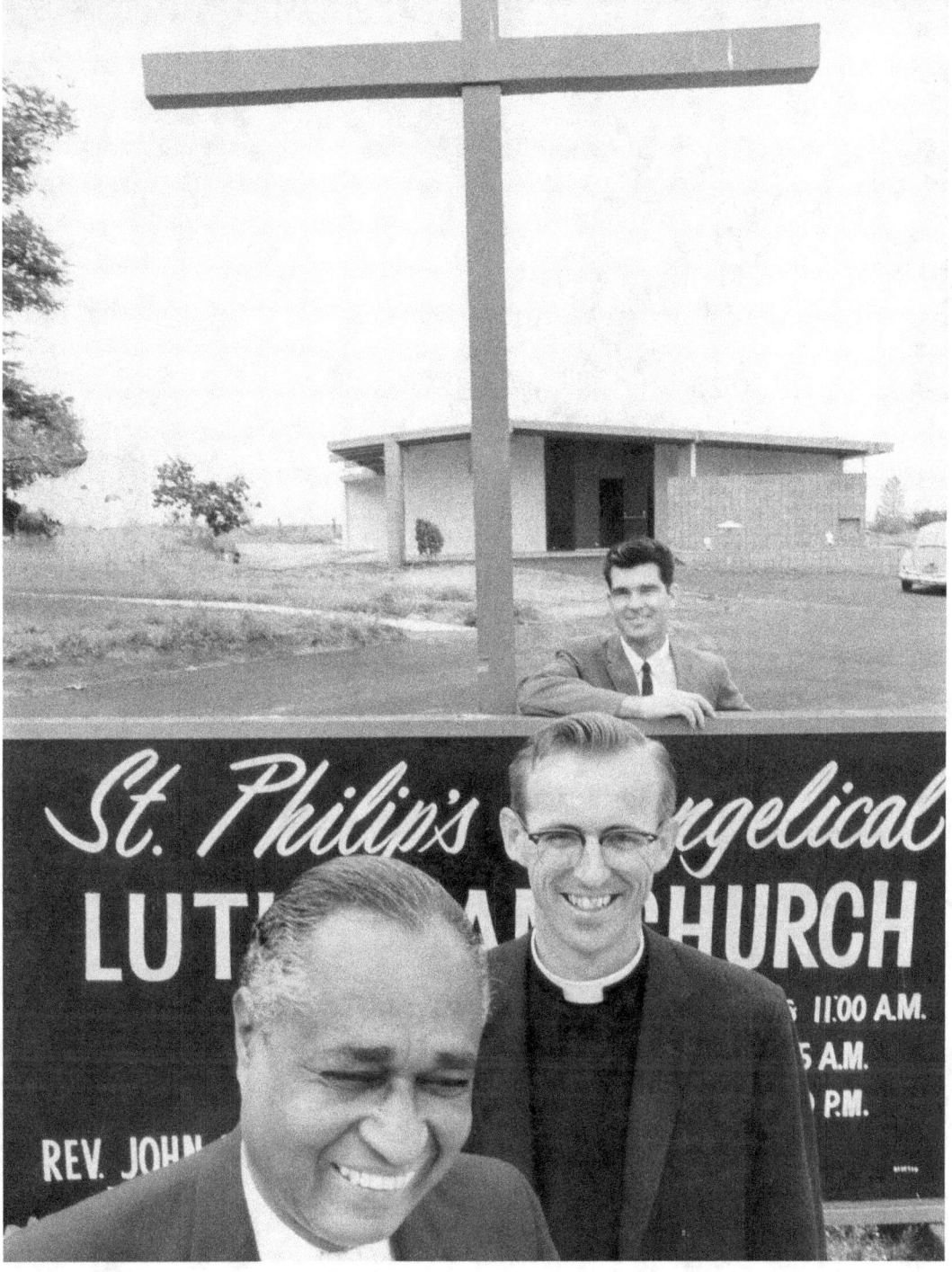

"Reverend John C. Wetzel, pastor of St. Philip's Lutheran Church in Pacoima, wants to establish a congregation of people from different races and economic backgrounds at his church. Board members include Hawley Arnold, Mr. Wetzel, and David Nesmith." June 1, 1963. (George Brich)

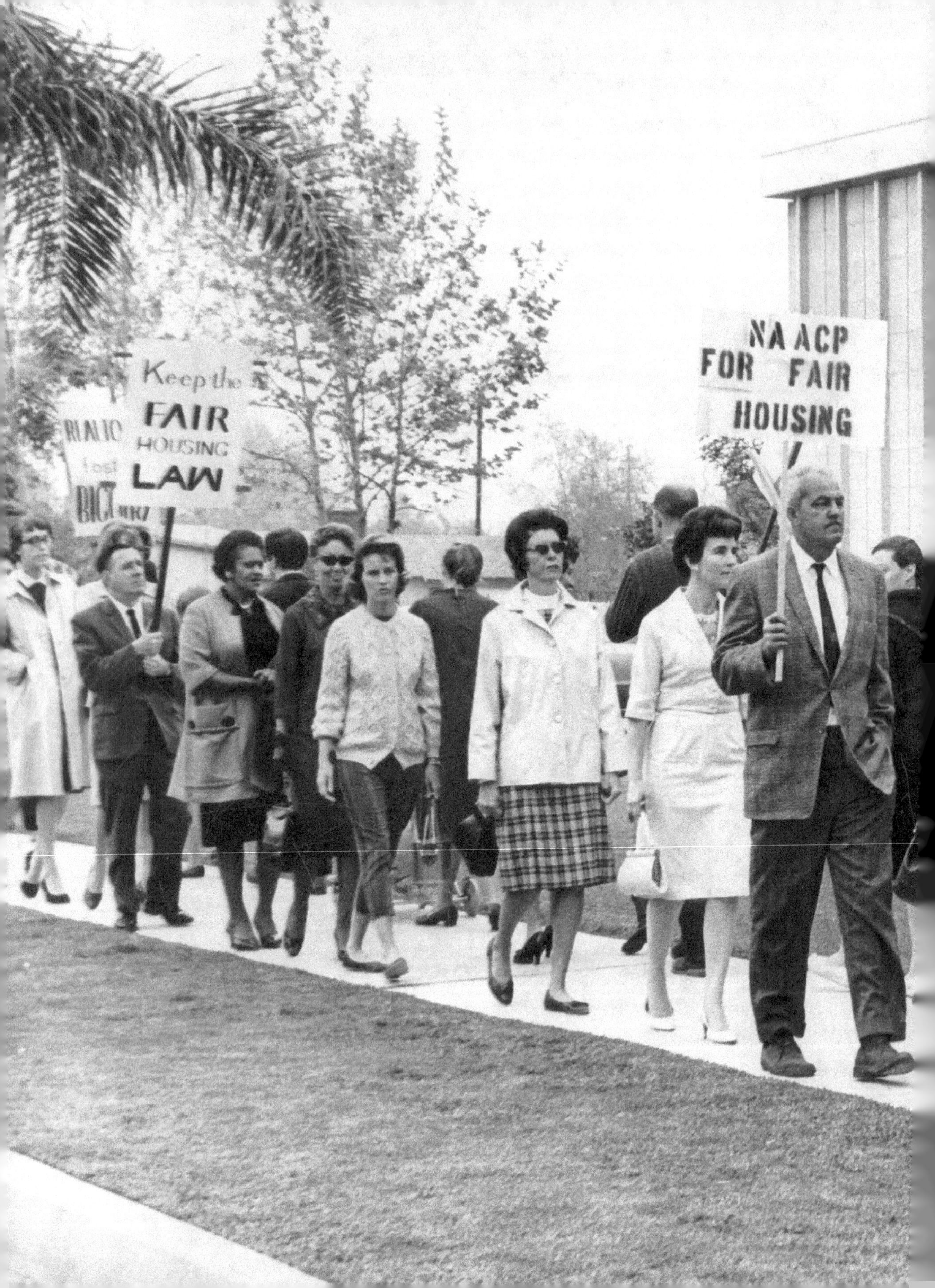
Keep the
FAIR
HOUSING
LAW
NAACP
FOR FAIR
HOUSING

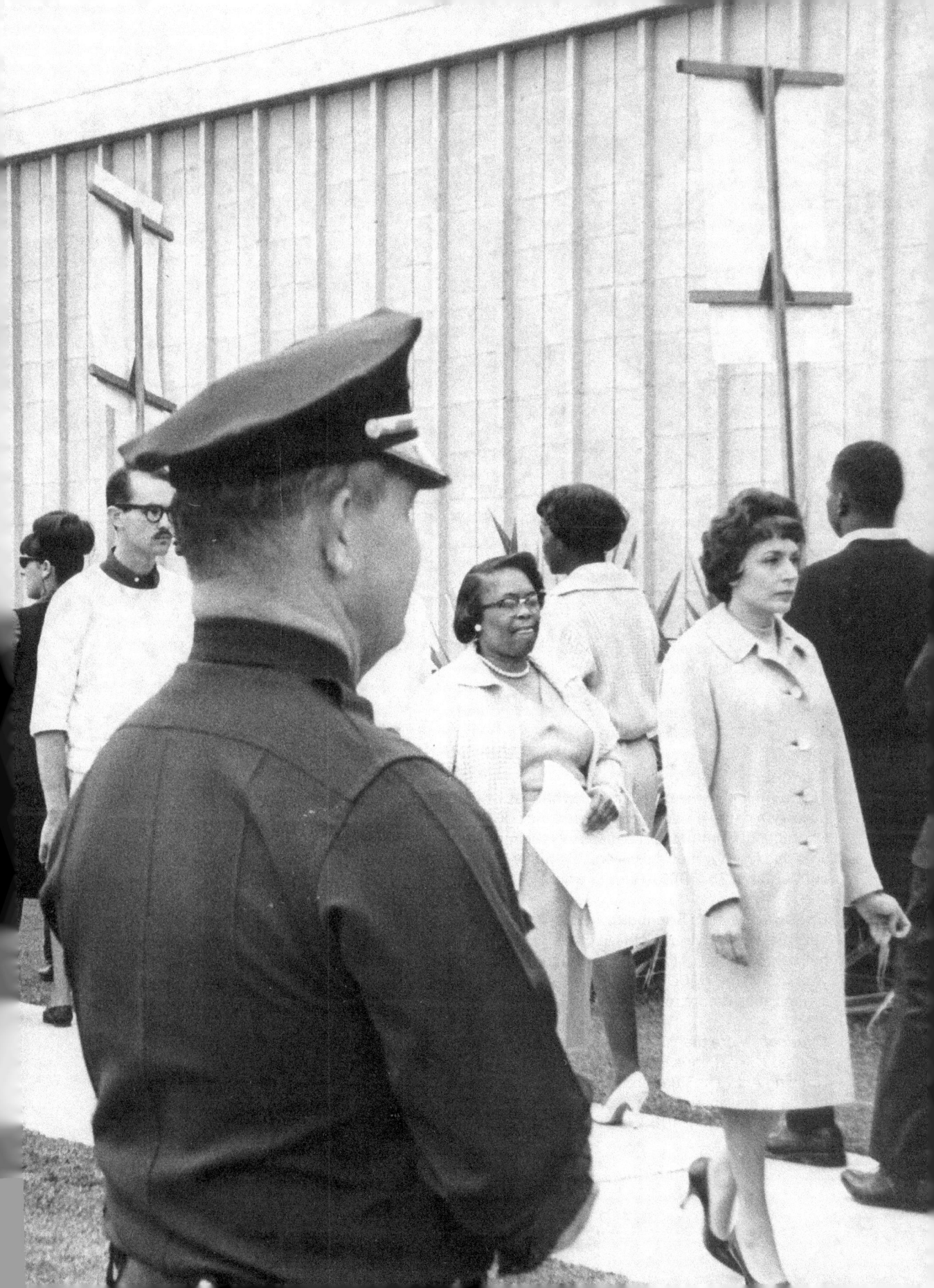

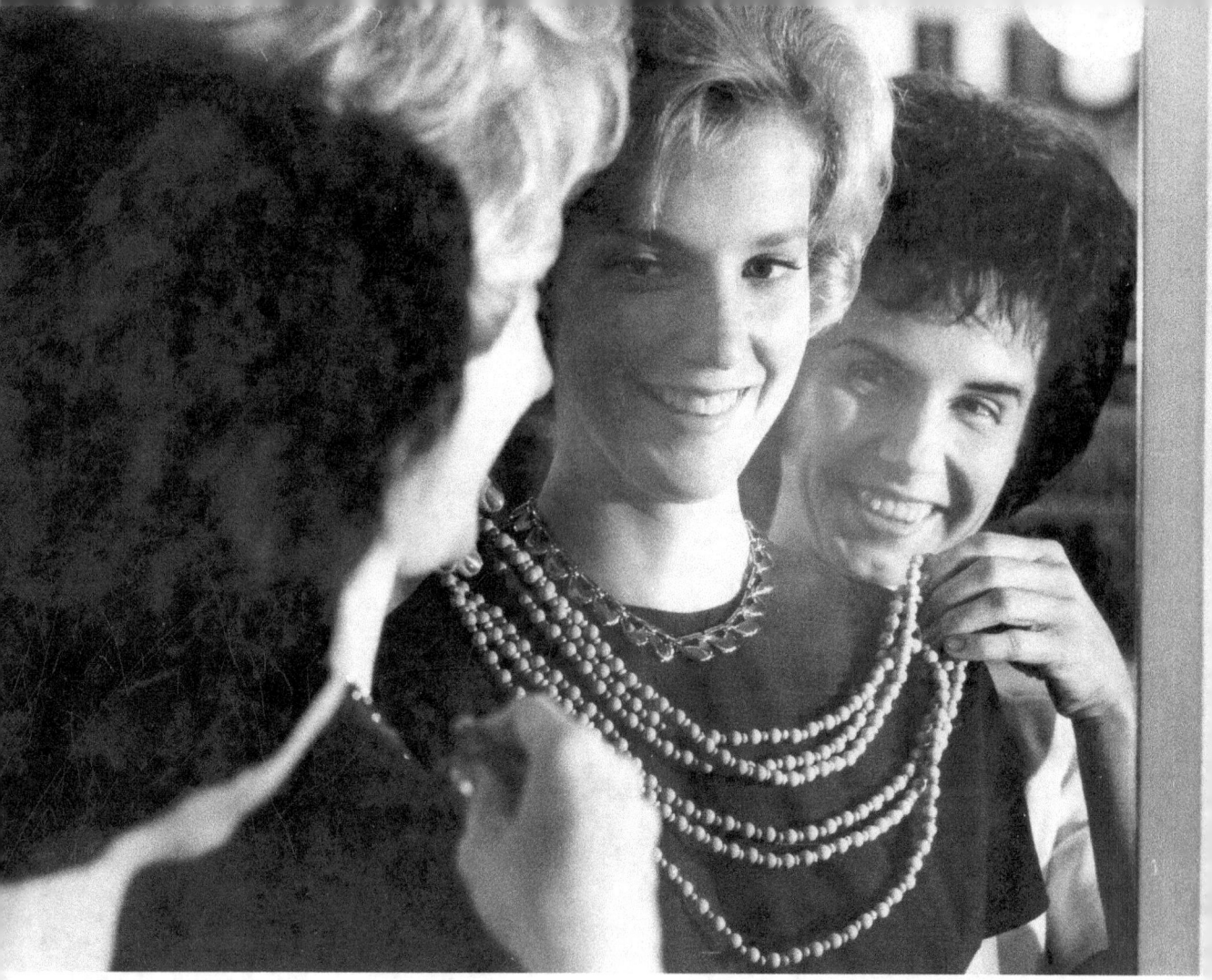

"Instrumental in the breaching of what has been a male preserve in the Valley until now is Shirley Lowery, a petite brunette who heads the newly formed Women's Division of the Canoga Park Chamber of Commerce....'Because of the rapid growth of the regular chamber we felt the time was ripe for a women's division...'." Shirley Lowery places jewelry on Robin Brickett for auxiliary show. March 25, 1963. (George Brich)

Opposite: "Marilyn Eisenberg, an 18-year-old 'Freedom Rider' returned home Monday and told of her 39 days in a Mississippi jail. Sitting in the den of her family's house she held a stack of mail in her hands—some of the mail was encouraging, much of it on the 'hate' variety." The Freedom Ride was sponsored by CORE (Congress of Racial Equality), and Eisenberg plans to raise funds for the organization before returning to college. August 29, 1961.

Overleaf: "More than 100 pickets marched yesterday in front of Valley Board of Realtors Inc. offices, 7232 Balboa Blvd., Van Nuys, to protest realtors' support of initiative to repeal Rumford Housing Act." The Rumford Fair Housing Act of 1963 stated landlords and property owners could not deny housing to any person based on their ethnicity, religion, sex, marital status, or physical handicap. March 4, 1963. (Jeff Robbins)

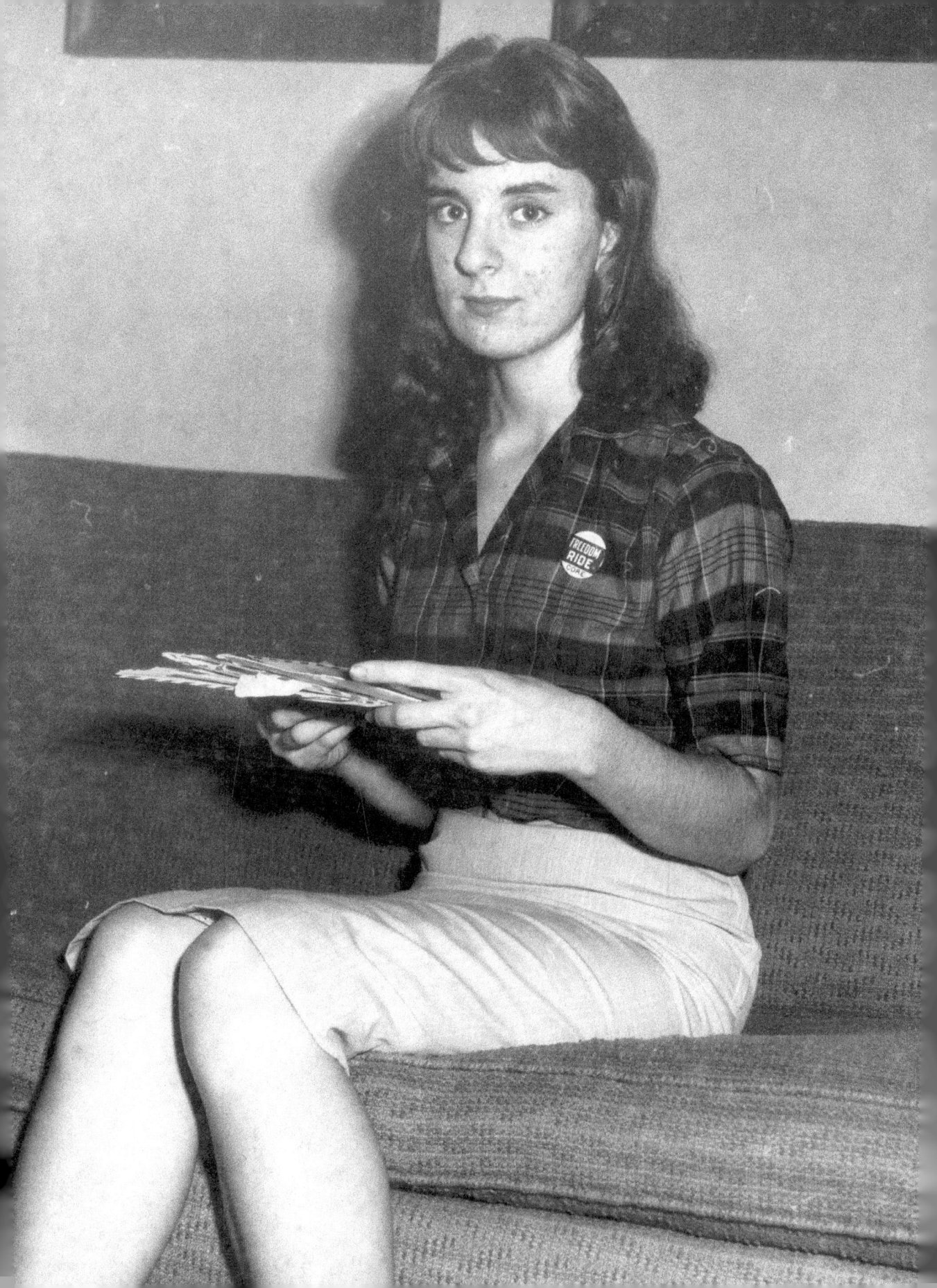

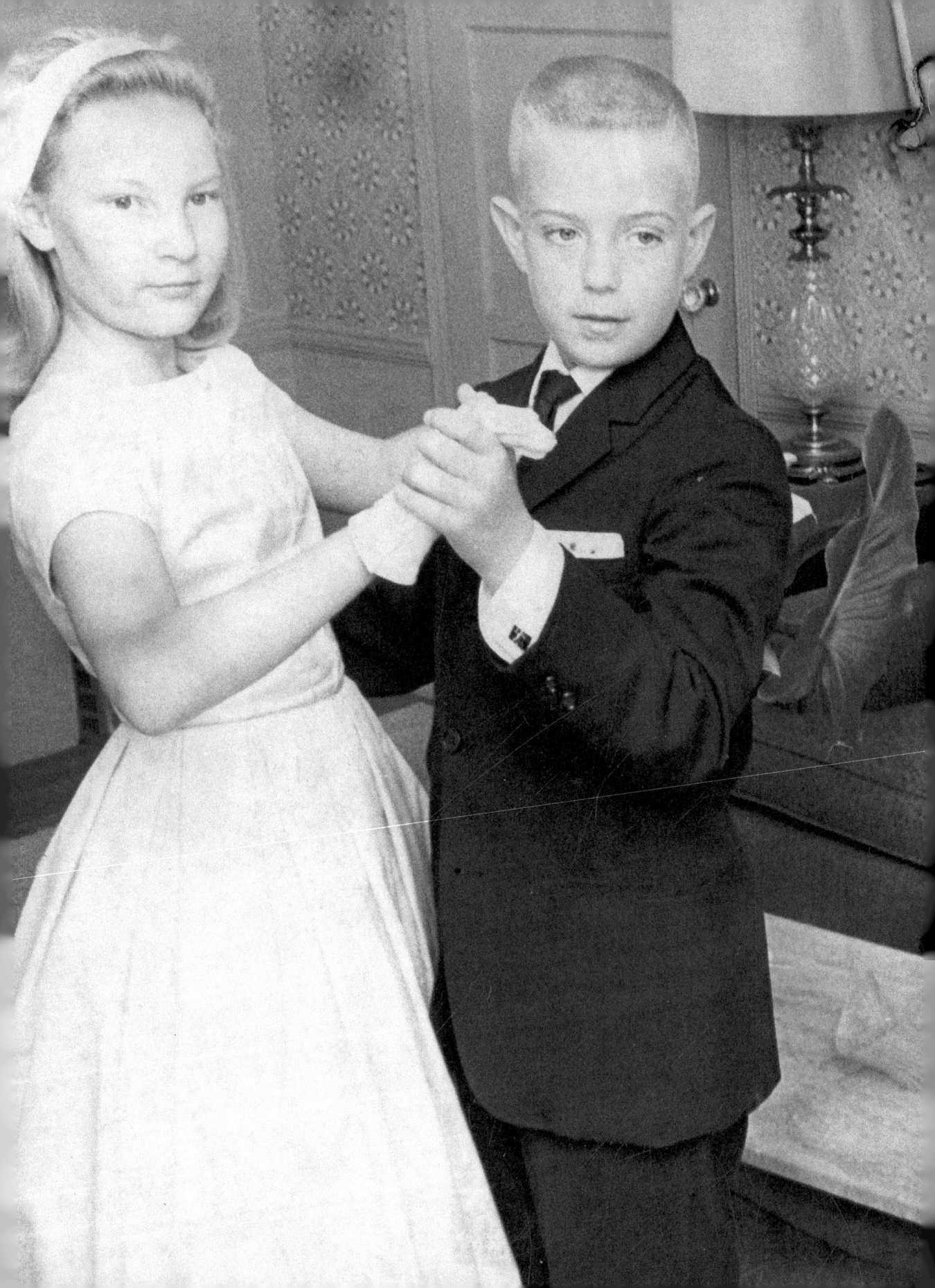

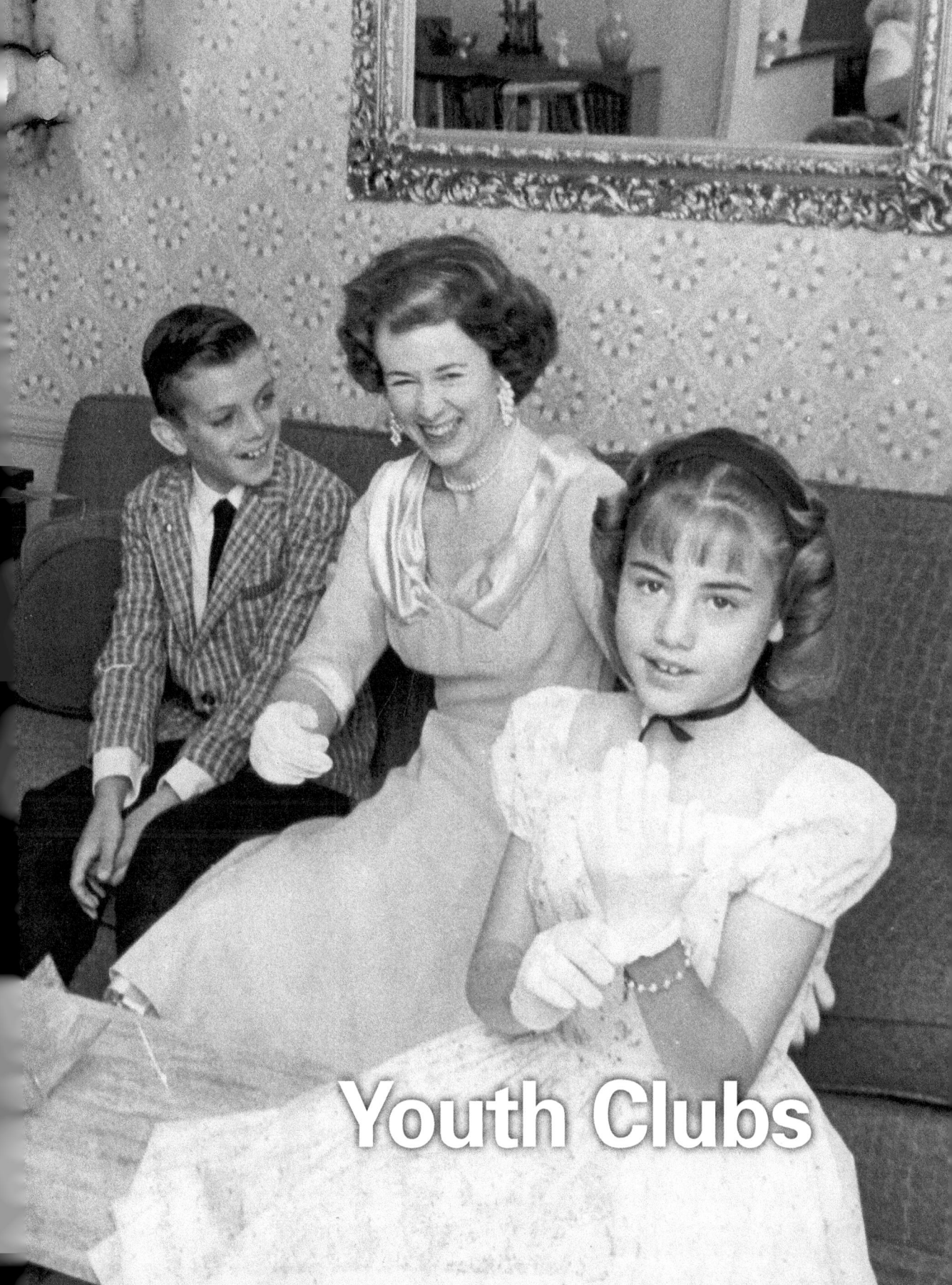

Youth Clubs

Opposite: "Canoga Park's Bethel 100 inducts honored queen of the International Order of Job's Daughters, Barbara Raych." Raych is center with her two attendants. December 20, 1960.

Overleaf. "The Cotillion Club of Van Nuys will culminate its season of social activities for young people with a family party at 7:30 p.m. Thursday in the Golden Valley Auditorium, 13506 Sherman Way, Van Nuys. Practicing dance steps are Kathleen Hearn, 11, and George Beck, 10, both of Panorama City. Looking on are Ricky Caprio, 11, North Hollywood; Mrs. Eleanor Hempel, club director, and Susan Fountas, 11, Panorama City. A father-daughter, mother-son waltz promenade will launch the evening's festivities." April 25, 1962. (Alan Hyde)

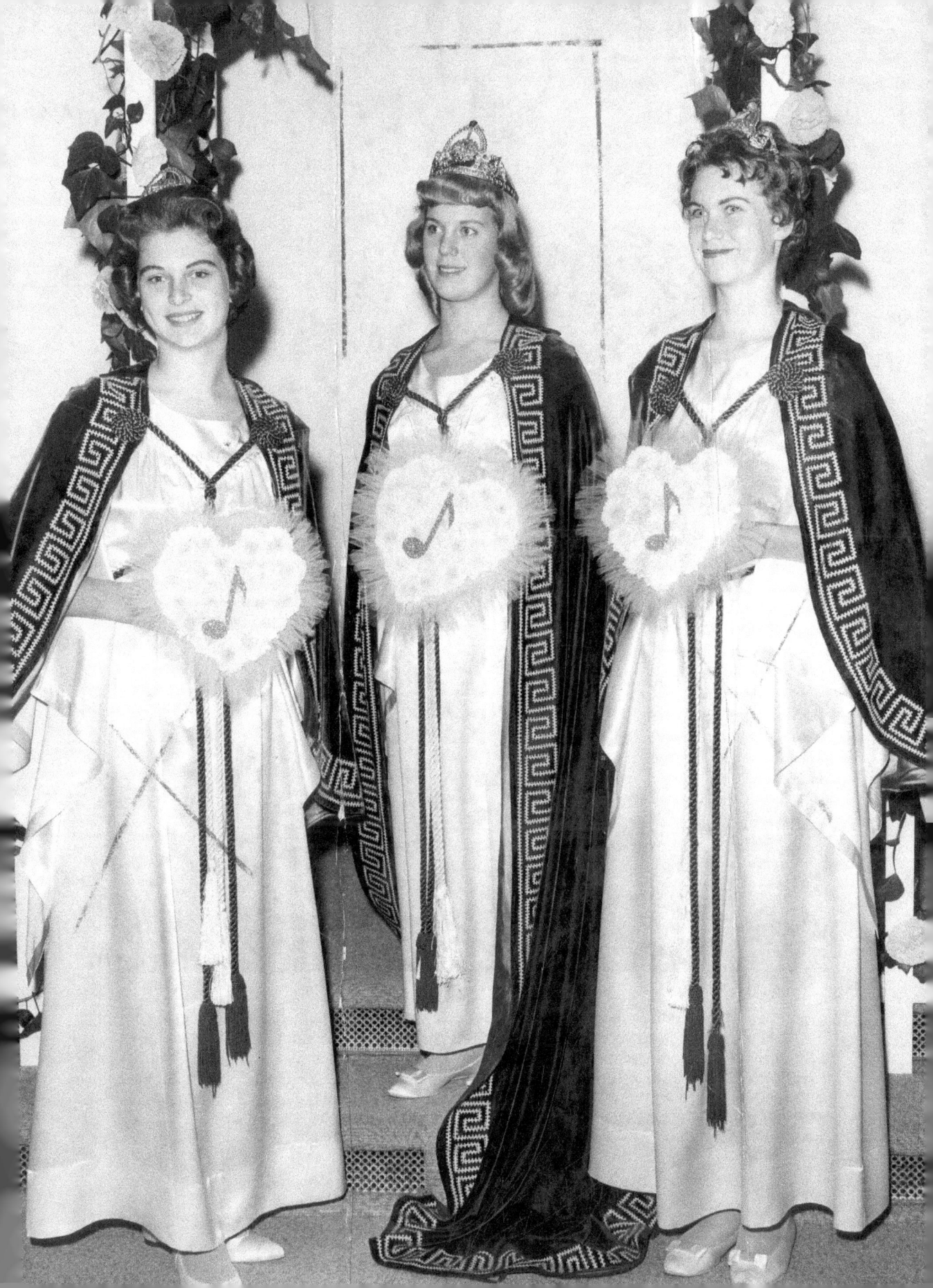

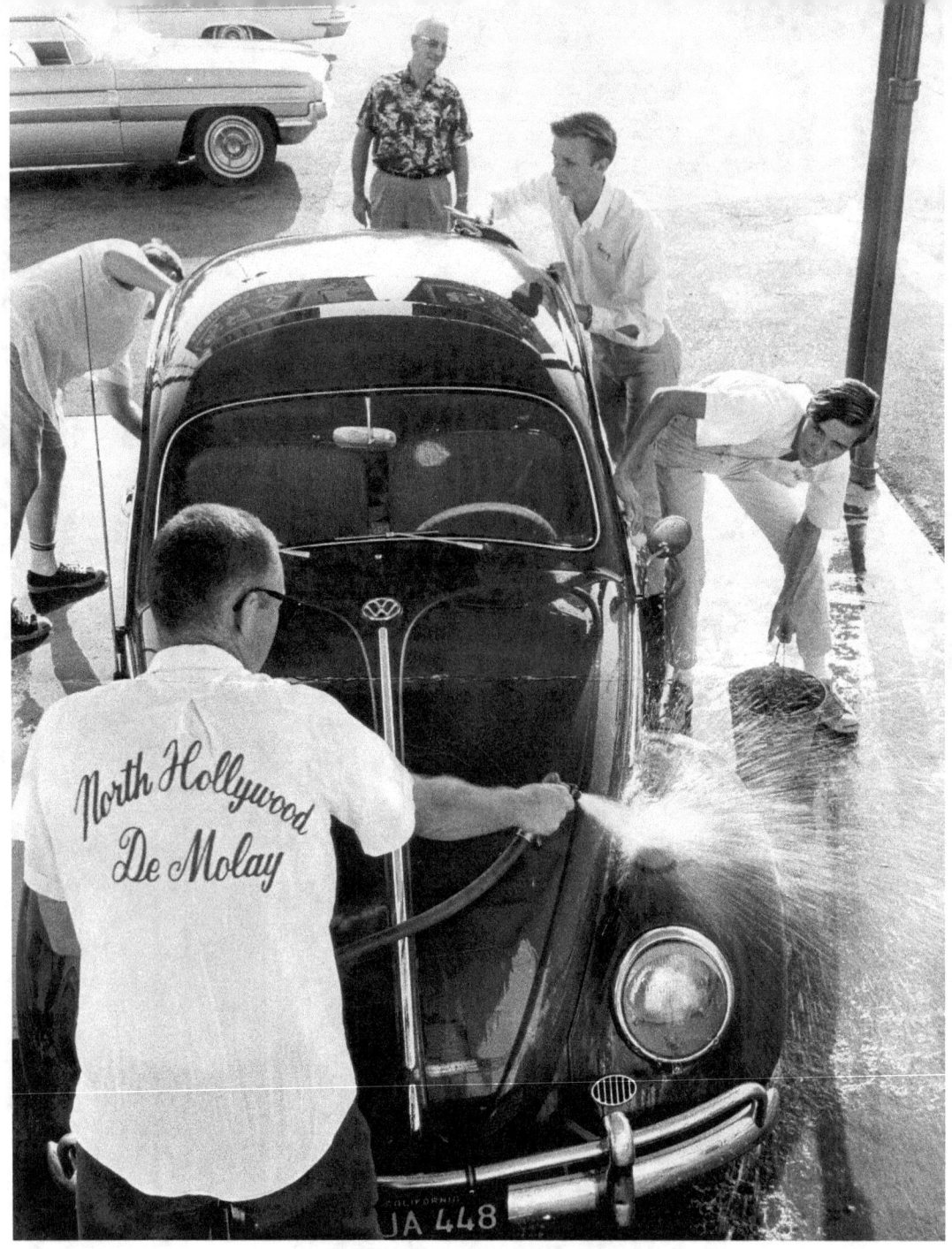

"Members of the North Hollywood Order of De Molay will grab up pails, hoses and rags for a real old fashion 'suds down' next Saturday at Ted Weiss' Chevron Station, 10960 Moorpark St., North Hollywood. Members of the club, who will assist at the car wash, are (back, from left) Albah Blake, advisor; Terry Rothenbach, 17; Buff Crossley Jr., 16; (front from left) Bill Firth, 17, Sr. Councilor, and Denny Nelson, 14. The car wash will be held between 9 a.m. and 4 p.m. Proceeds will aid the club's treasury." July 20, 1964. (George Brich)

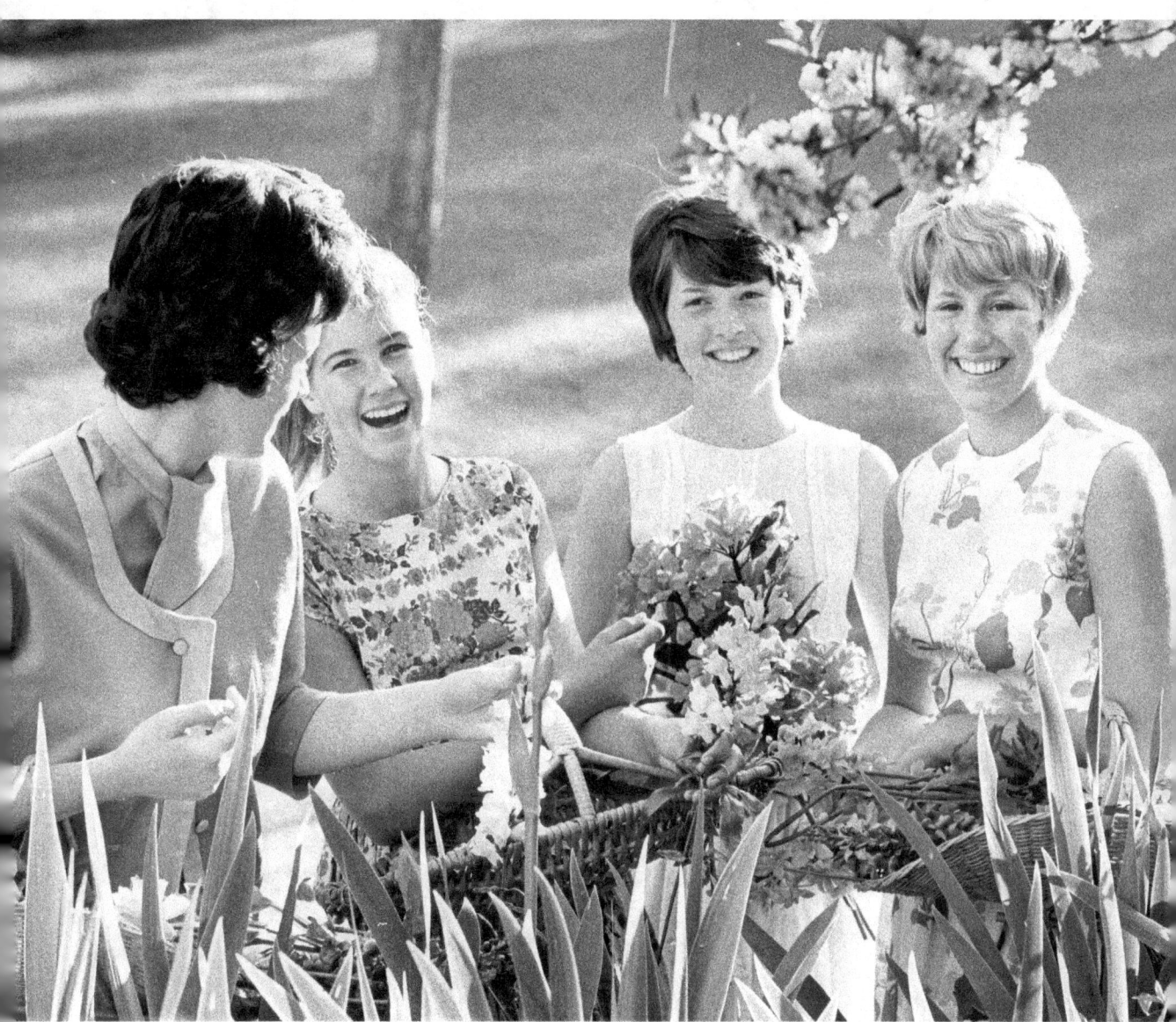

"Valley Debutantes of the Assistance League pick flowers for their May Basket Tea at
Sportsmen's Lodge, Studio City. From left, Karel Kavanaugh, 14, Studio City; Robin Munro,
13, and Kathy Dale, 15, Toluca Lake, and Cindy Rule, 15, Van Nuys." April 25, 1963.
(George Brich)

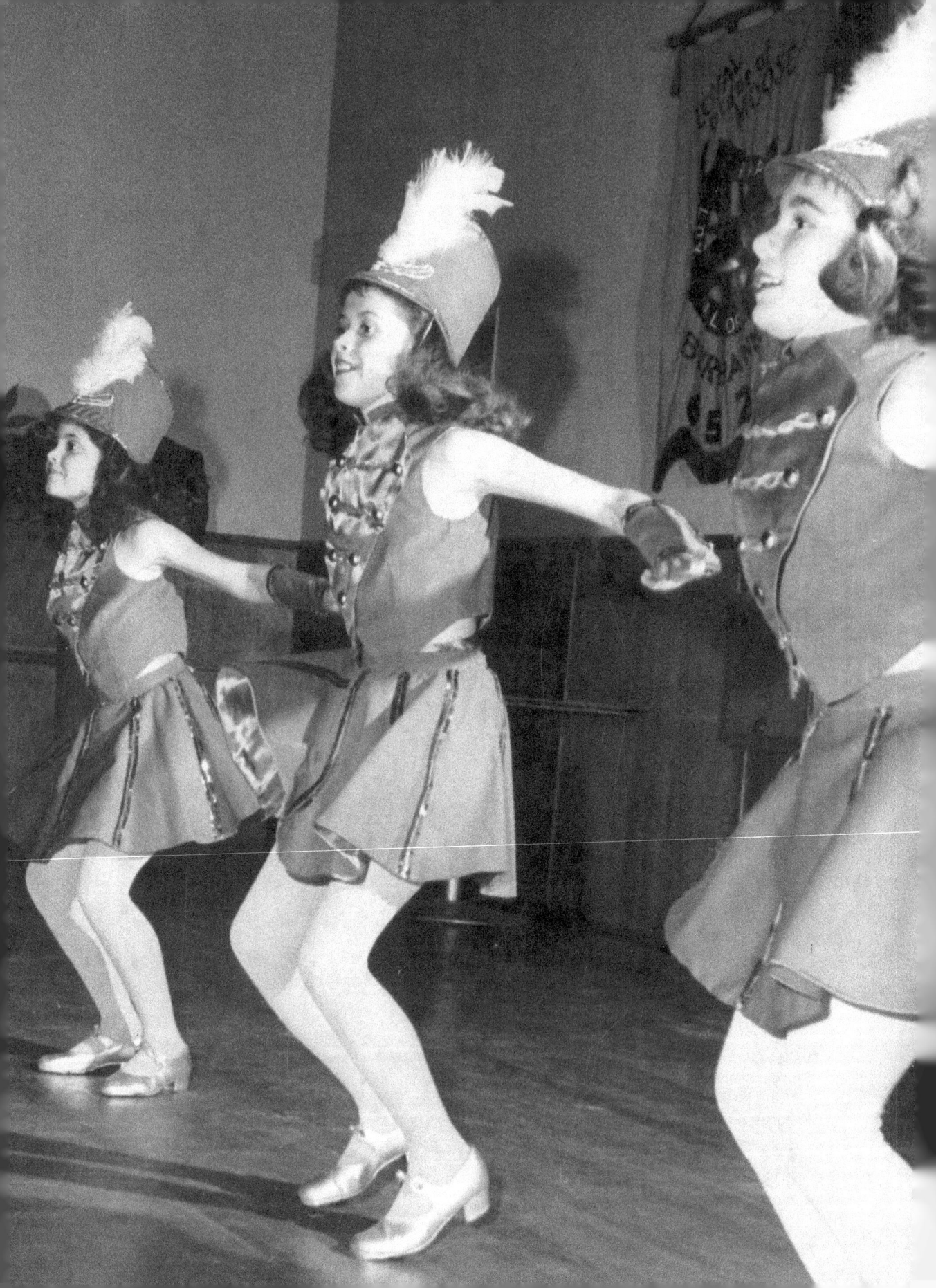

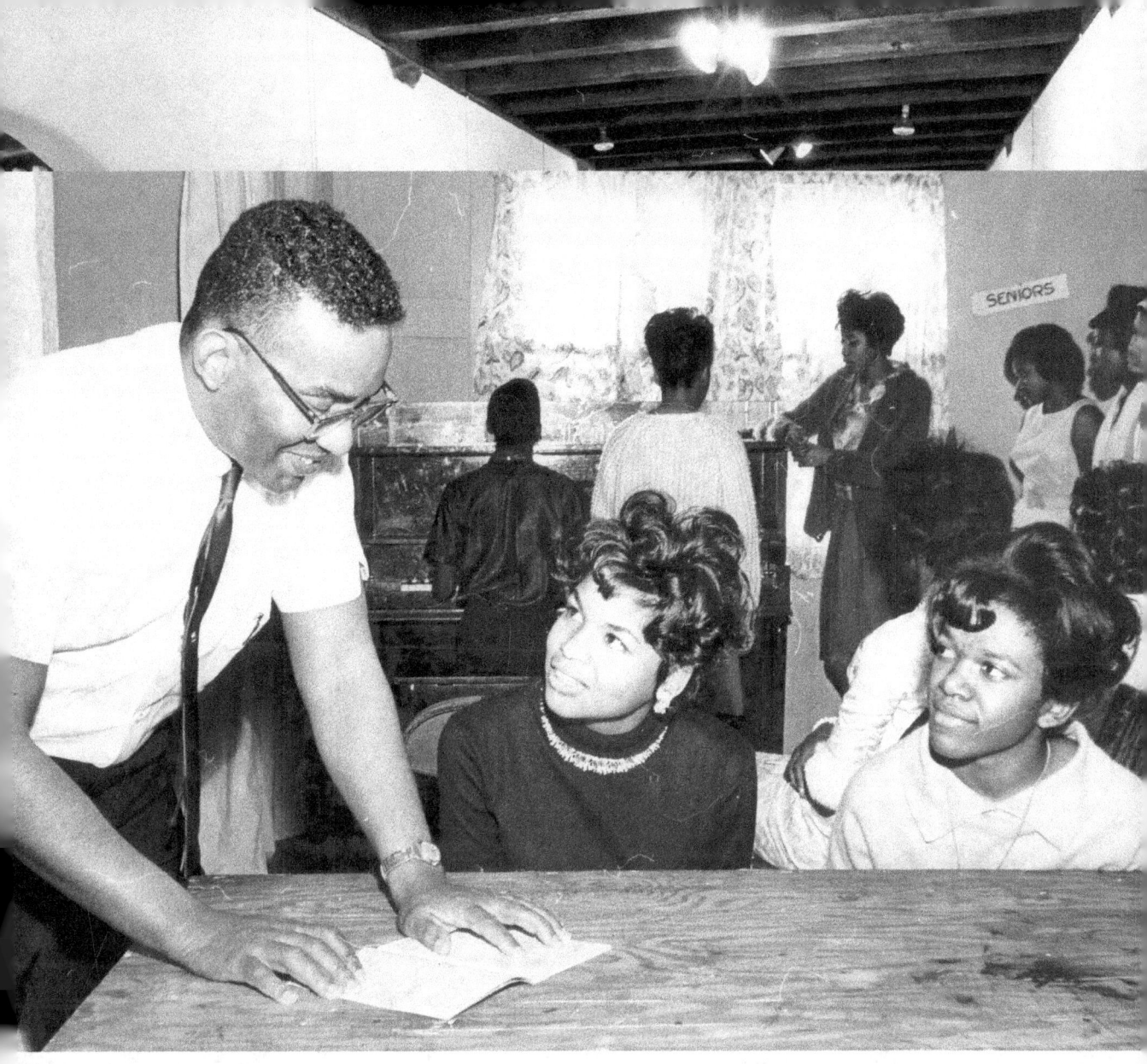

"Neighborhood Christian Services, a newly established social-religious service in Pacoima has helped Calvary Baptist Church expand, its youth program. Founded to provide social and religious guidance to community groups, the organization will work to combat antisocial elements in economically and educationally deprived groups, say its founders. In the left photo the Rev. Atha Baugh, director of NCS, holds a vocational counseling session with Karen Farris, 17, and Joyce Thomas, 16." February 15, 1964. (Gordon Dean)

Opposite: "Local finals in the annual 'Search for Talent' sponsored by the Exchange Clubs of District 10, San Fernando Valley, featured 18 acts of entertainment Friday at Moose Lodge, 1903 W. Burbank Blvd., Burbank. Winners of the junior division were Judy Nickerson, 9, 14753 Polk St., Sylmar, Donna Surgener, 9, 13868 Hubard St., San Fernando, and Regina Tremont, 9, 13868 Heron St. Sylmar, with a tap dance routine. April 28, 1961. (George Brich)

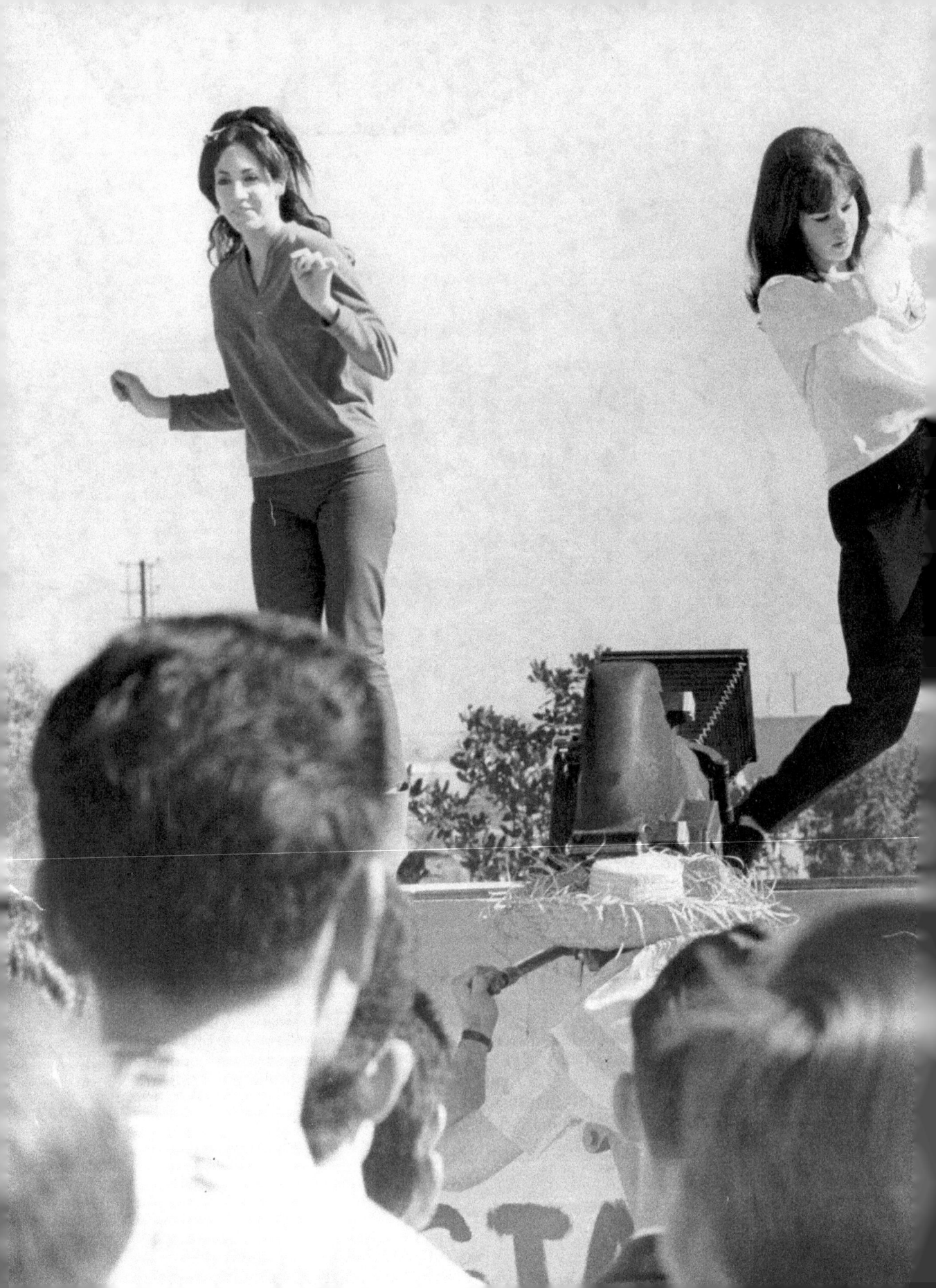

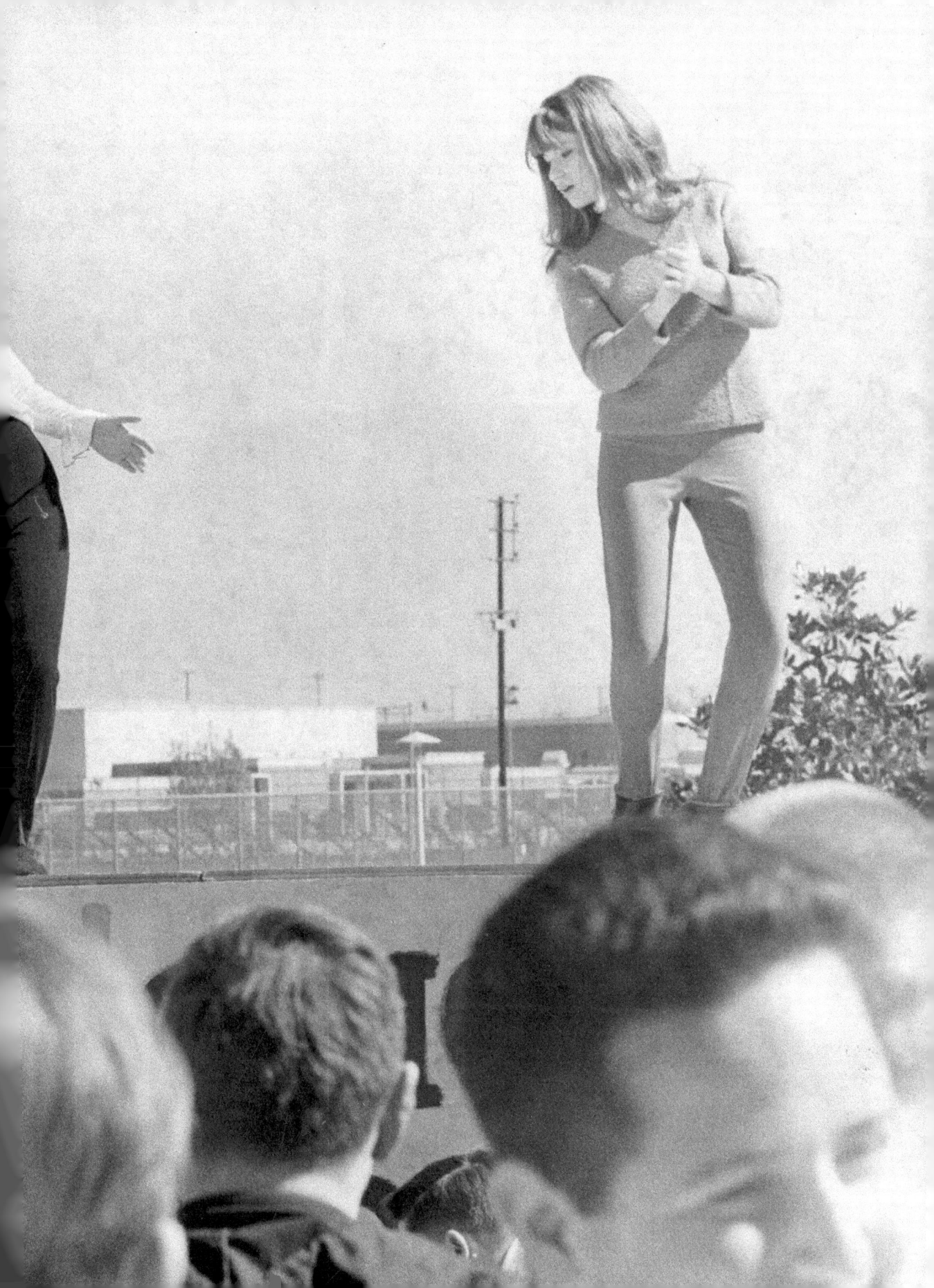

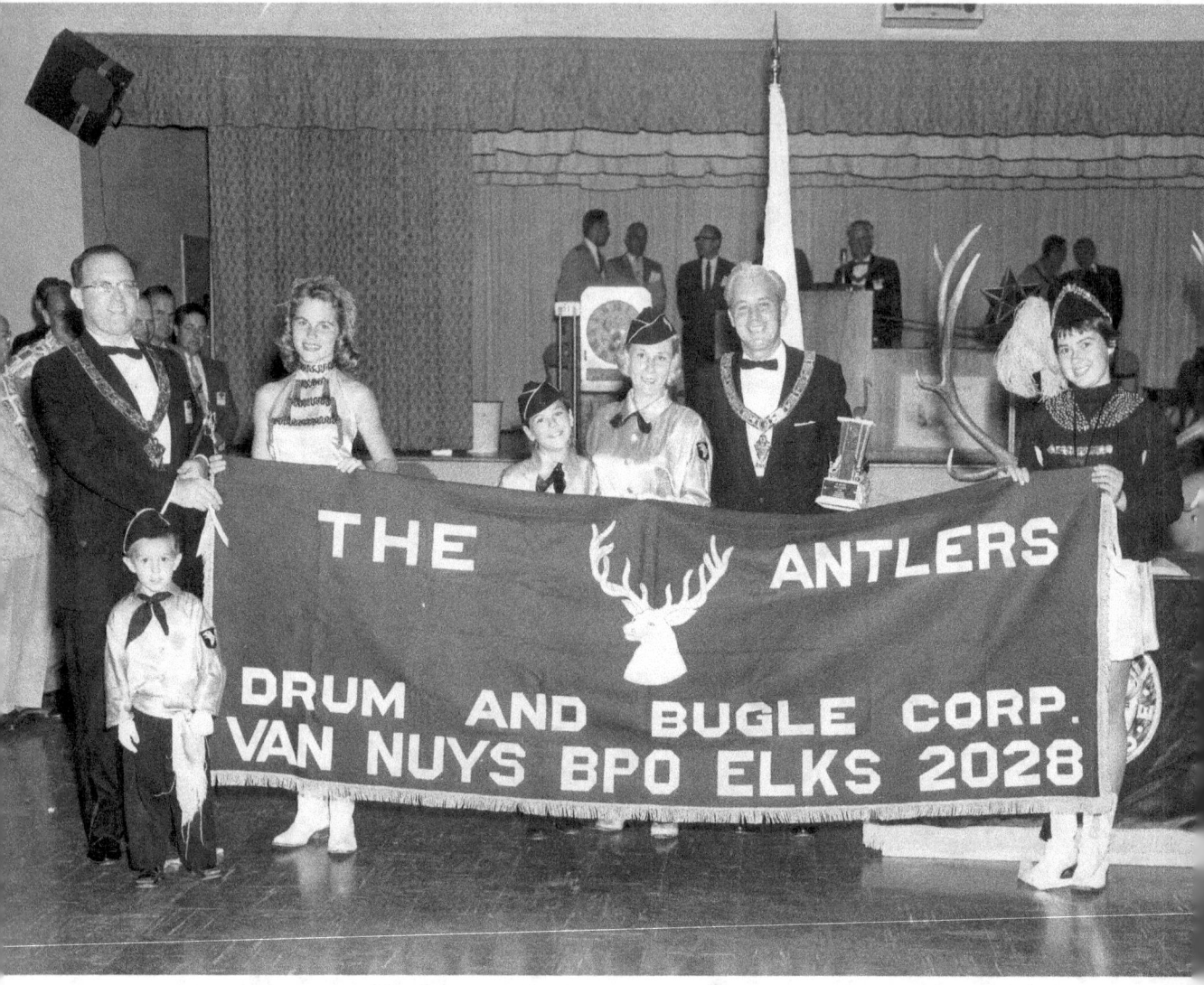

"Official banner presented to Antler Drum and Bugle Corps by Van Nuys BPO Elks 2028 is displayed by (from left), Terry Lee Popejoy, mascot; John Pulskamp; Carole Ann Polcar, solo baton twirler; Dianne Popejoy, lead drummer; Mrs. Mildred Popejoy, director; Glen Wyatt, exalted ruler, and Dianne Lazarus, drum majorette." Boys and girls between ages of 8 and 18 could join the Corps. July 21, 1958.

Overleaf: "In front of the Motion Picture Club's cameras, dancers (from left) Sue King, 18; Jackie Kornblatt, 18 and Carol Cherney, 18 did their stuff yesterday during Valley College's semi-annual Club Day. More than 30 groups, including the Art Club, Veterans, Sports Car Club and Home Economics Club set up booths and gave exhibitions." February 19, 1965. (George Brich)

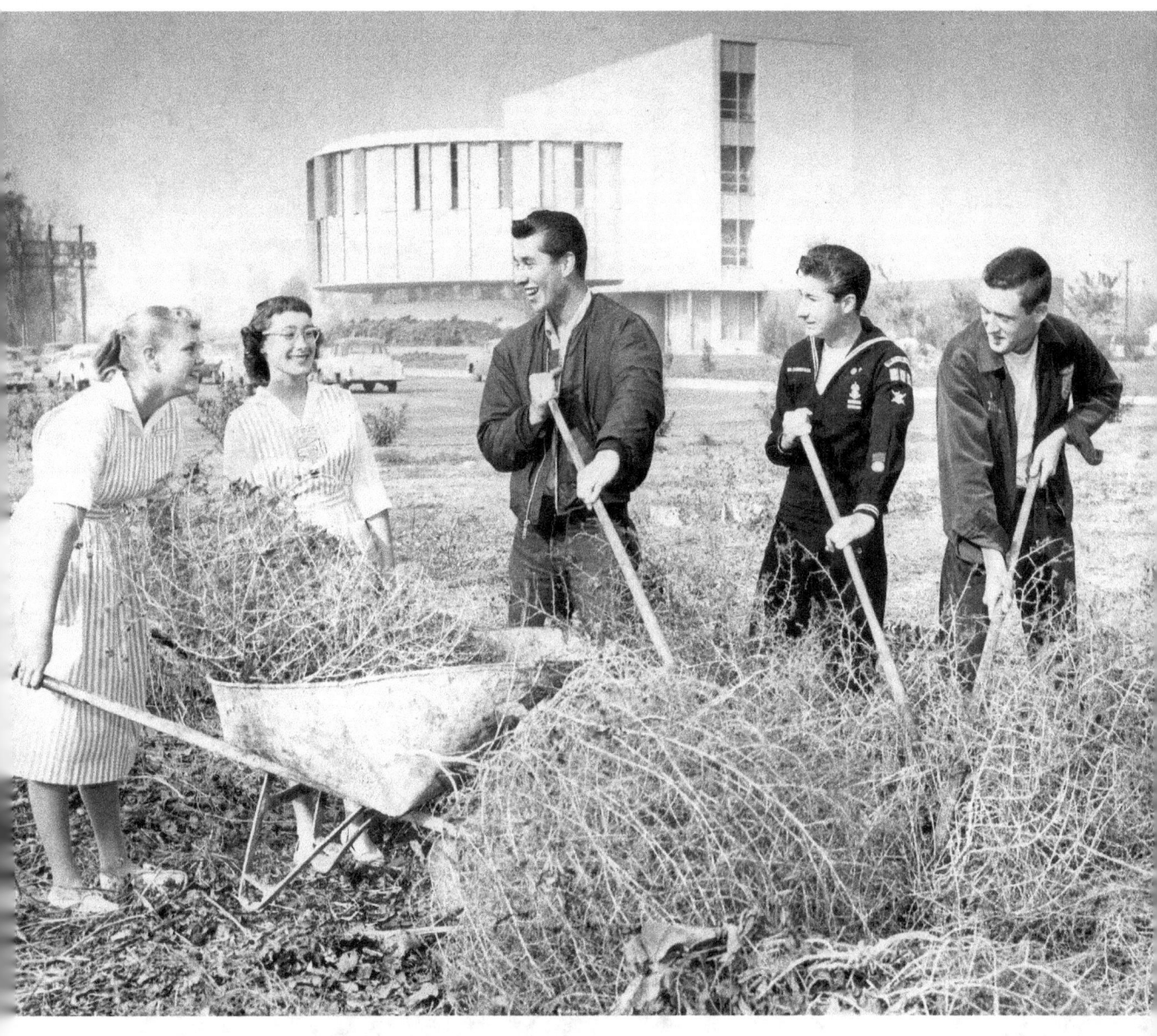

"Janet Kellenberger, 15, and Jackie Suess, 17, members of Candy Stripers (from left), aid Sea Scouts Bob Wheeler, 17; Steve Bidwell, 16, and Mike Strange, 15, in volunteer cleanup program of Valley Presbyterian Hospital. Sea Scouts, auxiliary of Explorer Scouts of America, and other organizations volunteer work hours for Van Nuys medical center." January 5, 1959.

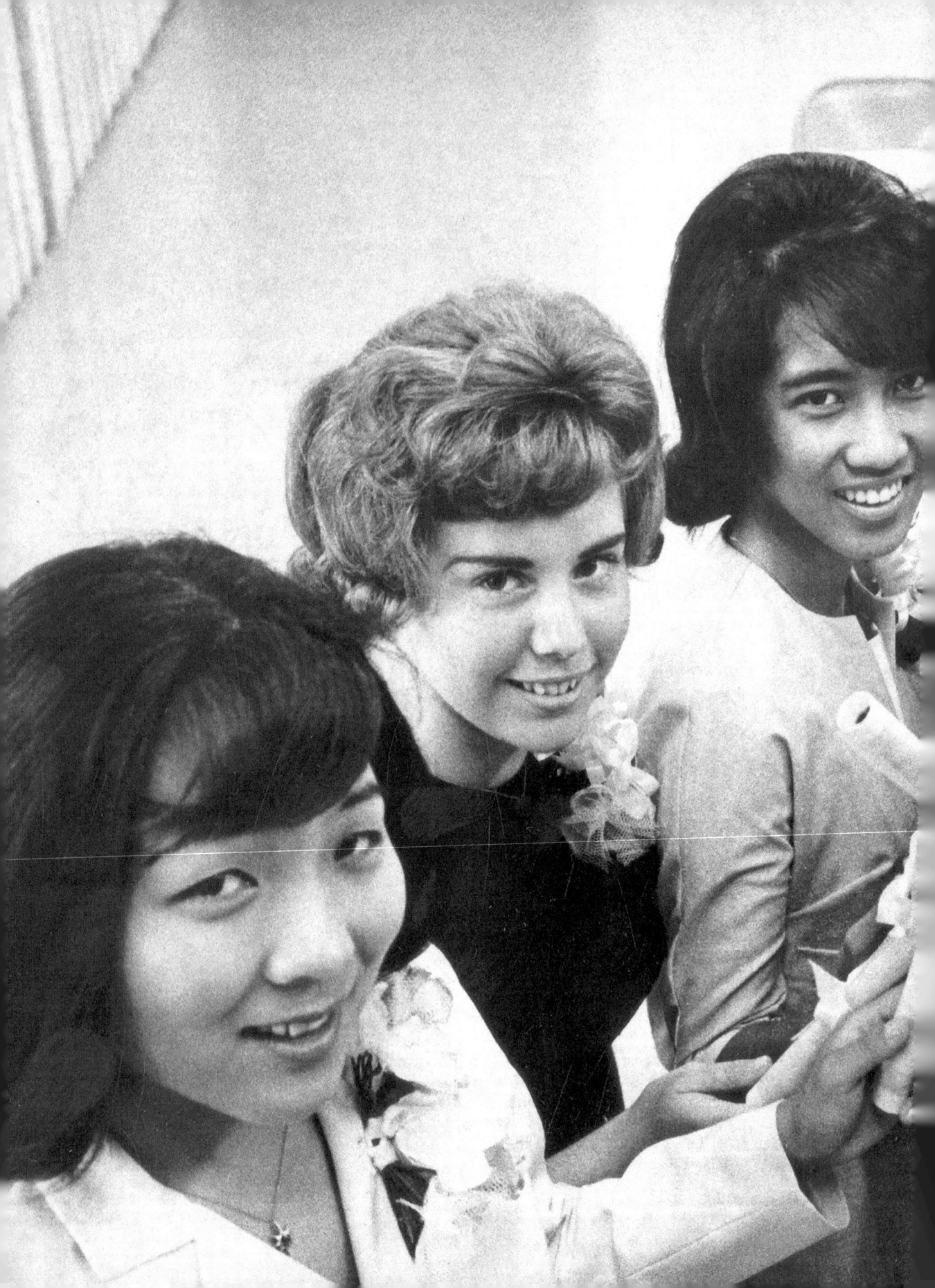

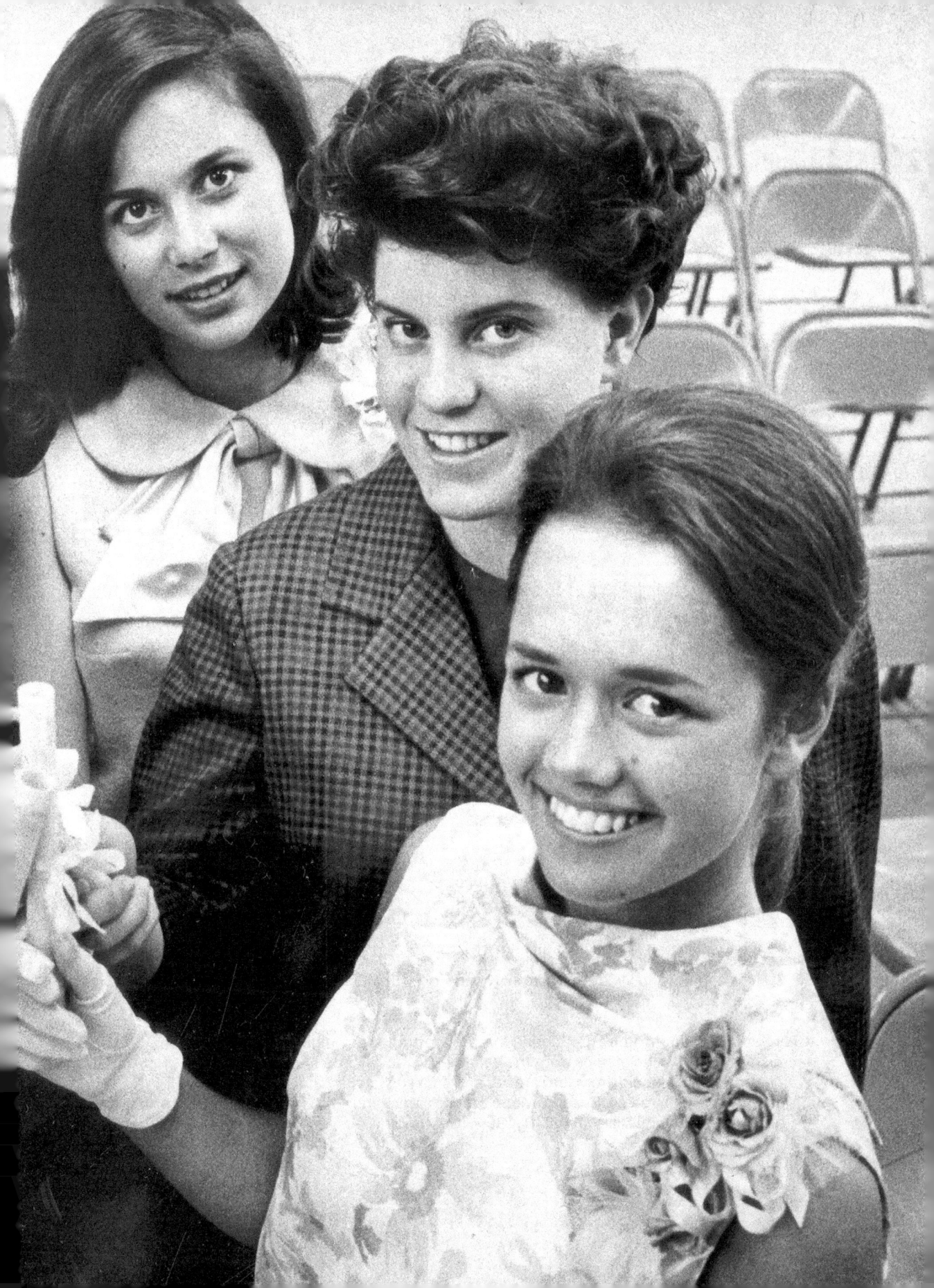

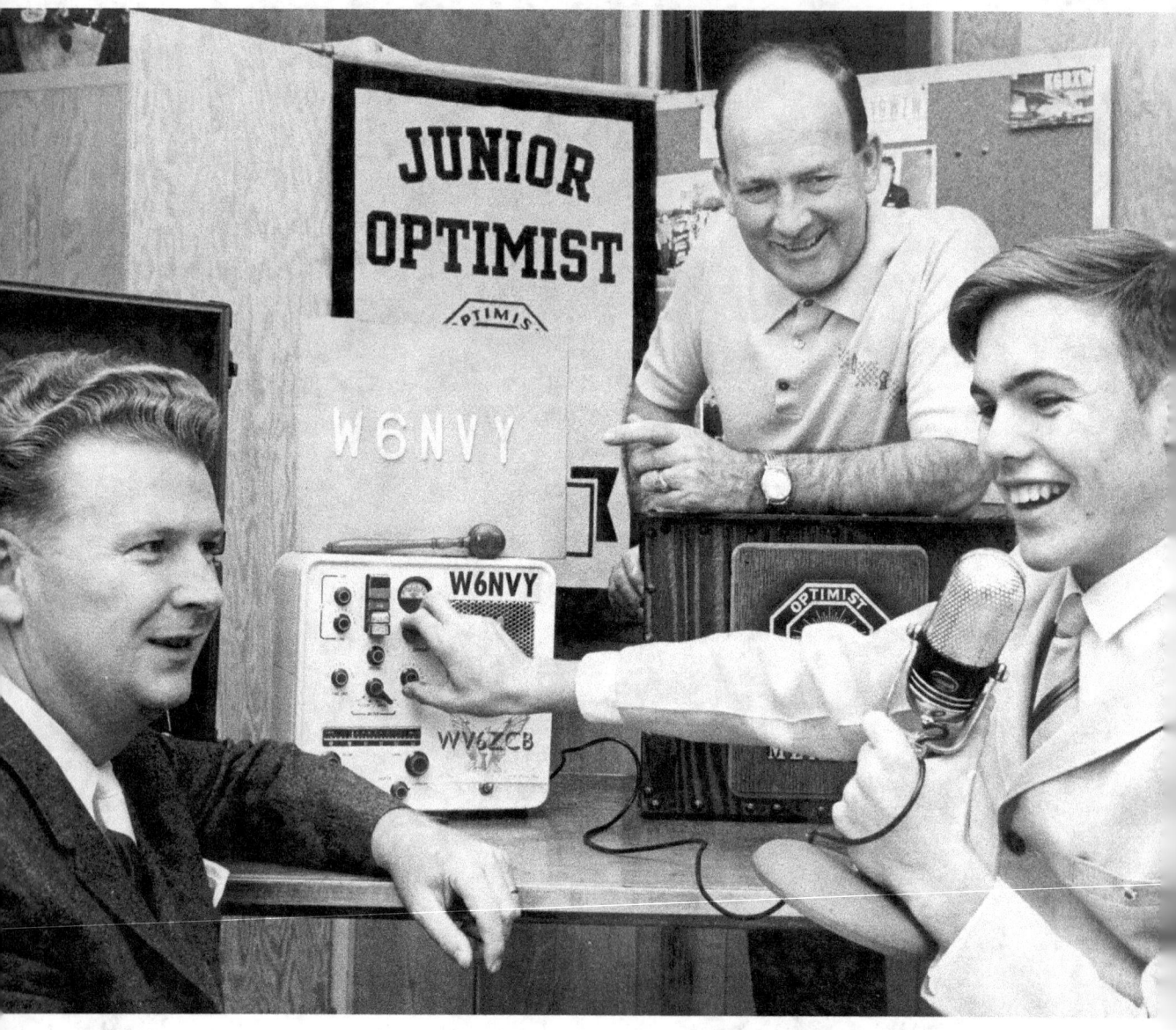

"North Hollywood Junior Optimist radio hams go on air. Cliff Wallace studies radio theory with Herb Roberts and Woody Franks, of North Hollywood Optimists." December 29, 1962. (Jeff Goldwater)

Overleaf. "Six young women graduating this month from Valley high schools are the recipients of $200 scholarships from the Valley University Women. [AAUW] Scholarship winners and their schools (from left) are Jeanne Tanaka, San Fernando; Ellen K. Burg, Birmingham; Dolly Eugenio, Reseda; Muriel Dance, Cleveland; Pam Rumbold, Sylmar, and Carole Bush, Woodland Hills." June 20, 1964. (George Brich)

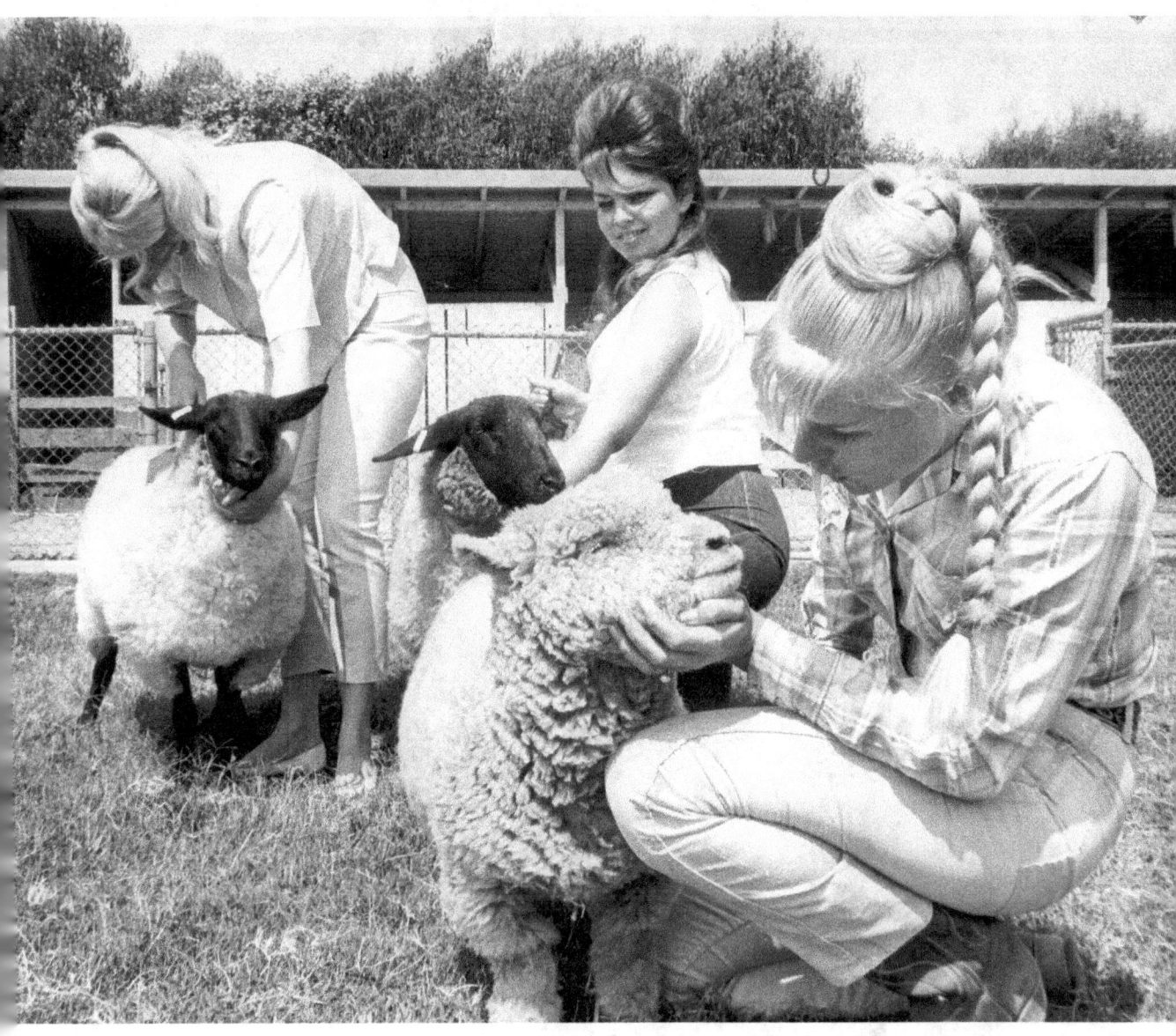

"Three Valley beauties hold the pets they will auction off tonight at the Future Farmers of America and the San Fernando Valley 4-H Club event at Devonshire Downs in Northridge. Holding pets above are Pamela Finch, Toni Martinez and Diane Evans (from left), all from Van Nuys. The proceeds will be given to the youth to help meet their costs of raising their livestock." August 2, 1963. (Gordon Dean)

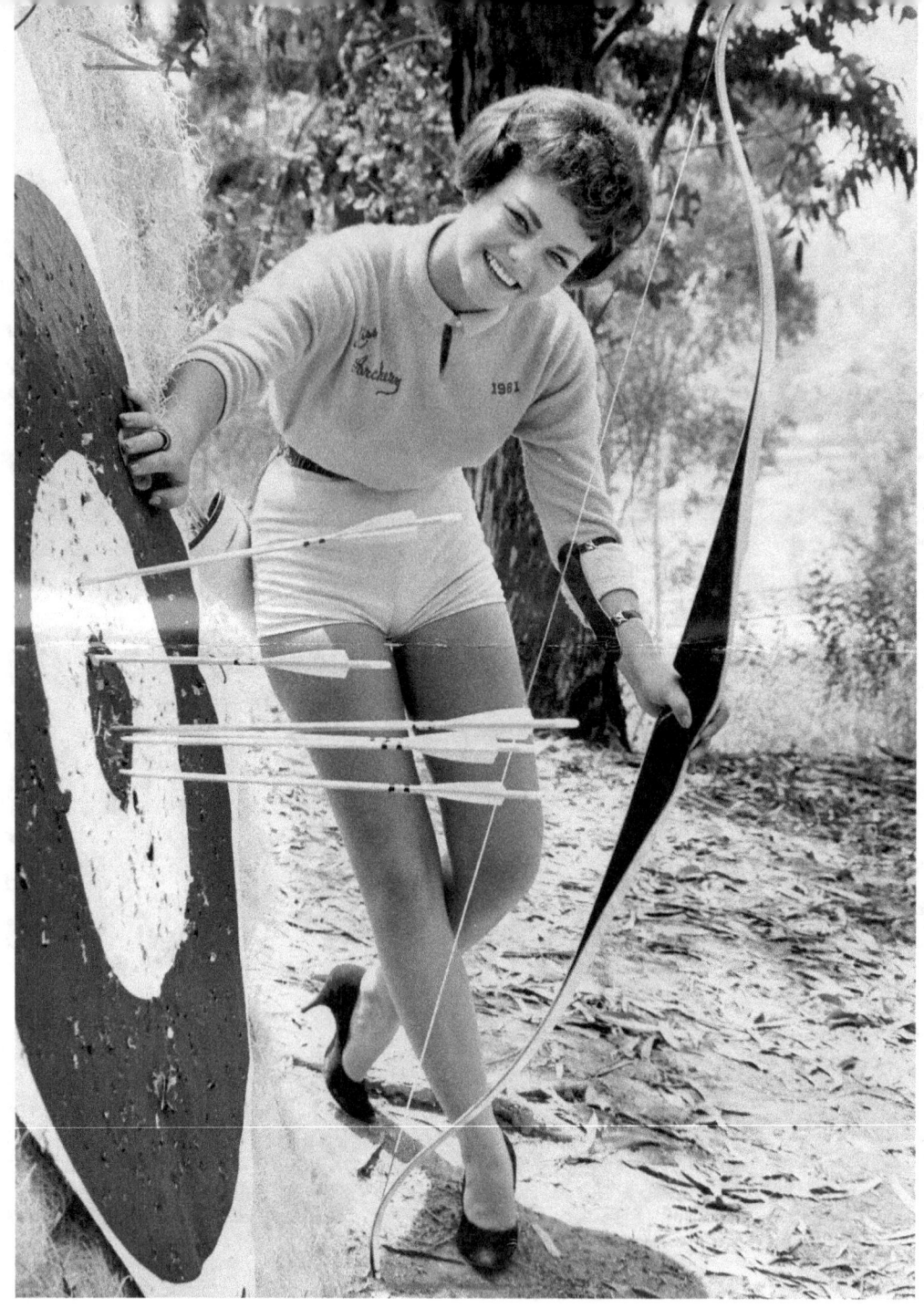

"Pretty Cathy Duncan, 17-year-old Burbank archer was caught practicing for the June 24th San Fernando Archery Club's field shoot." June 13, 1962. (George Brich)

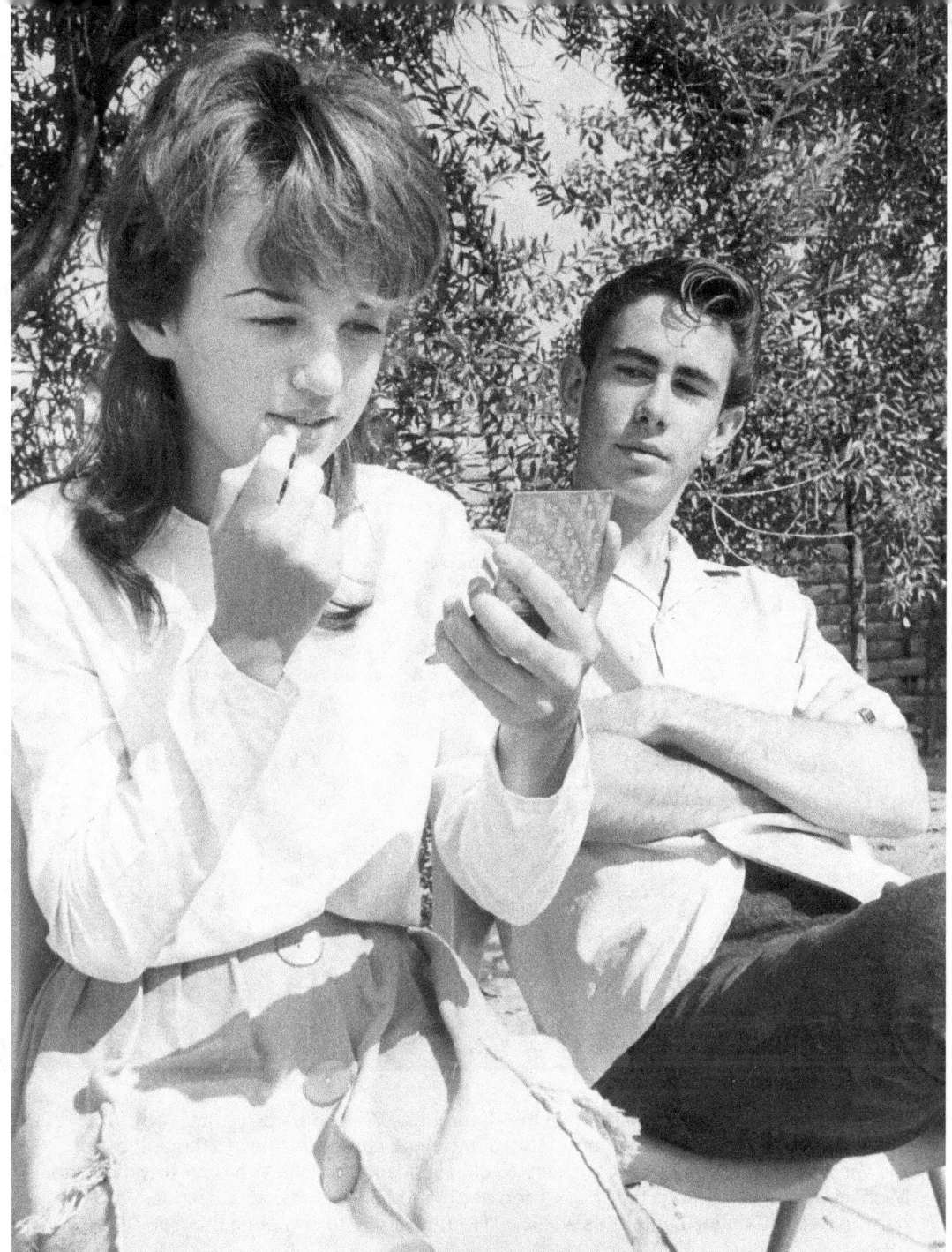

"Do's and don'ts of social etiquette are demonstrated by members of the Discuss-and-Do Club of the San Fernando Valley Youth Foundation, Van Nuys. Members of the co-educational group are taught social graces which include all facets of dating, grooming, restaurant manners, job etiquette and other items of interest to the club members. Rick Gill, 18, Encino, looks on disapprovingly as Sue Gantinbein, 14, Reseda, puts on lipstick in public." August 31, 1962. (Alan Hyde)

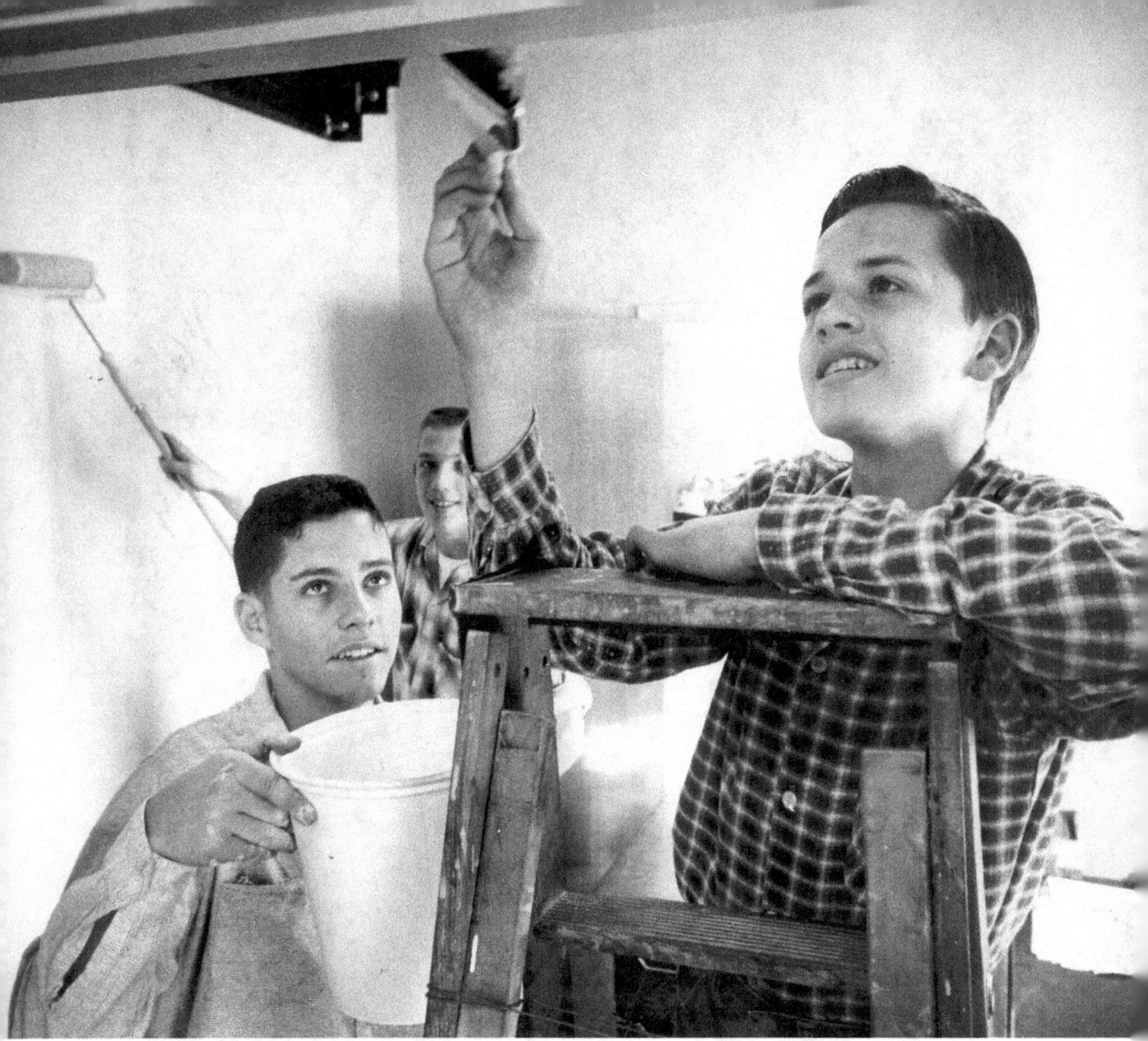

"Lobby, offices and conference room of the Community Chest Service Center, 14419 Burbank Blvd., Van Nuys, have a new look today, thanks to the efforts of 20 members of the Van Nuys High School Key Club, service club sponsored by the Van Nuys Kiwanis Club. Michael Odenheimer (left), 16; Chuck Thomas, 16, and Bill Combs, 15, on ladder who participated in painting center this week, will return April 7 to complete their job." April 2, 1962. (George Brich)

Opposite: "Three youngsters of Les Petite Femmes, a Y-Teen Club, from Sun Valley Junior High School, give a demonstration of their baking techniques prior to Friday's Bake Sale from 4 to 9 p.m. in the patio of the East Valley YWCA, 5703 Laurel Canyon Blvd., North Hollywood. The three young ladies are Diana Tabanera, 12, Adele Tones, 13, and Charlene Young, 13, all of North Hollywood. Proceeds from the sale will be used by East Valley YWCA to establish other Y-Teen Clubs." November 28, 1964. (Steve Young)

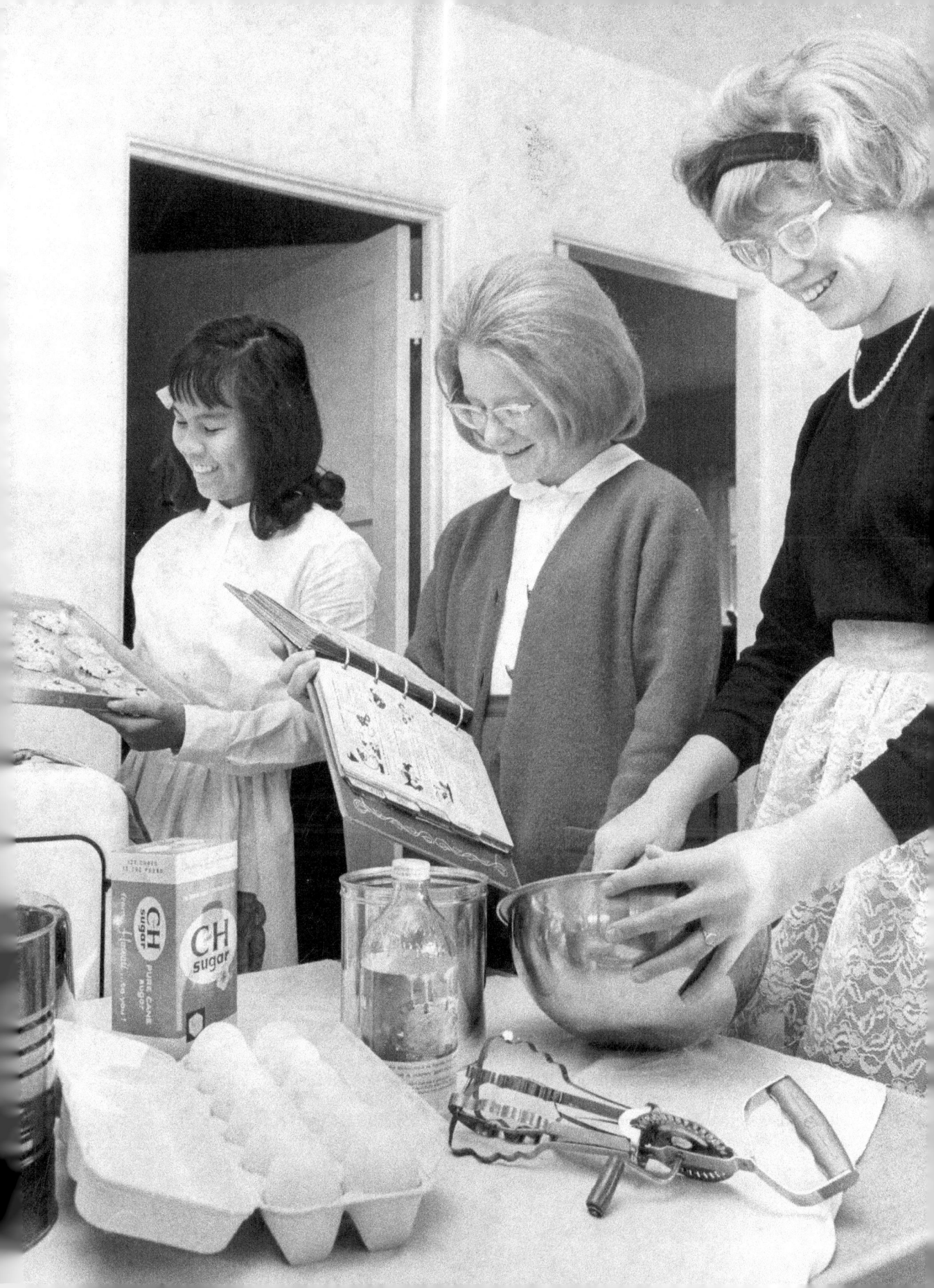

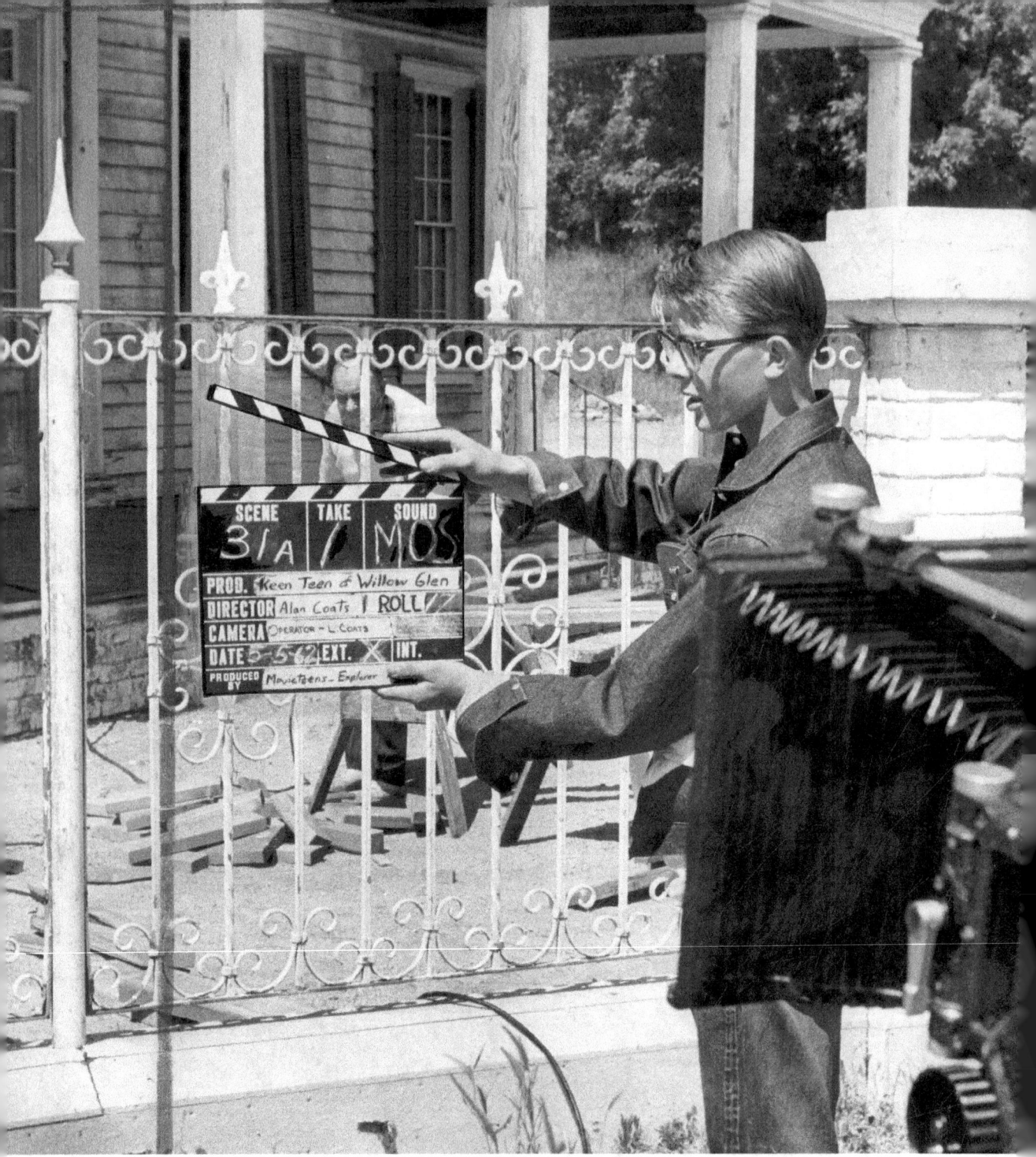

"Burbank Explorer Post 25 scouts shoot black-and-white 'epic' at Disney Studios. The teens, all sons of Disney Studio employees, are known as the Movieteens Richard Burau, 15, holds slate that lists scene and take numbers." July 28, 1962. (Alan Hyde)

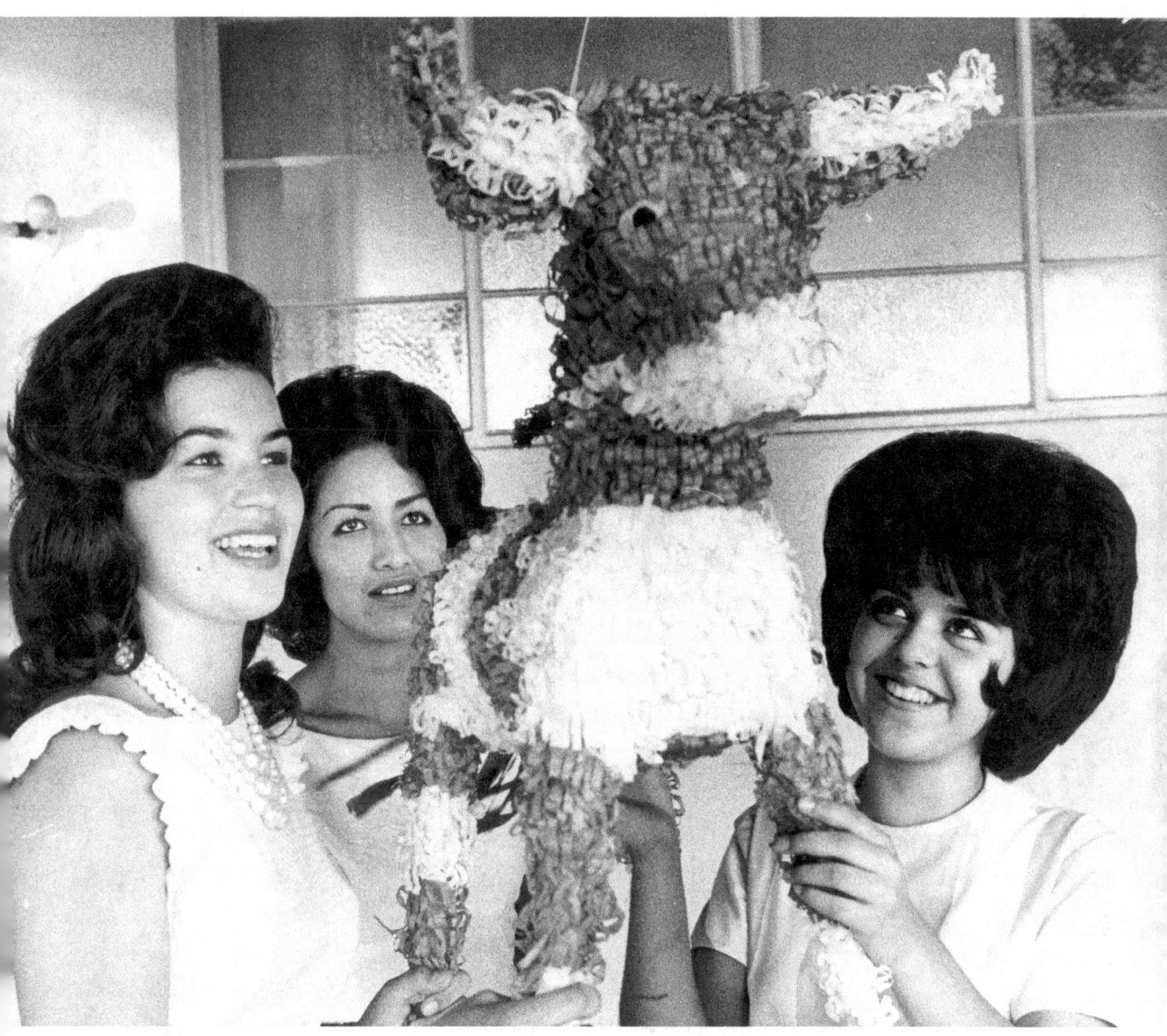

"Guadalupe Catholic Youth Organization members (from left) Alice Fonseca, 17; Connie Gallhos, 20, and Ruby Martinez, 15, are shown checking a pinata for their group's 10th annual fiesta at the CYO center at 21600 Hart St., Canoga Park. Booths and games for both adults and children are planned." July 25, 1963. (George Brich)

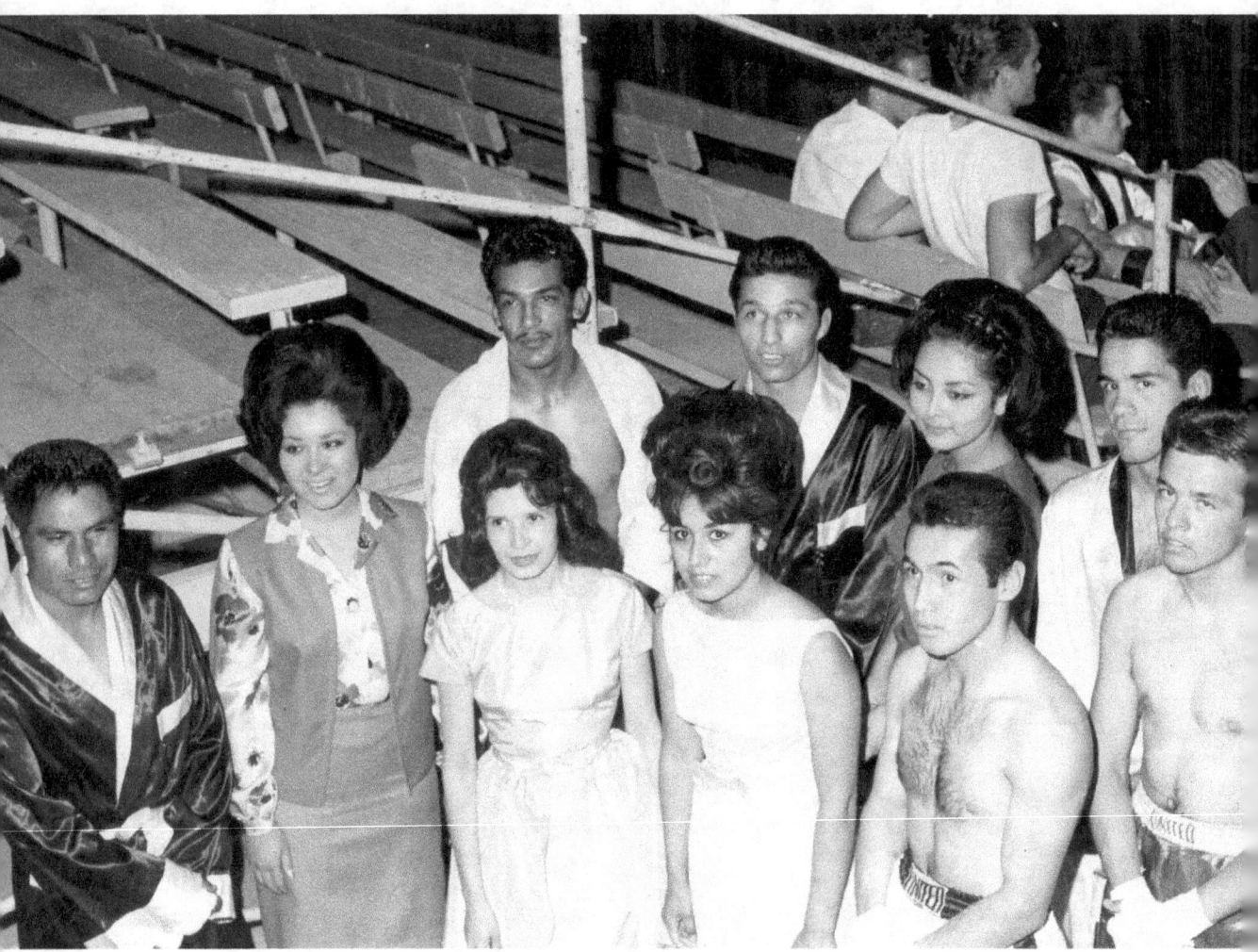

"Members of the Valley Latin Knights will sponsor the Valley Garden amateur boxing show Wednesday night in commemoration of the 102nd anniversary of Mexican freedom. One of these seven Latin beauties will be crowned queen at the fiesta at Van Nuys Carpenter's Hall Sunday. From left to right in the back row are: Manuel Dias and Anna Ortega (Burbank), Johnny Padilla and Diana Rey (San Fernando), and Butch Contrearas. Pictured in the front row are Hernandi Hernandes (North Hollywood), Isabel Abrera (Van Nuys), Bernie Magdallenes and L. Marques." April 28, 1964.

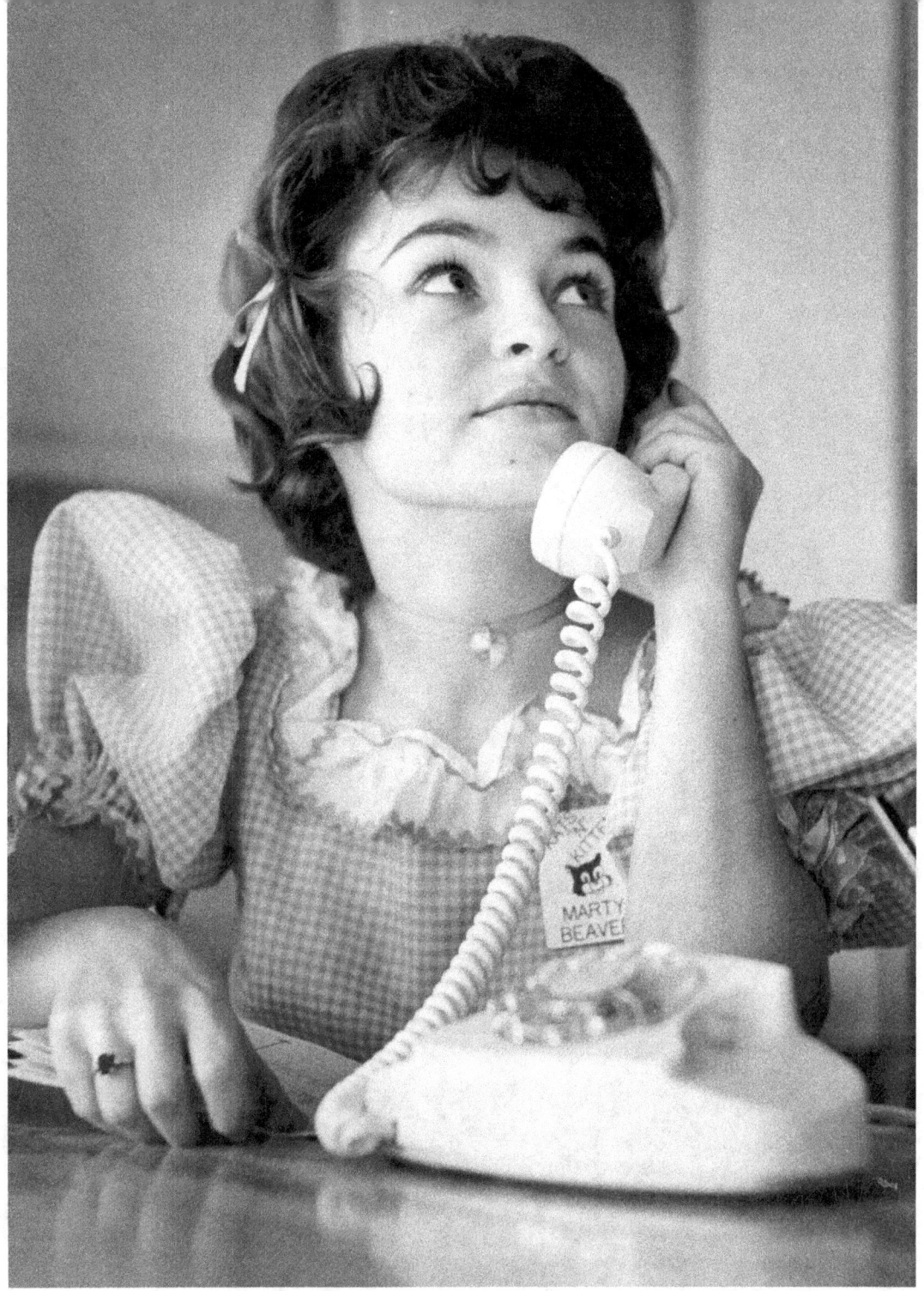

"Marty Beaver, 15, Northridge, answers square dance telephone requests." She is a Cleveland High School sophomore and president of the Teenage Square Dance Association, which represents 18 teenage dance clubs in the Los Angeles area. December 30, 1961. (George Brich)

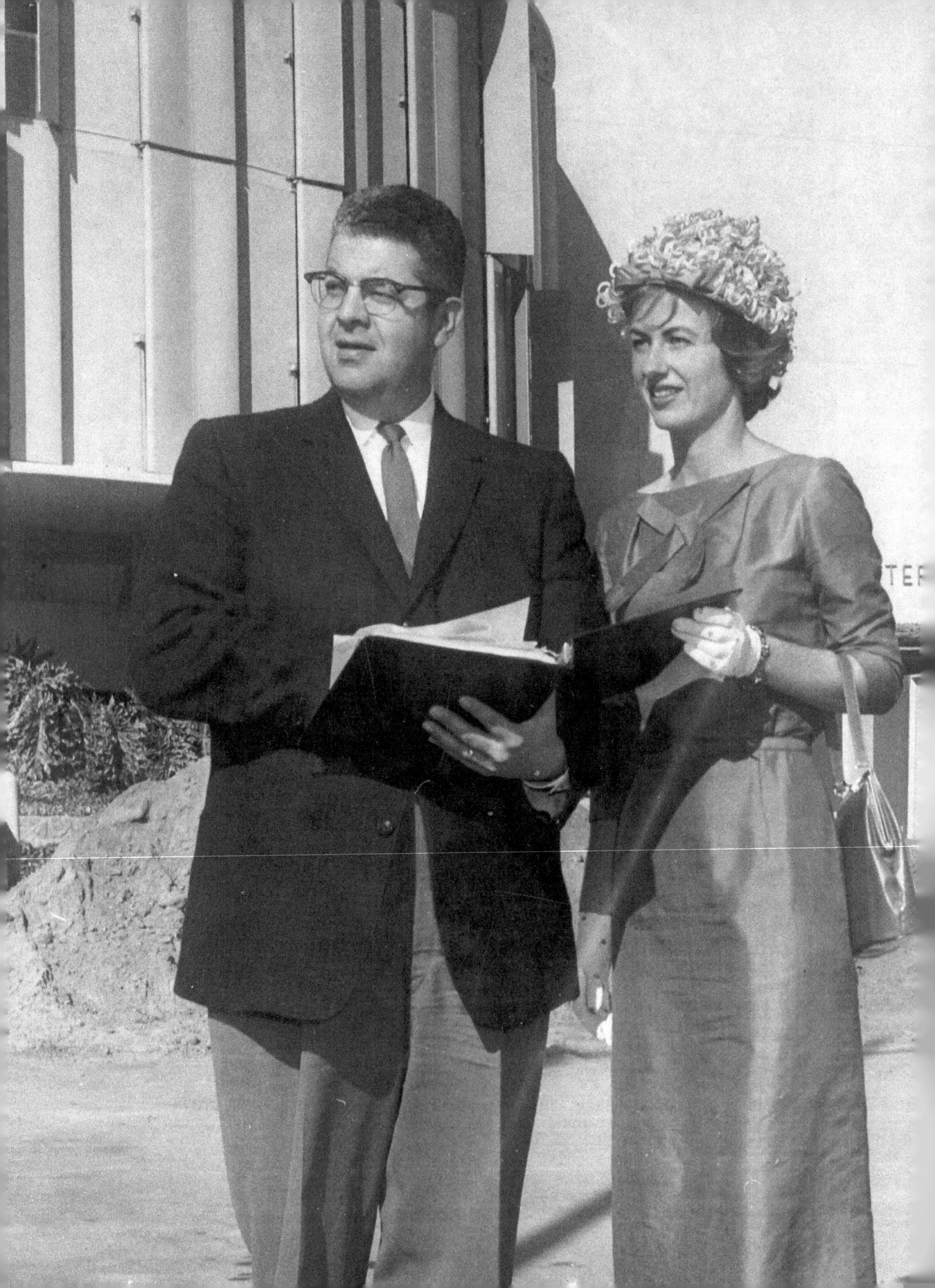

Fundraising

Overleaf: "Valley Presbyterian Hospital administrator Henry X. Jackson explains to Mrs. C. Richard Burdge how funds from Carrousels' benefit will further construction project. Looking over progress of the 'phase two' program are Mrs. Harry McCague (background left) and Mrs. Robert V. Miller Jr. who is heading the group's Spring Prelude." February 2, 1961. (Gordon Dean)

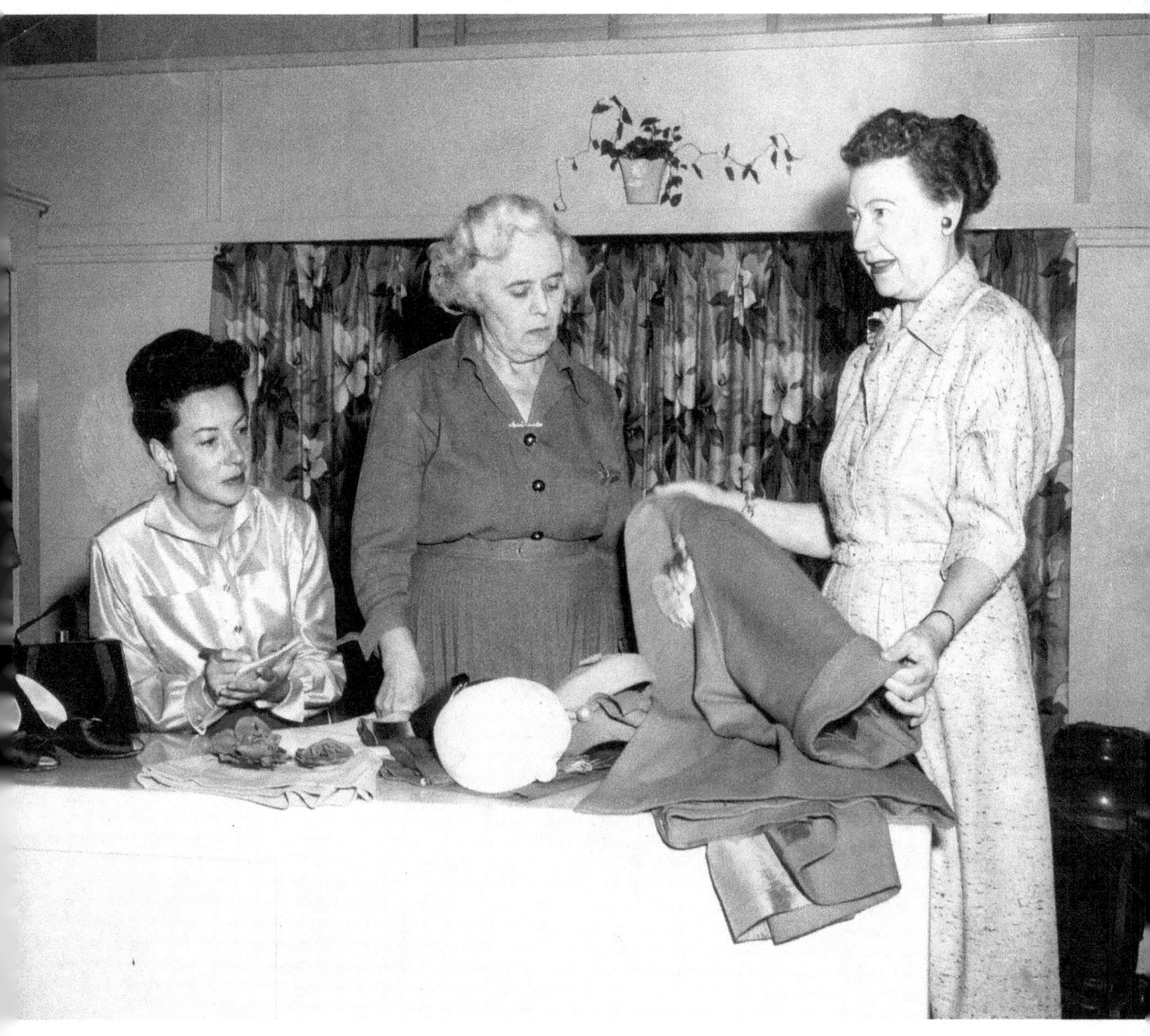

"North Hollywood Zonta Club members Mrs. Lucille Raport, Dr. Blanche Beakley and Mrs. Mae Miller (from left) list items for rummage sale Wednesday. Mrs. Raport heads sale committee, and Dr. Beakley is club president." April 24, 1954.

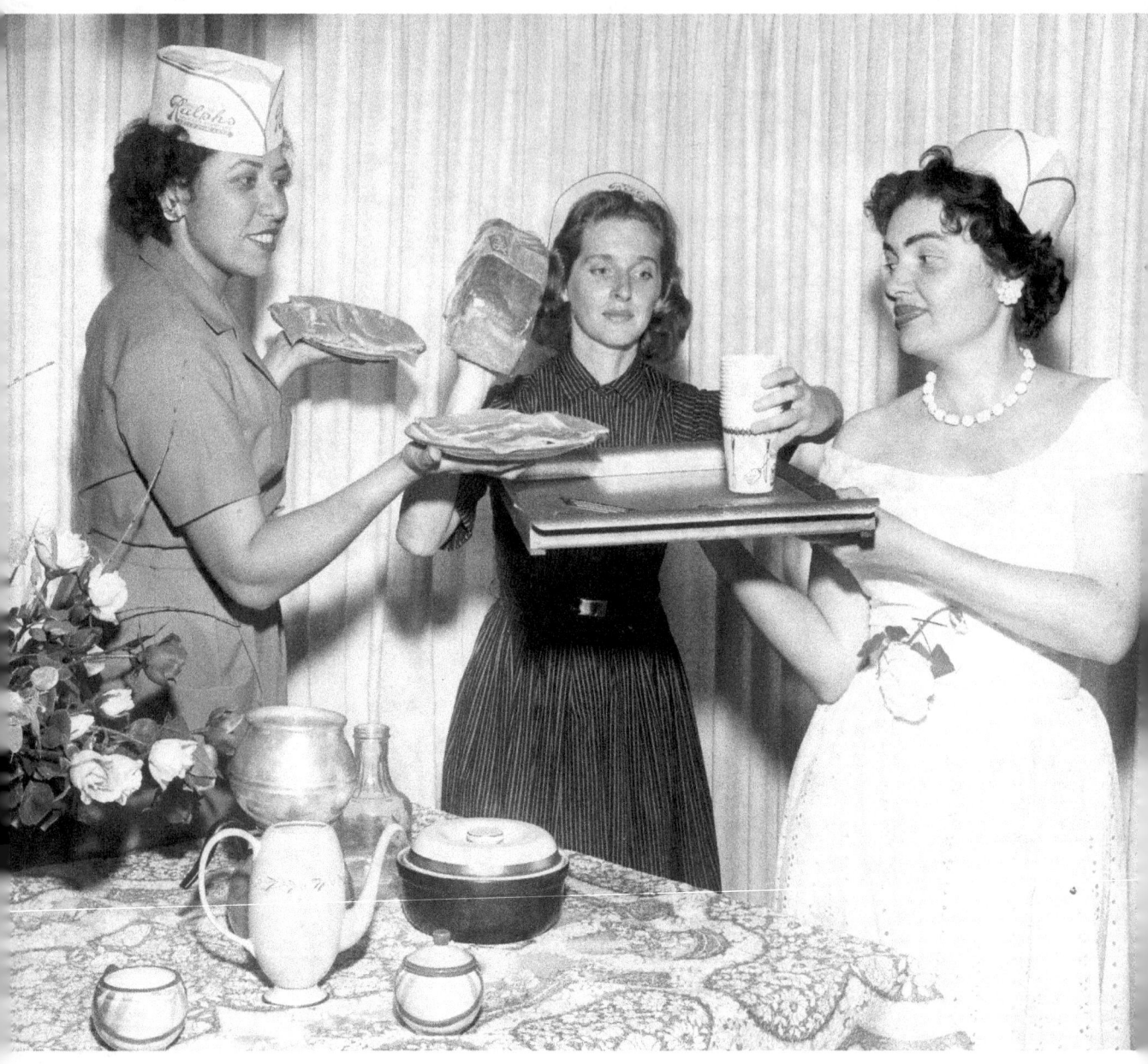

"A gourmet breakfast sponsored by Valley Hills B'nai B'rith Women, will be held from 9 a.m. to 1 p.m. Sunday at Ralphs Granada Hills, 17020 Chatsworth. The menu will include flapjacks, scrambled eggs, lox and bagel with cream cheese, donuts and coffee." September 8, 1960. (Gordon Dean)

112

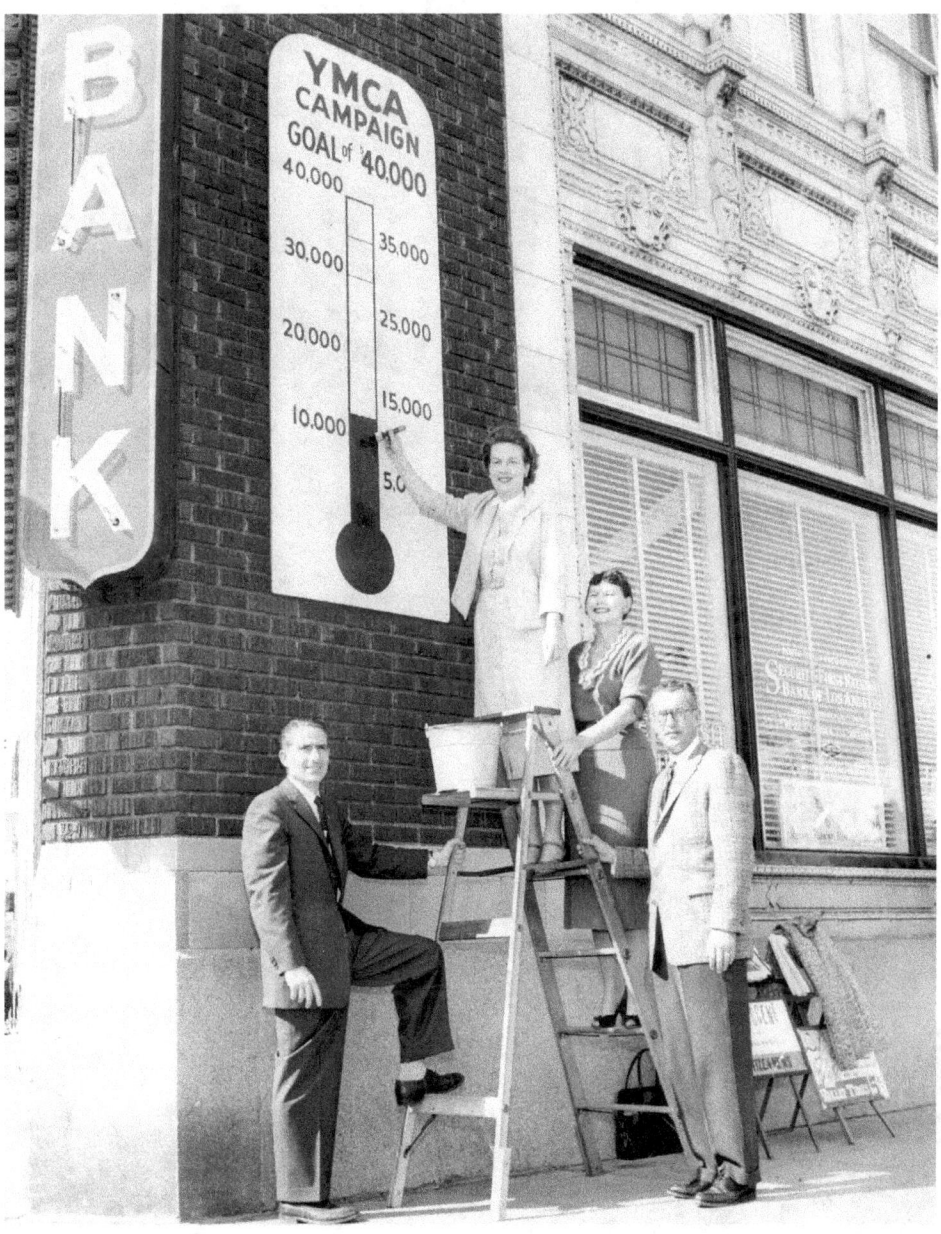

"Workers add latest totals to chart depicting North Hollywood Area YMCA's fund drive goal of $40,000. From left are Herbert Penfield Jr., campaign chairman; Mrs. Donald Cassels, rummage sale chairman; Mrs. Jack Hollebecke, president of Opti-Mrs. Club, and Lemoine Blanchard, Initial Gifts chairman." Bank building is located at 5303 Lankershim Blvd. February 10, 1958.

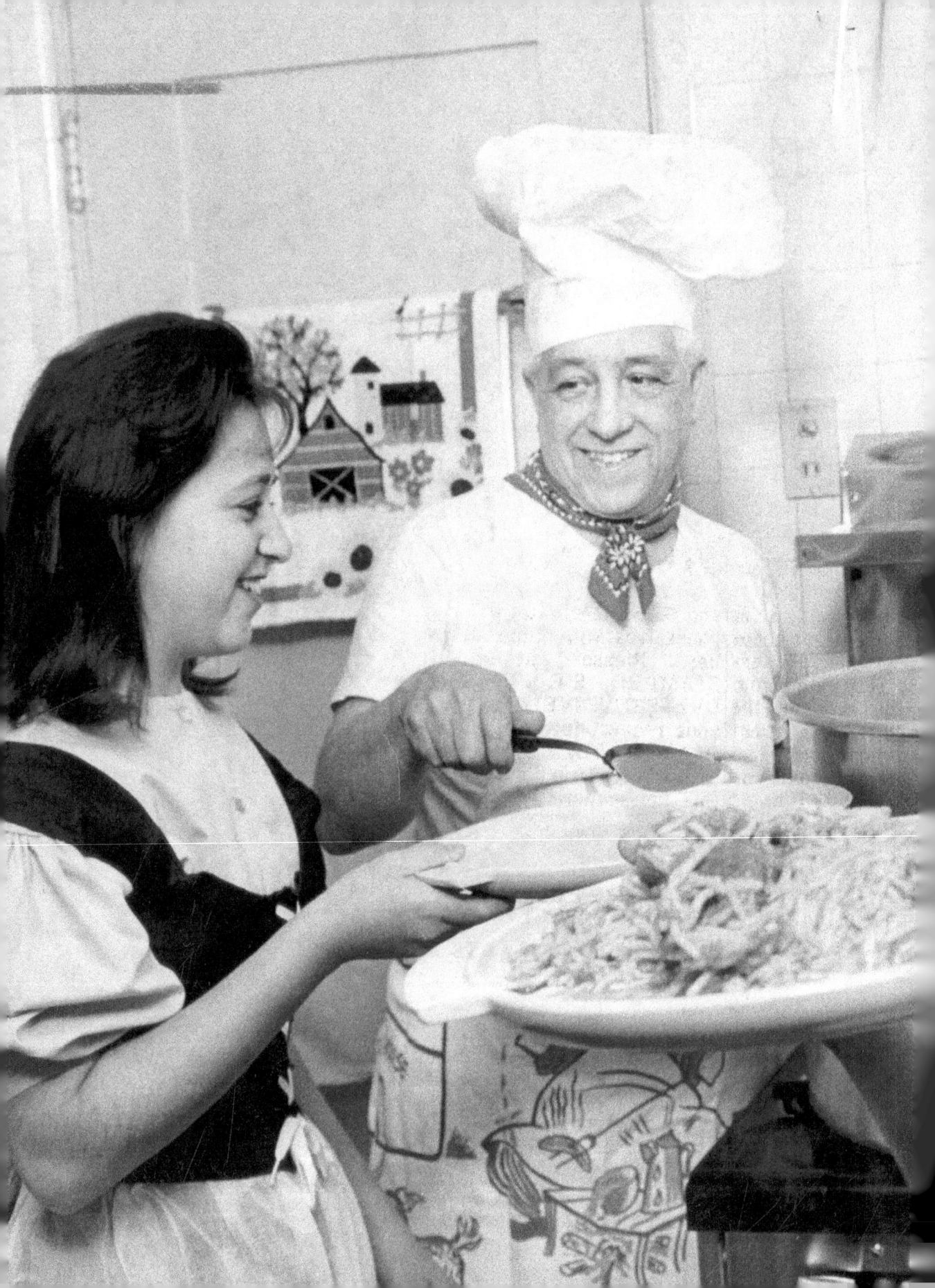

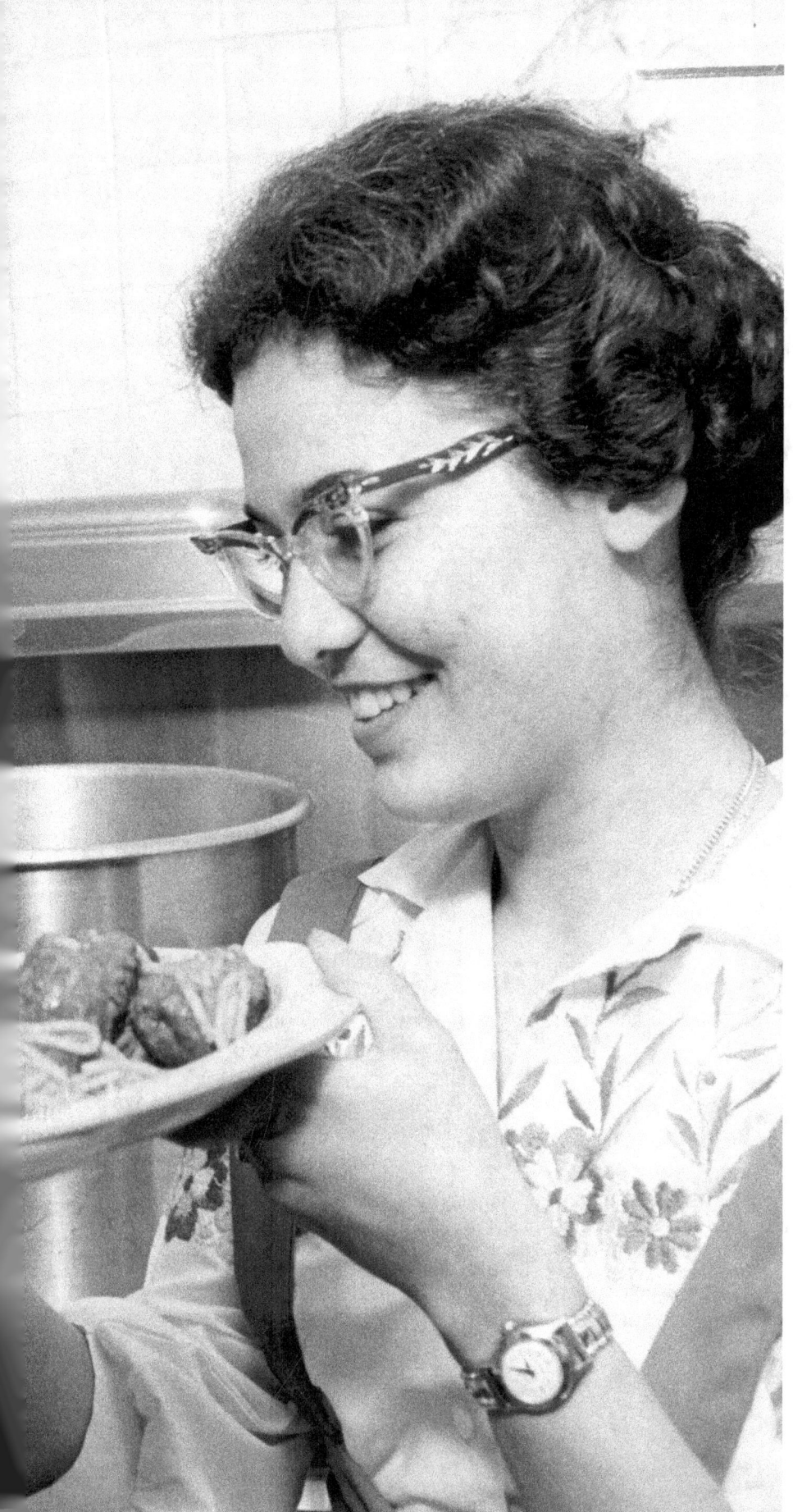

"Preparatory Institute of Notre Dame, training school for high school girls who plan to become religious teachers, will benefit from the annual spaghetti dinner April 1 of the Tujunga Branch, Italian Catholic Federation, from 12:30 to 6 p.m. on the school grounds, 9919 Sunland Blvd., Sunland. Tasting sample of steaming spaghetti prepared by chief chef Gene Galbo are Joan LeSage (left) and Marie Alfaro, included in peasant costumed students who will serve at event." March 24, 1962.
(Jeff Goldwater)

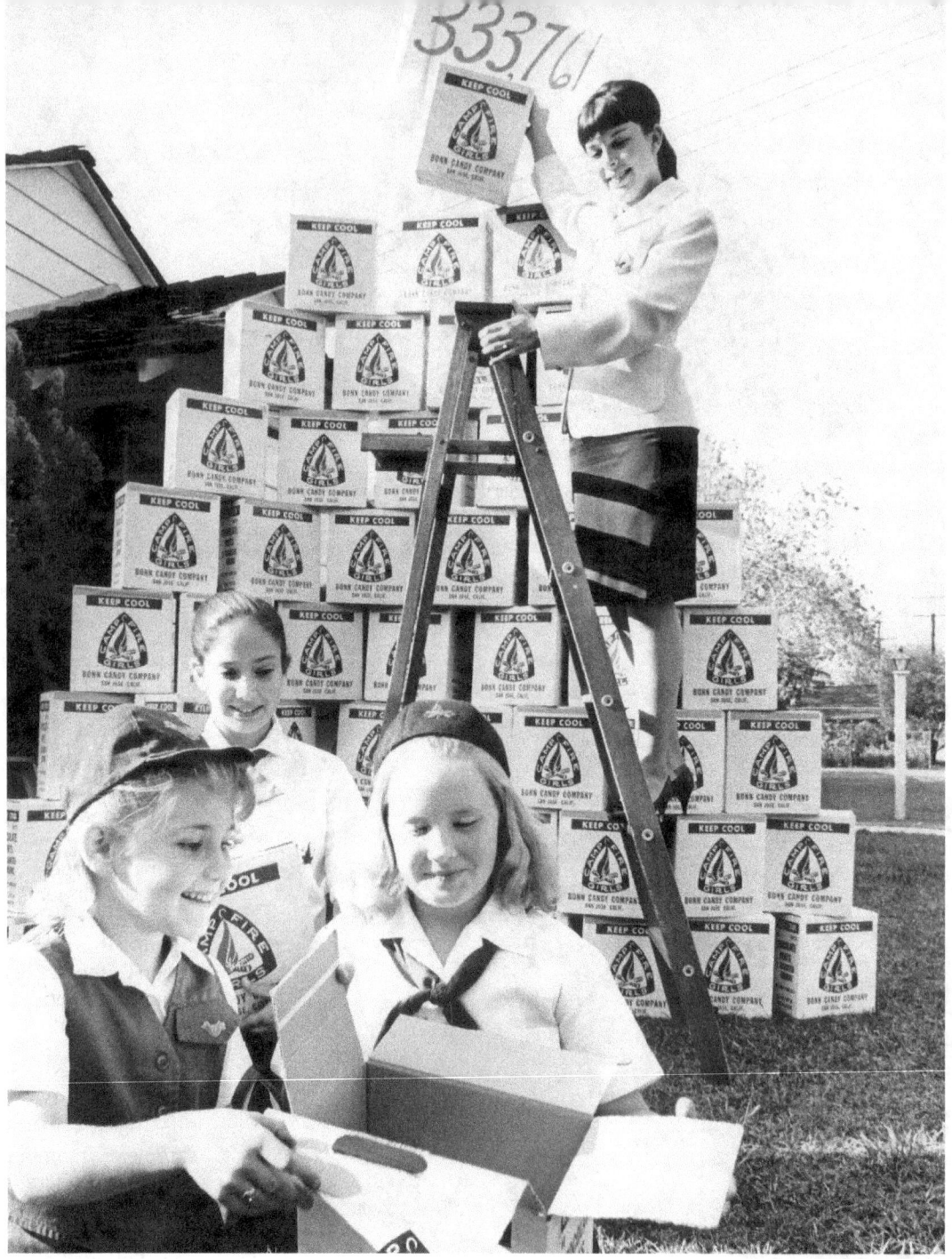

"Today thousands of Camp Fire Girls throughout Los Angeles will begin their once-a-year sale of chocolate covered mints and creams. They need to sell 333,761 dollar boxes in order to meet expenses. Members from Blue Birds, Camp Fire Girls, Junior Hi Camp Fire Girls and Horizon Clubs will scour neighborhoods and set up stands in business locations. Getting ready for the Valley drive are (from front), Kim Kimball, 8, Jamie Forrest, 13, Andrea Appleton, 10. Standing on ladder is Nancy Vasey, 15." April 23, 1965. (George Brich)

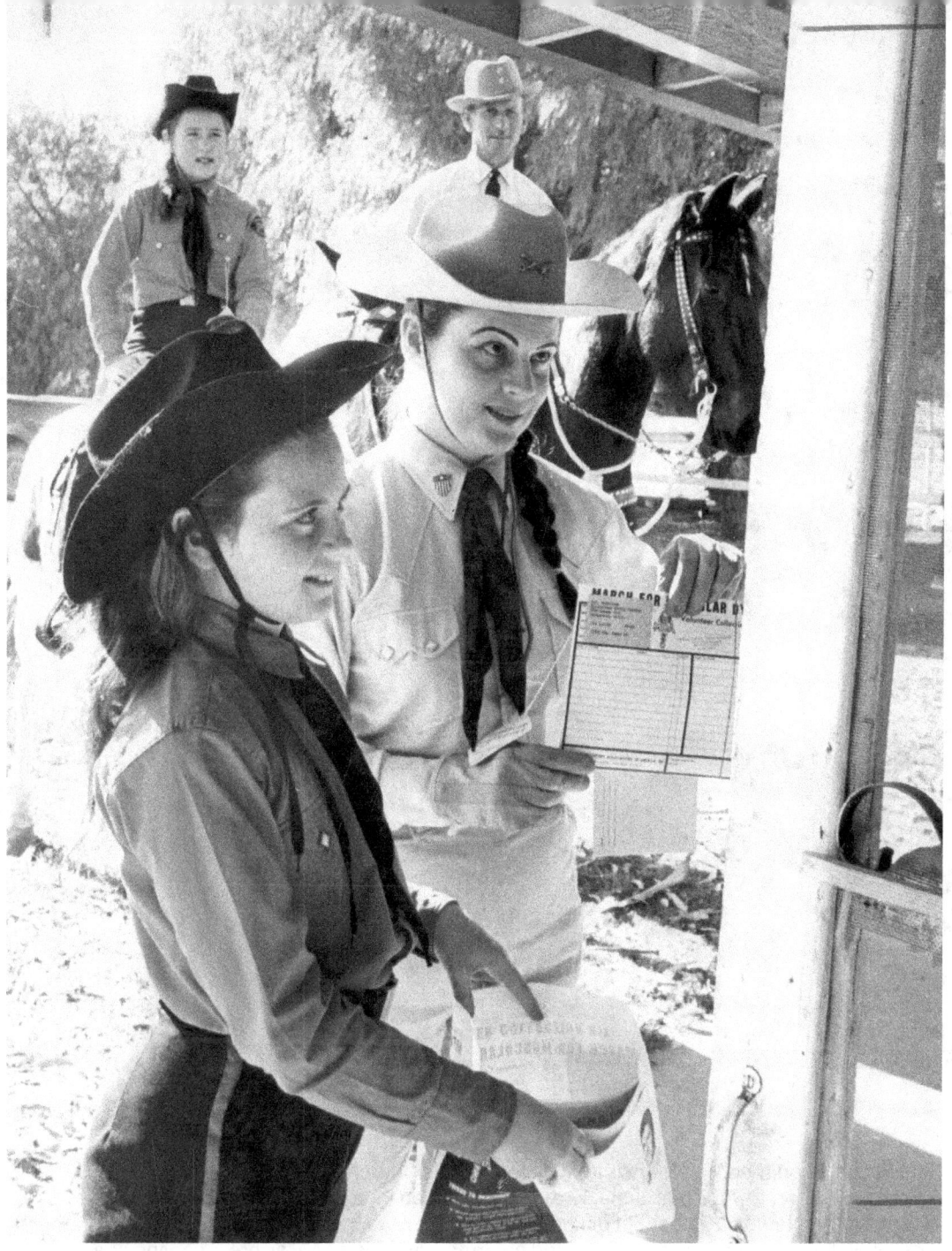

"Members of the Canoga Cavaliers, a group comprised of West Valley youth, taught horsemanship and equestrian discipline, and participated in various community services. Karen Skarrow (left) and mother, Mrs. Alexander Skarrow, 9332 Yoland Ave., Northridge, knock on neighbor's door for muscular dystrophy drive. On horses are Gilda Wyatt and Col. Charles Weisbaum." December 16, 1960.

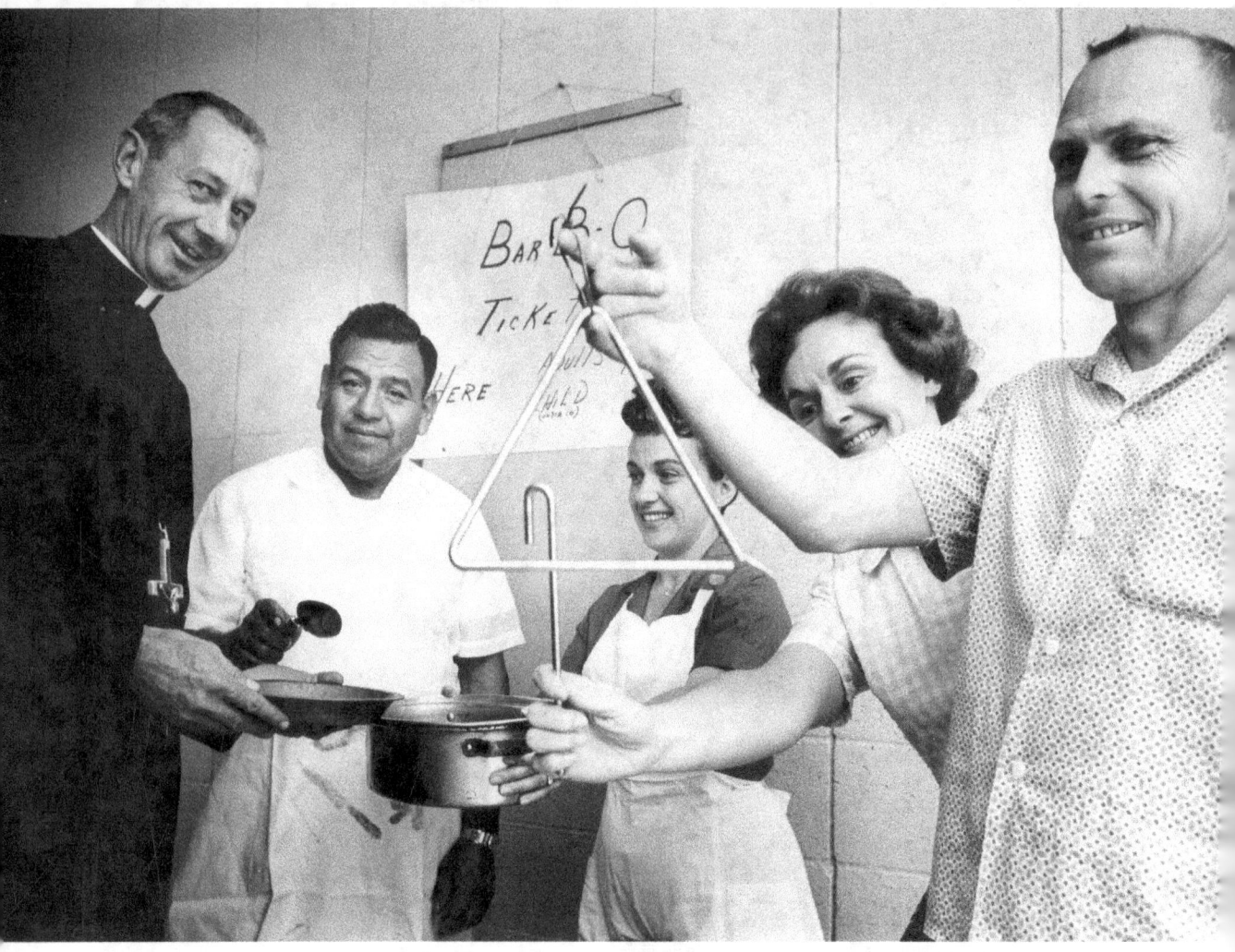

"Parishioners and friends of Mary Immaculate Catholic Church, Pacoima, will hear dinner bell sound from noon to 7:30 p.m. June 17 at Old-Fashioned Pit Barbecue and County Fair at Saxonia Park, Newhall, for benefit of church. Taking turns in sounding bell are (from left) Father Joseph Billman, pastor; John Alcazar, food chairman; Mrs. James Martorelli, serving chairman; Mrs. Clifford Fentriss, and Chic Bowling, event chairman." June 9, 1962. (George Brich)

Opposite: "The Mothers' and Dads' Club of Chaminade Preparatory School, 7500 Chaminade Ave., Canoga Park, are planning a Spring Dinner-Dance for the benefit of the school building program. Looking at a model of the proposed school are (from left), the Rev. William O'Connor and Brother Hugh Hoganson, of Chaminade; Mrs. A. H. Clarke, president, mothers' club, and Mrs. Robert Shadduck." May 11, 1964. (George Brich)

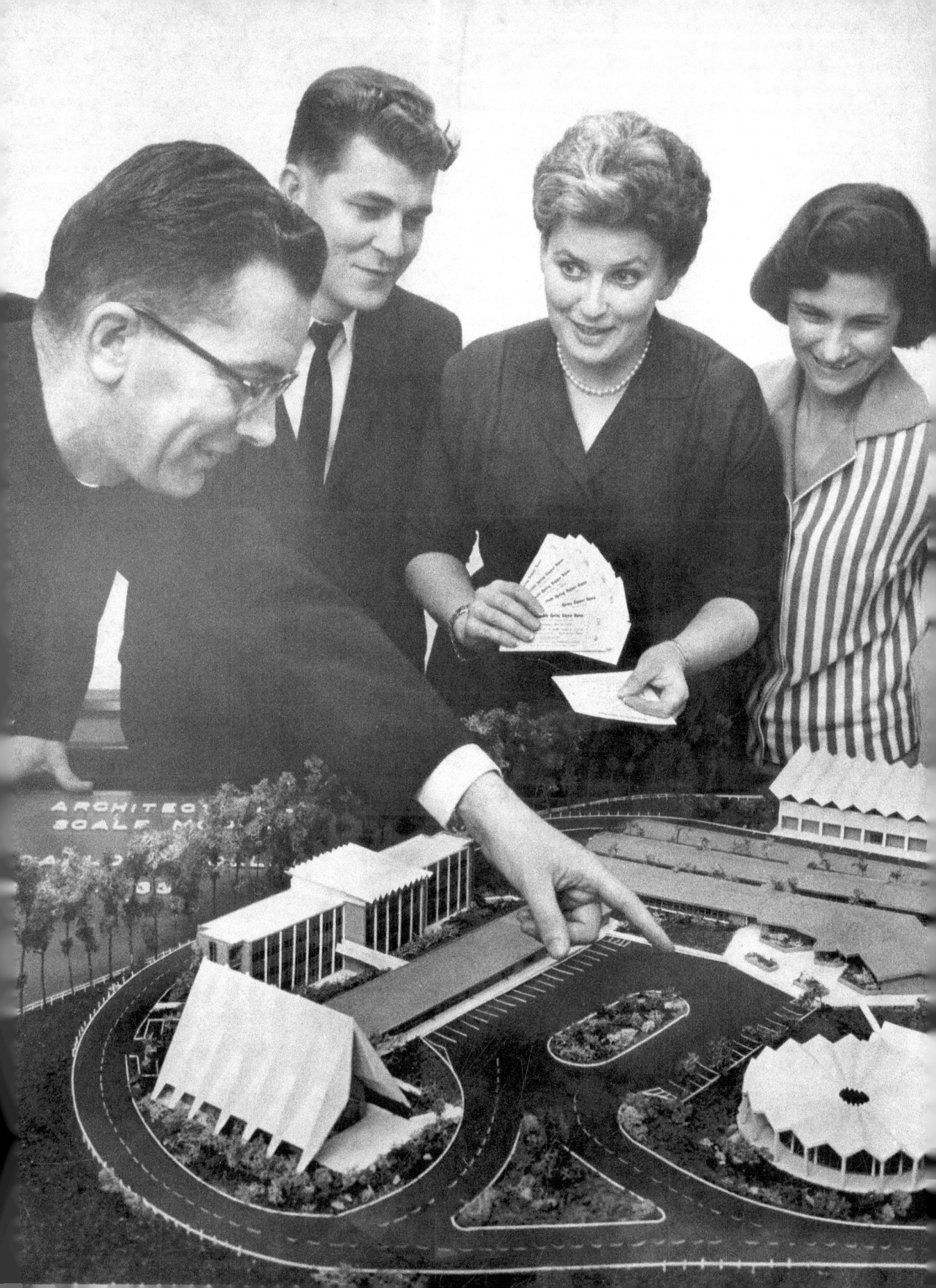

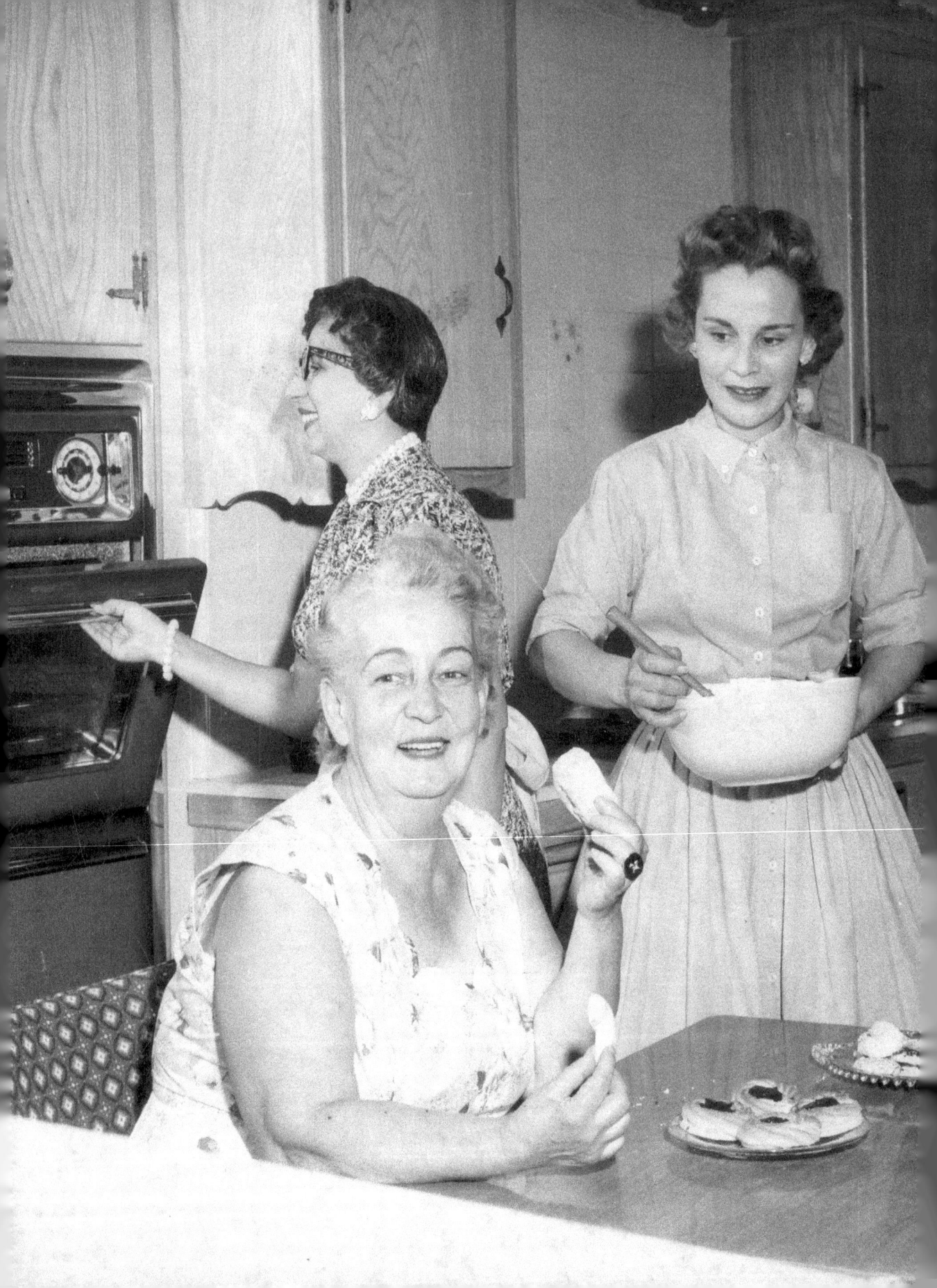

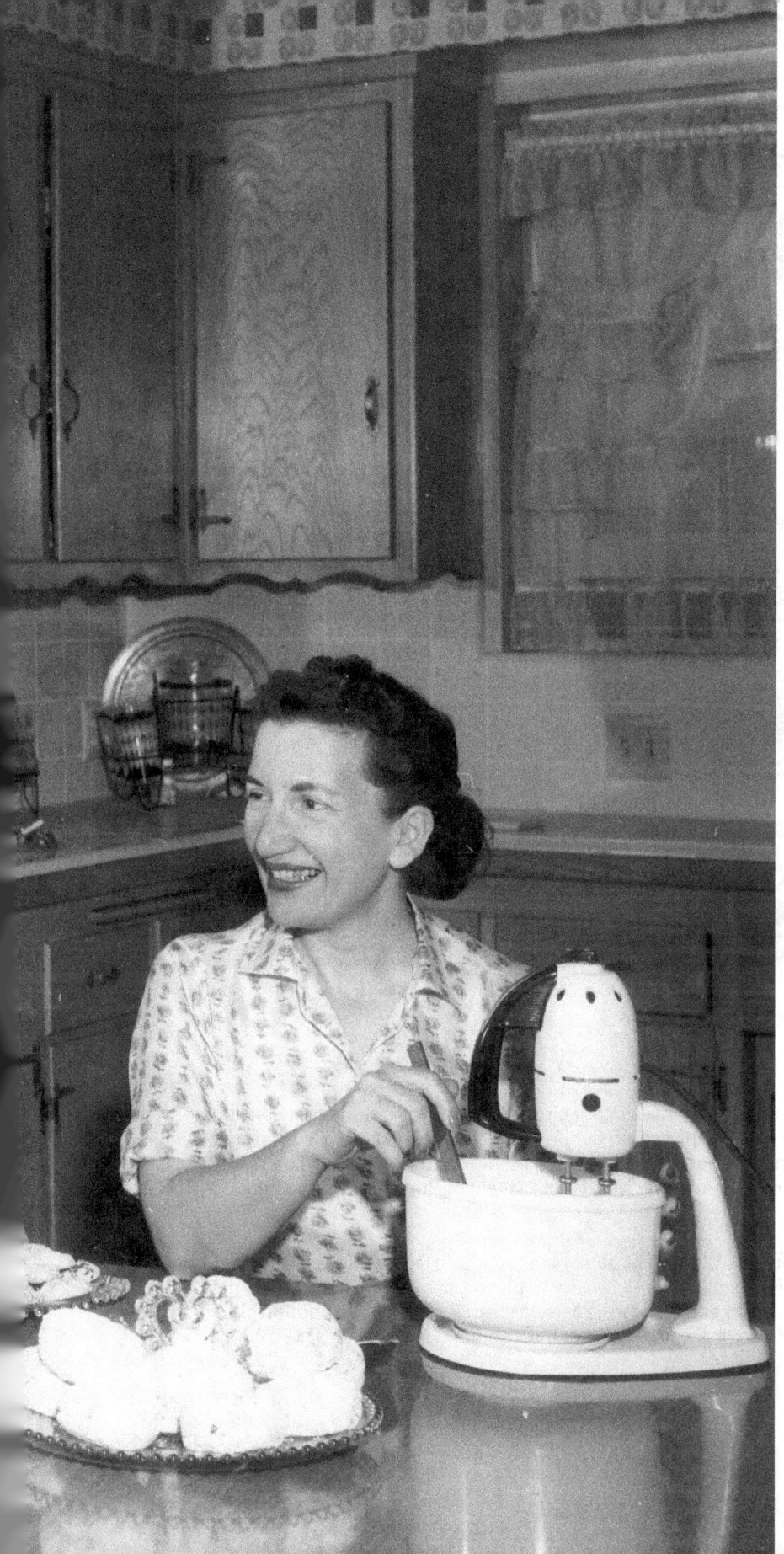

"Members of the women's division of the Greek Orthodox Community of San Fernando Valley prepare luscious pastry for benefit May 30-June 1 bazaar-carnival. Sampling results at table is Mrs. George Katsampes, pastry booth chairman. Cooks (from left) are Mmes. Theodore Maropulos, William Davis and Ernest Prodromos." May 28, 1958. (Gordon Dean)

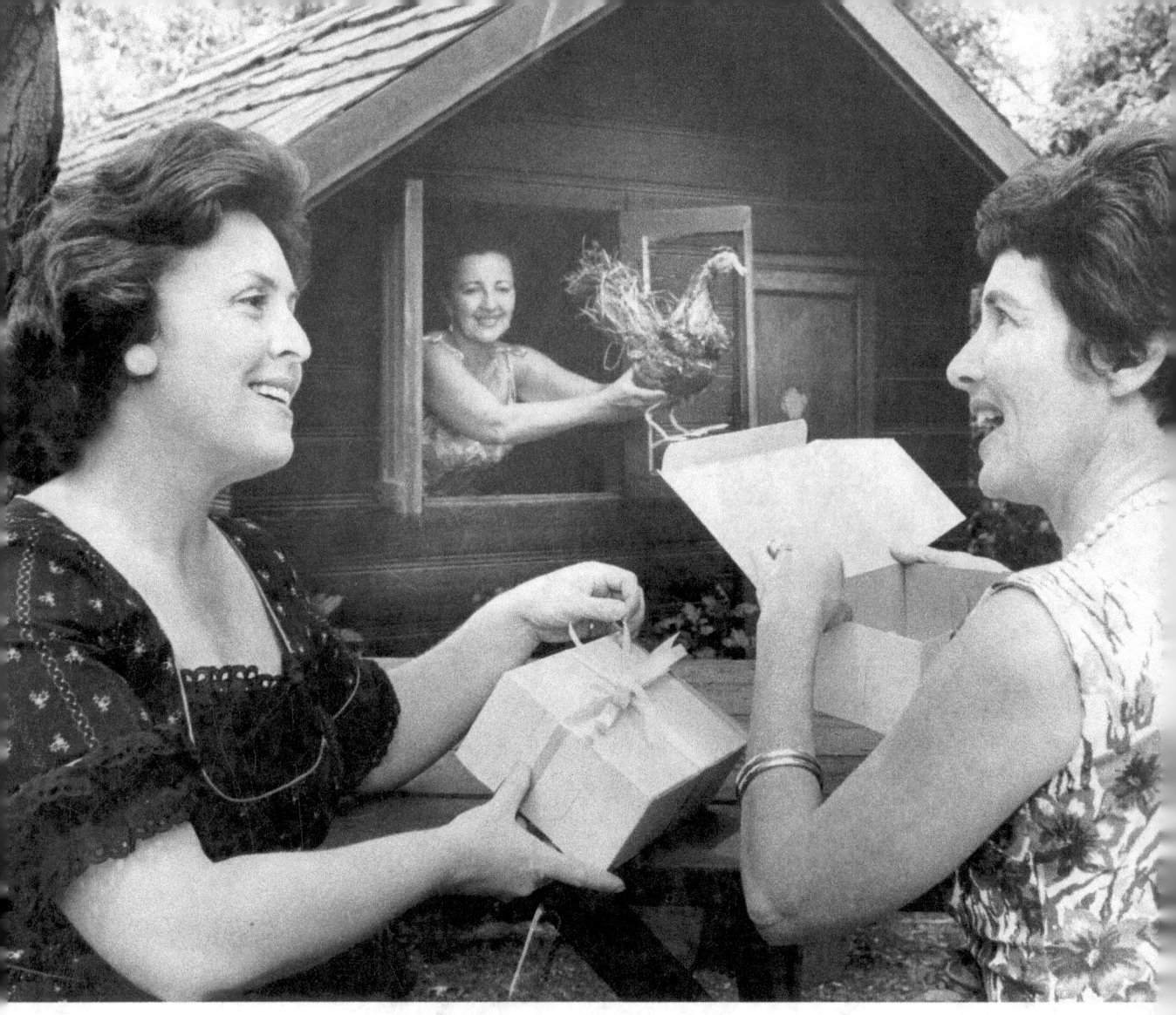

"Mrs. George Ungar of Van Nuys releases straw bird she hopes will get the first box June 12 at the 'Early Bird Box Luncheon' sponsored by the San Fernando Valley Child Guidance Clinic Founders Guild. Preparing lunches for event at Sherman Oaks home of Mrs. Leo Hirsh are Mrs. Gerald Drum of Sherman Oaks, left, and Mrs. Burns Steele of North Hollywood." June 2, 1961. (George Brich)

Opposite: La Cadena Women's Club of Burbank plan Signature Dance at Oakmont Country Club to raise funds for high school scholarships. "About to place a symbolical mortar board on the head of Mrs. Atton Hansen, ticket chairman, is Mrs. William E. Wood, subscription chairman. Mrs. John Bodley, decorations chairman, is approving third person." November 9, 1959. (George Brich)

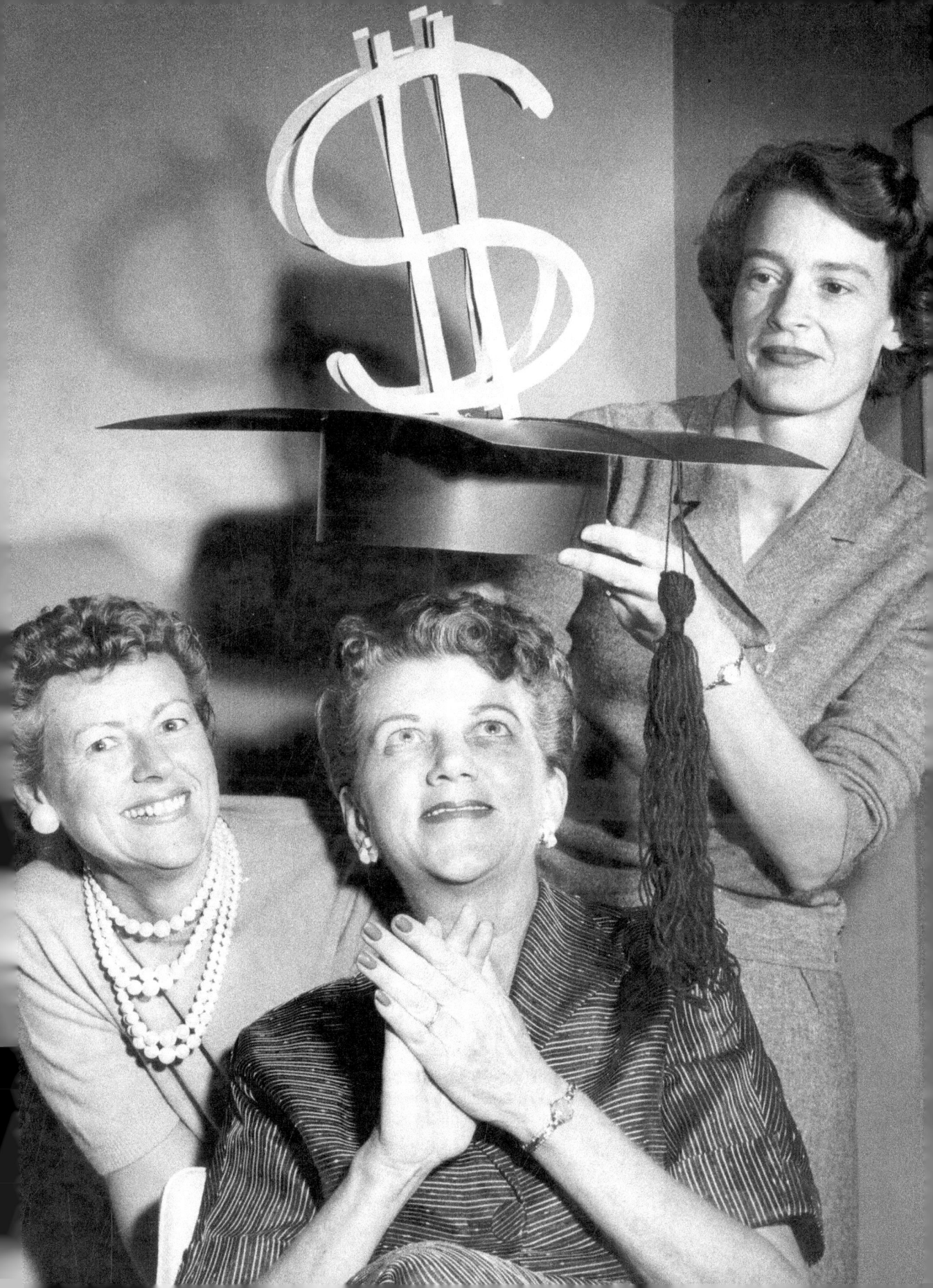

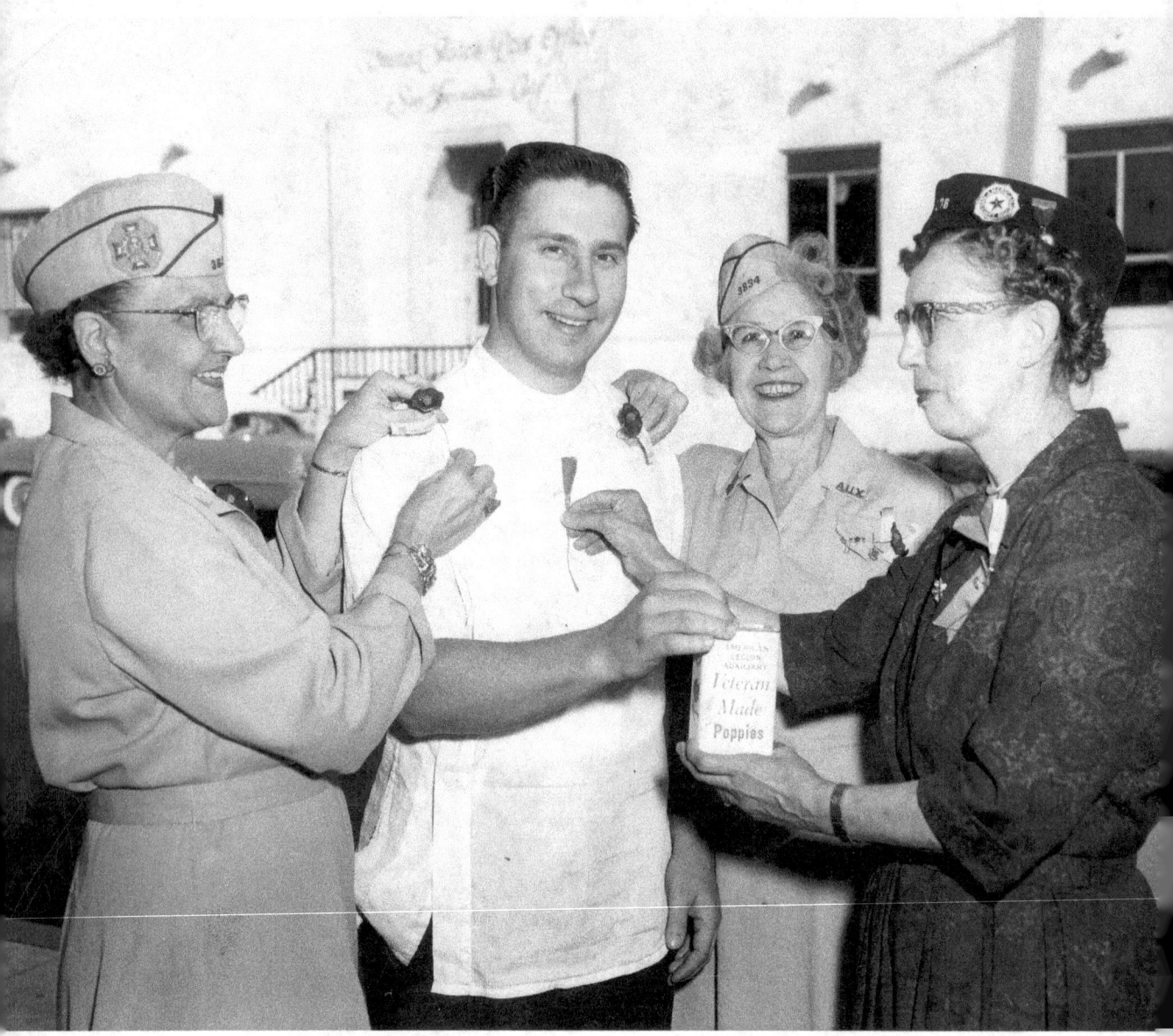

"First Buddy Poppy is purchased by barber Lee Wolfe, World War II veteran, heralding upcoming Poppy Days in San Fernando, May 22-23. Vying for first sale are (from left), Mrs. Reta Richardson, president of San Fernando Post 3834, Veterans of Foreign Wars Auxiliary; Mrs. Trecia Martin, American Legion Post 176 Auxiliary poppy chairman, and Mrs. Myrtle Graham, Post 176 Auxiliary president. Both groups join in poppy sale." May 11, 1959.

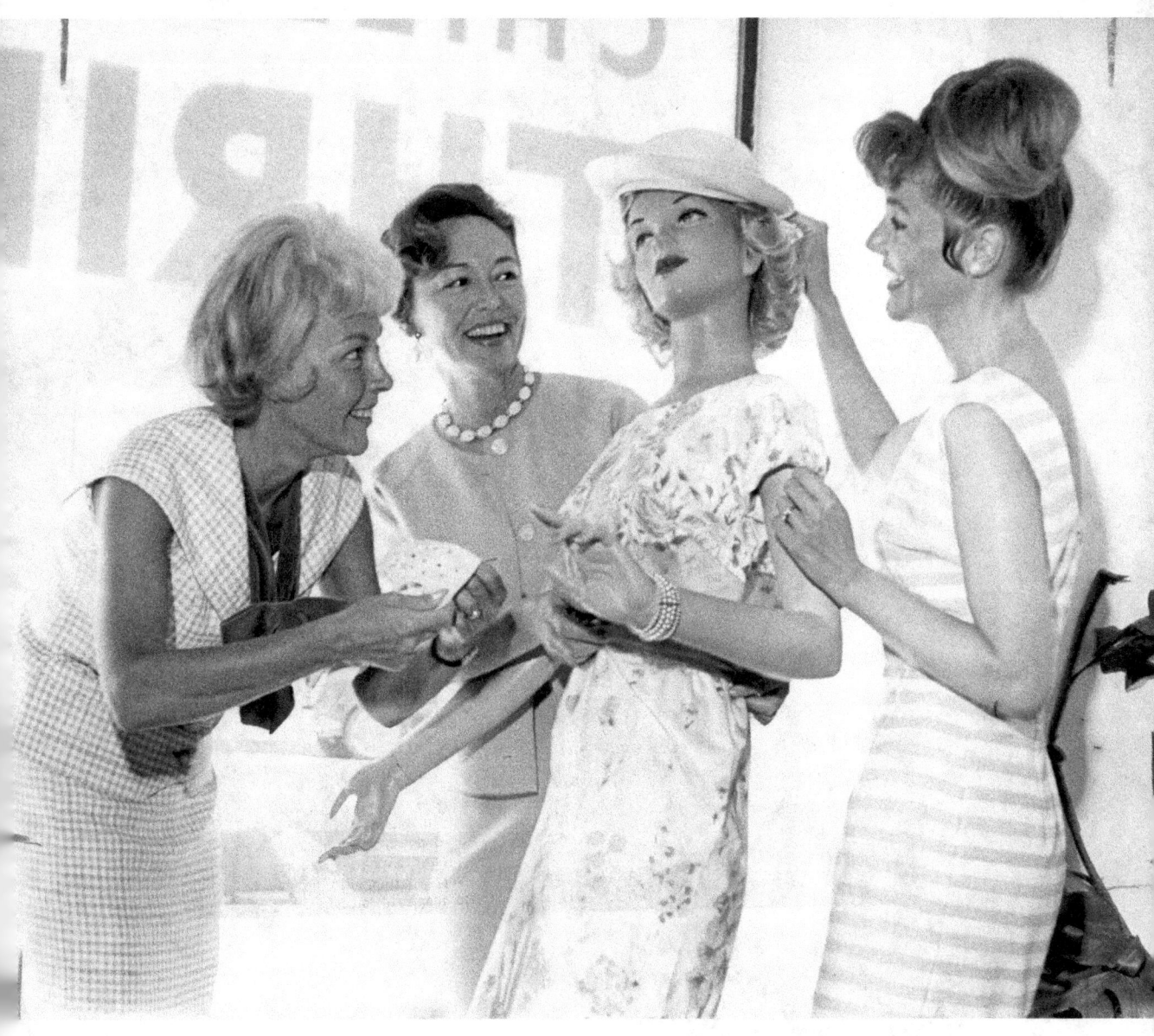

"Valley Heart Guild members prepare mannequin display for Children's Hospital Thrift Shop in Reseda. From left are Mmes. Howard J. Liggett, H. Douglas Gamble, chairman, and Ballard Huntley, all of Woodland Hills." May 28, 1964. (Bob Miller)

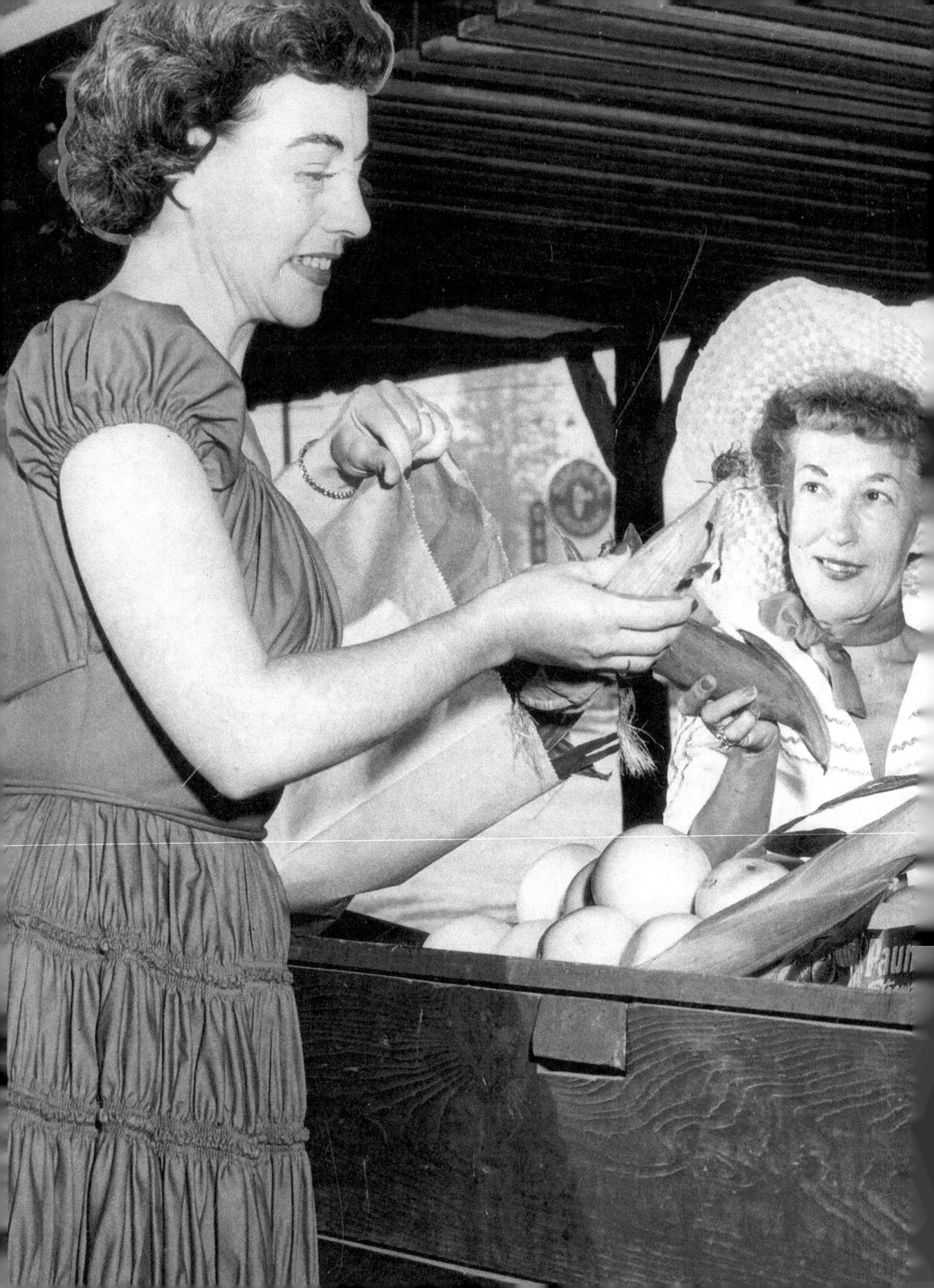

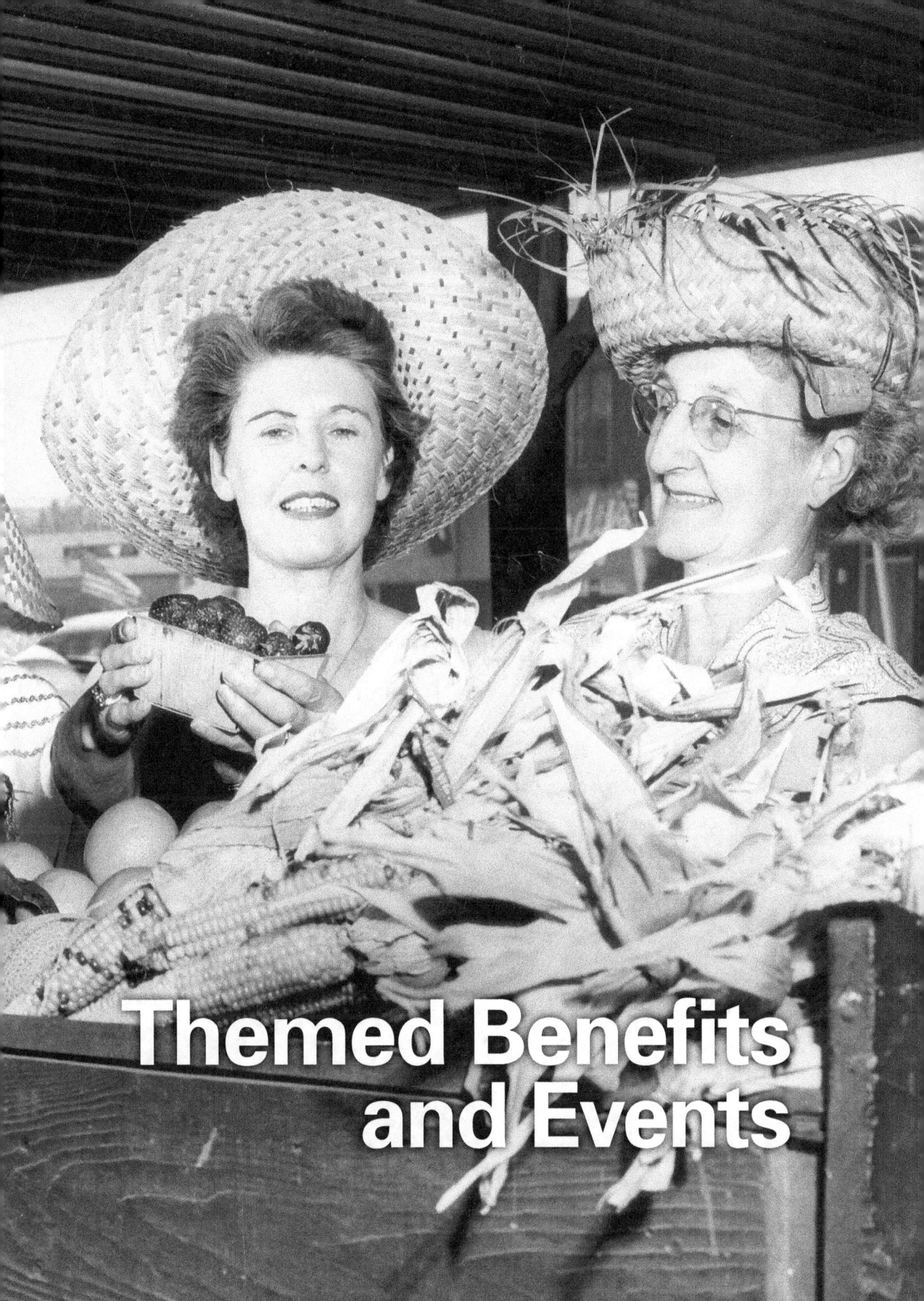

Themed Benefits and Events

Overleaf: "Mrs. D. Wendell Reid shows wares ready to sell at Van Nuys Woman's Club country fair scheduled Saturday as Mmes. Paul Murray, Martin Fritzen and Harold Kreutzinger (from left) give merchandise a nod of approval." May 27, 1954.

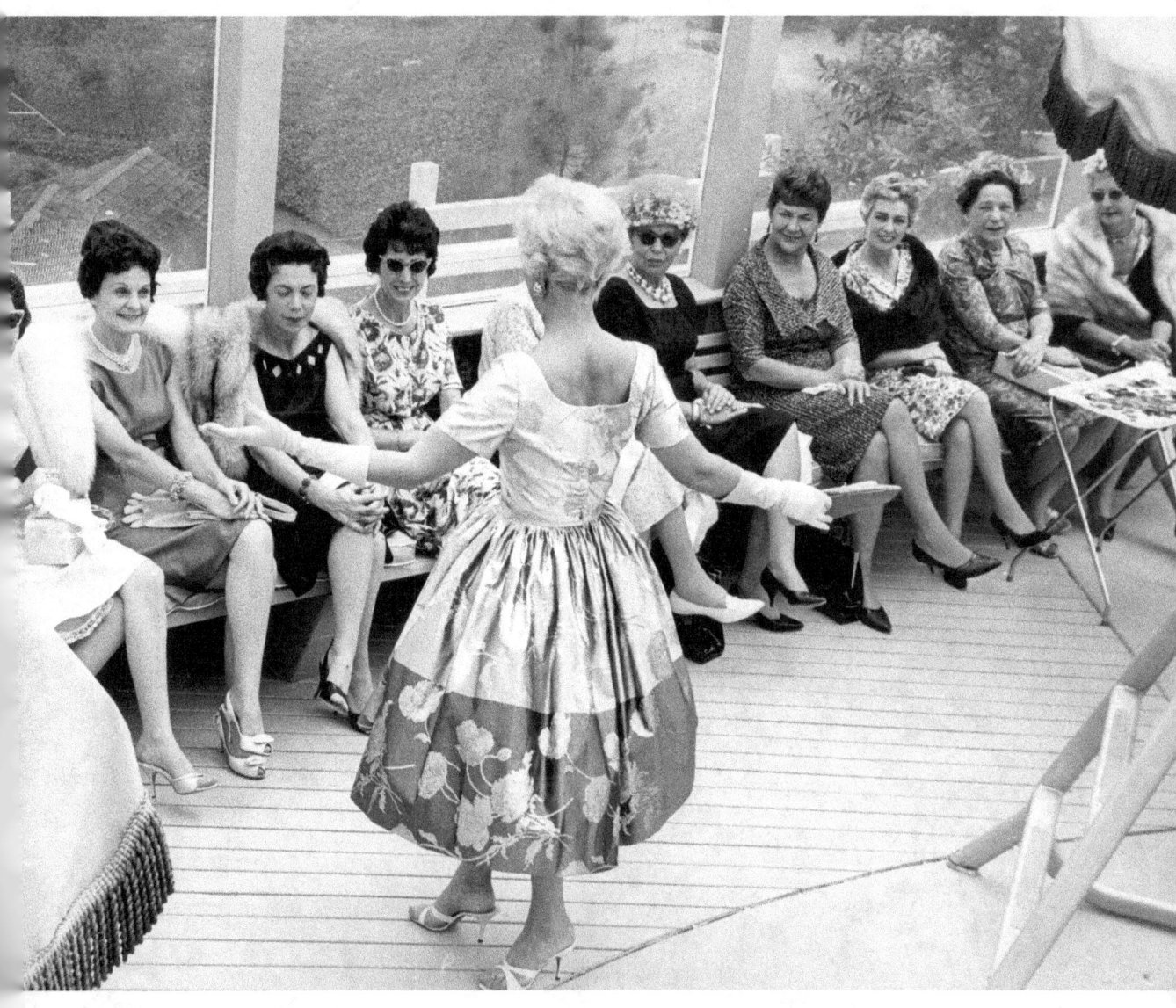

"Members of the Home and Garden section of the Encino Women's Club gather at the home of Mr. and Mrs. J.A. Marion, 4060 Valley Meadow Road, for the annual June garden party and fashion show. A captive audience sees the newest lines in resort wear. Fashions ranged from casual daytime cottons to graceful summer formals." June 17, 1961. (George Brich)

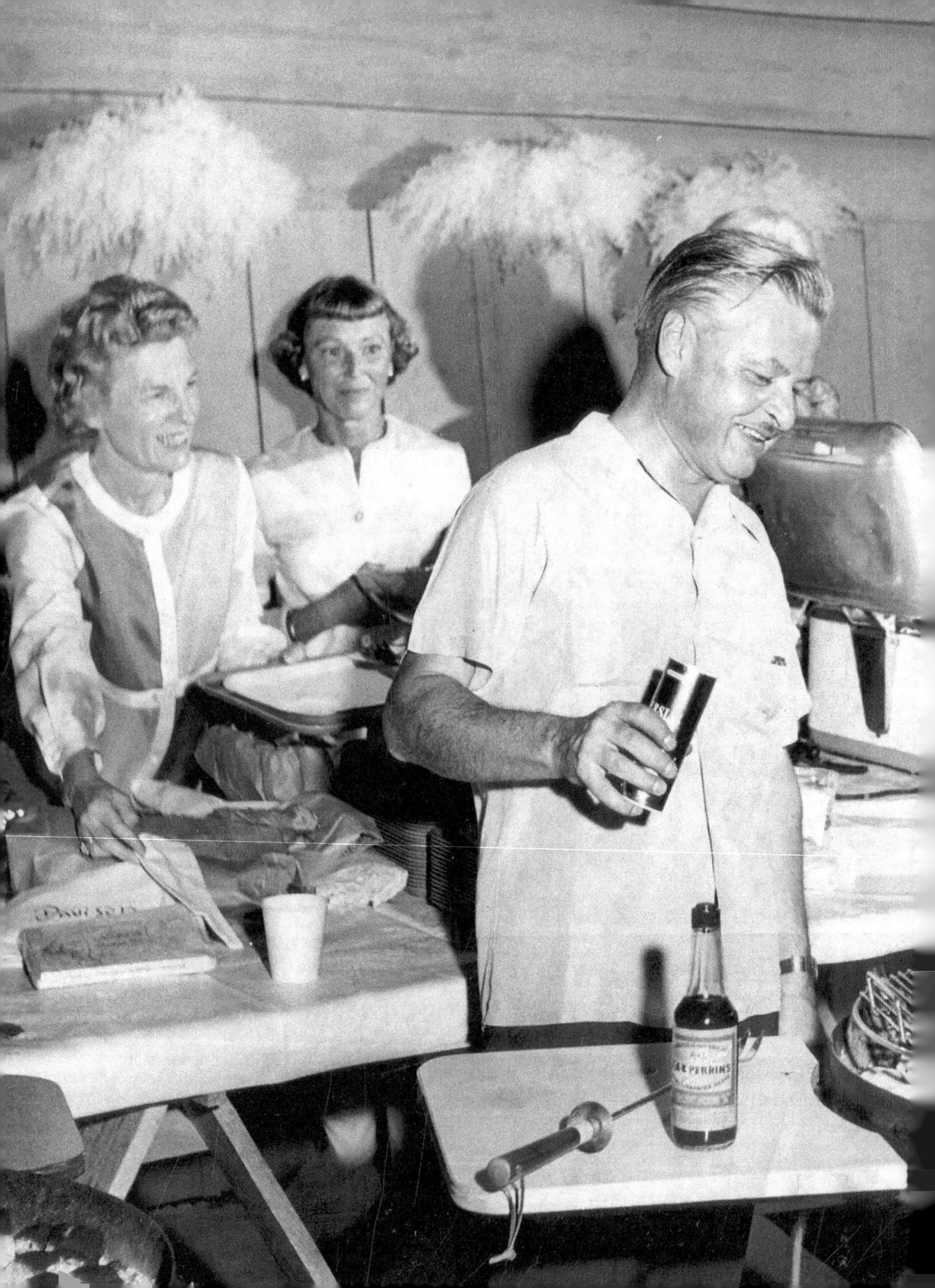

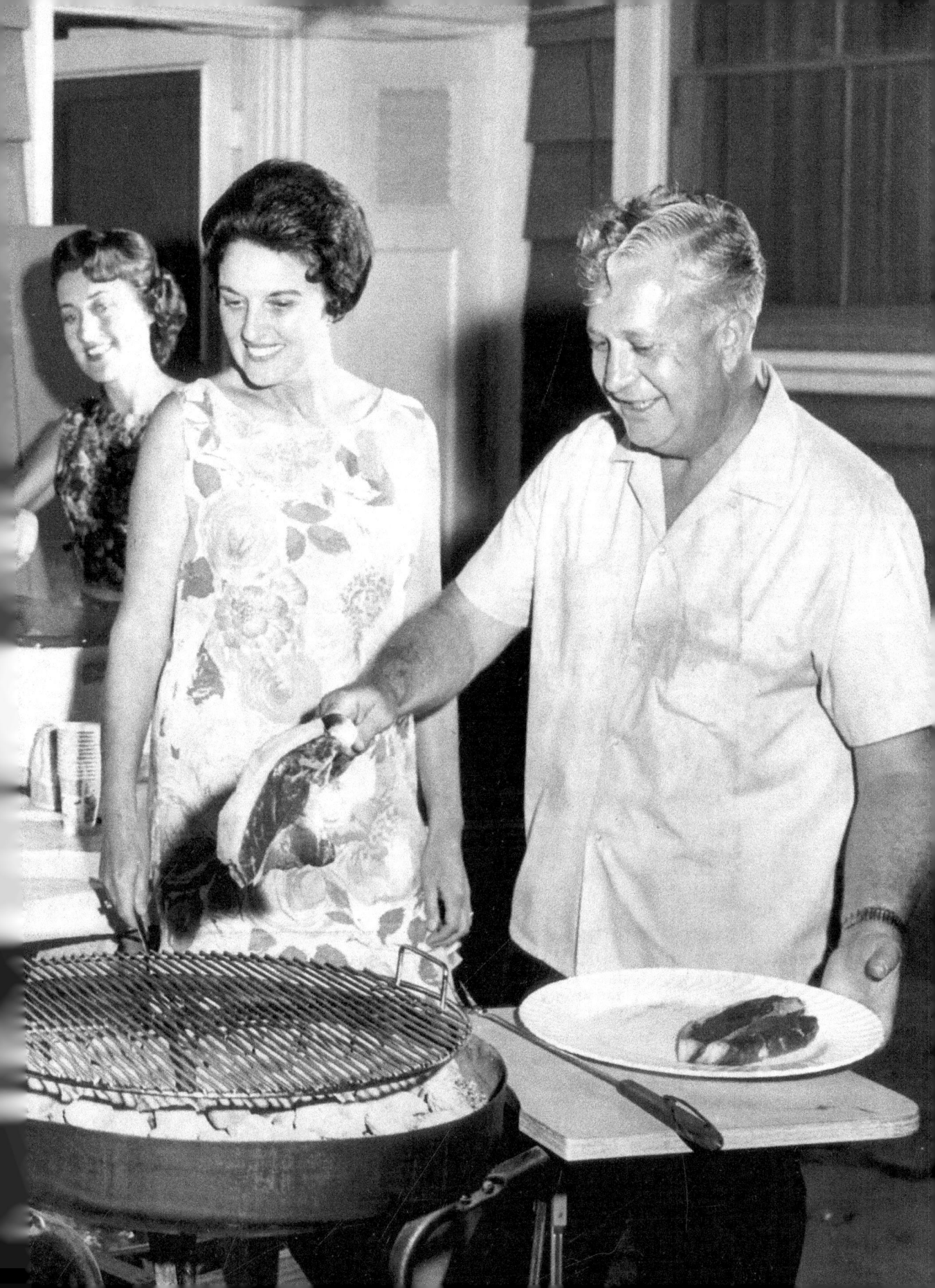

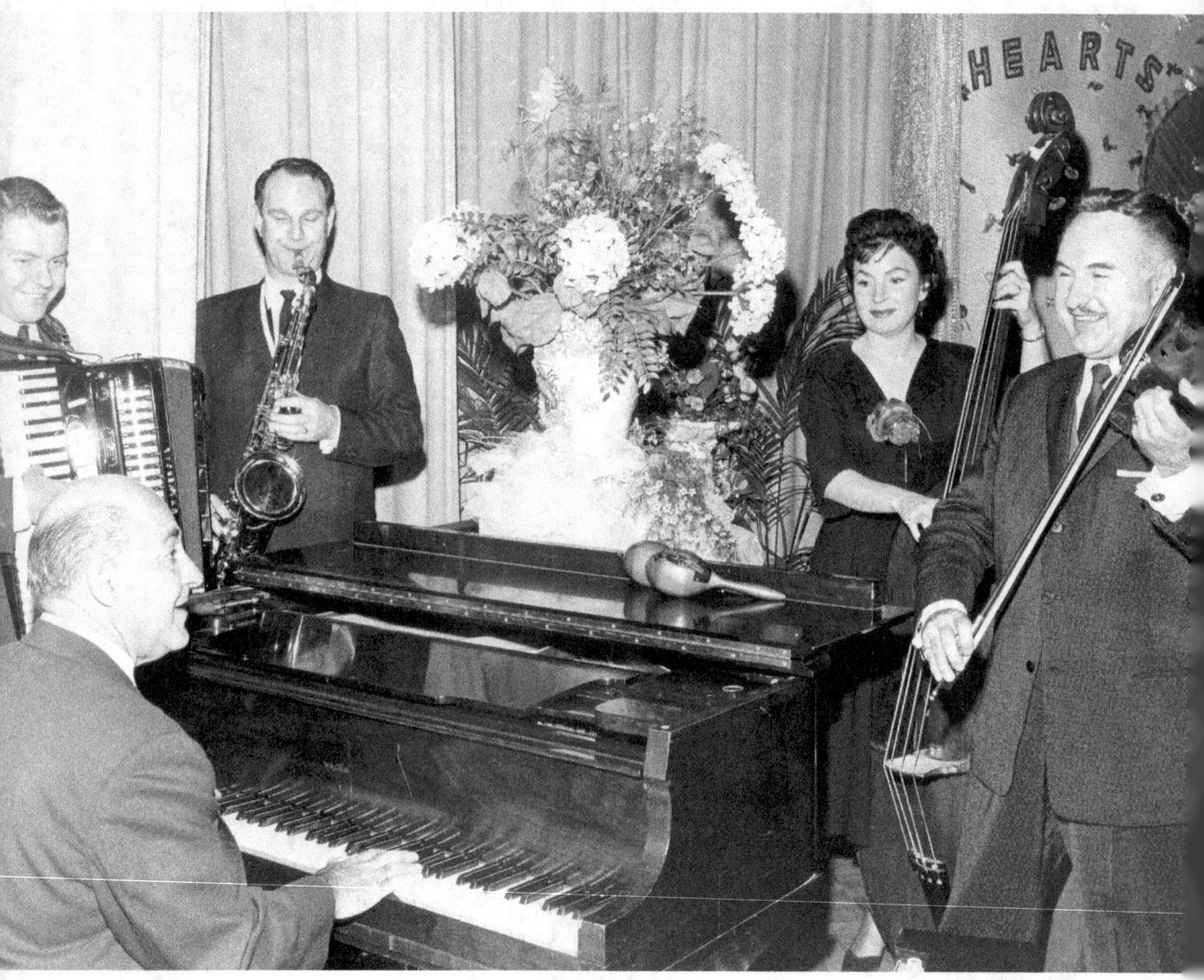

"George Liberace provides background music with Millie Springer, who plays bass and sings at the 'Hearts and Flowers' benefit luncheon at Villa Cabrini Academy in Burbank sponsored by Patronesses." February 23, 1961 (Alan Hyde)

Overleaf. "Stanley Moe, left, and Leon K. Madsen reveal their recipes for barbecuing steak to Mrs. Clifford Hegness and other members of the Valley Heart Guild for Childrens Hospital. In background are Mmes. Walter Wetzel (left), George Klein and Robert Rapp. Husbands of guild members prepared steaks for summer party." The party was held at the Moes' Van Nuys home. September 18, 1963. (Larry Leach)

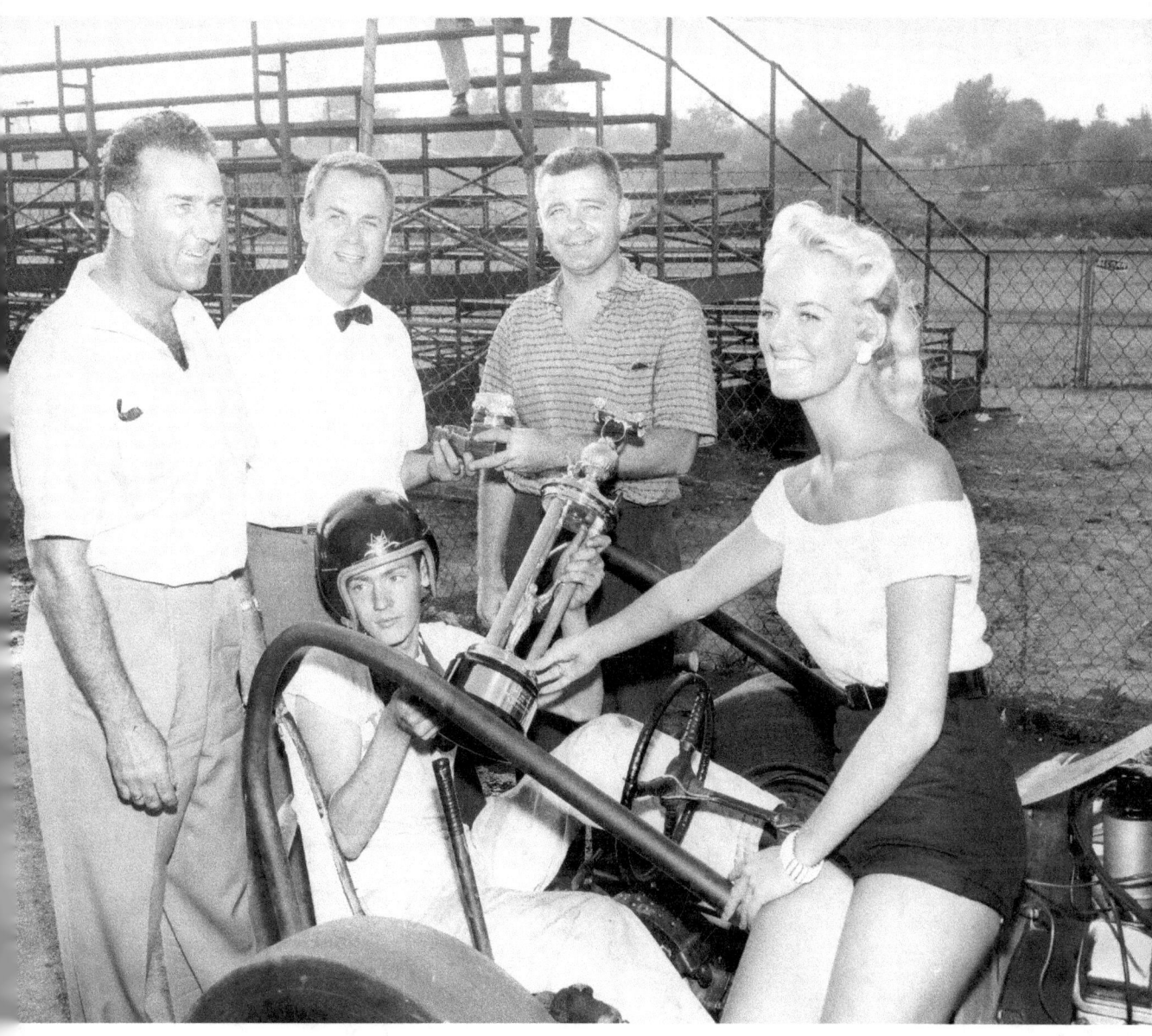

"Tom Indovina, 18, 4532 Woodley Ave., Encino, accepts trophy as top elimination winner at Kiwanis benefit drag strip races. Bob Aiton, left, district governor of Kiwanis presents award with help of Orlanda Munyon, Miss Panorama City. Herb Lightfoot (second from left) presents trophy to Jerry Firestone, winner of Panorama City Kiwanis interclub competition." August 27, 1956.

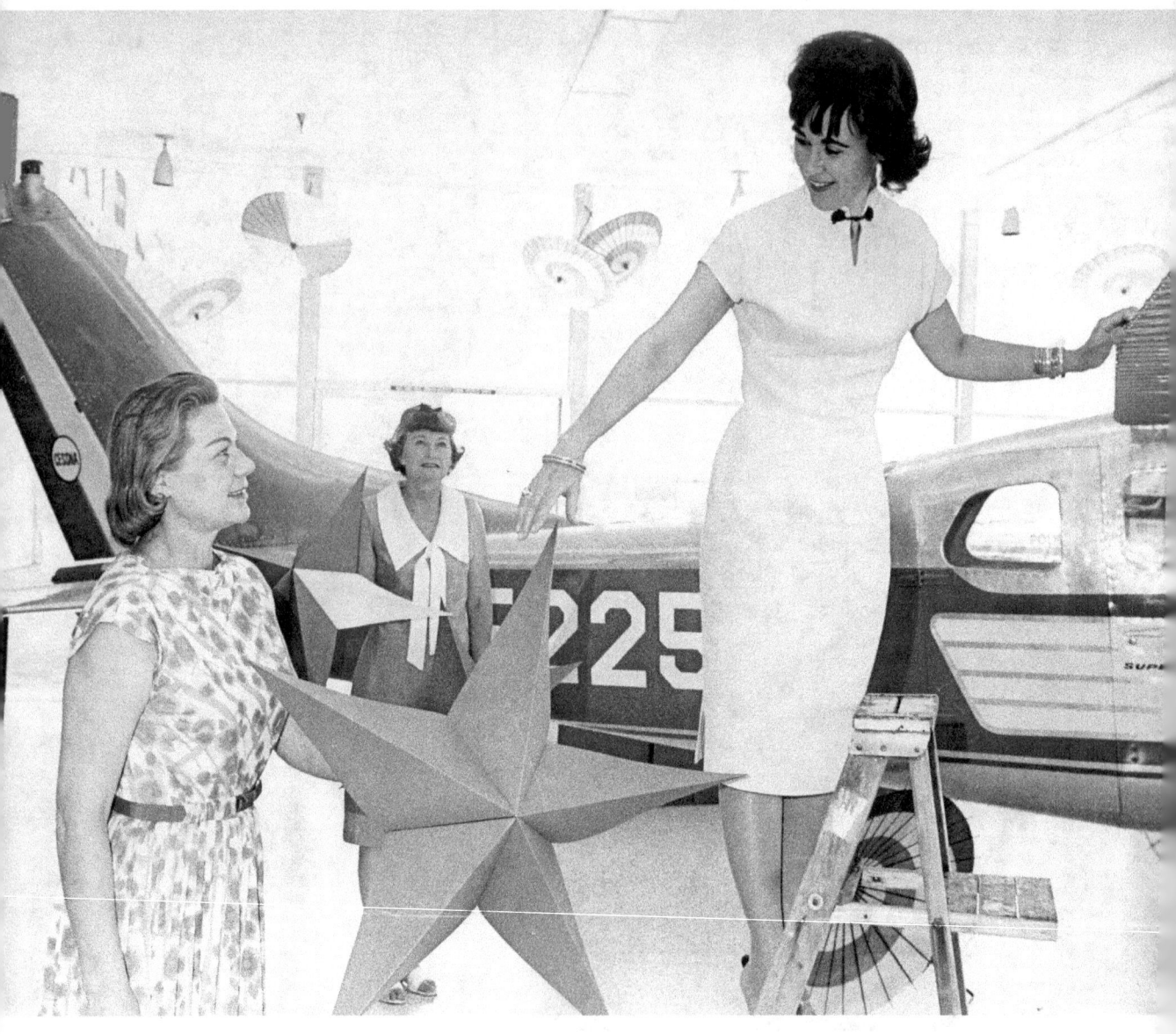

"Soar to Victory, a dance sponsored by the Icarian Flying Club as a benefit for the U.S. Olympic Soaring Team, will be held at 8 p.m. tomorrow at the Van Nuys Skyways Hangar, 16700 Roscoe Blvd.,Van Nuys. Working on decorations are (from left), Mrs. Esther B. Athons, Van Nuys, private secretary to Walter R. Von Der Ahe of Van Nuys Skyways; Mrs. Jack Hollebeke, North Hollywood, decorations committee chairman for the Icarian Club, and Mrs. Barbara Bottenfield, Northridge, switchboard receptionist at Van Nuys Skyways." September 11, 1964.
(Gordon Dean)

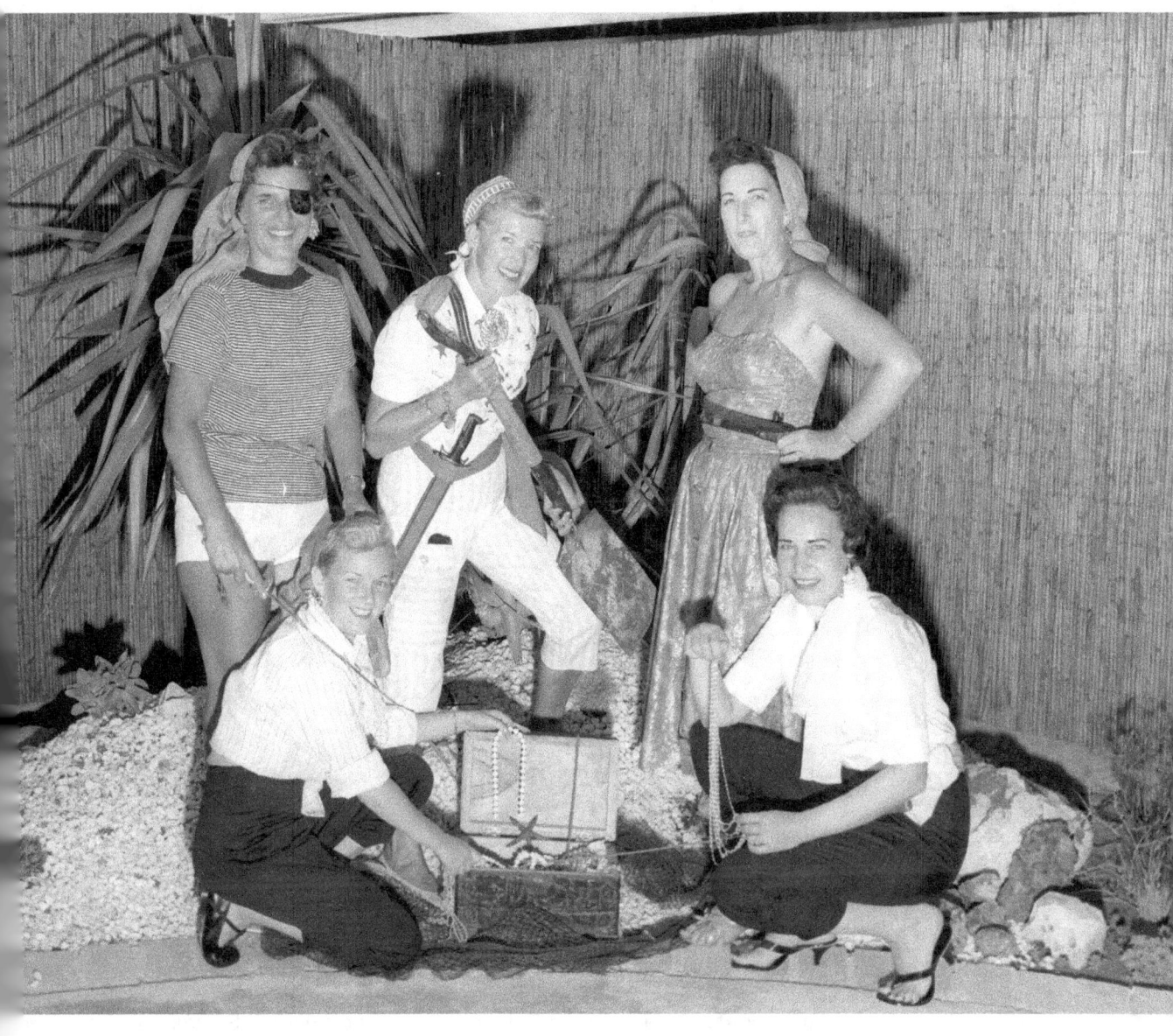

"La-Junta Waldron and Elise Smith (foreground from left) inspect contents of pirate chest, the 'Pipsi Lal' for which members and guests will search at Tarzana Business and Professional Women's Club's festive summer benefit party on Sunday. 'Buccaneers' in background are Marie Louise Spencer, Esther Barnes, and Eileen Morgan (from left)." July 22, 1959.

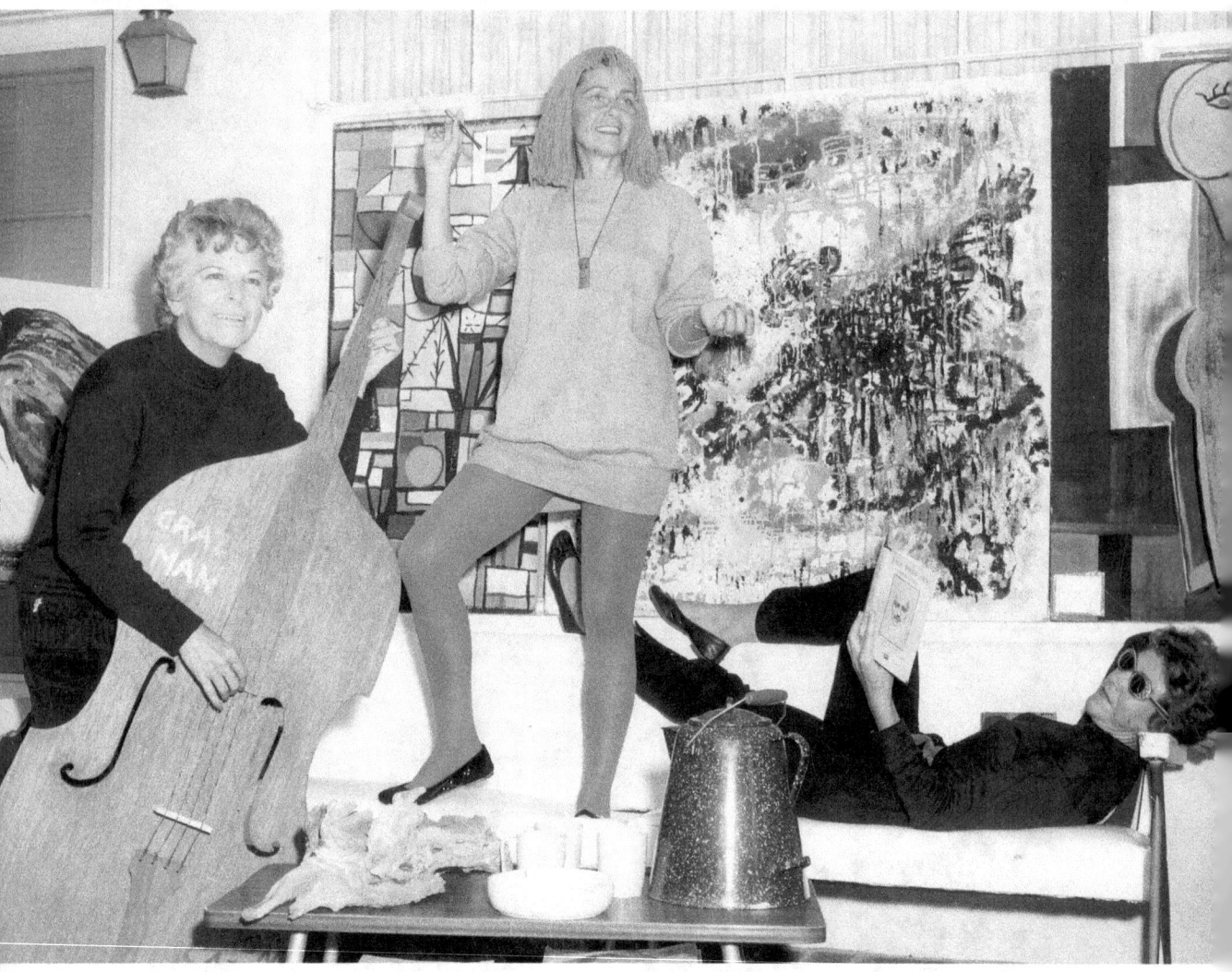

"The Studio City gardens of Mr. and Mrs. Lawrence Shriver will turn into a combination of San Francisco's North Beach and Los Angeles' Venice when members of the North Hollywood Circle of the Florence Crittenton Home stage a beatnik benefit with cocktails and dinner on Saturday. Collecting objects d'art and donning tights and 'sloppy Joe' shirts for the event are Mmes. H. Claude Baker, Bernard N. Smith and Evie G. Stacey (from left)." September 22, 1959. (Gordon Dean)

Opposite: "Bucks for Bonnets' themes hat auction and brunch March 16 to be sponsored by the Prospectors Guild of Valley Presbyterian Hospital at Lakeside Golf Club. Elizabeth Talbot-Martin (left), who will be mistress of ceremonies and auctioneer at fete, gives sneak preview of hats to Mmes. Herman Balleweg, decorations chairman, and Richard Molnar, right." March 9, 1961. (George Brich)

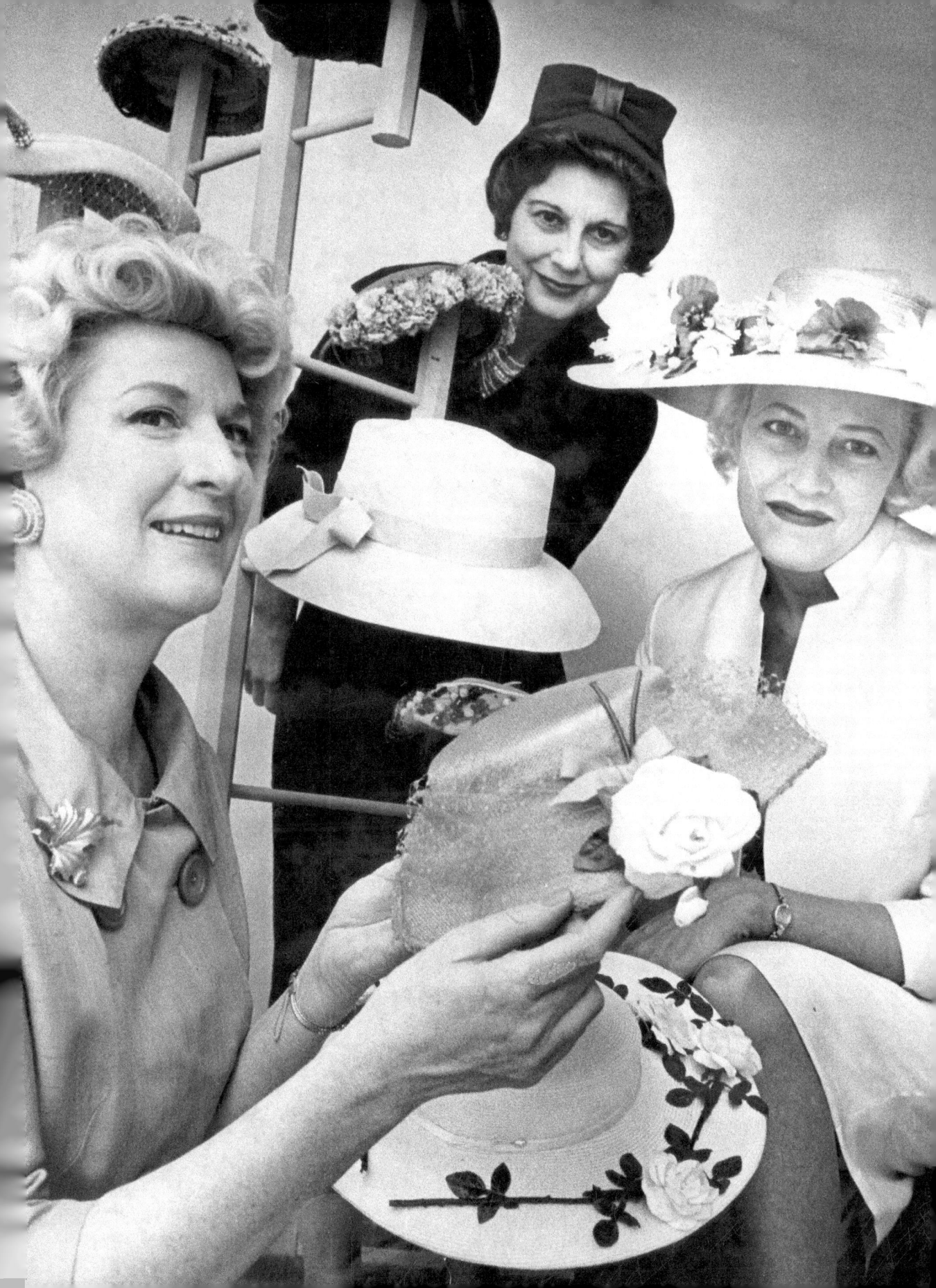

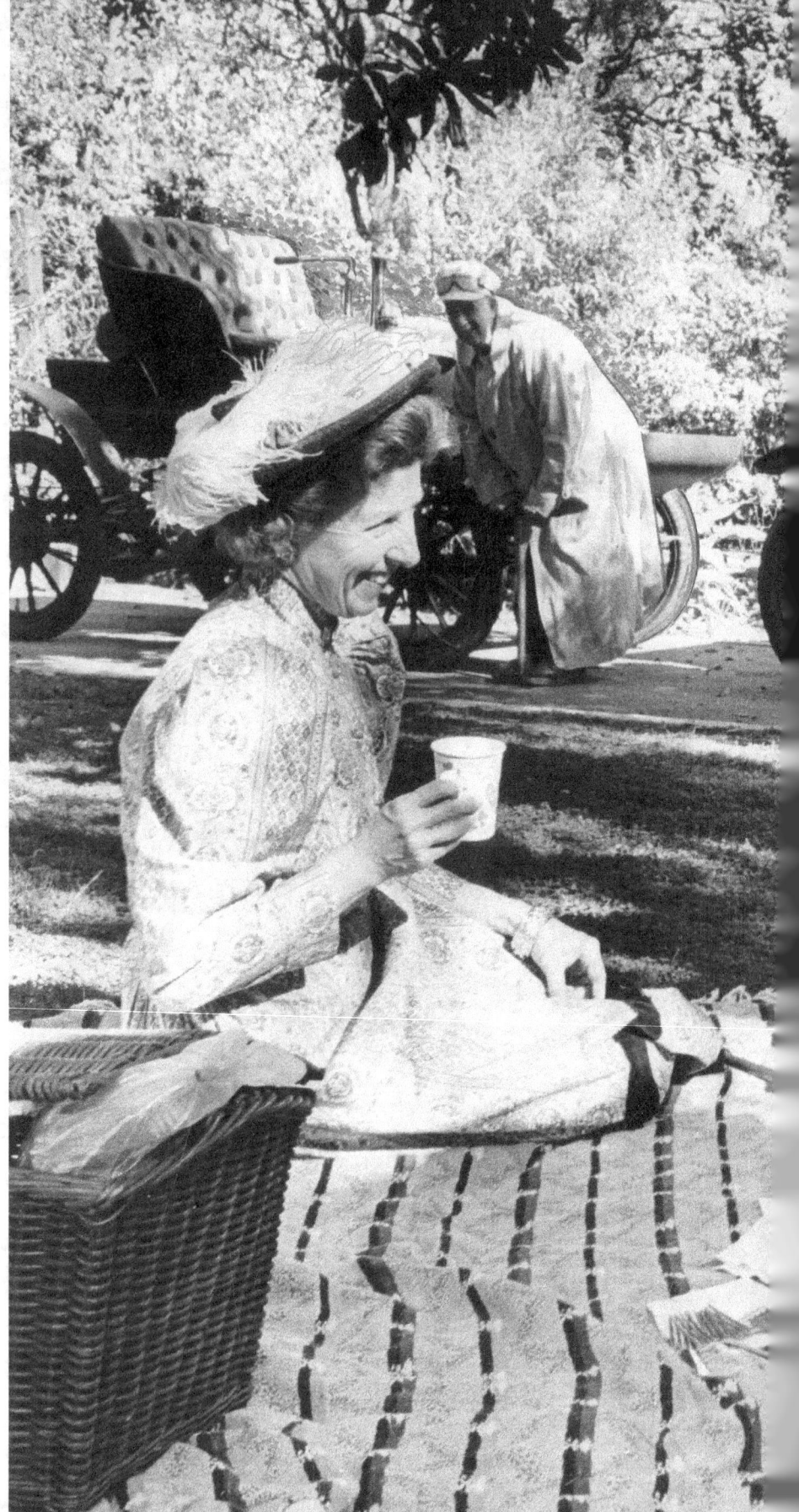

"At the Horseless Carriage Club picnic for antique car aficionados, John Carra stands by his Pierce Arrow while (from left) Mrs. Robert F. Ball, Juda Ball and Mr. Ball prepare for lunch." February 12, 1962. (Jeff Goldwater)

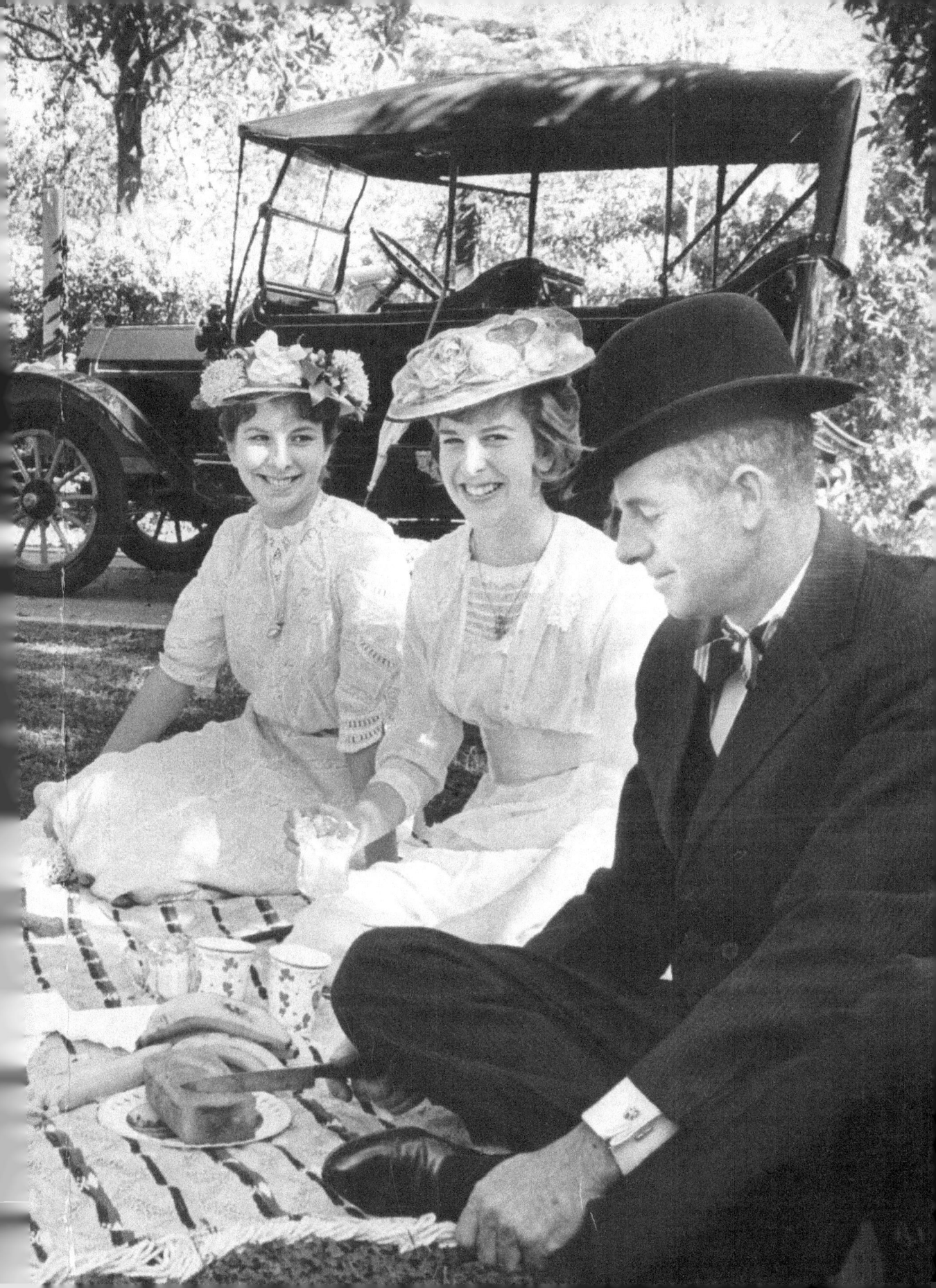

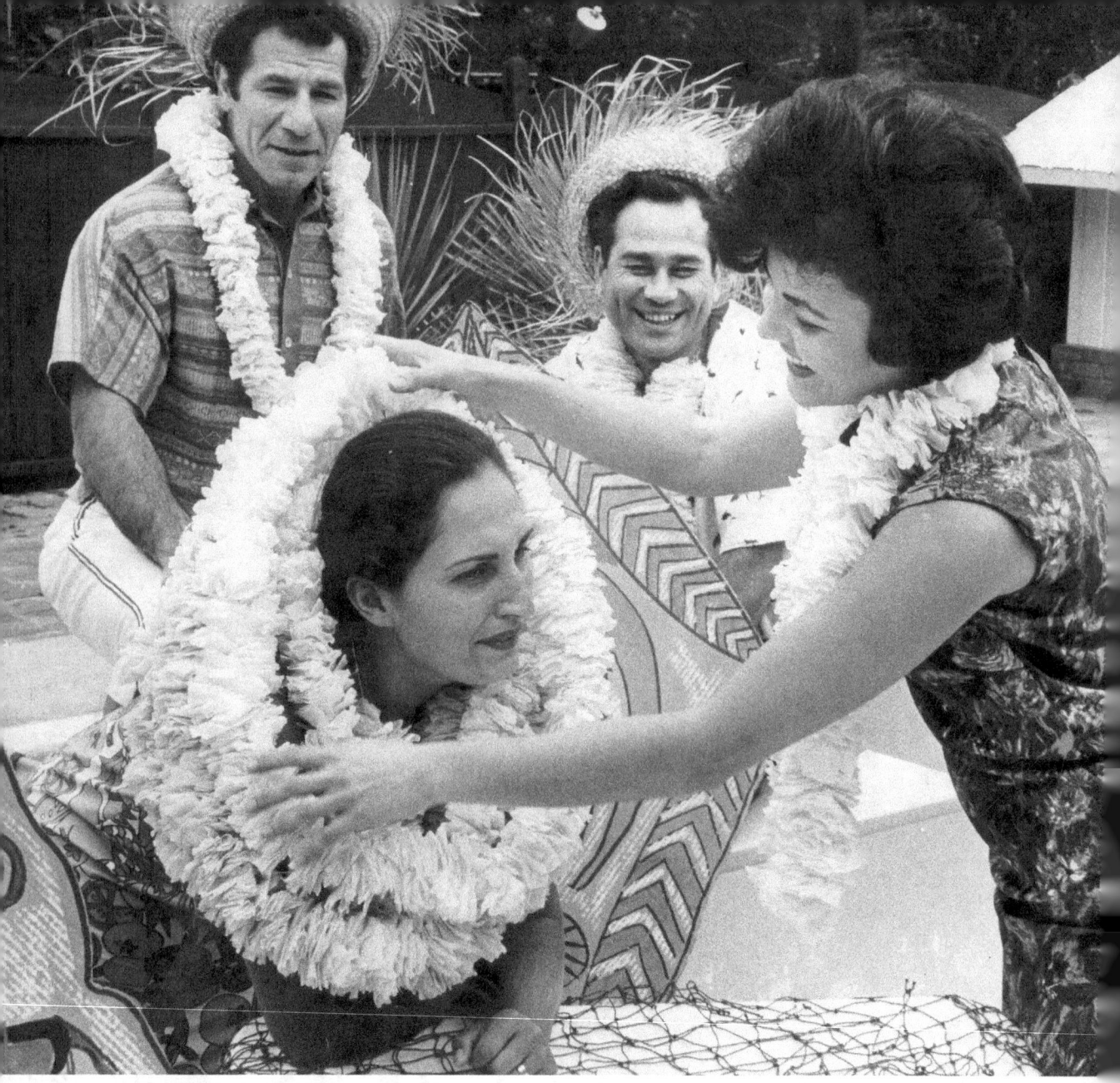

"More than 300 persons will attend a Hawaiian luau sponsored by the newly organized Mr. and Mrs. Society of St. Peter Armenian Apostolic Church, Van Nuys, on July 11. Planning the affair are (from left), Mr. and Mrs. Buck Kartalain, and Mr. and Mrs. Levon Chaloukain. Funds from the social affair will be used to construct a new church." June 27, 1964. (George Brich)

Opposite: "Four members of Hilltoppers of Assistance League paint and shine giant hourglass in preparation for second annual Hourglass Award Tea Jan. 29 at Sportsmen's Lodge. Chairmen working on project are (from left), Mmes. Wallace F. McDonald, organizational contacts; Claude Coats, reservations; Ralph Head, fashion show coordinator, and John Christ, in charge of properties." January 7, 1957.

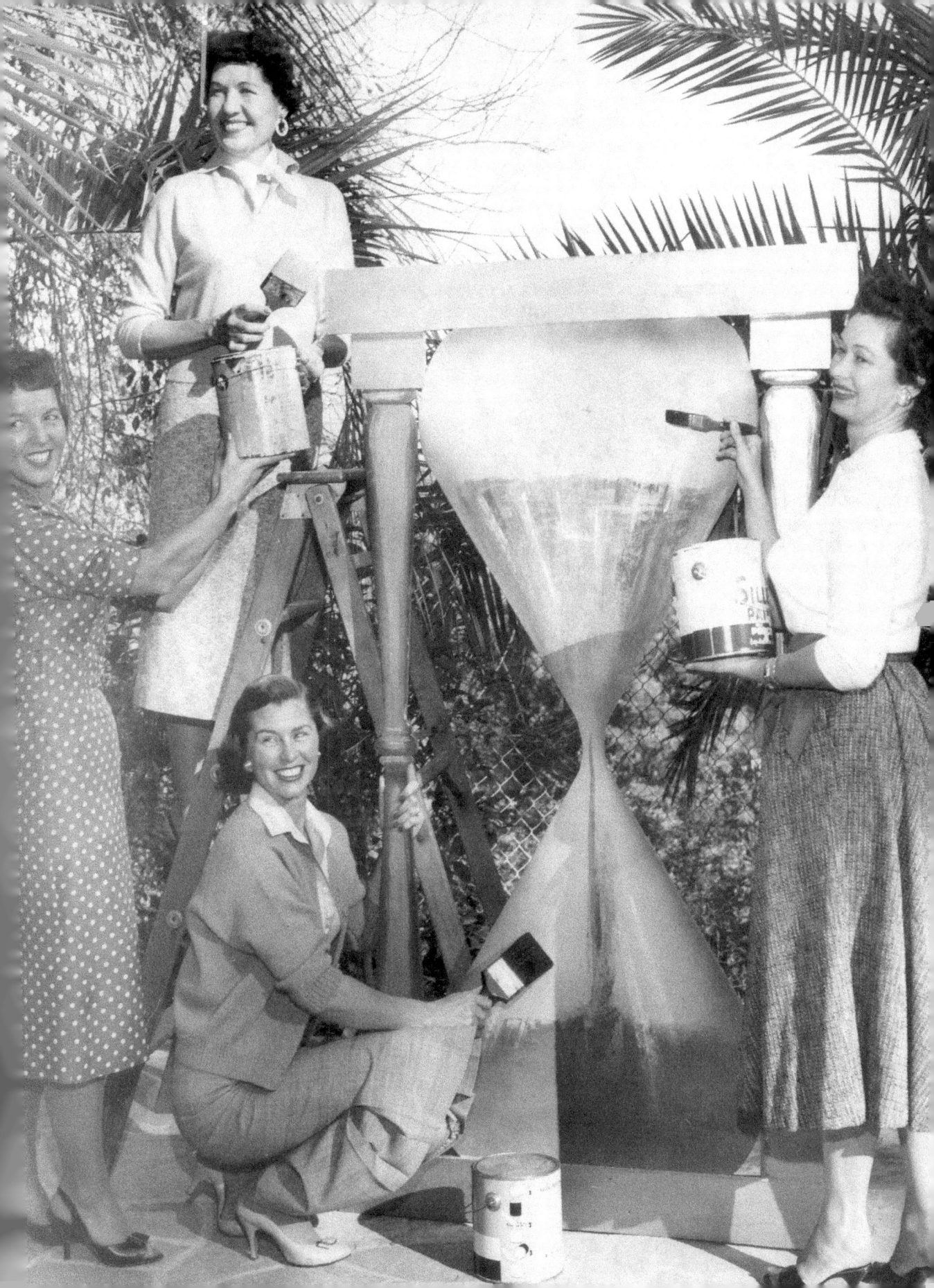

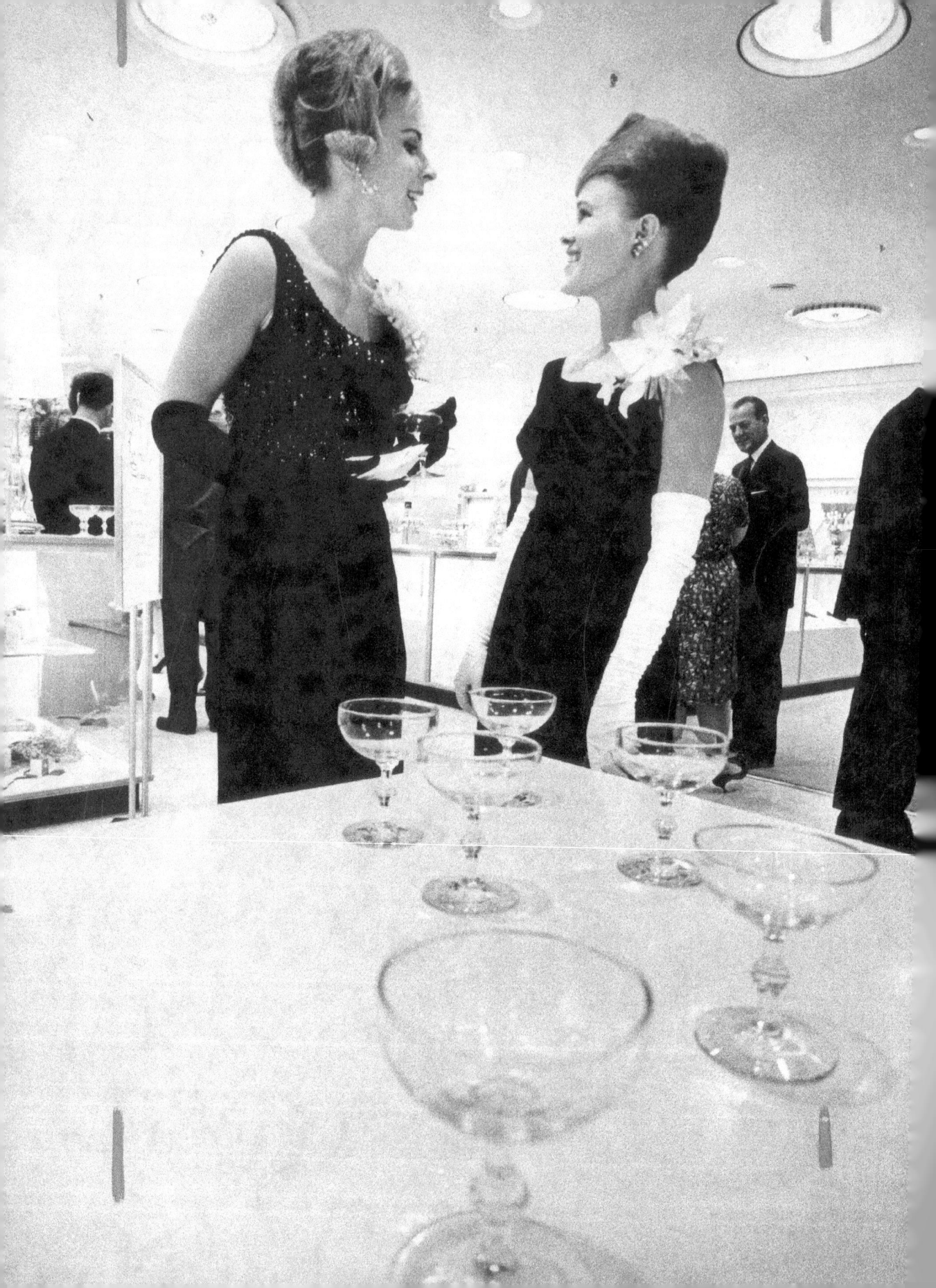

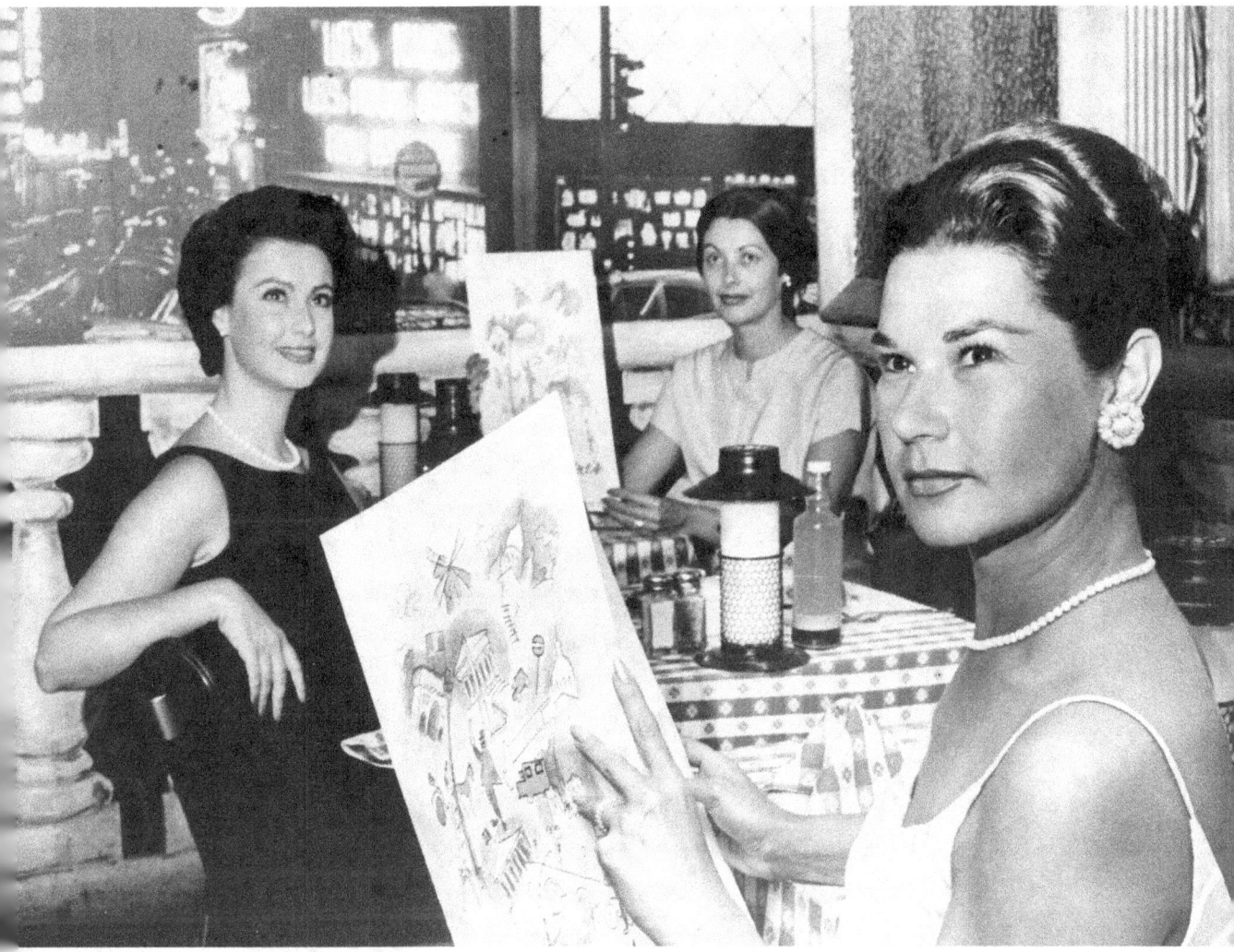

"Street cafe in Paris will be one of novelties in decorations at Assistance League-sponsored premiere of California International Automobile Show at Pan Pacific Auditorium. Valley women (from left), Mmes. Truman Van Dyke, North Hollywood; Robert F. Anderson, North Hollywood, and William M. Pollack, Sherman Oaks, go over plans at Robaire's French Restaurant, 13849 Ventura Boulevard in Sherman Oaks." August 29, 1961. (Jon Woods)

Opposite: "A gourmet back-to-school fashion show highlighted the teen extravaganza at the Fountain of Youth Benefit christening of the new Broadway Topanga Plaza. Assisting with arrangements (photo at left) are Mrs. Roy Lovejoy, membership chairman of the Canoga Park Junior Women's Club, sponsors of the event, and Mrs. Herbert Saxton, president." August 27, 1964. (George Brich)

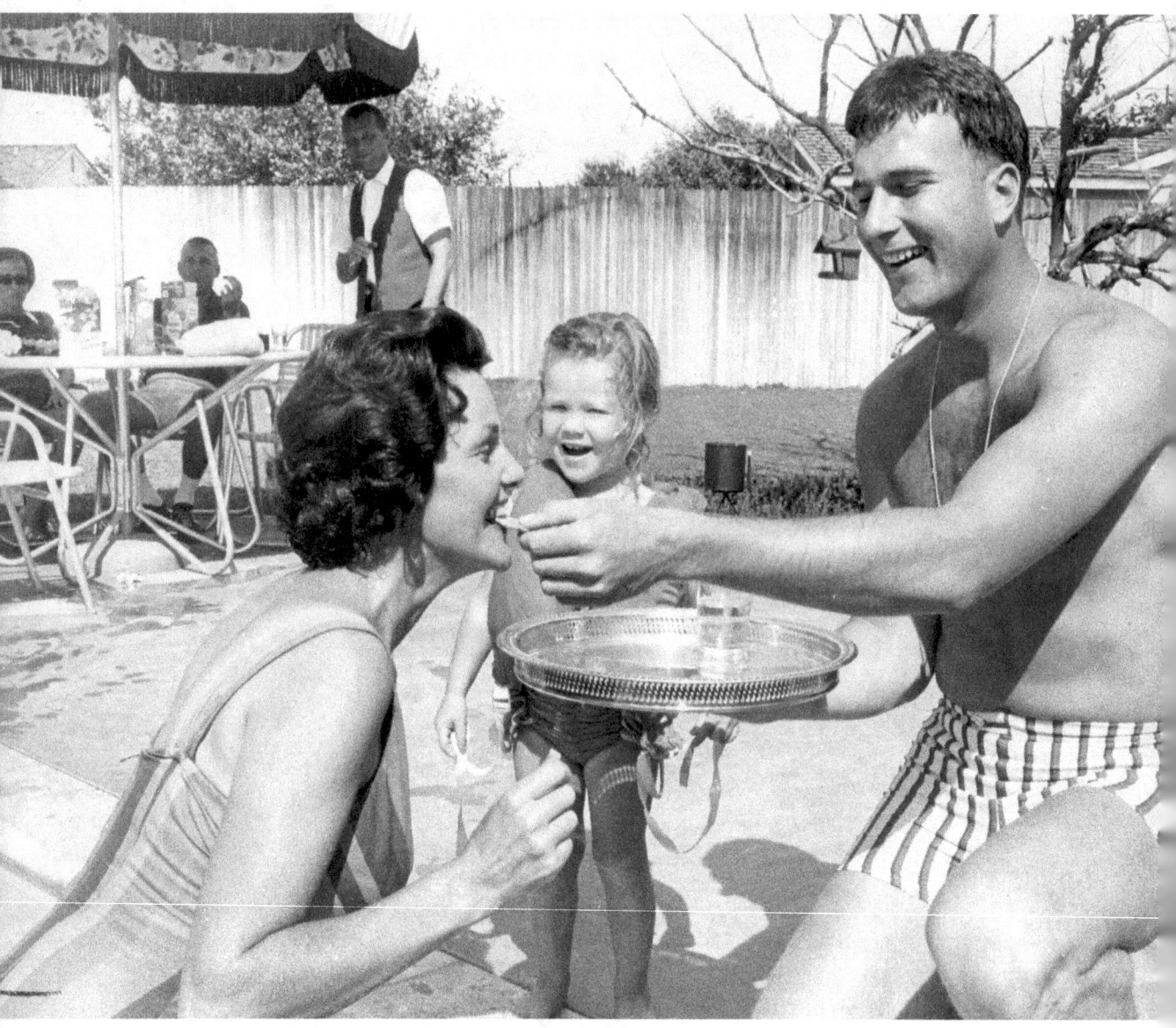

"At the Northridge home of the John Warrens, wives of members of the Matador Booster Club gave a Champagne swim party for the purpose of introducing prospective members of the club. Quarterback Max Choboian serves snack to Mrs. John Warren as her daughter, Jane, 2¹/₂, looks on." August 6, 1963. (Bob Martin)

Opposite: "North Hollywood Opti-Mrs. Club members are having a great time as they prepare decorations for 'Fiesta al Fresco Carnival.' From left are Mmes. Branson S. Hand Jr., Northridge, the hostess; Robert Wilcomb, North Hollywood, ways and means chairman, and Clayton E. Preston, North Hollywood, food preparation chairman." July 4, 1964. (George Brich)

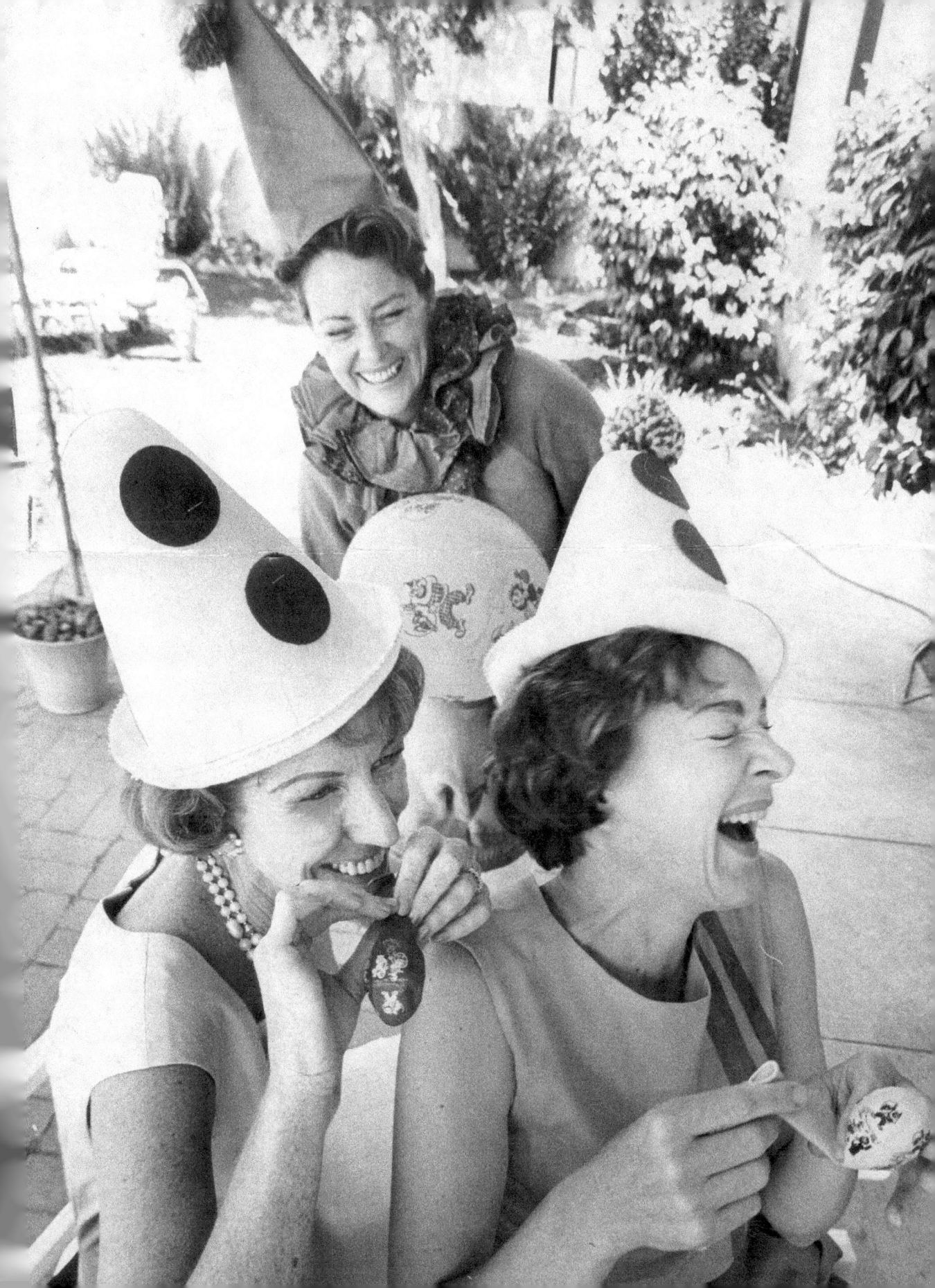

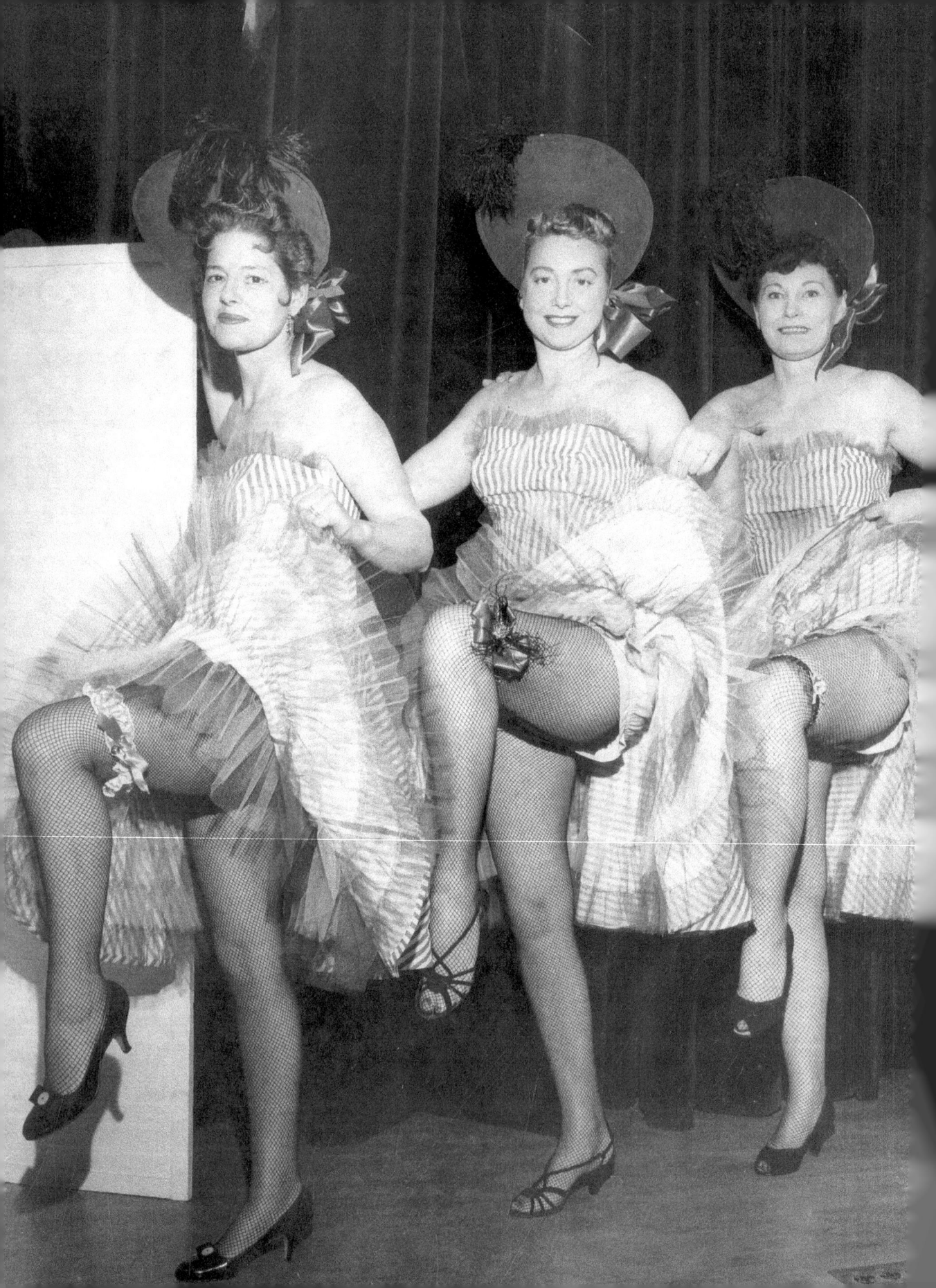

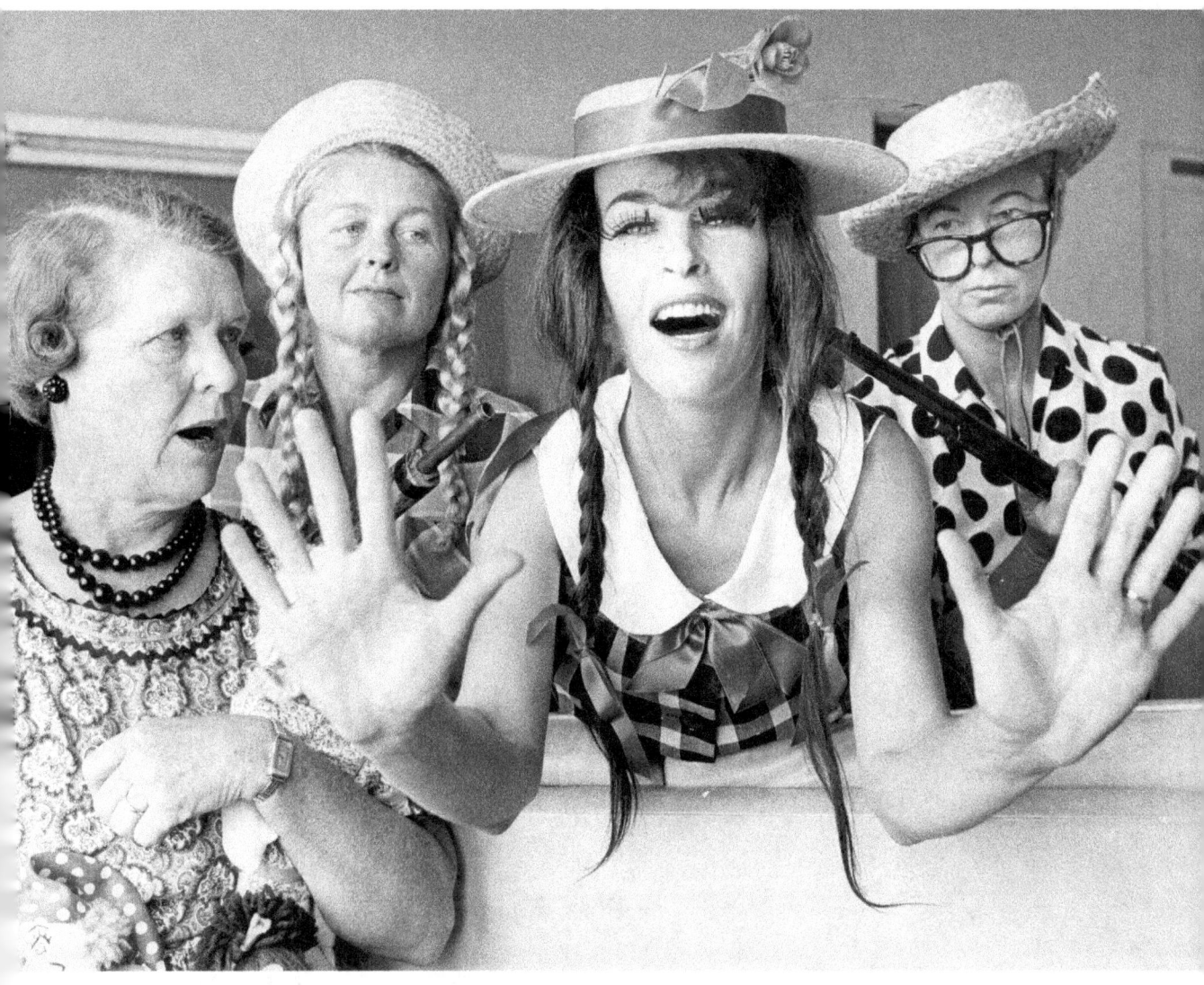

"Burbank Emblem Club members dress in their 'hillbilly' costumes for their Home Town Jamboree to be held Saturday at the Elks Club. From left are Mmes. Alfred Jones, Henry Koester, Robert Bennett and Harry Jandt." August 23, 1963. (Larry Leach)

Opposite: "Members of North Hollywood chapter, Order of Eastern Star, rehearse entertainment they will stage at cancer benefit dinner April 12 at North Hollywood Masonic Temple, 5122 Tujunga Ave. From left are Mmes. Bette Le Franche, Harriet Mansfield and Helen Hollebeke. Mrs. Mansfield is directing entertainment." April 8, 1958.

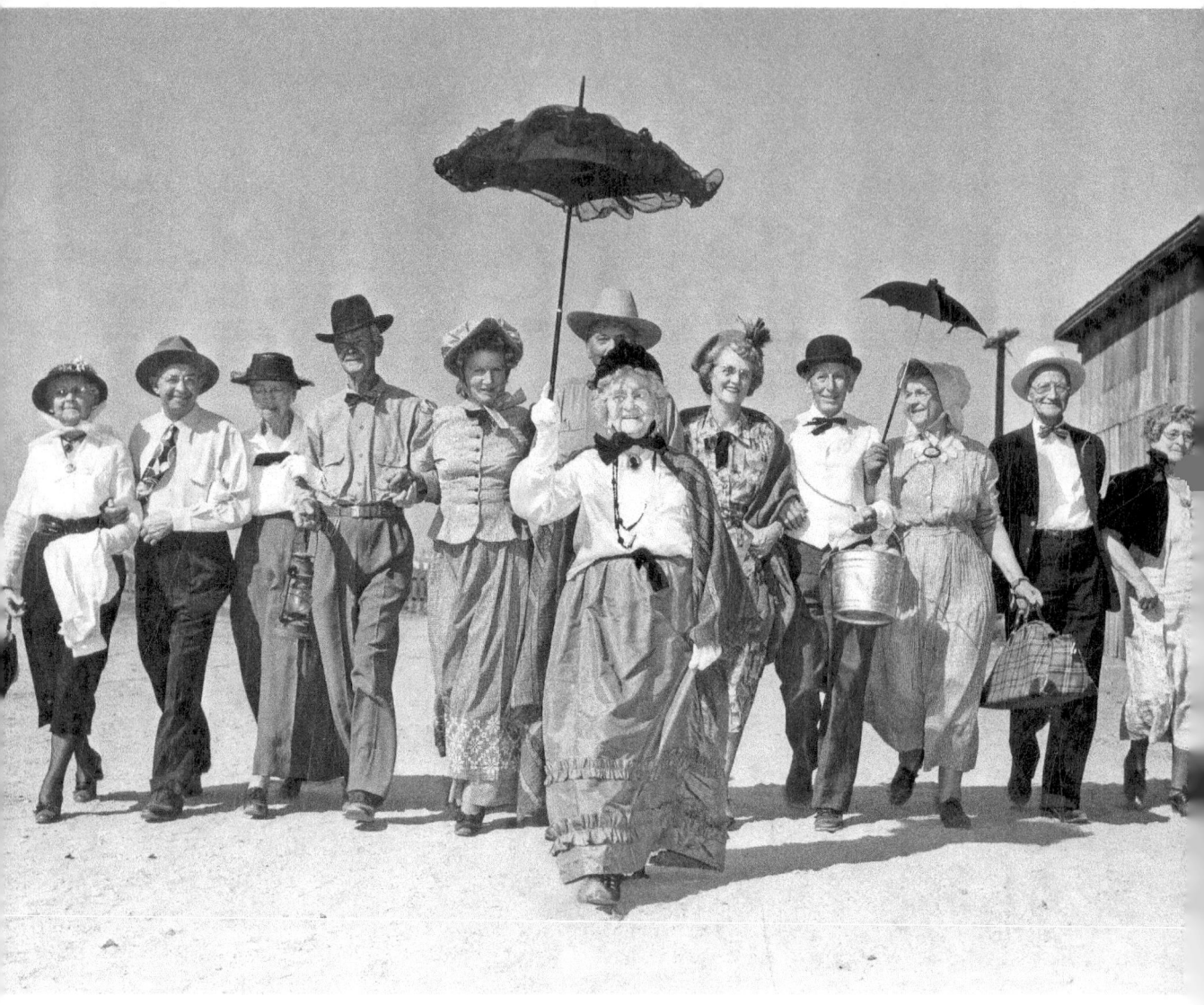

"In marching formation displaying costumes they will wear at Pioneer Picnic in North Hollywood, and led by parasol wielding Mrs. Bessie Westerfield are (left to right) Emma Prince, Oscar Nobles, Lynn Wilcox, I E. Ijams, Frances Muir Pomeroy, Fred Weddington, Ivy Nobles, Alfred Prince, Clara Wilcox, Charles Osborne, Susie Osborne." The picnic is held at the North Hollywood recreation Center and is a celebration for early Valley settlers. Mistress of ceremonies is Frances Muir Pomeroy, of the San Fernando Valley Historical Society. October 18, 1948.

Opposite: "The annual Mardi Gras benefit event at the Encino Community Center, hosted by the Toluca Guild Juniors of Childrens Hospital. Sampling food from buffet table at are Mr. and Mrs. Dennis Morrow, Encino." May 11, 1964. (Bob Martin)

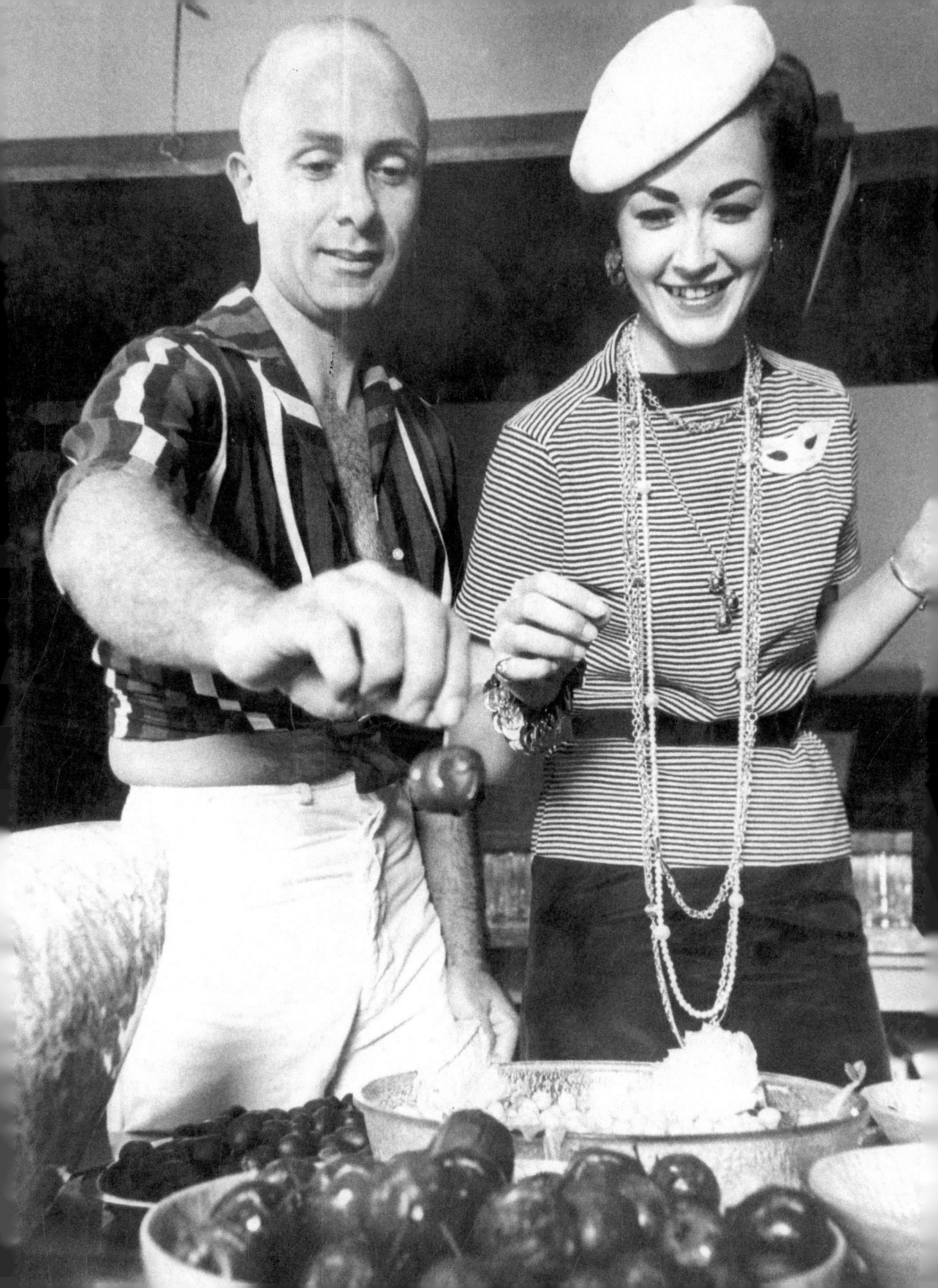

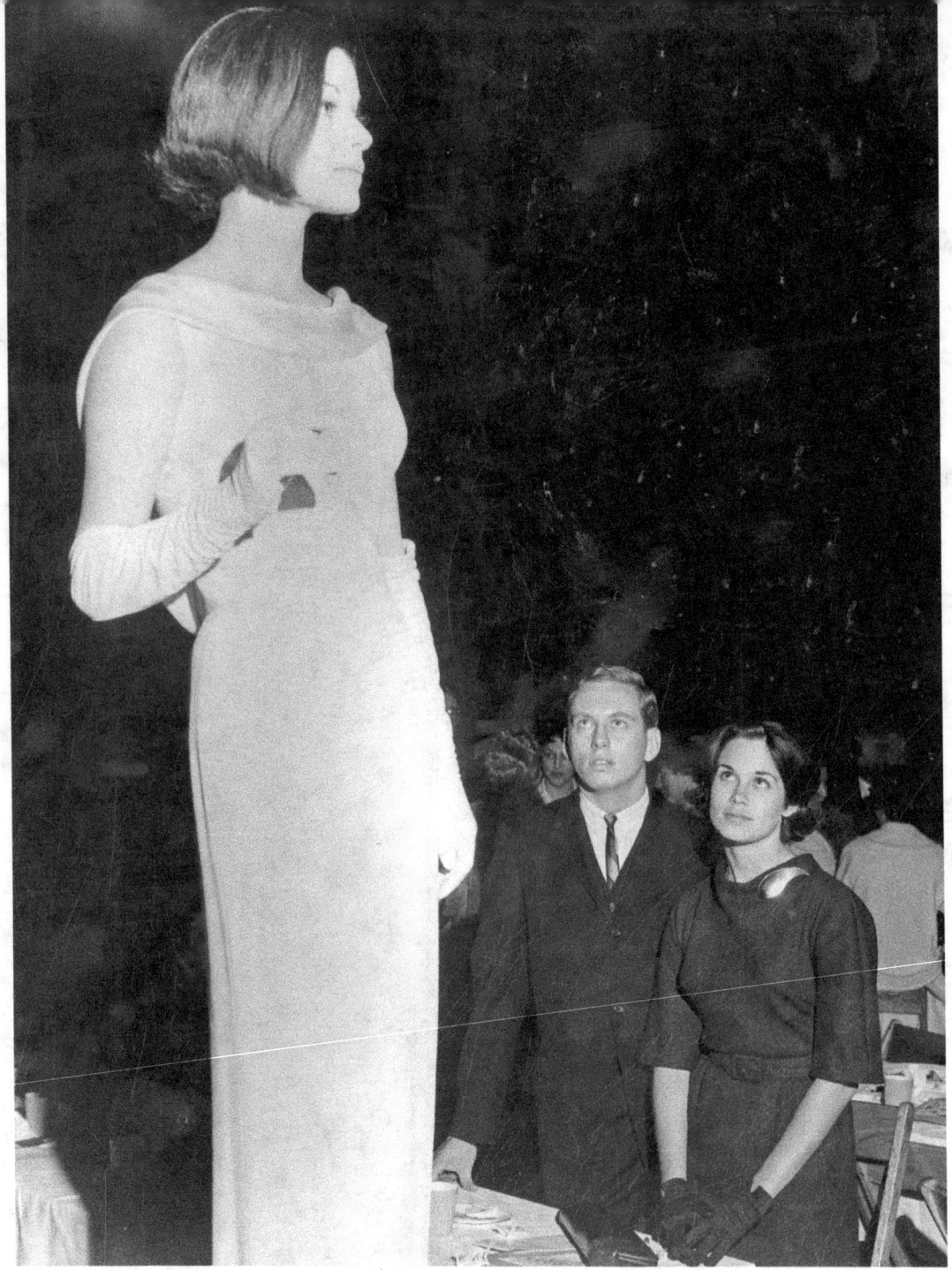

"At the Encino estate of the George Gobels, members and guests of the Cadenzas, Women's Auxiliary of the San Fernando Valley Symphony Association, gathered for their third annual Starlight Buffet and Fashion Show. Fashions were presented by Broadway, Valley, on a specially constructed revolving stage. Gloria Comacho models as Kent Evans and Barbara Ross admire the gown." September 12, 1961. (Bob Martin)

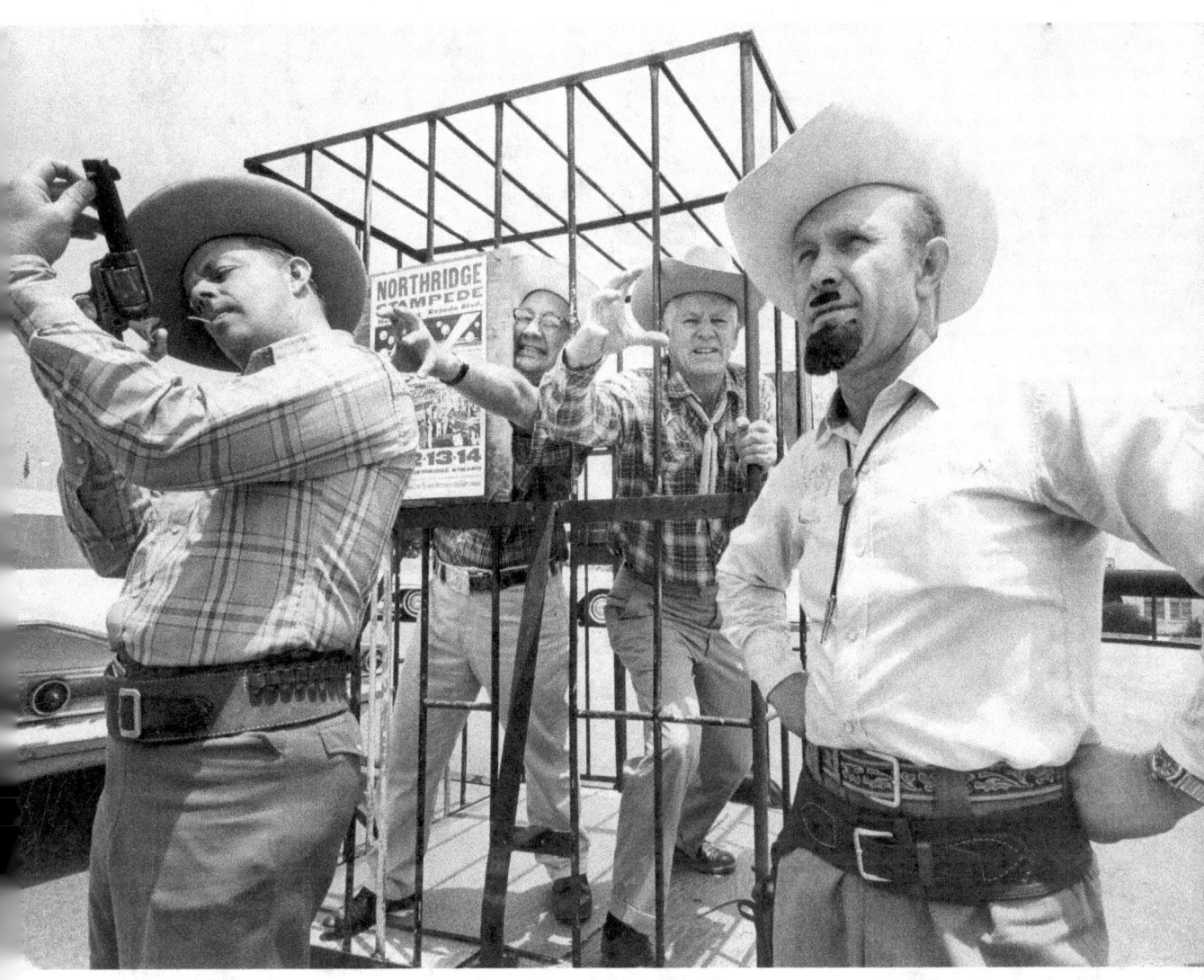

Northridge Kiwanis Club members promote the Northridge Stampede barbecue and carnival at benefit Nordoff Street and Reseda Blvd by enforcing the beard growing tradition. "Byron Mabon, left, general chairman, checks his six-shooter while prisoners, from left, Bernard Piotrowski and George Gilmore, express their disapproval. Herb Wohland (right), the only man with a beard, reportedly warned Mabon that he'd better get his beard growing or he would end up behind bars also." June 10, 1964. (Gordon Dean)

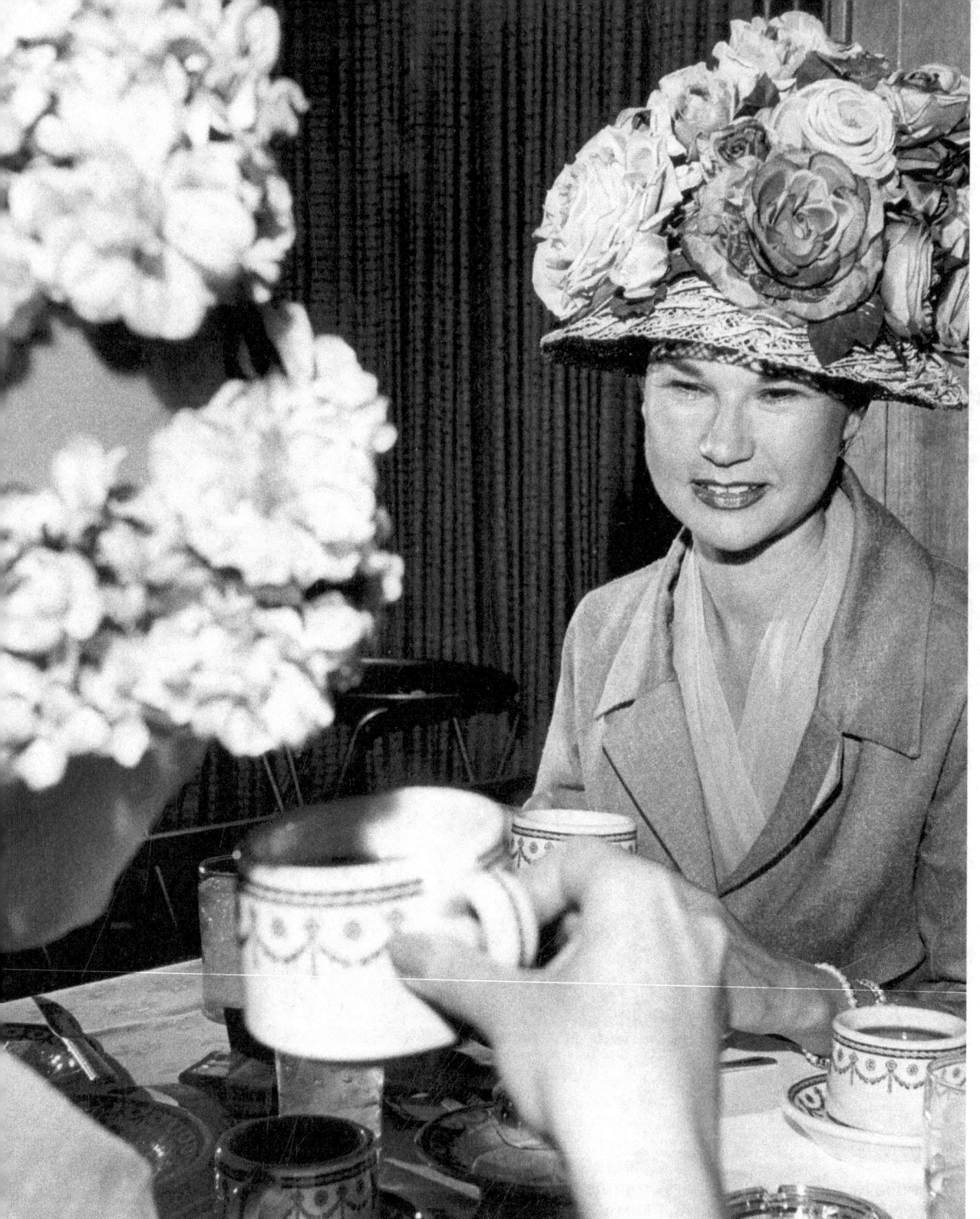

"Mrs. William Pollack wears a spring hat at the Valley Panhellenic Association's 'Emerald Elegance' fashion-luncheon benefit at Sportsmen's Lodge. Funds from the event will be used for scholarships for Valley high school girls." April 3, 1961. (George Brich)

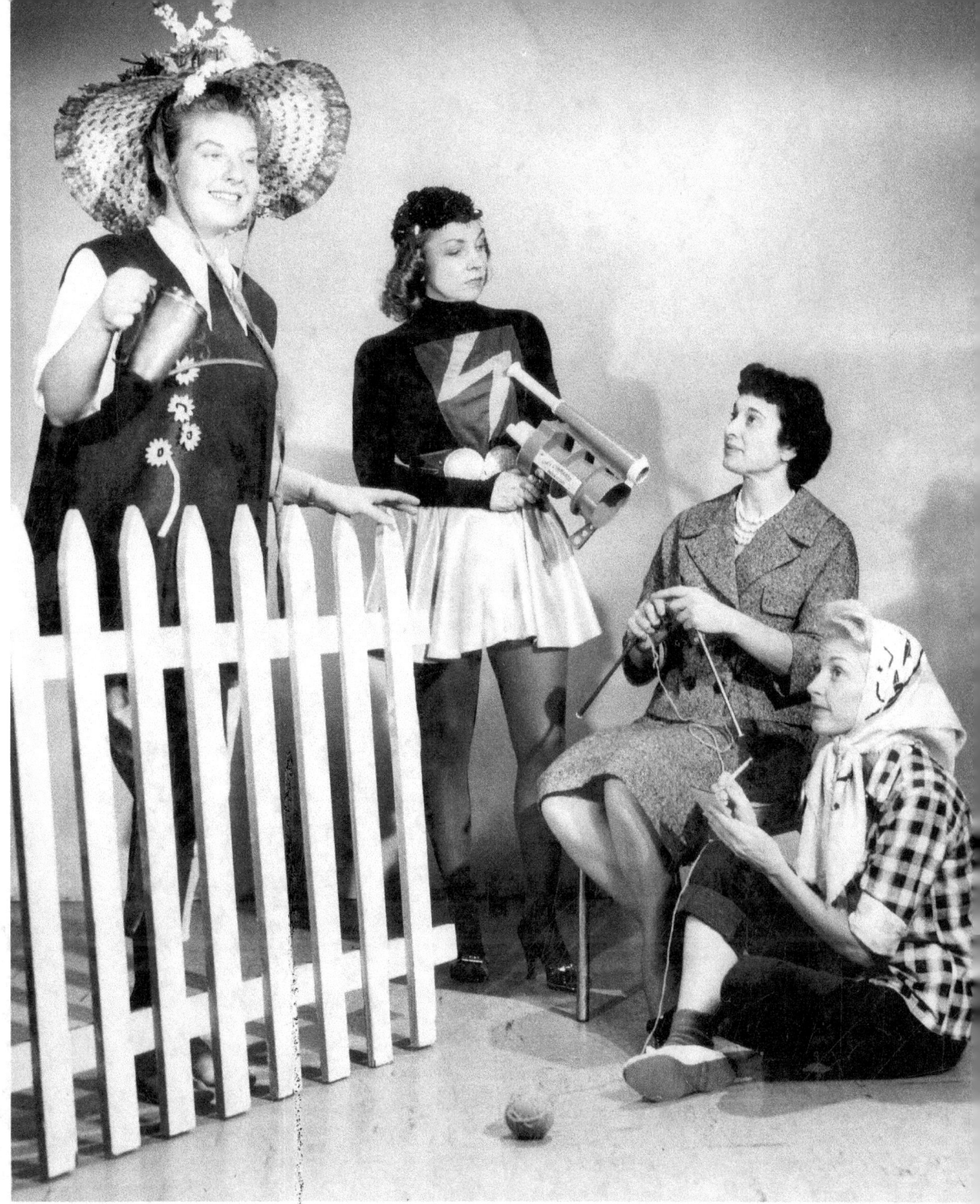

"Unfriendly 'visitor' from Mars gives peaceful earth wives bad time in scene from Encino PTA benefit play to be staged Thursday and Friday. From left are Mmes. Roger Kirkpatrick, Jack Werner, Barton Pohl and Richard Irving." March 16, 1958. (William H. Wilde)

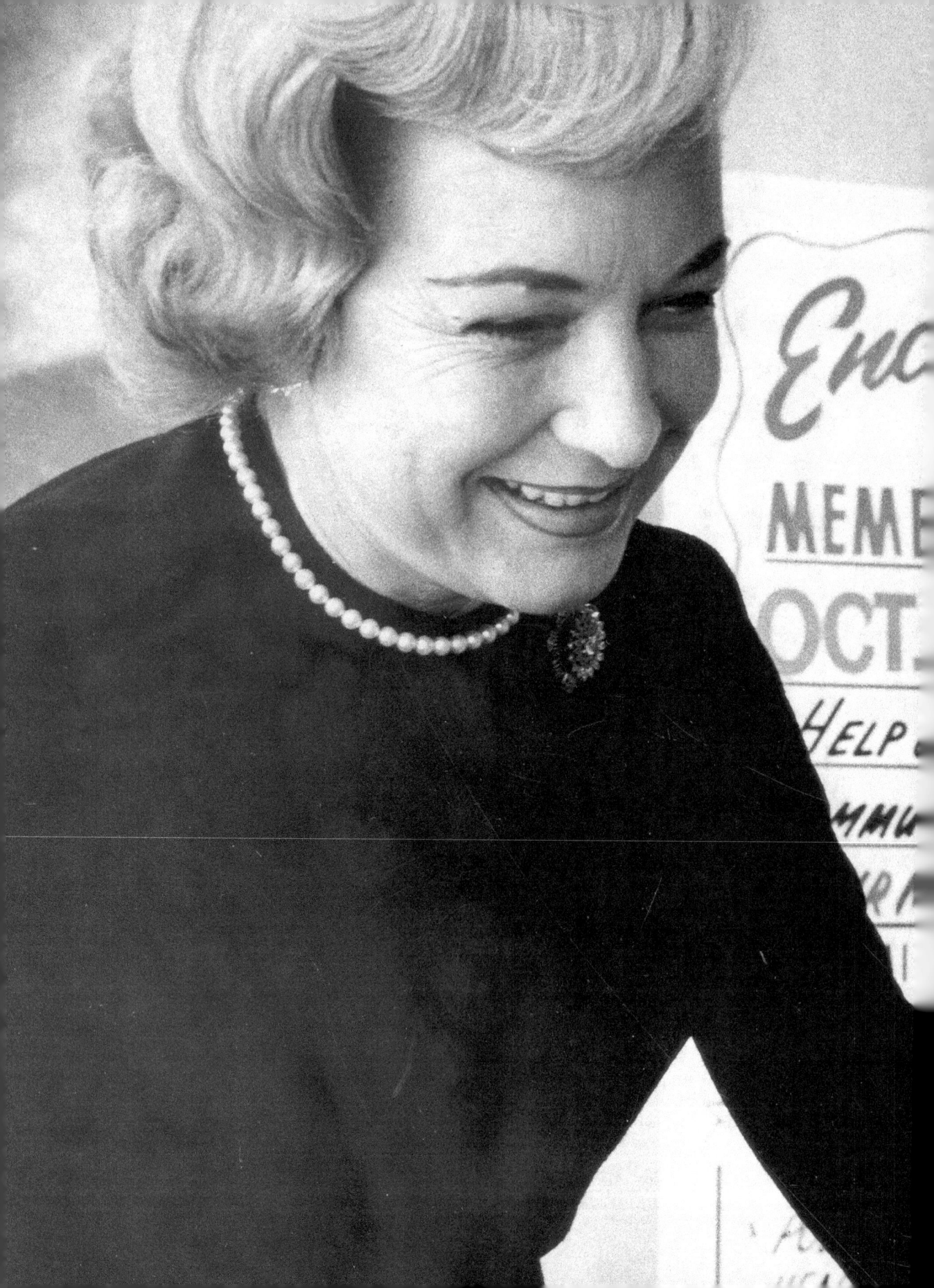

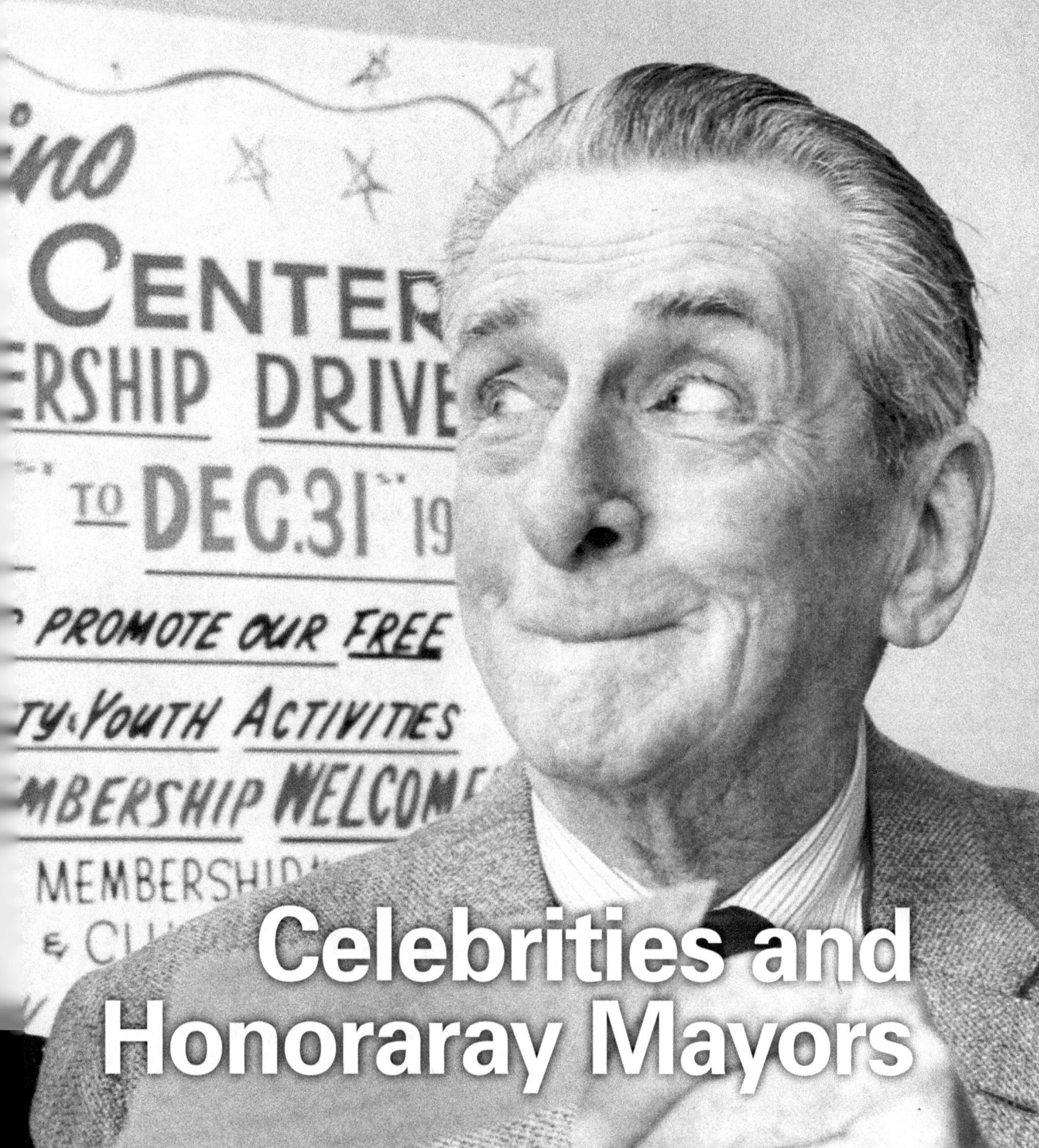

Celebrities and
Honoraray Mayors

Overleaf: "Actor Edward Everett Horton, honorary governor of the San Fernando Valley and long-time Encino resident, renews his membership in the Encino Community Center. Mrs. Eugene Gelson, a member of the center's membership committee, assists Horton with his registration. The center, 4935 Balboa Boulevard, is a non-profit corporation for youth and recreation purposes." December 5, 1961. (George Brich)

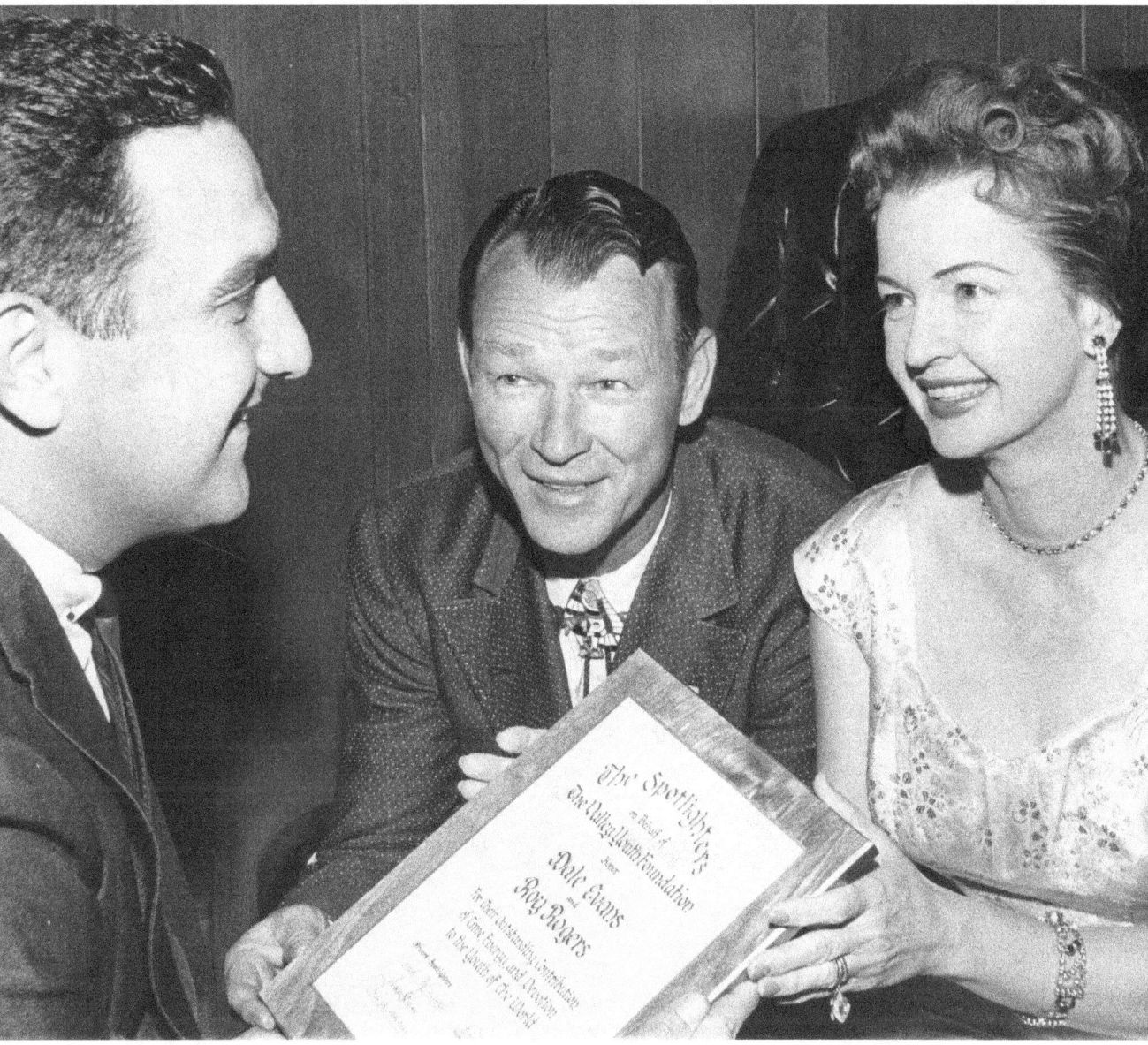

"The Spotlighters, on behalf of the Valley Youth Foundation, honored Dale Evans and Roy Rogers, honorary mayor of Chatsworth, for their outstanding contribution of time, energy and devotion to the youth of the world." October 6, 1960. (Jon Woods)

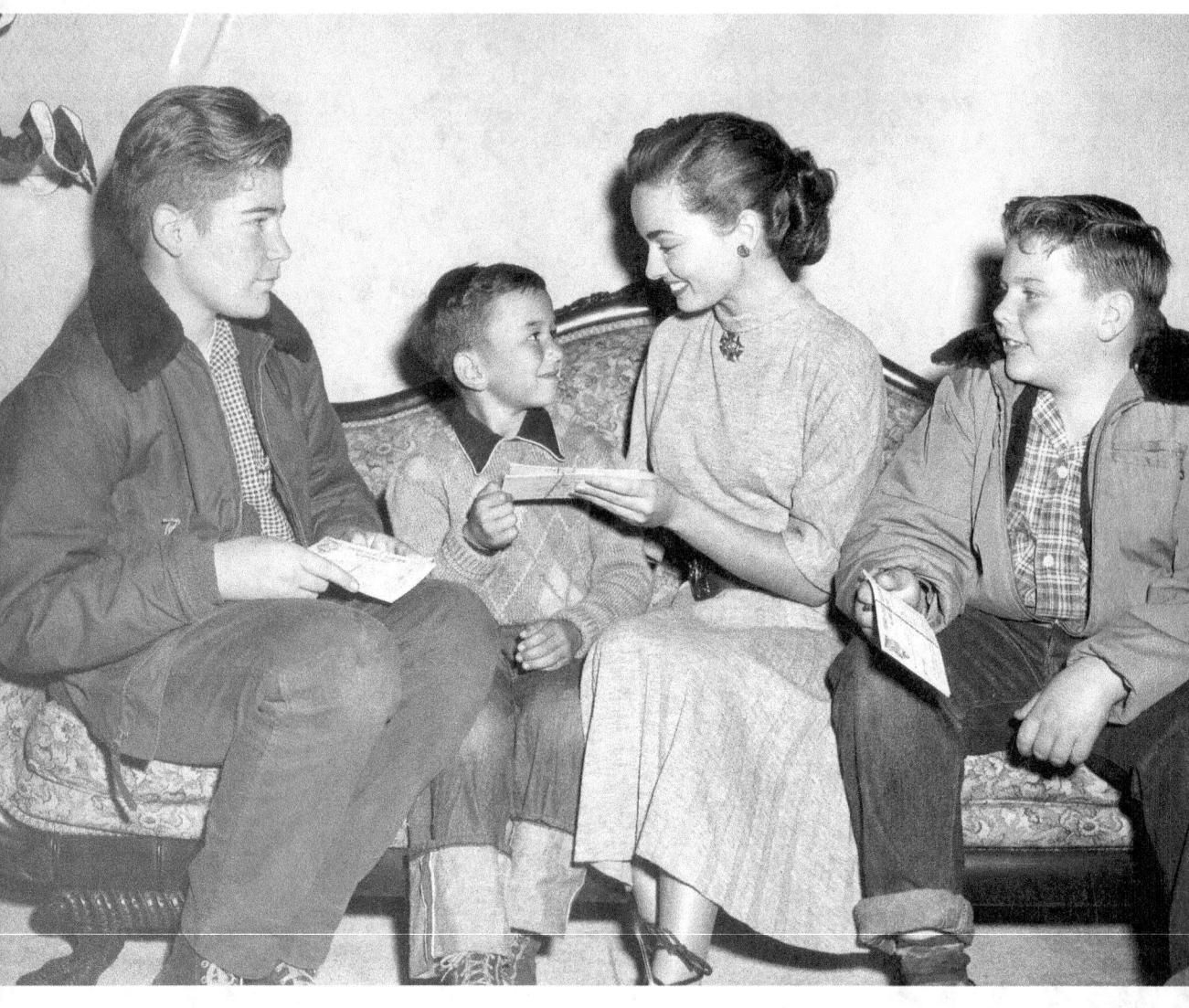

"Star Ann Blyth of Toluca Lake promises (left to right) David Kupp, Edward Mirsky and Dick Dillman she will make personal appearance in boys' Biosphere Explorer's Club show Saturday night at John Burroughs High School. Show will raise money for truck for club." December 12, 1949.

Opposite: "Liberace is shown with Miss Mildred Darby (left) and Mrs. Donald Huish, as they get in tune for Sherman Oaks Woman's Club's May 24 luncheon and fashioncade at the George Liberaces." Liberace served two terms the honorary mayor of Sherman Oaks. May 1956. (Dave Siddon)

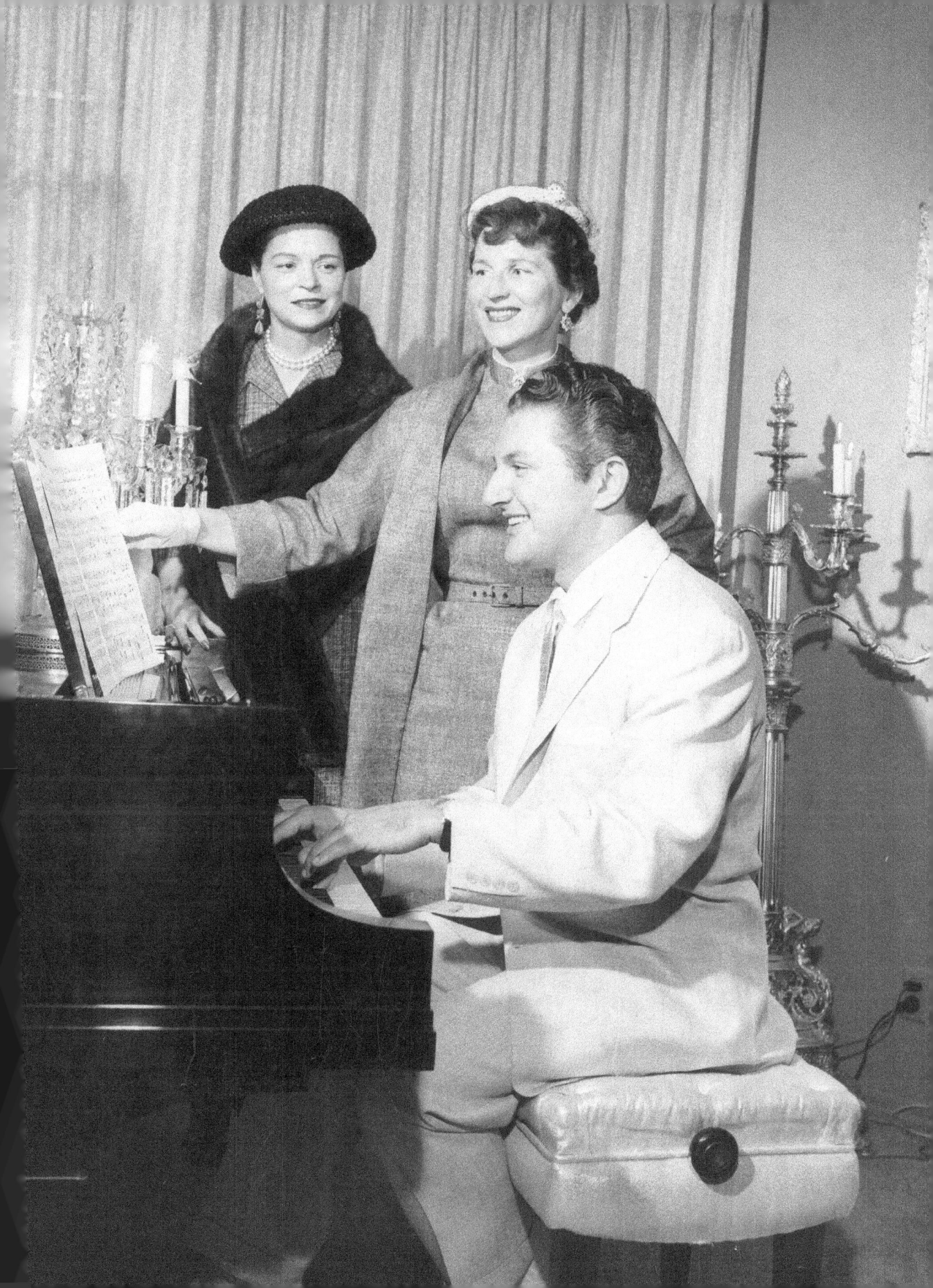

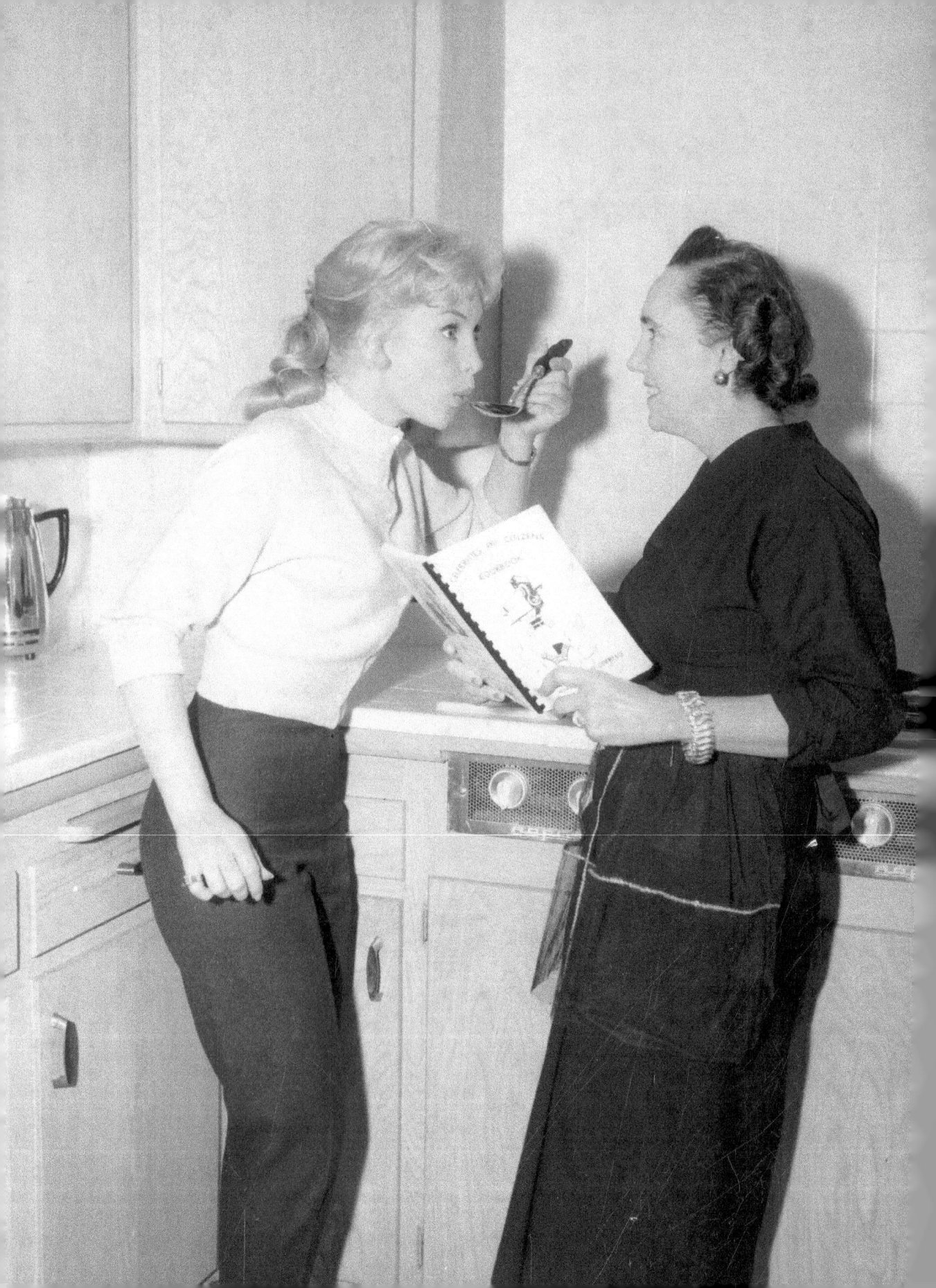

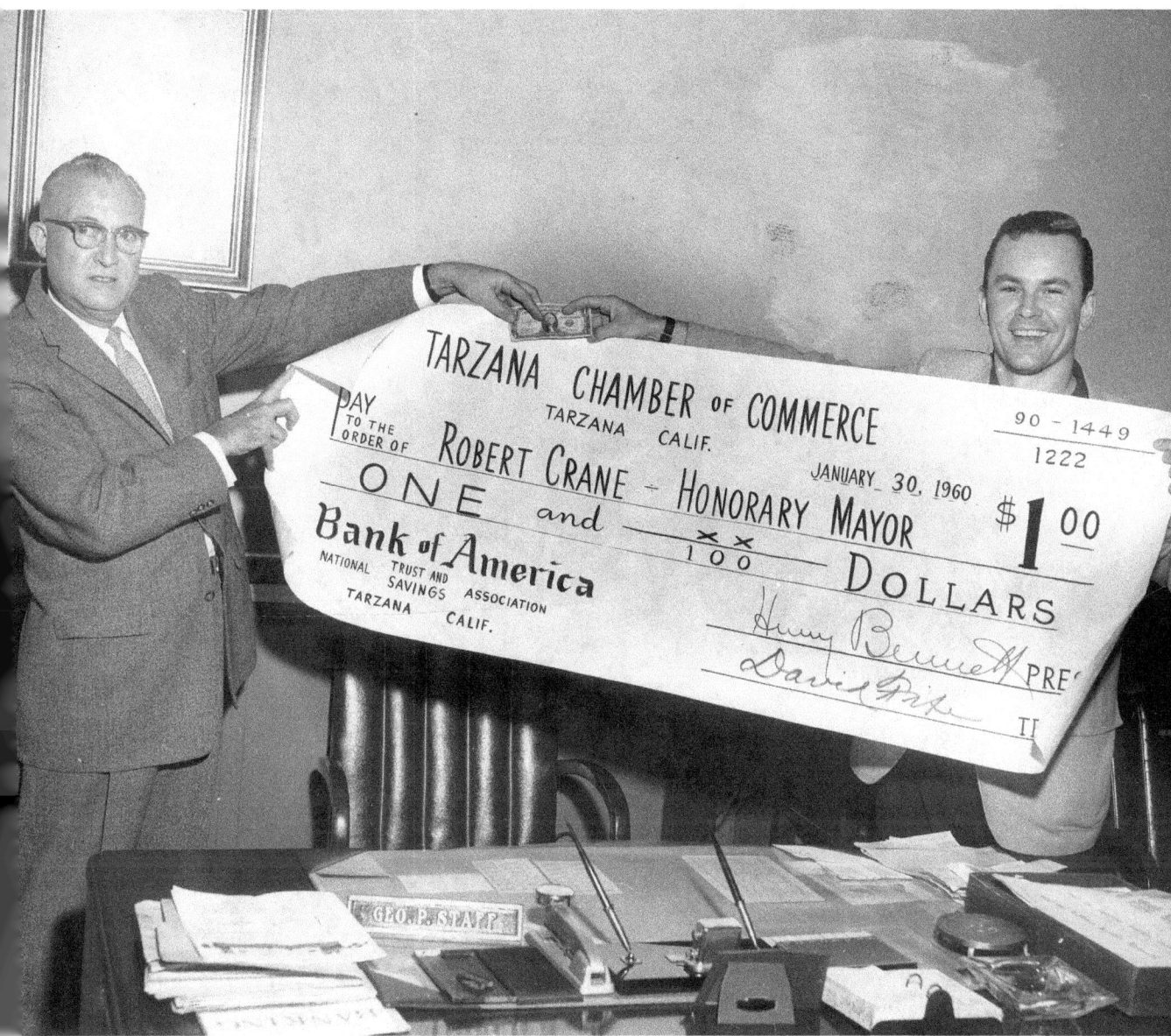

"Bob Crane dollar-a-year second term honorary mayor of Tarzana, cashes check from Chamber of Commerce, Bank of America branch next door to KNX studios where he is a radio station morning host." February 12, 1960.

Opposite: "Sherman Oaks actress Barbara Eden samples spaghetti sauce dreamed up by another film queen, Marilyn Monroe, whose recipe for sauce is included in *Celebrities and Citizens' Cookbook* being made available to public by women's division of Sherman Oaks Chamber of Commerce. Division is headed by Mrs. E. J. Turner (right)." March 23, 1960.

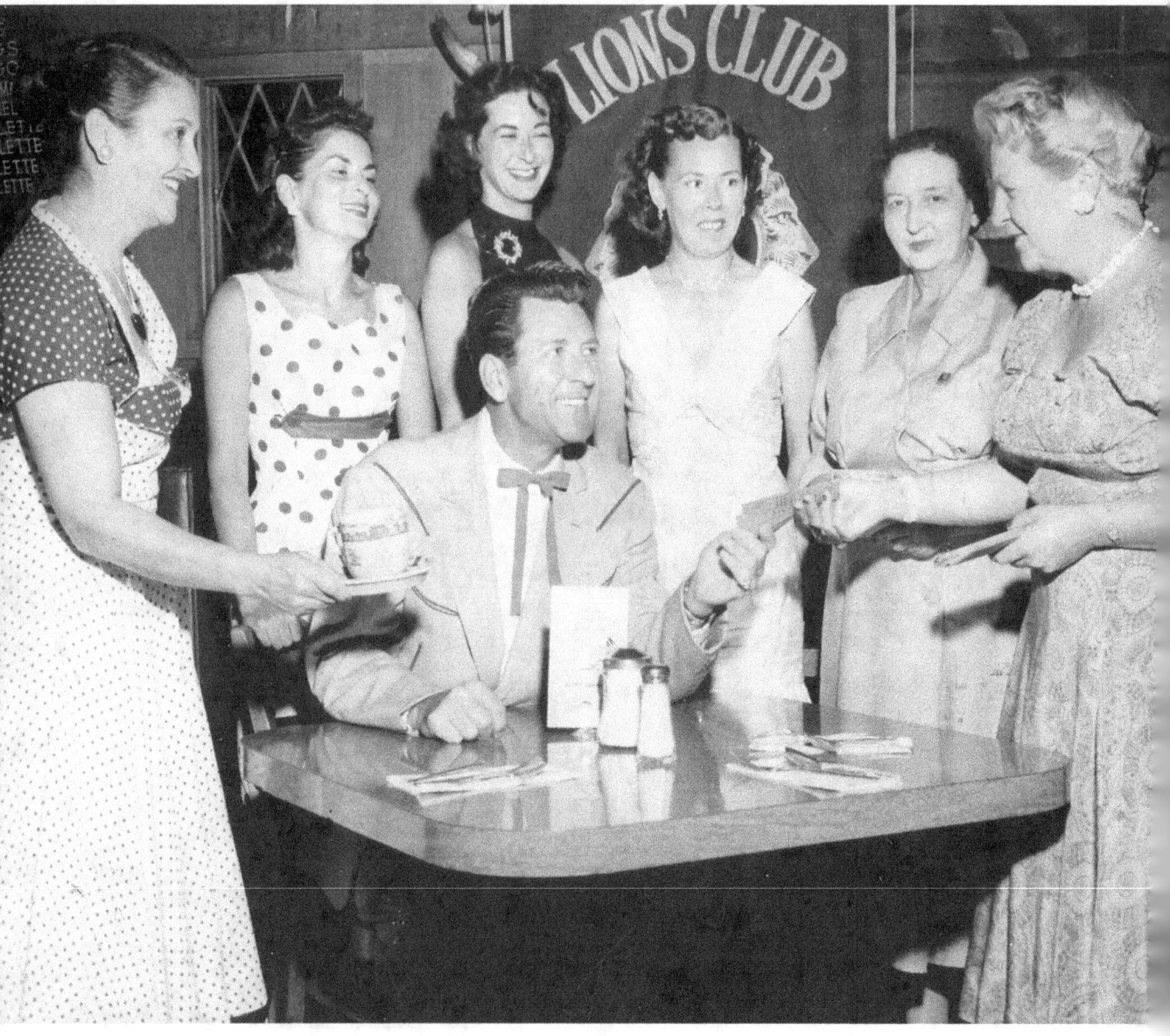

"Doye O'Dell, Western television entertainer, gets tickets for Studio City Lions Club's second annual pancake breakfast from Mrs. D. Arthur Lowe. Others who will be on hand Sunday morning to provide service are (from left) Mmes. Morris Levin, Curtis B. Danning, Dan Le Vantine, Al Snellings and Edward Lunin. Event will be at Bonds Market, 12160 Ventura Blvd." August 23, 1956.

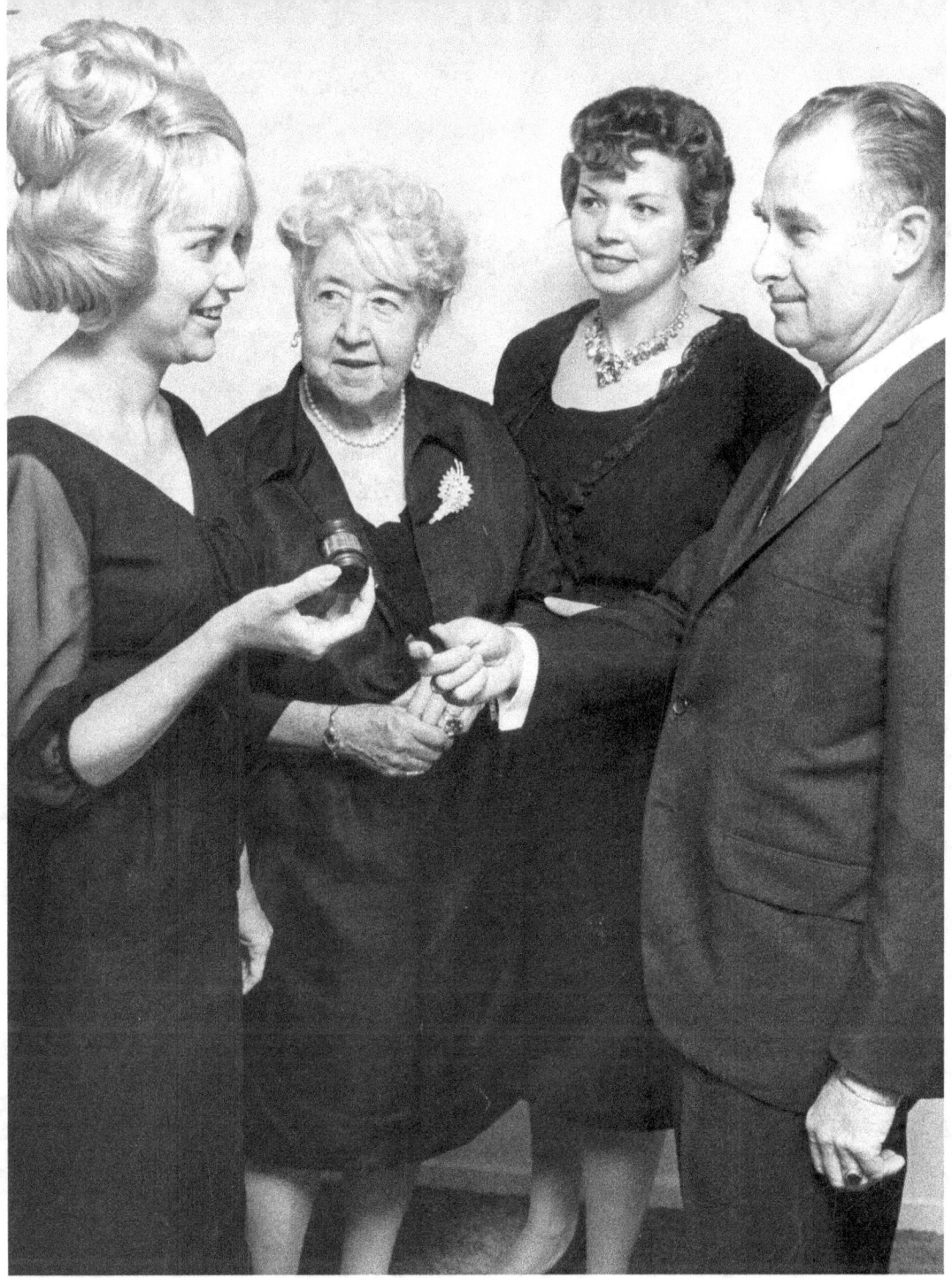

"Mrs. Charles (Shirlene) Alling (left) receives gavel of office as new president of the North Hollywood Jaycettes from Eddie Holohan, North Hollywood Chamber president and installing officer. Offering congratulations are actress Verna Felton (honorary mayor of North Hollywood) and Mrs. Tom (Linda) Church, new Jaycettes vice president. Ceremony was held at Golden State Motor Lodge, Burbank." March 10, 1965. (Bob Martin)

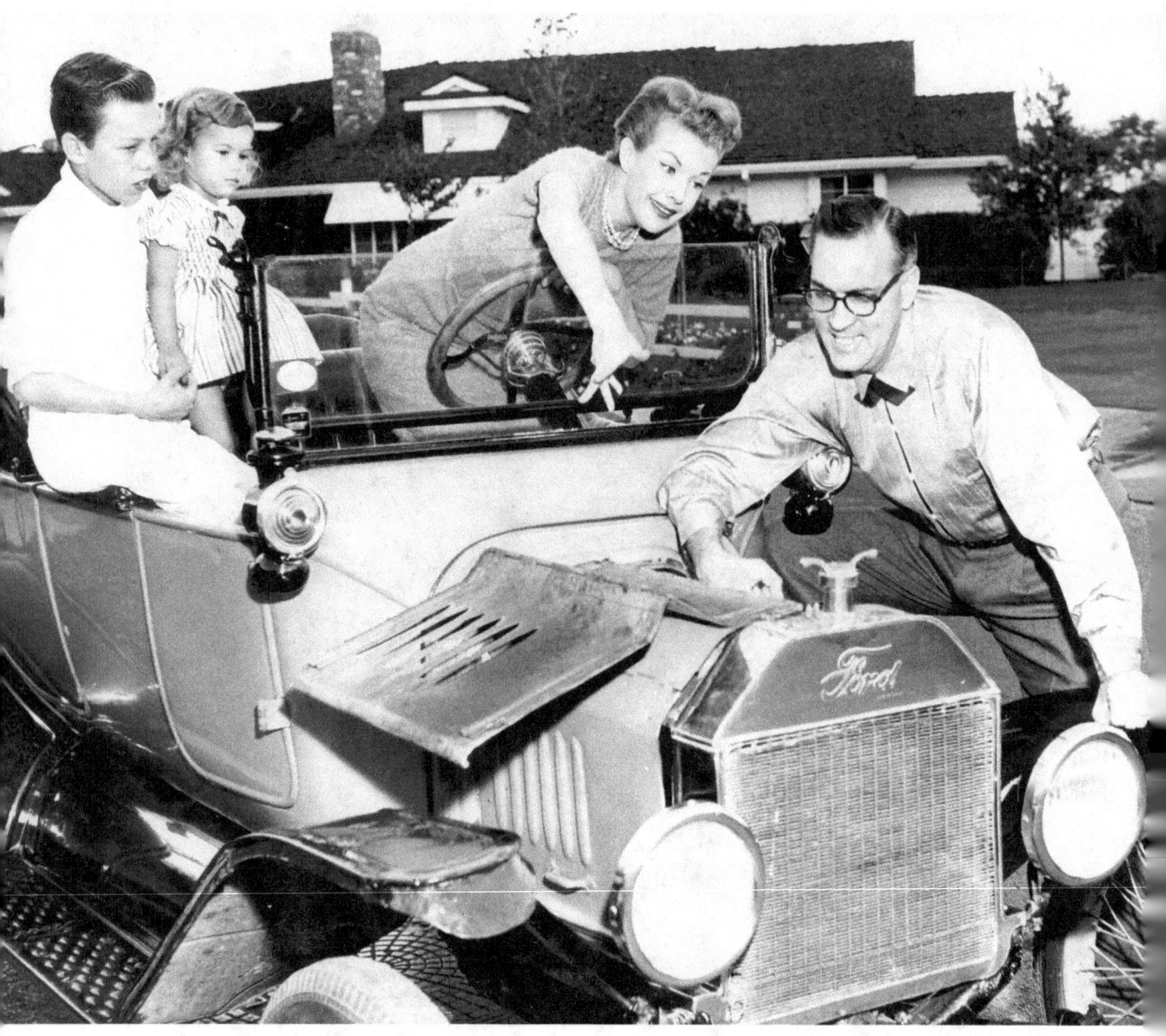

"Gail Storm, television personality, will ride in 1916 auto as Grand Marshal of Bethlehem Star Parade's second division Saturday. In auto to be driven by her husband, Lee Bonnell, president of Sherman Oaks Kiwanis Club, will be Bonnell children, Paul, 11, and Susanna, 2 (seated left), and their brothers, Phillip, 15, and Peter, 13. Horseless carriage is entry of Kiwanis group." December 5, 1958.

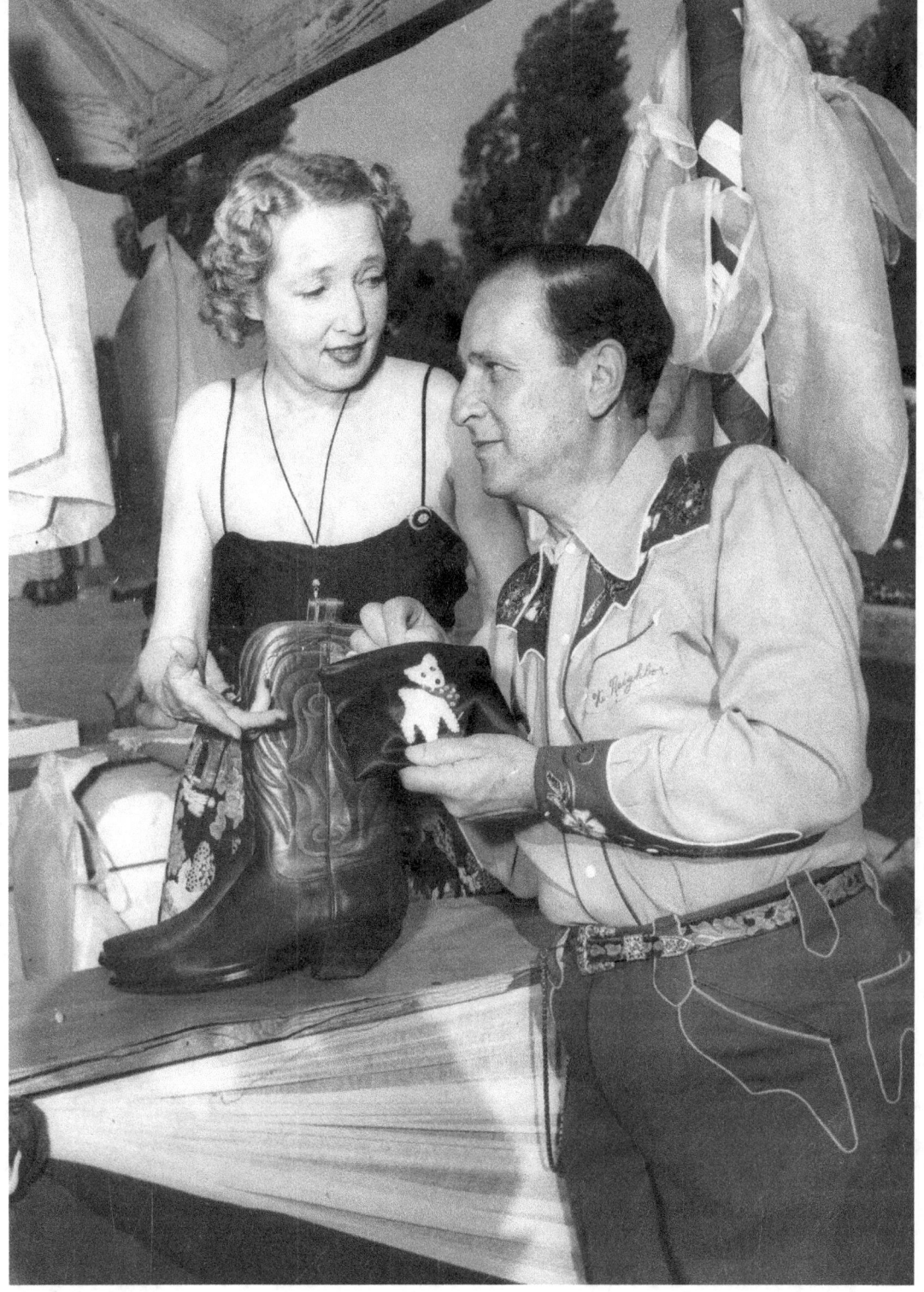

"Mrs. Victoria Mix, widow of Tom Mix, sells comedian Bud Abbott pair of her late husband's cowboy boots for $100 at the 12-30 Club's annual bazaar, held at the Abbott home in Encino. Proceeds go to the club's charity fund." June 6, 1949.

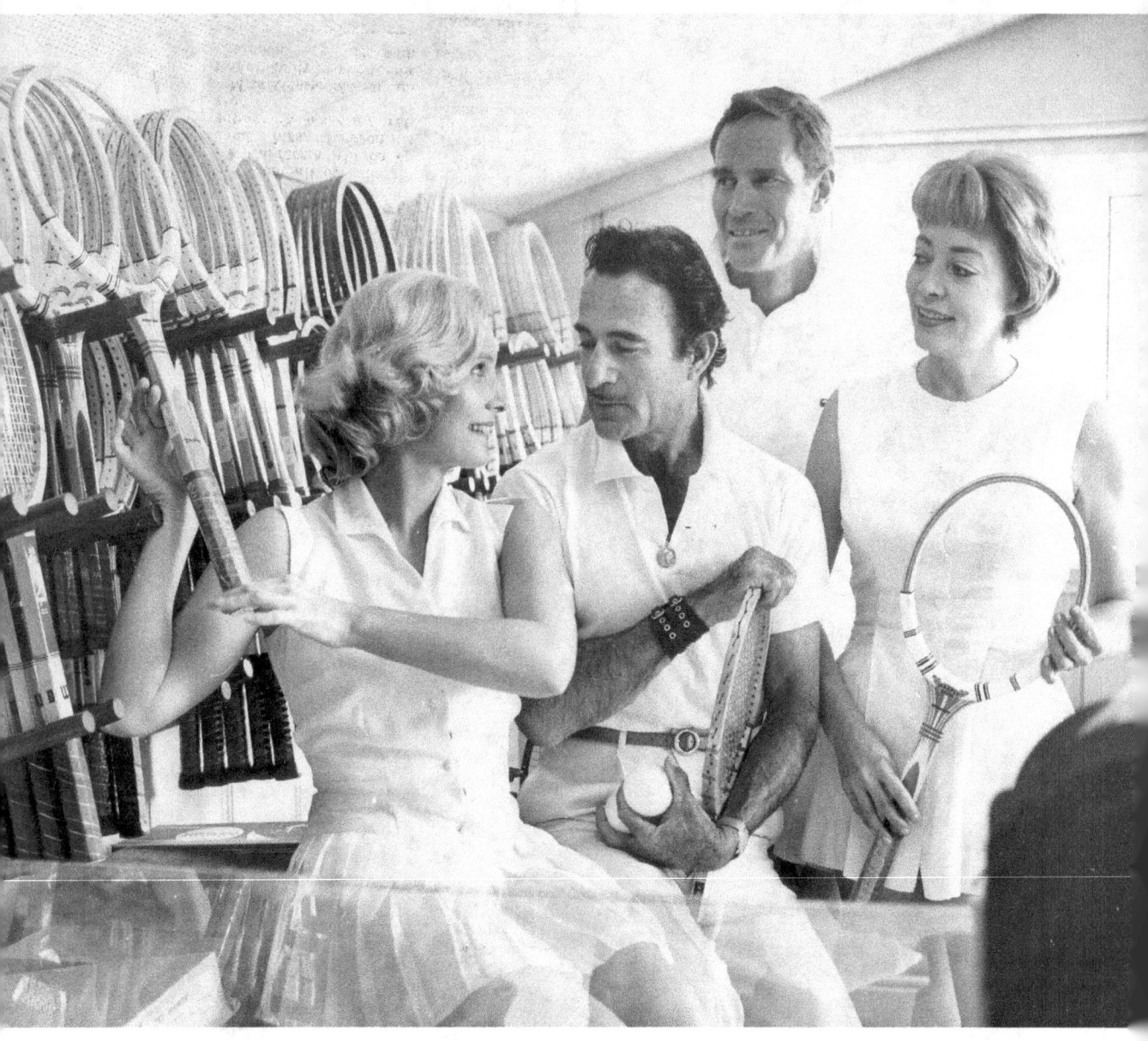

"Selecting racquets for the 31st annual Motion Picture Tournament which will be held at the Lake Encino Racquet Club are Miss Marion Moses, Gilbert Roland, Charlton Heston, tournament president, and Miss Marie Windsor." March 23, 1965.

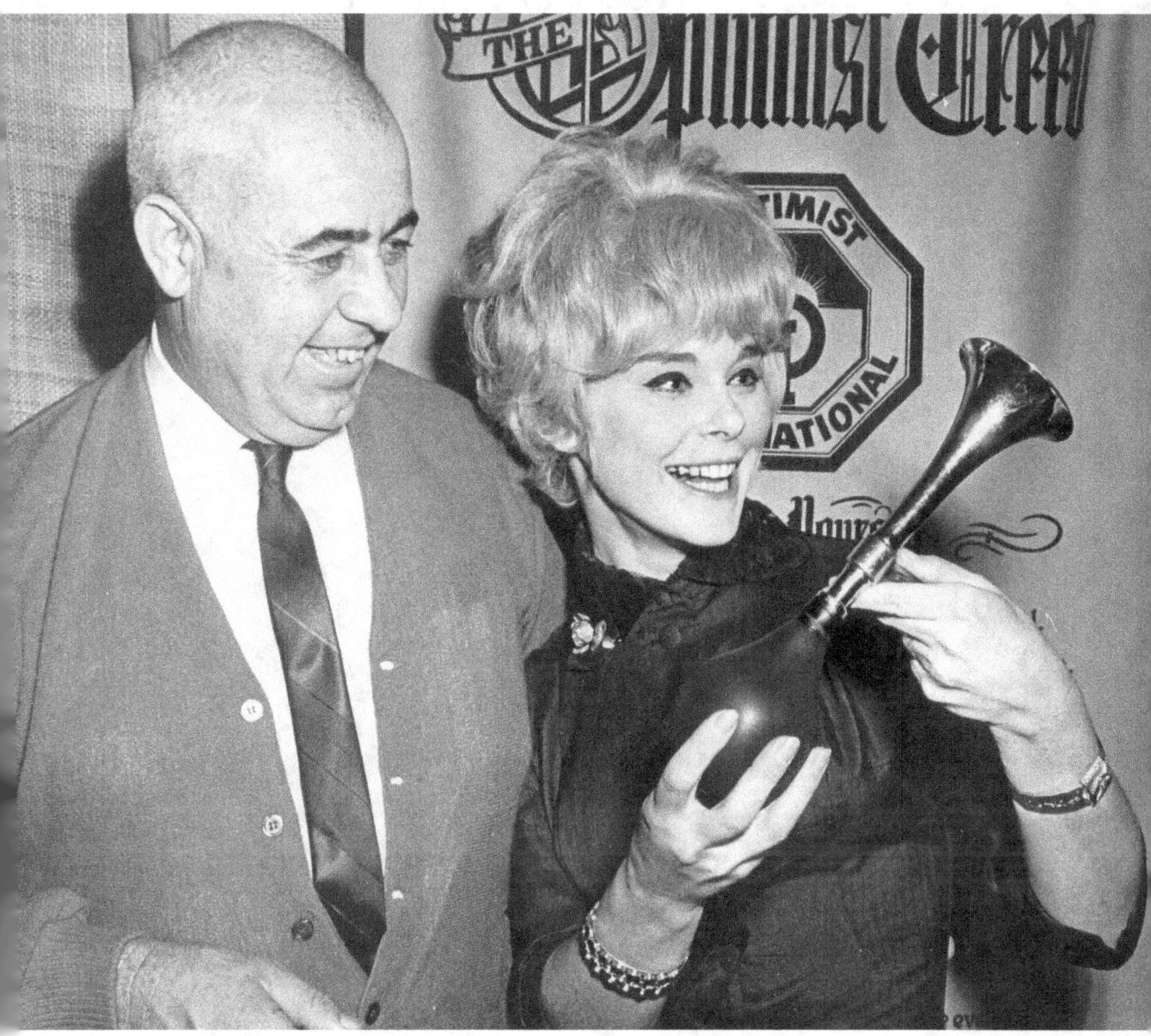

"Max Green, Studio City Optimist president, shows actress Elke Sommer how to make money. Hoot the horn and fine a member. Miss Sommer was guest speaker before the club at Tahitian Restaurant in Studio City." January 6, 1965. (Bud Maurer)

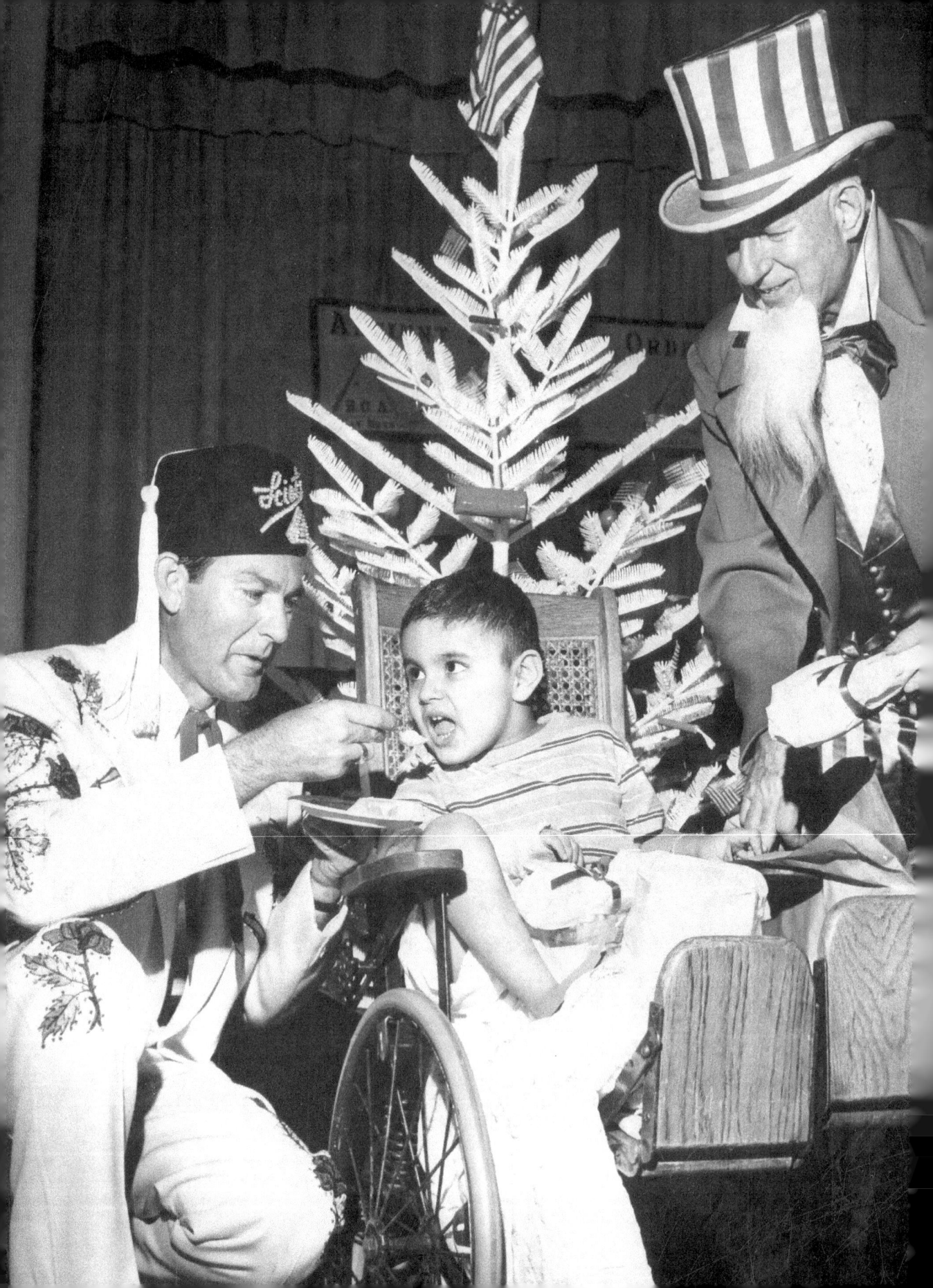

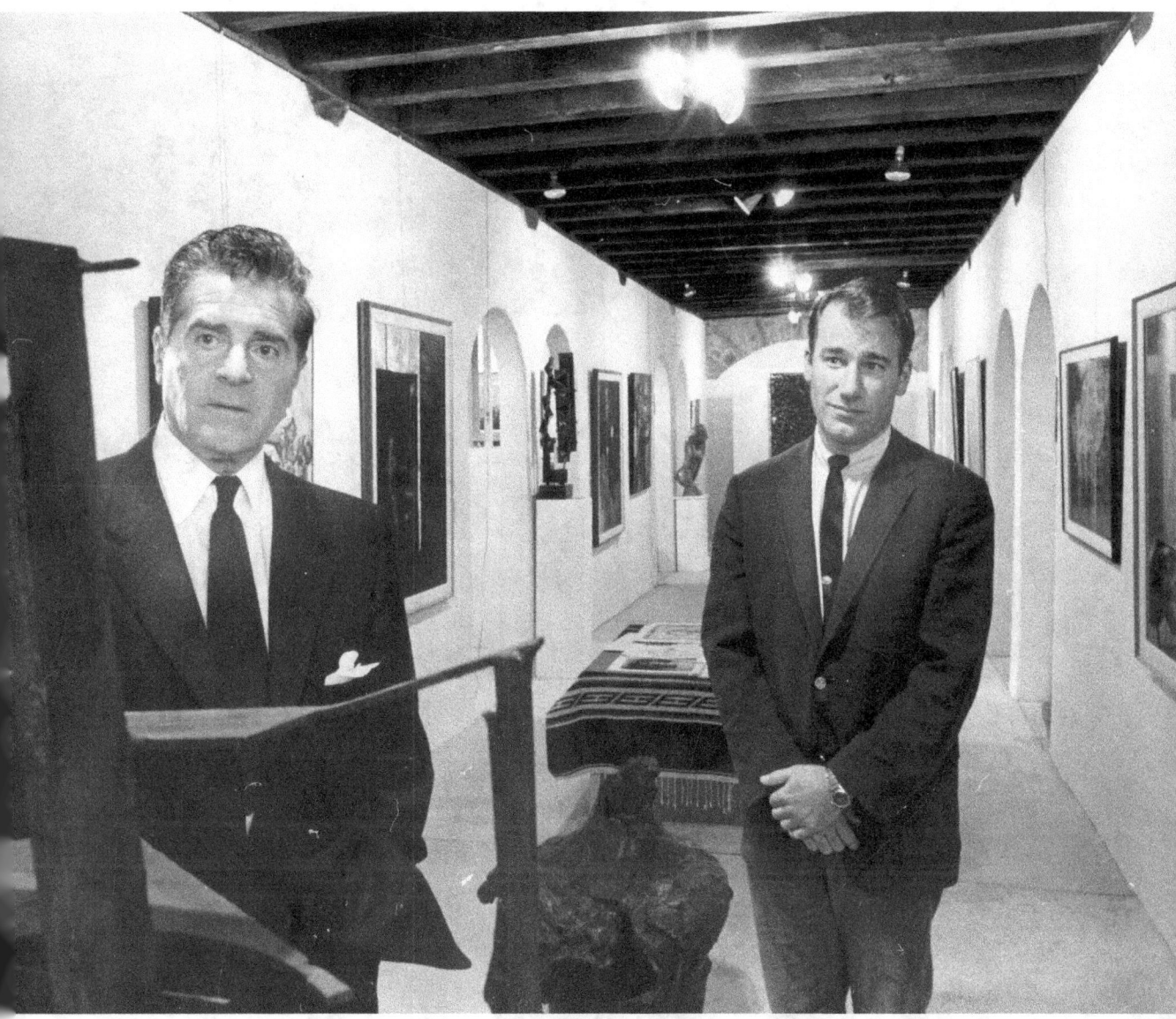

Actor Francis Lederer (left), honorary mayor of Canoga Park, renovated the stables on his estate into the Canoga Mission Community Art Center, 23030 Sherman Way. The center's director, David Brockman (right) discusses sculpture. March 16, 1965. (George Brich)

Opposite: "Western singer Tex Williams (left), in masonic dress, feeds red, white and blue ice cream to Ignacio Lizarraga, 5, while Harry Stellmacher, portraying Uncle Sam, 'Santa of July,' hands out gifts at special '4th of July Christmas Party' for 75 youths at Orthopaedic Hospital. Special party was sponsored by Ancient Egyptian Order of Sciots, Valley Masonic group." May 22, 1960. (Jon Woods)

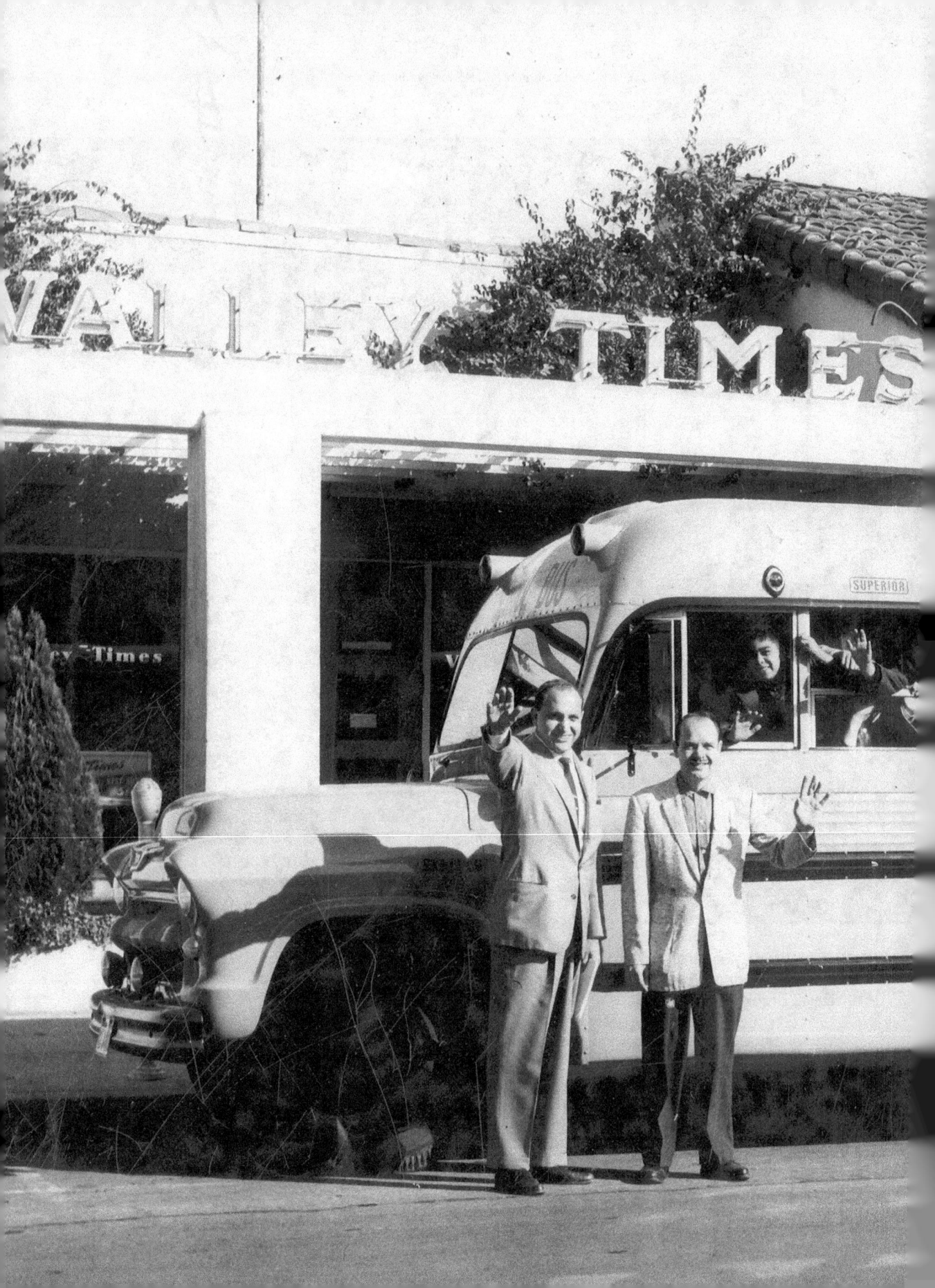

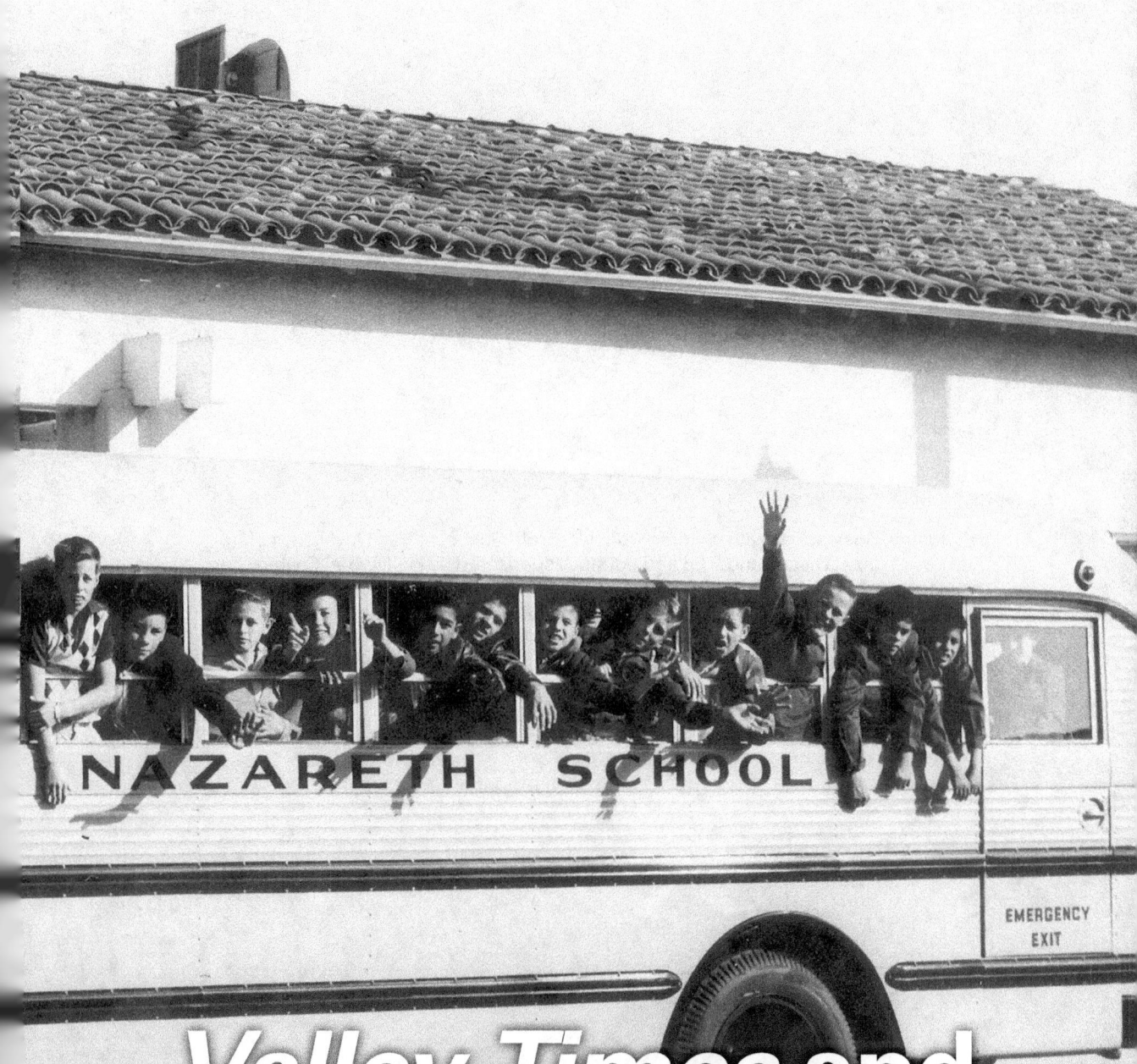

NAZARETH SCHOOL

EMERGENCY
EXIT

Valley Times and the Community

Overleaf: "Bus packed with children from Nazareth School of Van Nuys takes off for full day of fun at Disneyland. Trip and outing is sponsored by Hollywood Civitan Club, whose members take school children on trips every weekend. In front, supervising departure, are Joe Guadnola, left, president of club, and Dr. Kenneth Smith, club director." The bus is in front of *Valley Times* offices at 11109 Magnolia Boulevard in North Hollywood. November 5, 1956.

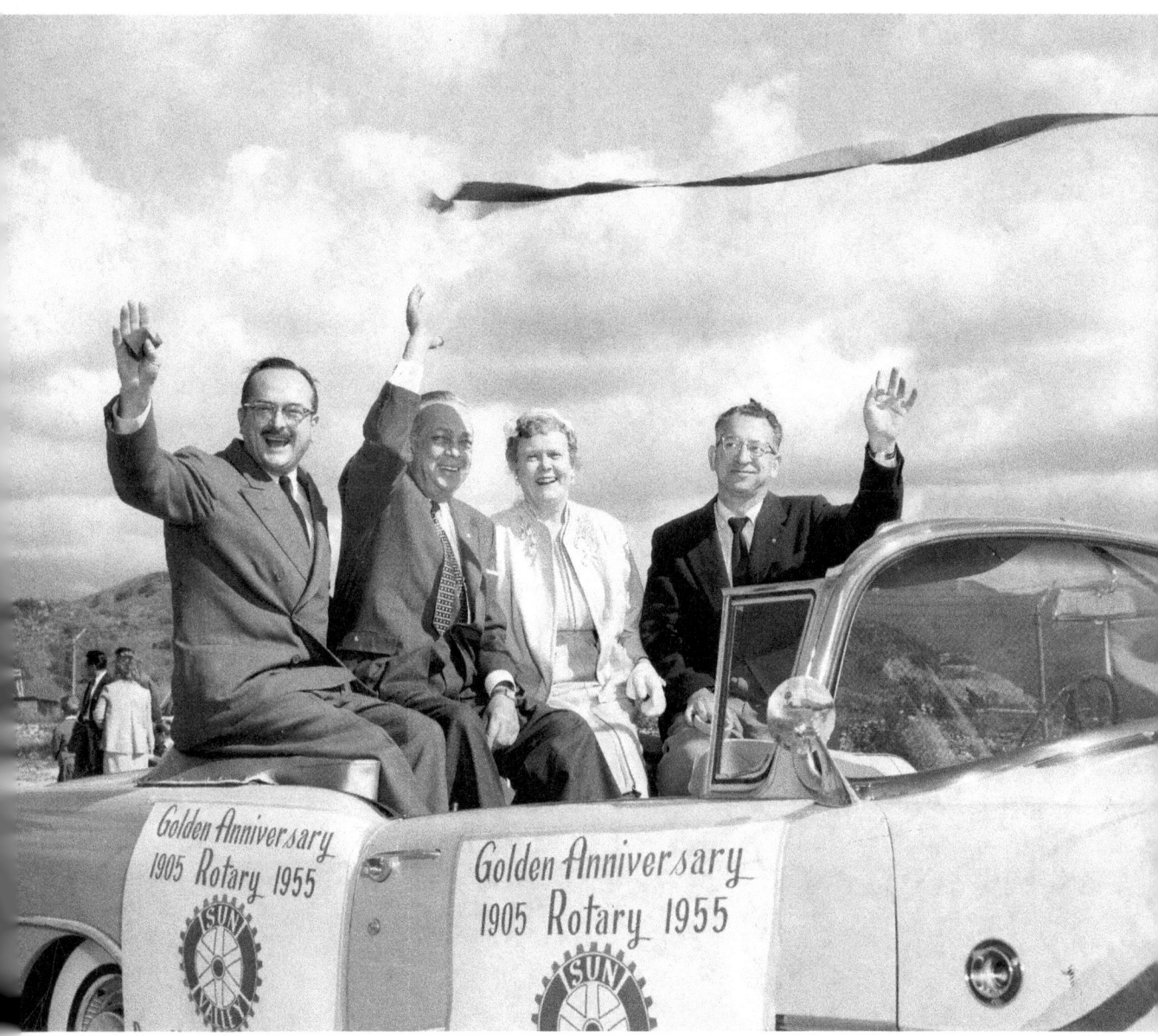

"Rotary officials wave from auto at Sun Valley Rotary Club motorcade marking 50th anniversary of Rotary International. From left are Dr. James Wells, chairman of the Sun Valley club's golden anniversary observance; Russell Quisenberry, governor of Rotary district 160-B [and publisher of the *Valley Times*] and Mrs. Quisenberry, guests of honor; and Dr. Dean Ames, president of Sun Valley Rotary." February 28, 1955.

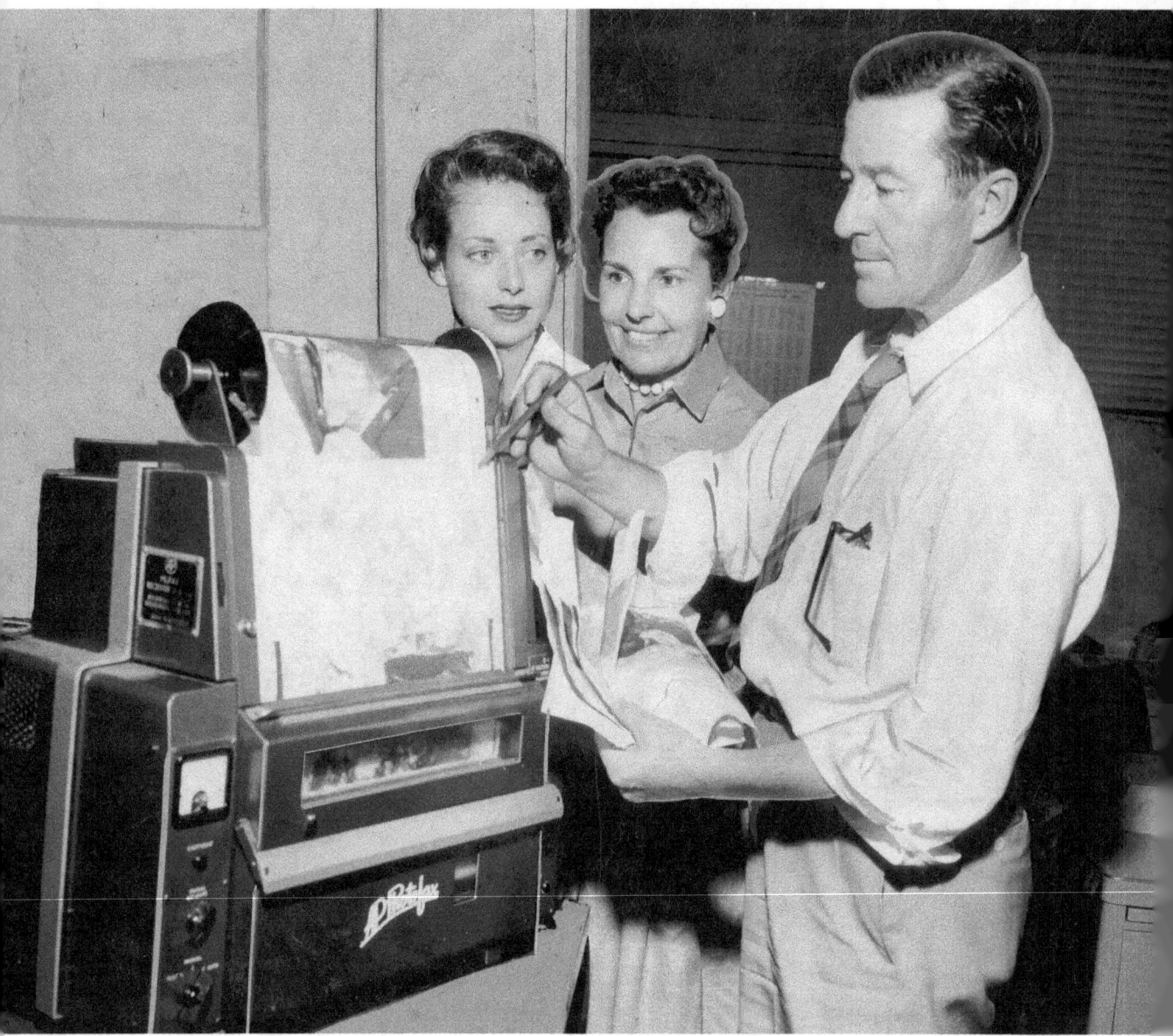

"Stopping by the *Valley Times* editorial offices recently to discuss Theta Sigma Phi's annual 'Ladies of the Press' breakfast, two members of the professional fraternity (from left), Mrs. J. Arthur Mesch of Burbank and Mrs. Lloyd Gregg Jr. of North Hollywood, are shown the new AP Photofax machine by Clifford Jackson, city editor." September 28, 1955.

Opposite: "Emery Potter, *Valley Times* office manager (left), is installed as Chef de Gare of Valley Voiture 1303 of 40 et 8 Honor Society of American Legion, by Sevy Benson, center, past Chef, and Ralph E. Goodall, Grand Chef of California." June 8, 1958.

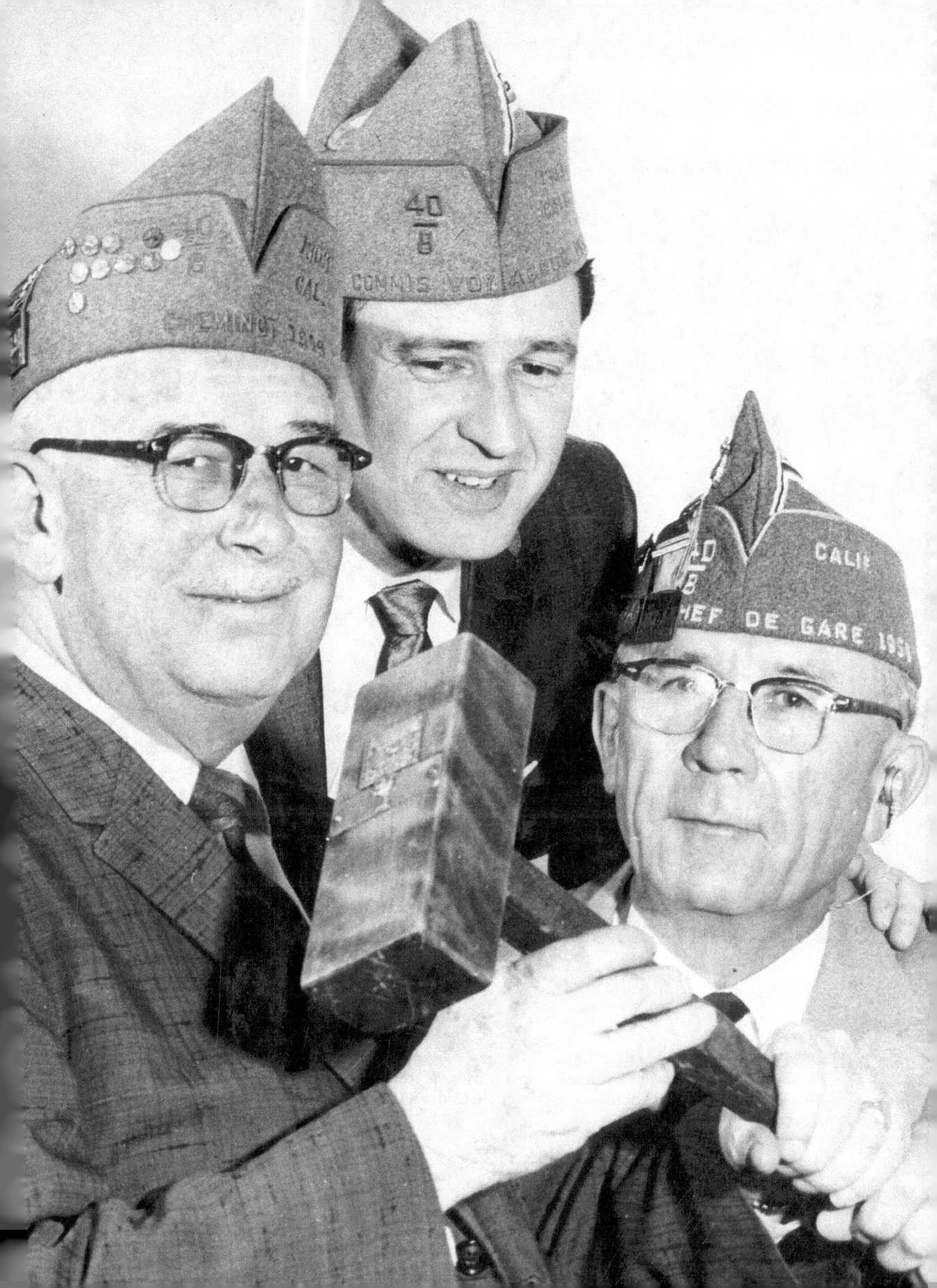

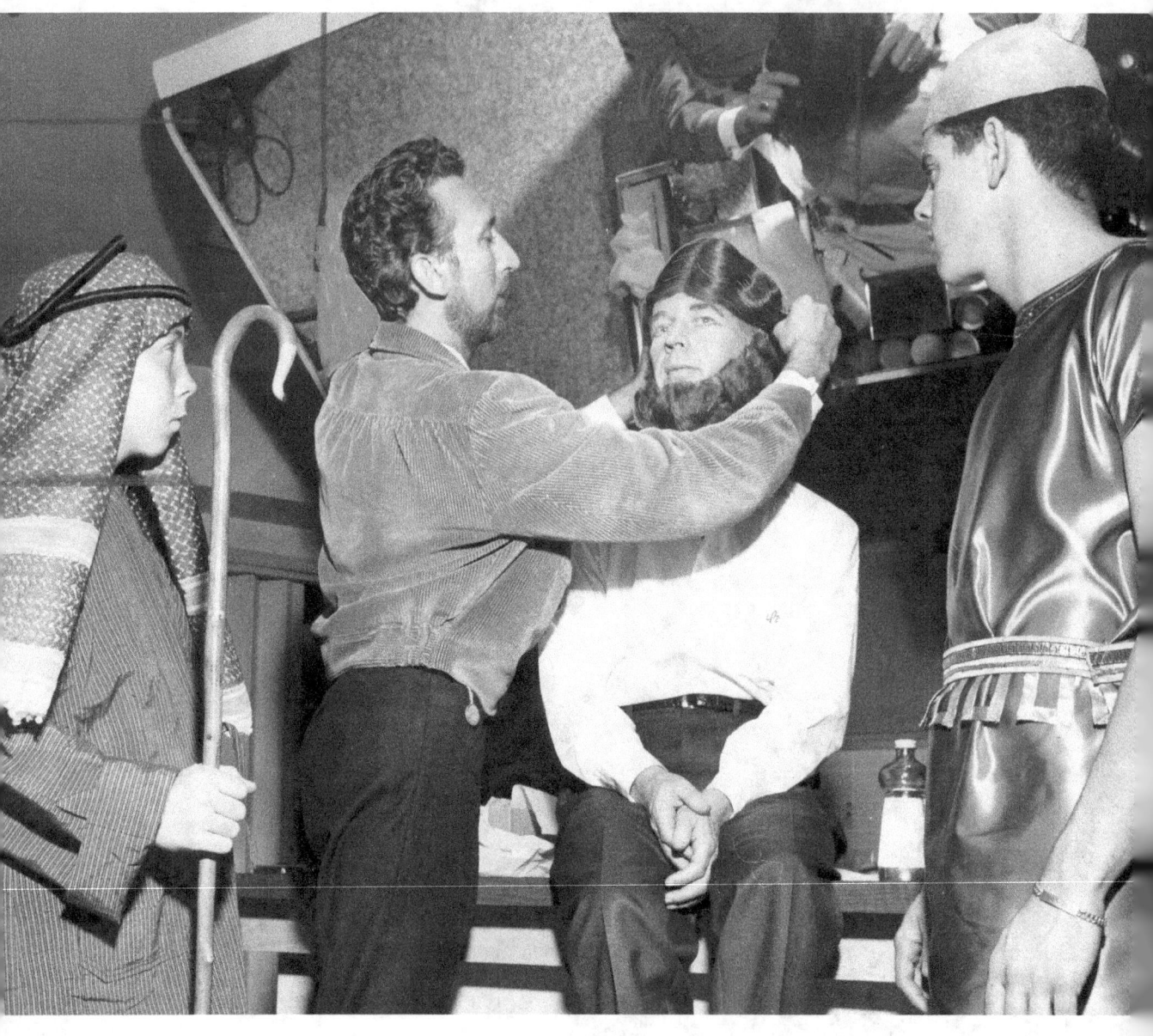

"Movie and television actor Kay Kuter transforms *Valley Times* Newspaper journalist Larry Paulson into a religious figure for the upcoming Bethlehem Star Parade in Van Nuys." November 13, 1962.

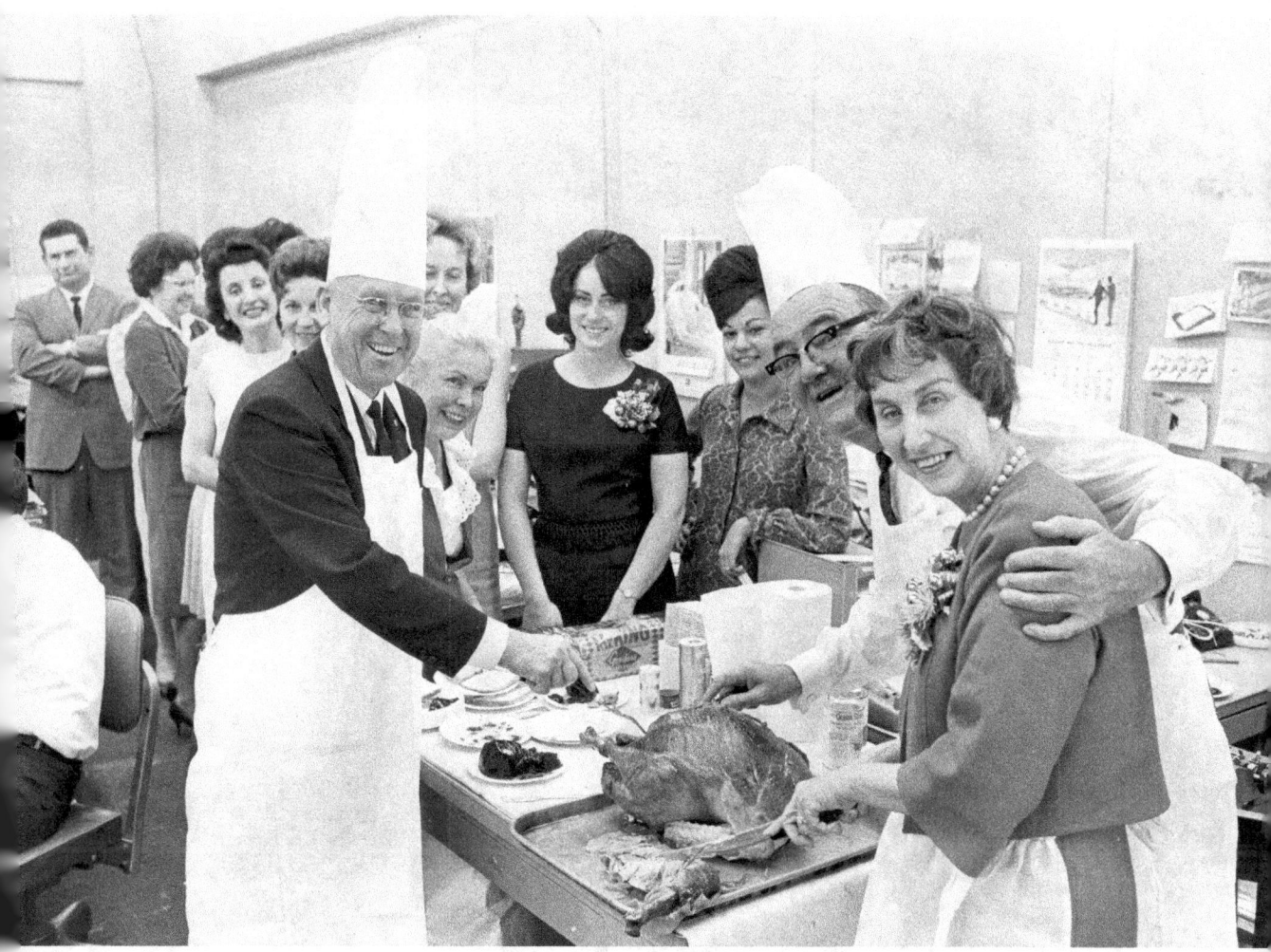

"Employees of the *Valley Times* were entertained Tuesday at a turkey dinner hosted by the North Hollywood Chamber of Commerce. In foreground (from left) are Barney Oldfield, chamber manager; Noel Merson, P.B.X. operator, Mayerene Barker, reporter, and Loretta Morrow, display advertising staff, all of the *Valley Times*; Ted Gifford, public relations representative, and Ruth Ennis, receptionist, both of the chamber." December 25, 1963. (Larry Leach)

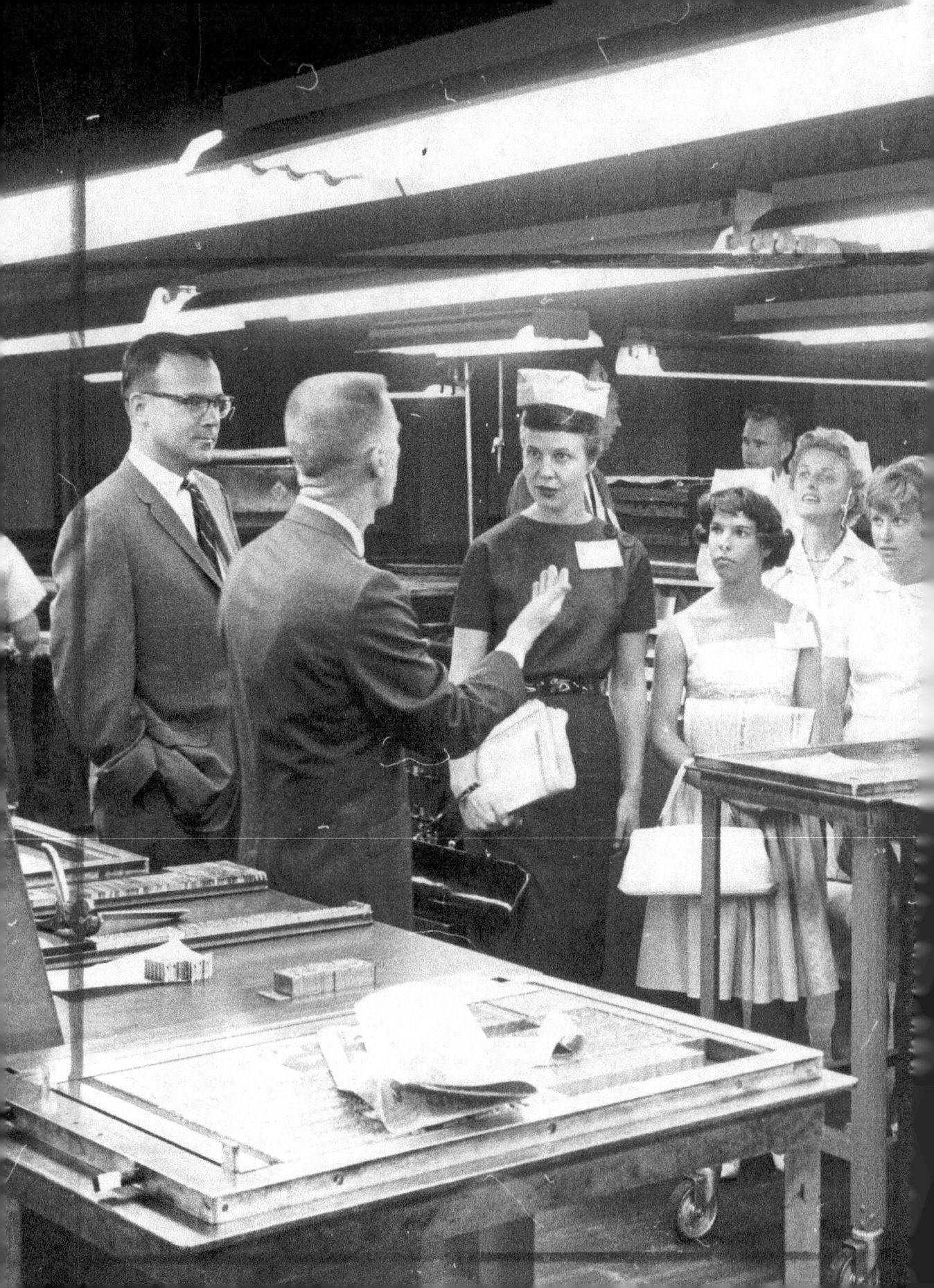

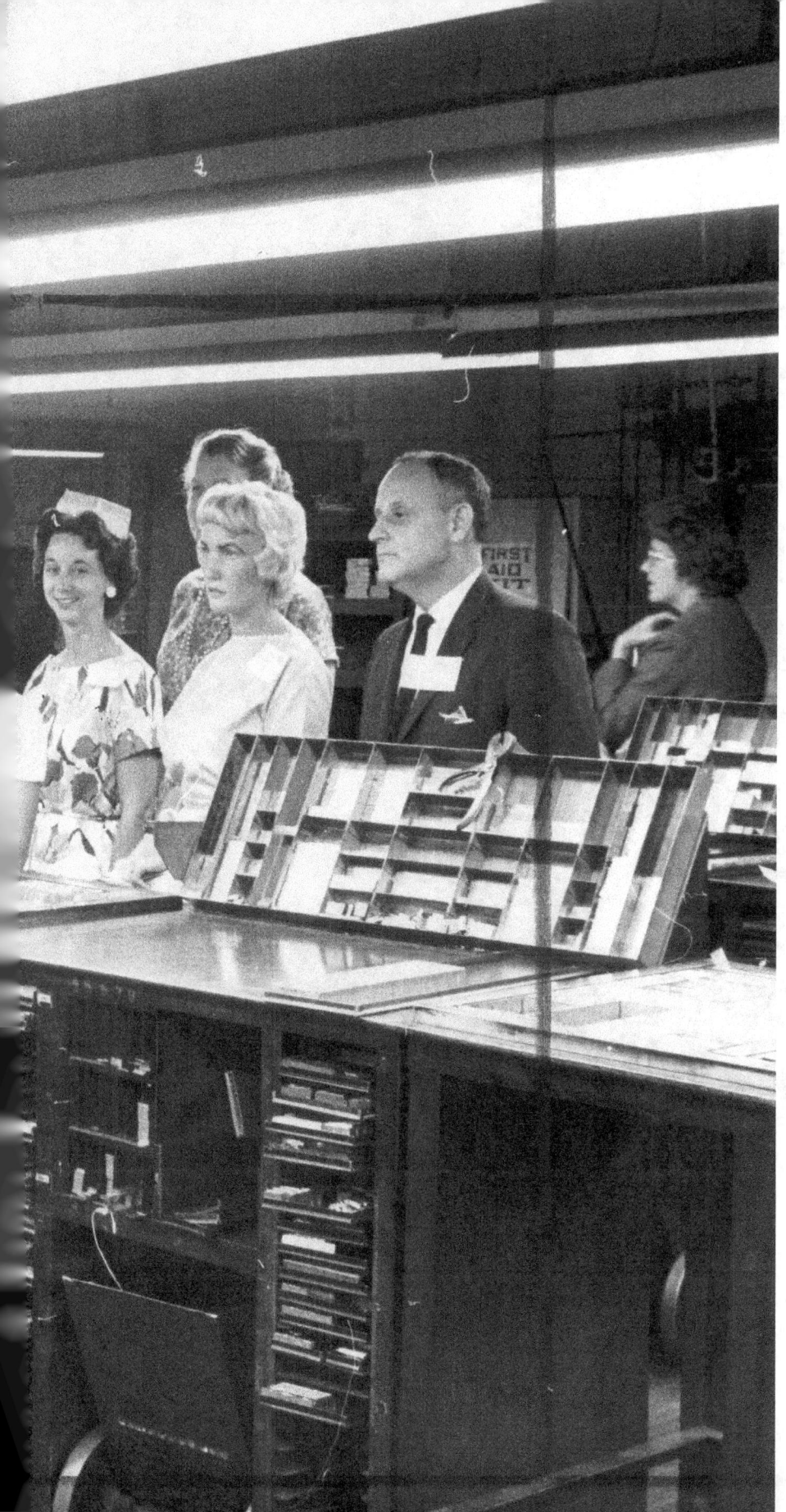

"Jack Burley (left), business manager of the *Valley Times TODAY,* and Larry Paulson, *Valley Times TODAY* columnist and photographer, discussed Thursday the newspaper's operation with a group of Burbank teachers and students touring Valley business concerns. The tour was part of the Burbank Chamber of Commerce's sixth annual Business-Education Day. September 7, 1962. (Gordon Dean)

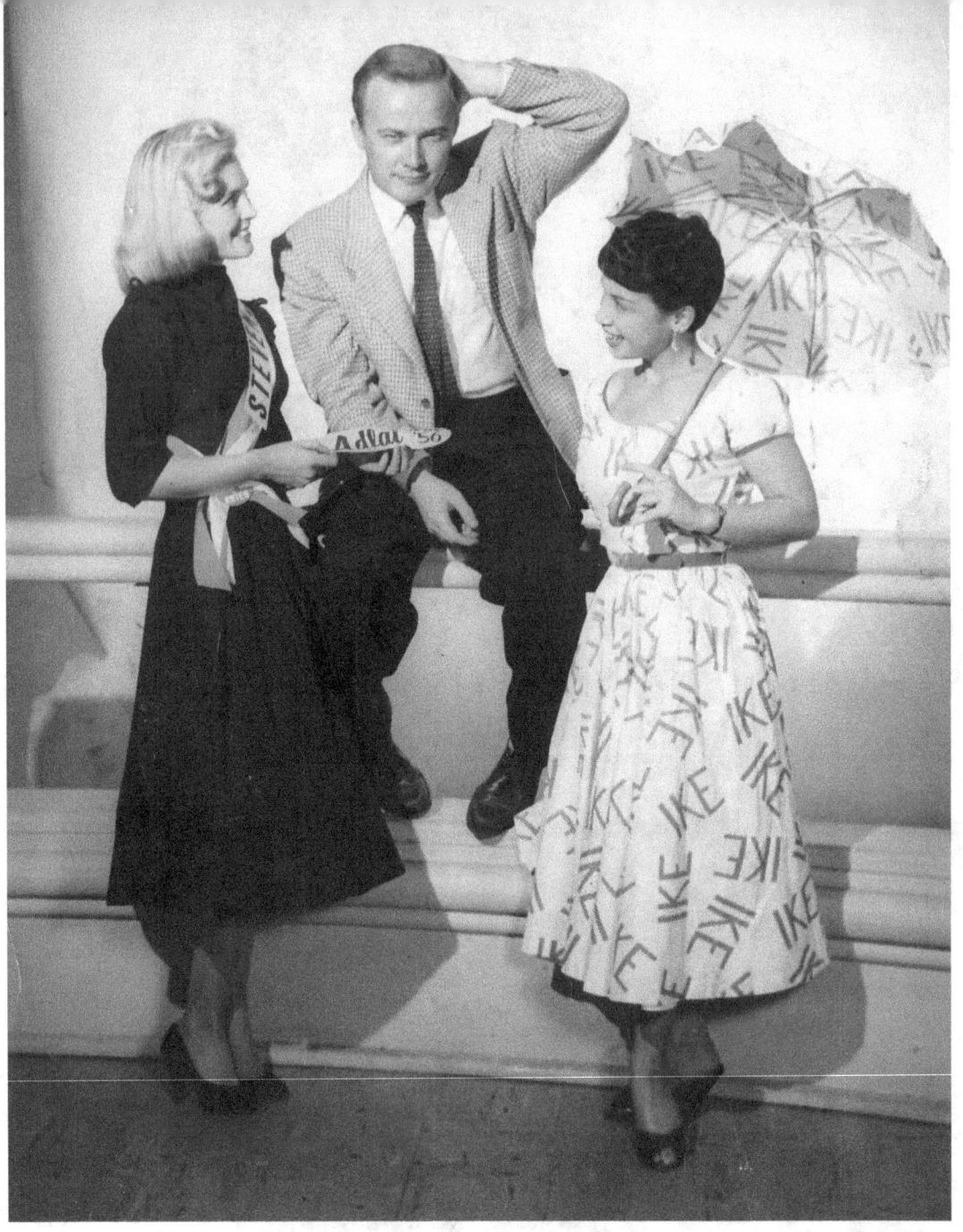

"Vladimir Chernik, *Valley Times* reporter and naturalized citizen, who will ballot in first national election, is typical of undecided voters weighing arguments of Democrat Jeri Sands, 23, Sun Valley housewife, and Republican Marlene Giangiuli, 18, Valley Junior College coed. Chernik is asking readers' help." November 2, 1956.

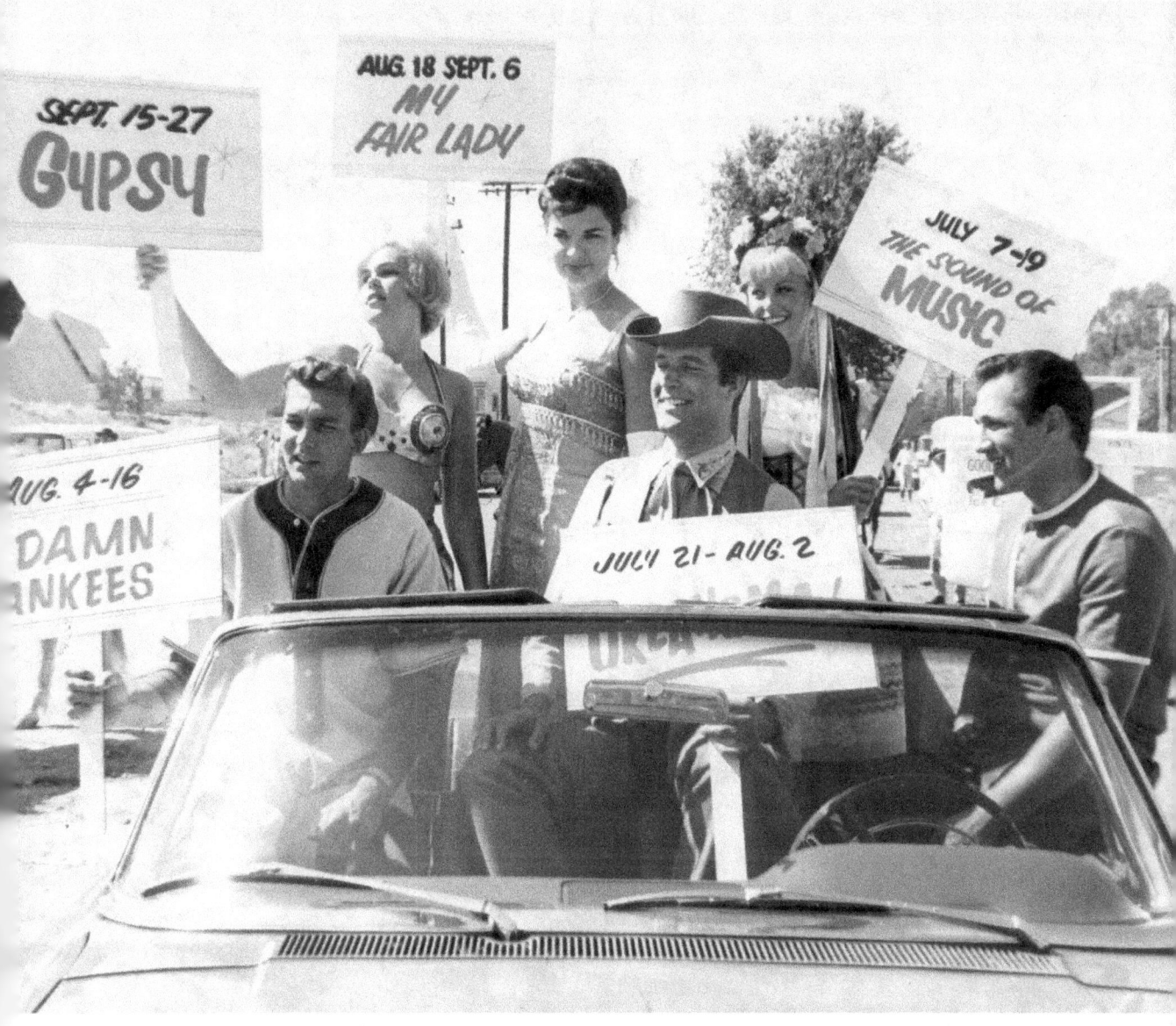

"An entry in the Woodland Hills American Legion Parade announces the summer musical comedy schedule of the Valley Music Theater. Holding signs bearing show titles and their dates are (from left) John Glidwell, Sassy O'Hara, Kirsten Smirnoff, George Brich, Joy Dunn and Bob Miller." George Brich and Bob Miller are *Valley Times* staff photographers. July 6, 1964. (Bob Martin)

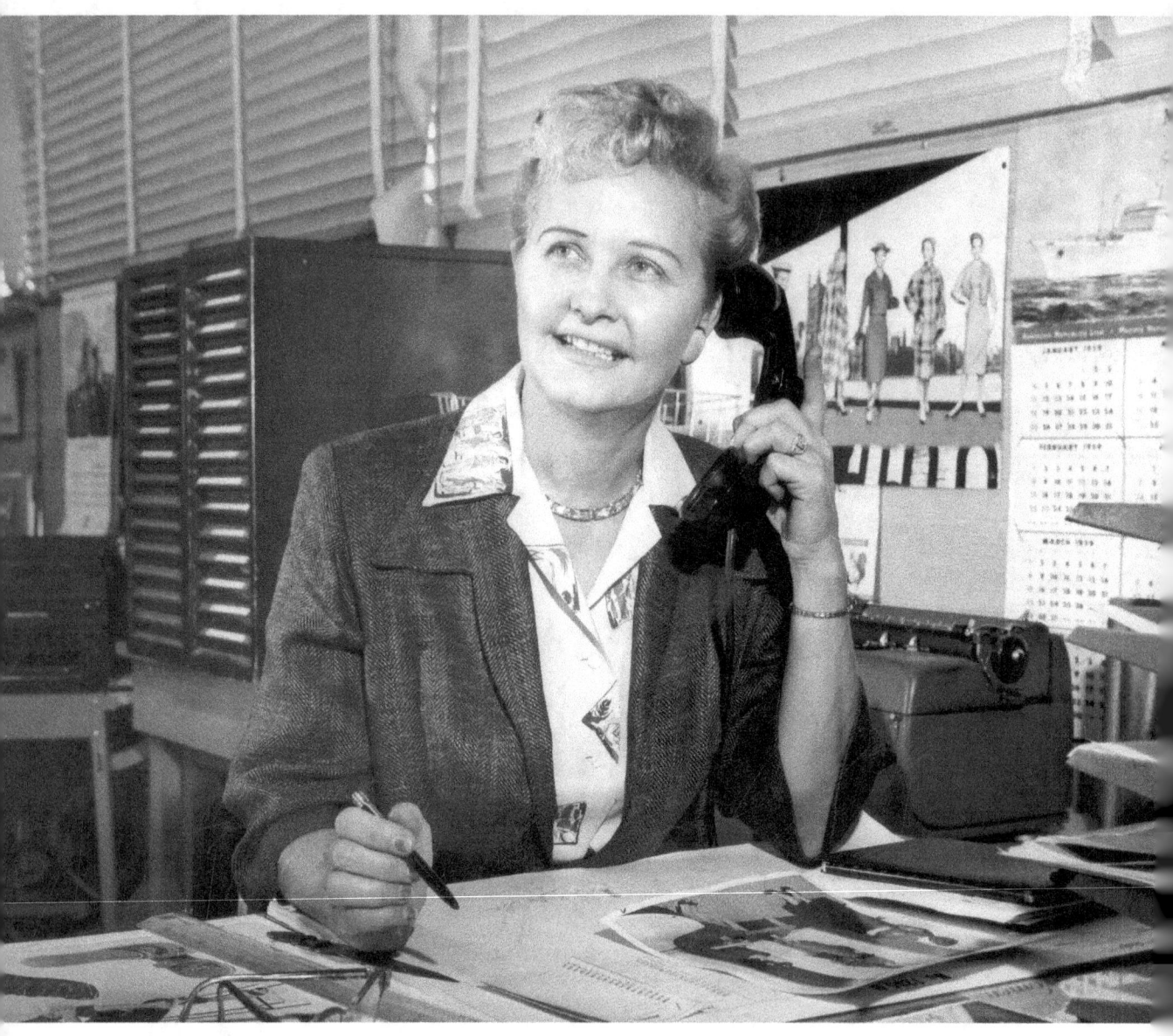

"Frances Marion Dewberry, *Valley Times* women's editor. Dewberry has been on staff at the Valley times since September 1948 working as editor, reporter, photographer, feature writer and columnist. She was elected, in 1958, as the national president of Theta Sigma Phi, professional fraternity for women in journalism and is president of Zonta Club of North Hollywood, international organization for women in business and the professions." October 1959.

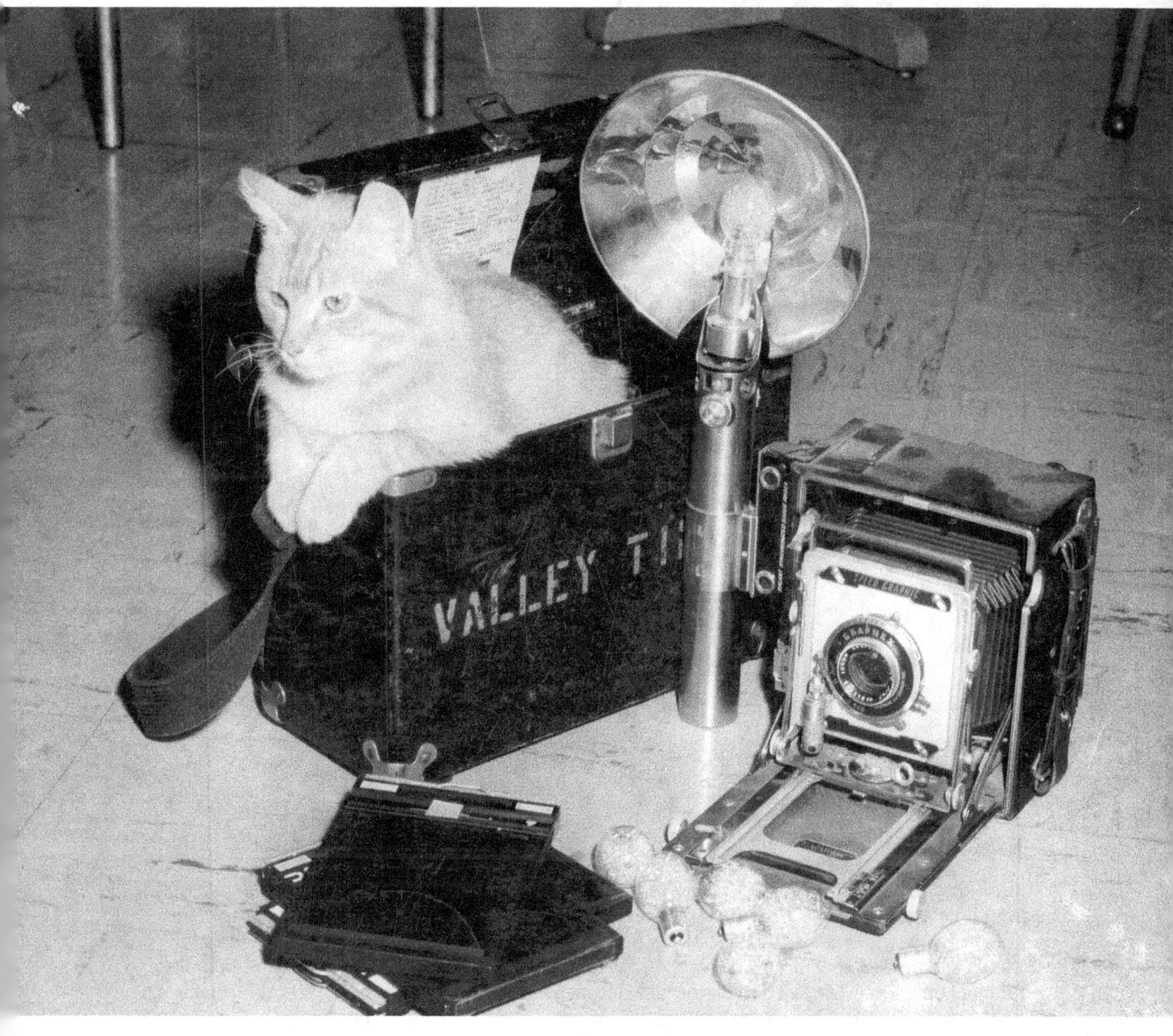

"Stray cat rudely awakened early today when *Valley Times* photographers came to work. 'The buff-colored feline apparently slipped into photo lab last night, slept and then sneaked out when offices opened.'" May 20, 1960.

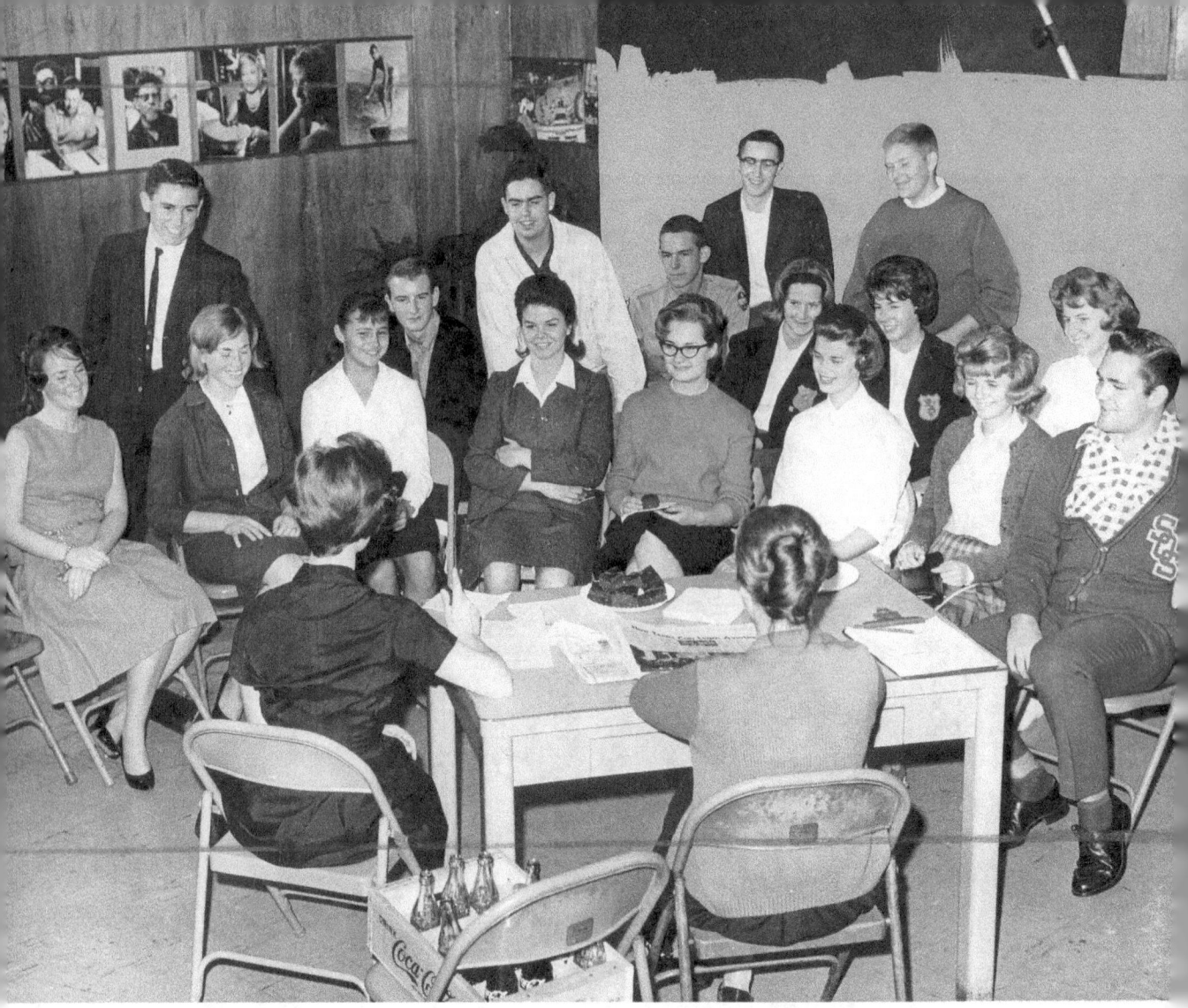

"Introducing...The *Valley Times TODAY* Youth Advisory Board. It consists of about 30 teen-agers representing every public, private and parochial high school in the Valley area. The purpose is to keep the *Valley Times TODAY* Youth Page writers informed of what's going on in the high schools and among teen-agers." (From left to right) Carol Cameron, Bill Cormier, Charla Ballard, Stefanie Lupo, Pat O'Malley, Jim Fitzgerald, Jennie Ducharne, Tony Sword, Carla Hendricks, David Lapp, Linda Avent, Susan Smith, Carol Wilmes, Mark Oliff, Linda Lee Anicich, Sharon Wheeler and Dave Skiles. (Backs to camera) *Valley Times TODAY* Youth Editor Lynda Elyea and Carol Wolff, Youth Page assistant. December 8, 1962. (Larry Paulson)

Opposite: "Joan Dew left, *Valley Times TODAY* Fashion Editor, presents Mrs. Ralph B. Howell of North Hollywood with an award from the Millinery Institute of America naming her one of the 'Best Hatted Women of the Year' in a nationwide contest. In recognition of her award, Joseph Rumelt, Millinery Manager-Buyer for May Co. Valley, gives Mrs. Howell her choice of a new spring chapeau." Mrs. Howell was president of North Hollywood junior woman's club. May 26, 1962. (Larry Paulson)

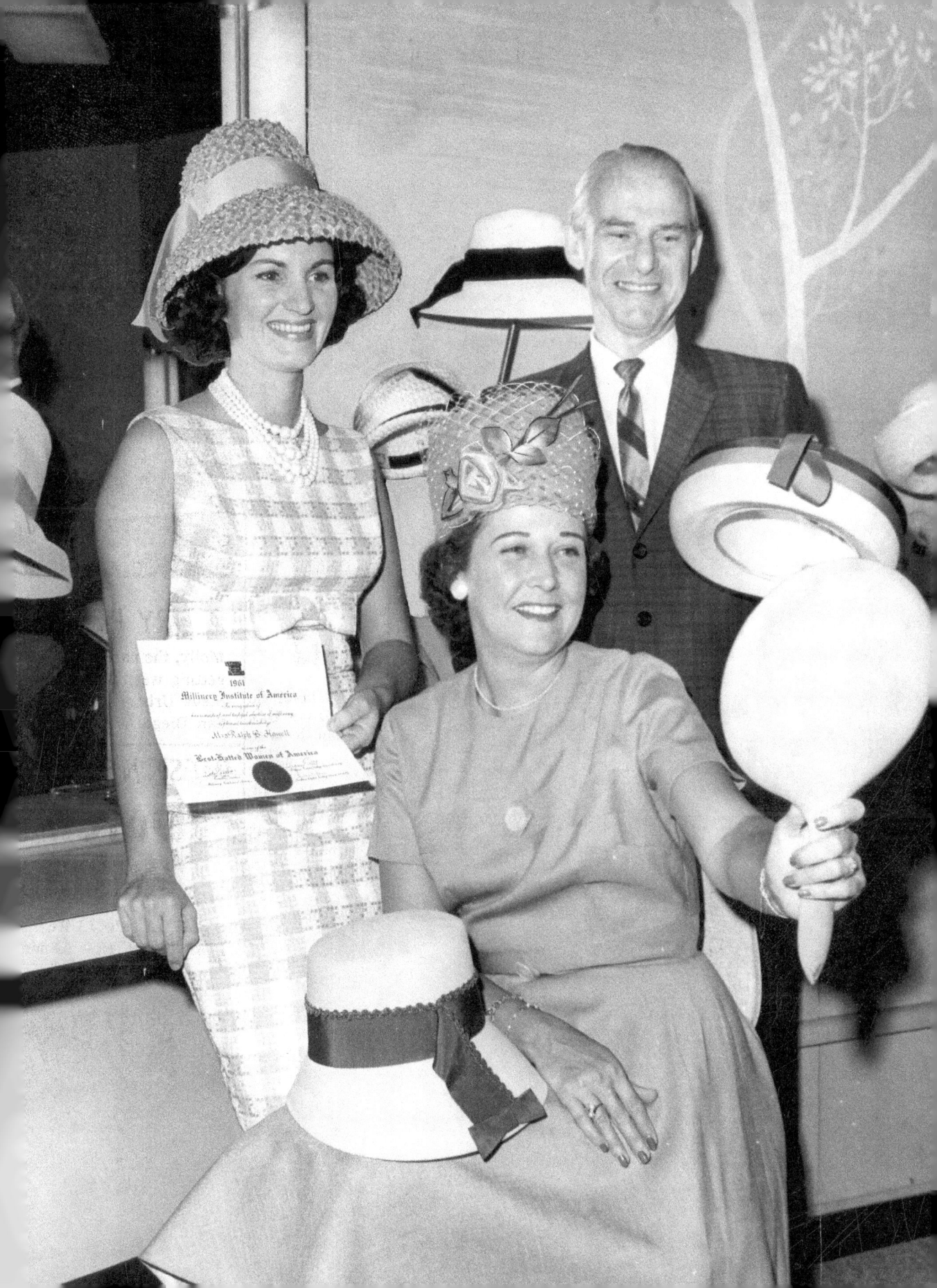

Afterword

In March 2012, Kevin Roderick, founder, publisher and editor of *LA Observed* and author of *The San Fernando Valley: America's Suburb* presented an overview of the *Valley Times* image archive, held by the Los Angeles Public Library (LAPL). The library had been in possession of the collection since 1981 when it was acquired as part of a massive donation of images from Security Pacific National Bank. The bank had obtained the *Valley Times* photos from a private collector who had won the photos in an auction after the newspaper was forced to fold in 1970 due to its owner, Lammot Du Pont Copeland Jr., filing one of the largest personal bankruptcies in United States history.

As I sat listening to Kevin and viewing the images, I was surprised to discover the long-forgotten significance of the *Valley Times* photographers and the work they produced. The *Valley Times* "photogs" were the first in the region to make the switch from 4x5 to 35mm film, resulting in rich narrative photo spreads that were unparalleled in the region's many competing newspapers. This included the *Los Angeles Times* who, supposedly as a response, launched a weekly San Fernando Valley edition in 1956 which was expanded to biweekly distribution in 1960. Roderick had tracked down George Brich, a former *Valley Times* photog who had been among what the newspaper claimed were the "5 good reasons why you get the get the finest news photography in your *Valley Times*." To hear these two speak so highly of this long defunct and largely forgotten newspaper was a revelation.

Since assuming ownership of the *Valley Times*, LAPL had not done a whole lot with it. In fact, the collection was frequently referred to as the *Hollywood Citizen News* collection, another local paper which had folded on Copeland's watch. Roderick's presentation put a fine point on the necessity to make the long-buried images readily accessible in this age of digitization. However, for me to single-handedly organize a collection of roughly 70,000 prints was not feasible.

When I turned to the board of Photo Friends and brought up the possibility of raising a quarter of a million dollars to bring in additional staff for the organizing and digitizing of the *Valley Times*, I thought they would tell me I was nuts. They probably should have, but instead they climbed aboard my crazy train, and with president Amy Inouye leading the charge, went full steam ahead. The past four years of *Valley Times* fundraising has not be easy, nor always pleasant, but in the end…we did it!

As we prepare to open "Service, Society and Social Change: Post-War Clubs from the *Valley Times* Newspaper," and publish this supplemental catalog, I can proudly say that under the full-time care of archivist Christine Adolph, the *Valley Times* collection is now fully organized and beautifully preserved in archival safe folders. Of those 70,000 images, roughly 45,000 were taken by *Valley Times* photographers and are either already online or on their way to being digitized.

During our campaign, we received coverage in the *Daily News* and a front page feature in the *Los Angeles Times*. I presented to the Los Angeles City Council where LAPL and Photo Friends accepted commendations for the efforts to preserve the collection, and we received additional support from Councilmembers Tom LaBonge and Paul Koretz. We mounted exhibitions at Central Library, the Museum of the San Fernando Valley, and LaBonge's Sherman Oaks field office, and I gave presentations about the collection at libraries, historical societies, women's clubs, universities, retirement homes, and synagogues. We even had a *Valley Times* Day at Antonio's Pizzeria in Sherman Oaks. It has been heartening to know others in the community are as excited about this collection as we are, and that our work will ultimately result in an archive readily accessible to anyone through the Los Angeles Public Library website.

As we officially bring closure to this project, I want to personally thank all of the community members who spread the word about this project, along with library staff, the *Valley Times* Advisory Council, and especially Amy Inouye and the board members of Photo Friends. This was a hard-earned victory, but the *Valley Times* photos and the stories they tell were well worth the effort.

—Christina Rice, Senior Librarian
Los Angeles Public Library Photo Collection
June 2016

Thank Yous!

Nicole, Possert, Kim Creighton, Matthew Mattson, Diana Sauceda, Angie España, Maria Novoa, Julie Minton, Lisa Ondoy, Stacy McKenna, Sophie Duran, Fernando Sauceda, Terri Garst, Wendy Horowitz, Kristine Protacio, Dawn Coppin, Andrew White, George Brich, Kevin Roderick, Hailey Branson-Potts, Antonie Boessenkool, Kelly Goff, Linda Stewart, Cindy Mediavilla, Darla Gunning, Alex Lunardon, John Bwarie, Brady Potts, Mary McCoy, Emma Roberts, Glen Creason, Cindy McNaughton, Michael Kirley, Debbie Savage, Kelly Wallace, Julie Huffman, Llyr, Heller, Dan Dupill, Ruth Seid, and Giovanna Mannino.

Special thanks to those who help fund the *Valley Times* project: Steve & Christy McAvoy, the Ralph M. Parsons Foundation, Galpin Motors, Tom LaBonge & Staff, Paul Koretz & Staff, John Randolph & Dora Haynes Foundation, Robert Cannon, Friends of the Chatsworth Library, Los Angeles Press Club, Ross Hopkins, Alain Khella, the Los Angeles Breakfast Club, AT&T, Friends of the Platt Library, Secret City, Institute of Museum and Library Services, California State Library, and the *Valley Times* Advisory Council.

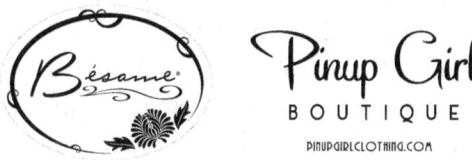

About the Author

Christine Adolph has worked with the Los Angeles Public Library Photo Collection as an archivist for the Valley Times digitization project since 2013. Before earning an MLIS from San Jose State University, she received a BFA from California Institute of the Arts School of Film/Video and worked as a wig specialist, planned exhibits for a video arts collective, and digitized historic photographs for the Antelope Valley Indian Museum State Historic Park in Lancaster. She currently lives in Glendale with her husband and two dogs. As a Los Angeles native, who has also lived in Sherman Oaks and North Hollywood, she will always have a passion for San Fernando Valley history.

About the Photo Collection

The Los Angeles Public Library (LAPL) began collecting photographs sometime before World War II and had a collection of about 13,000 images by the late 1950s. In 1981, when Los Angeles celebrated its 200th birthday, Security Pacific National Bank gave its noted collection of historical photographs to the people of Los Angeles to be archived at the Central Library. Since then, LAPL has been fortunate to receive other major collections, making the Library a resource worldwide for visual images.

Notable collections include the "photo morgues" of the *Los Angeles Herald Examiner* and *Valley Times* newspapers, the Kelly-Holiday mid-Century collection of aerial photographs, the Works Progress Administration/Federal Writers Project collection, the Luther Ingersoll Portrait Collection, along with the landmark *Shades of L.A.*, which is an archive of images representing the contemporary and historic diversity of families in Los Angeles. Images were chosen from family albums and copied in a project sponsored by Photo Friends.

The Los Angeles Public Library Photo Collection also includes the works of individual photographers, including Ansel Adams, Herman Schultheis, William Reagh, Ralph Morris, Lucille Stewart, Gary Leonard, Stone Ishimaru, Carol Westwood, and Rolland Curtis.

Over 110,000 images from these collections have been digitized and are available to view through the LAPL website at **http://photos.lapl.org.**

About Photo Friends

Formed in 1990, Photo Friends is a nonprofit organization that supports the Los Angeles Public Library's Photograph Collection and History & Genealogy Department. Our goal is to improve access to the collections and promote them through programs, projects, exhibits, and books such as this one.

We are an enthusiastic group of photographers, writers, historians, business people, politicians, academics, and many others, all bonded by our passion for photography, history, and Los Angeles.

Since 1994, Photo Friends has presented a regular series called *The Photographer's Eye,* which spotlights local photographers and their work. In 2011, Photo Friends inaugurated *L.A. in Focus,* a lecture series that features images drawn primarily from the Photo Collection. We have presented programs on L.A. crime, the San Fernando Valley, Kelly-Holiday aerial photographs, and L.A.'s themed environments, among others.

With initial funding from the Ralph M. Parsons Foundation, Photo Friends sponsored *L.A. Neighborhoods Project* by commissioning photographers to create a visual record of the neighborhoods of Los Angeles during the early part of the 21st century (all now part of the collection). To ensure the library's collection will continue to reflect such an important part of Los Angeles's history, a generous grant enabled Photo Friends to hire five contemporary photographers to document present-day industrial L.A. These images have become part of LAPL's permanent collection and are available through the Library's photo database. Photo Friends also curates photography exhibits on display in the History Department.

Photo Friends is a membership organization. Please consider becoming a member and helping us in our work to preserve and promote L.A.'s rich photographic resource. All proceeds from the sale of this book go to support Photo Friends' programs.

photofriends.org

This catalog was published in conjunction with a photo exhibit at
Los Angeles Central Library's History & Genealogy Department—
Service, Society and Social Change
Post-War Clubs from the Valley Times *Newspaper*
July 7, 2016 - January 15, 2017

Service, Society and Social Change:
Post-War Clubs from the Valley Times *Newspaper*
Edited by Christina Rice
Copyright © 2016 Photo Friends of the Los Angeles Public Library
Images © Los Angeles Public Library Photo Collection

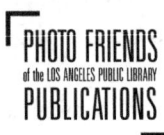

Published by:
Photo Friends of the Los Angeles Public Library
c/o Future Studio
P.O. Box 292000
Los Angeles, CA 90029
www.photofriends.org

Designed by Amy Inouye, Future Studio Los Angeles

Special quantity discounts available when purchased in bulk by corporations, organizations, or groups.
Please contact Photo Friends at: **photofriendsla@gmail.com**

ISBN-13: 978-0692732038

Printed in the United States